THE
SCOTTISH ECONOMY

A
STATISTICAL ACCOUNT OF SCOTTISH LIFE
BY
MEMBERS OF THE STAFF OF
GLASGOW UNIVERSITY

EDITED BY
A. K. CAIRNCROSS

CAMBRIDGE
AT THE UNIVERSITY PRESS
1954

PUBLISHED BY
THE SYNDICS OF THE CAMBRIDGE UNIVERSITY PRESS

London Office: Bentley House, N.W.1
American Branch: New York

Agents for Canada, India, and Pakistan: Macmillan

Printed in Great Britain at the University Press, Cambridge
(Brooke Crutchley, University Printer)

CONTENTS

CONTENTS

LIST OF TABLES

vii

LIST OF TABLES

viii

LIST OF FIGURES

PREFACE

This book is not an attempt to present a comprehensive picture of the Scottish economy. Such a picture would require far more historical depth; and the statistical perspectives that have been sketched here would need to be filled out with more of the colour and detail of everyday life. We have felt, however, that the picture could not begin to take shape at all without some such effort as we have made, and that the peculiarities of the Scottish economy could most readily be brought out by analysing those features of Scottish life that can be measured quantitatively. This is not the straightforward task that it may seem: reliable statistics for Scotland do not exist in the same profusion as statistics for Great Britain, and there are often problems of statistical comparability which make it difficult to establish the degree of similarity with the rest of the country and the direction which changes in the social and economic structure are taking. On the other hand, the task has been greatly eased by the appearance of the results of two major censuses—the Census of Production for 1948 and the Census of Population for 1951. It is at least a reasonably up-to-date picture, even if an inadequate one, that is given in the following pages.

Our first thought in preparing this volume was to produce a Scottish version of *The Social Structure of England and Wales*—a study that has been the staple reading of a whole generation of students of social economics. At a very early stage, however, we abandoned this idea and decided on a more elaborate and more analytical approach, describing the existing structure in the context of a twofold comparison with an earlier period and with the rest of Great Britain. Although this is not a companion volume to the work by Carr-Saunders and Caradoc Jones, however, it owes a great deal to that work and may help to illuminate some parts of it.

The present volume derives also from an older, native tradition, that of Sinclair, Cleland and Giffen, to name only three of the distinguished Scotsmen who helped to develop the use of statistics as a technique for the analysis of social and economic structure. We hope that it will be found not unworthy of that tradition.

We have been helped in the preparation of this volume by a large number of people, some mentioned in it, some not. To all of them we offer our thanks. We are indebted to Miss E. C. Hatrick and Miss M. Murdoch for much typing and re-typing of the various manuscripts, and to Mr B. Weber for preparing the index. We have been enabled to publish the volume by a guarantee from the Carnegie Trust for the Universities of Scotland.

A. K. C.

January 1954

CHAPTER 1

INTRODUCTION

By A. K. CAIRNCROSS

The Scottish economy is an integral part of the British economy, sharing the same currency, supplying a common market, subject to identical rates of tax. There is complete freedom of movement between Scotland and the rest of the United Kingdom and a strong equalizing tendency, therefore, alike in prices and wages, in the terms of employment and conditions of living. Whatever other significance the Border may have, it is not a barrier between two separate economic systems but a line between two segments of a single economy.

Yet the segment lying north of the Border is a distinct society with a unity and cohesion of its own. It is not merely that it coincides with an ancient kingdom in which the fire of nationalism still burns: although the fact that Scotland is a country in its own right, differing from England and Wales in memories and aspirations, temperament and tastes, institutions and culture, lends additional interest to a study of its social and economic problems. There is also a sufficient degree of segregation from the rest of the economy, and a sufficient diversity within Scotland, to allow one to speak of a Scottish economy, functioning as a unit and with an independent momentum; and there is a sufficient amount of statistical information about this economy to enable one to describe and analyse it.

It is on this statistical information that the following chapters draw. They represent more a description of the Scottish economy as it has developed over the past century than an analysis of the problems that beset it currently. They are not a complete description even of those features of Scottish life that lend themselves to quantitative description. For example, nothing is said of the transport system and distributive services on which the functioning of the economy so much depends. But they do review, in a way that has not previously been done, the economic and social structure of the country so as to bring out—generally by comparison with the larger economy of Great Britain—the dominant trends.

The picture that emerges is one of an industrial economy that shows signs of lagging behind the rest of the country. It is, above all, an urban economy, with a scattered agricultural fringe. Over one-third of the population of five million live within twenty miles of the centre of Glasgow and a million more in or around Edinburgh, Dundee and Aberdeen. On the other hand, in the seven crofting counties in the North, forming almost half of the total area of

Scotland, there are less than 300,000 people—about as many as the population of the county of Angus; and in the seven southernmost counties, from Berwick to Wigtown, there are not much over 250,000 people. Three-quarters of the population are packed into the comparatively small quadrilateral bounded by Ayr and Greenock in the West and Edinburgh and Dundee in the East. Practically all the industry of the country is carried on in this central belt, the only exceptions of any importance being the Border woollen industry and the industries in and around Aberdeen; and within the central belt there is a heavy concentration on the Glasgow area, where over half the factories in Scotland are located.

This concentration has shown comparatively little change over the past fifty years. The rapid decanting of the countryside into the towns that went on all through the nineteenth century seems to have subsided in the middle of the twentieth and the distribution of the population has acquired a certain stability. The four large cities, for example, are hardly at all bigger than they were twenty years ago. At the same time, the size of the population has become more stable. In the last fifty years the increase has been only 14 % compared with 55 % in the previous fifty years. This stability has been reached at birth- and death-rates which, although higher than in England and Wales, are less than half what they were a century ago. The expectation of life is thus much longer—66 years as against about 40 in 1851—and there are at once more old people and fewer young people. Another change making for greater stability is that there are more married people.

The economic and social consequences of this greater stability are far-reaching. They mean, for example, a longer useful working life for the average man and woman; a rise in the status of women, who now spend less time in child-bearing and more with their children; a change in the structure of the household, the care of the aged coming to displace the care of infants as the main source of worry; a growth of more conservative habits; a revival of interest in rural activities; a decline in emigration.

In the nineteenth century the growth of population and of industry went hand-in-hand, to the accompaniment of unprecedented prosperity. From being a poor and backward agricultural country, Scotland leapt forward to the very forefront of modern capitalism, and won a handsome return for her pioneering efforts. The greater stability of the past half-century has not meant a corresponding stability in the national income, which has gone on rising except in the worst years of depression in the early 1930's. But the rise in total national income has been slower than in England and Wales, and there is abundant evidence that income per head in Scotland has remained below the average level south of the Border.

For this there may be a number of reasons. One is the bigger part that agriculture plays in the Scottish economy—agriculture drawing, as a rule,

2

a lower cash income per head than most industrial pursuits. The rather higher level of unemployment in Scotland operates in the same direction. But neither of these factors accounts for the difference in wage-earnings, which is of the order of 5–10 %. It seems likely that this is to be explained more by the absence of the newer industries, which tend to offer higher rates of pay, and still more by the absence of new products within existing industries—the comparative indifference of Scottish industry to advances in technology, to new equipment, new knowledge, and new opportunities for development.

It is possible also that if Scotland has dropped behind, this is partly to be accounted for by a narrowing of the material base of the economy, a switch in modern technology to materials not indigenous to Scotland and an inability or reluctance to use new ones. The fact that fuel and raw materials seem to be losing ground as localizing factors to markets and distributive and research facilities operates in the same direction. But fuel is no longer cheaper in Scotland than in England. Coal, the most precious of Scotland's natural resources, is now won at greater cost than in the main English coalfields. Of the metals produced in Scotland, steel is dependent on imported ore and imported scrap, and some of Scotland's former competitive advantages as a steel producer no longer exist. Aluminium is too costly to undersell imports from Canada. Of home-produced textile fibres, most Scottish wool is of carpet, not apparel, quality and much of it is exported, while the small amount of rayon manufactured finds only a negligible market locally. In plastics, Scotland has lagged far behind. Against all this are two circumstances of great potential importance. One is the presence of large unutilized coal reserves, admittedly at great depth but apparently of good quality; the other, which is of particular importance in the manufacture of the newer chemicals, is ease of access to supplies of pure water and pure air.

An important geographical shift is taking place in the raw material base and this may in course of time have important repercussions on Scottish industry. The output of coal comes increasingly from areas at some distance from Glasgow instead of mainly from the Lanarkshire coalfield, as in pre-war years. This change, together with the rise of the petro-chemical industry at Grangemouth and such developments as the new ardil factory in Dumfries, seems likely to exercise on Scottish industry a thrust away from the Glasgow area.

The prosperity of Scotland was built on heavy industries—especially those in the metal and engineering group. It is difficult to show the precise degree of dependence on those industries, since engineering covers a whole range of activities—half the factory workers in Britain are metal workers or engineers. But if one singles out those branches of engineering that are more strongly represented in Scotland than in the rest of the United Kingdom, all but one come within the heavy engineering group, the exception being the newly

3

established watch- and clock-making trade. Shipbuilding and marine engineering, constructional engineering, locomotive-building, foundry-work, and the making of iron and steel tubes are all heavily concentrated in Scotland while the vast new industries that have grown up in England—motor vehicles, aircraft, radio and electrical apparatus—are almost entirely absent. The dominant manufacturing industry of Scotland is shipbuilding; and it is neither surprising nor inappropriate that the products by which Scotland is best known and of which she is proudest are the great liners that have been launched on the narrow Clyde.

This dependence on heavy industry has grown rather than diminished. As has happened in England and Wales, the metal and engineering trades have grown steadily, in relation to the rest of the industry of the country and now account for about half the total industrial production. But whereas the growth in England and Wales has been mainly in the medium and lighter sections of engineering, in Scotland heavy engineering has retained its preponderance, not only within the engineering group, but in relation to other manufacturing industries. The typical factory in Scotland remains an engineering works, engaged in heavy mechanical engineering, and with a layout not very different from what was common fifty years ago.

In parallel with the growth of the metal trades, the textile and clothing industries have been contracting. It was mainly because of this contraction that in pre-war years more factories appeared to be closing down than opening up. During and since the war many new factories have been built, but they have so far produced only a minor change in the industrial pattern. In course of time, however, the new factories may come to play a highly important role, both by giving a broader industrial base and by providing fresh points of growth and development.

Partly because of the comparative insignificance of light engineering, mass production, in the American sense, plays little part in Scottish industry. The output of the main industries is organized less on a production line than on a batch principle or consists of custom-built products like ships. This has important consequences for the structure of Scottish industry since short runs tend to mean less specialized, less powerful and less up-to-date machinery, and a greater dependence on manual skill. They also mean a less organized market with more emphasis on meeting the special requirements of customers than on low costs.

With the absence of mass-production methods and the dependence on heavy industry have gone a lack of opportunities for women to find employment and a degree of trade union organization comparable with that achieved in England and Wales. Another consequence has been an unusual reliance on export markets. It would have been impossible to find employment within the limits of Scotland for such a large output of heavy engineering products,

4

except perhaps in ships built for Scottish owners, and engineering exports, therefore, have always been an important element in Scotland's trade. This has made Scottish industry highly sensitive to activity abroad and to the level of world demand, shipbuilding, for example, fluctuating closely with the volume of international trade. It is by no means certain, however, that other small countries like Denmark and New Zealand are any less dependent than Scotland on foreign markets over which they have no control.

In textiles, carpets, whisky, and a long range of consumer goods there is also a large export business. Much of this is with North America. Although it was Christopher Columbus who, by discovering America, 'let Glasgow flourish', it was many centuries before the discovery took effect. At the beginning of the present century, America may well have provided a larger market for Scottish products than England and Wales, although this is certainly no longer so. Scottish trade, both with North America and other countries, has at all times been greatly assisted by the migratory habits of the people. The large number who came to occupy important positions in industry and commerce overseas, or made their homes abroad as permanent emigrants have become reliable customers for Scottish exports.

The specialization of Scotland on heavy engineering and the high level of her exports involve certain risks. These were most evident in the years before the war when world markets were depressed and capital investment everywhere low. They were not nearly so evident before the first world war when export markets were booming and profitable and Scotland's largest industries were such as to meet the needs of those markets and make the fullest use of local skill and resources. The risks of specialization, however great, are no greater in Scotland than in the rest of the country. The new export industries that have risen to prominence since the war, particularly motor vehicles and aircraft, are concentrated in the south and are at least as dependent as shipbuilding on foreign orders. Moreover, some at least of the risks are balanced by the greater prominence of agriculture in Scotland. Although it is very far from being true that Scotland feeds herself, Scottish farms produce slightly more in relation to the food consumed in Scotland than do English farms in England, and the average Scottish farm is also less dependent than its English counterpart on imported feeding-stuffs.

The fruits of Scottish prosperity in the nineteenth century were not equally distributed. At no time has Scotland been a country in which there was economic equality. A century ago the organization of industry and commerce was almost as paternalistic, if not indeed as feudal, as Scottish agriculture. Current earnings were probably more unequal than in England and Wales. The bigger landowners, whose means had once been so limited, seem to have accumulated wealth faster than their neighbours south of the Border; while the large profits that were made, although they may have left the spread between rich and poor no wider than before, produced such a disturbance in the social scale under the weight of new fortunes that the traditional disparities began to be called in question. The present position, in which the State exercises a powerful influence in the direction of economic equality, both through high taxation and the social services, is more or less identical in Scotland and the rest of the country and needs no elaborate comment.

The rapid growth of wealth after centuries of poverty had unfortunate consequences for Scottish housing. The slums of Glasgow are not to be explained in terms of a shortage of accommodation, for they were far worse in 1911 when houses of all sizes stood empty by the thousand. They are due to social habits which were only partly the creation of bad town-planning and hasty building and were far more the product of earlier history. Glasgow and Edinburgh built tenements when they were little bigger than villages, much as Dallas and Fort Worth build skyscrapers in the middle of the Texan desert; and although Edinburgh learned to use the terrace and the square to house the professional and business classes, Glasgow was less successful, partly because the beauty of the surrounding country was more irresistible to the well-to-do. Glasgow's population, constantly fed from a country-side where housing conditions were often atrocious (e.g. in Ireland and in the Highlands) came to live in a state of gross overcrowding in tenement blocks near the centre of the city. Scottish working-class families did not habitually spend on rent what was usual in England, and even to this day may often prefer an overcrowded two-roomed house to one twice as large and not much more expensive. For this reason the subsidies necessary to improve housing standards in Scotland are likely to prove particularly heavy and are already laying on local authorities a most onerous financial burden.

Economic inequality in Scotland has never meant social inequality. Visitors have commented on the entire absence of any indication of servility or deference by the poorer classes and their rather strident national pride. In the eighteenth century they observed that the laird sent his son to the village school and that he was liable to be publicly reproved by a kirk session drawn largely from his tenants. Education and religion combined to nourish egalitarianism in a semi-feudal society while in the Highlands clan society had the same effect. In the twentieth century neither education nor religion has so powerful an integrating influence; and it is arguable that as economic equality has increased, social equality has declined. The laird is vanishing and his well-to-do successor need have no dealings either with the kirk or with the local school. His background and interests are increasingly unlikely to coincide with those of his neighbours; he is more likely to spend his time with others of his class and finds it easy and necessary to do so, both in his work and in his leisure.

Organized religion has lost much of its hold. In earlier centuries, it was the intellectual content of religion that gripped the average Scot rather than ceremony and ritual or emotional response. His love of argument and logic drew him to theology and rhetoric rather than to ethics, and he waxed fanatical over the state of the individual soul rather than over society. The fanaticism has since found other outlets, but love of argument remains a characteristic of the Scot.

The influence of the minister in Scottish history has been as profound as the influence of religion. Until the middle of the eighteenth century the clergy were the intelligentsia, almost the sole product of the Scottish universities; and the width of their interests and their power to raise the general level of education in their parish can be gauged from the *Statistical Account* of 1792–98 in which they furnished complete surveys of the physical and human features of their parish, including a sketch of its history and social structure. No such influence is exerted by the minister now. Instead of being almost the only graduate in his parish, he is now on the average one of thirty or forty. He is, by any standard, poorly paid by a comparatively apathetic congregation, but still provides an irreplaceable source of leadership.

Scottish schools have also been a levelling influence as well as one that has raised Scotland to a position of eminence in the history of thought and action. The university in particular has a far greater fascination for the able boy in Scotland than it has in England, and more Scotsmen go to a university. At one time Scotland had five universities compared with only two in England. Fifty years ago, the Scottish universities could rival Oxford and Cambridge in the eminence of their professors and the scholarship of their students. With the sheer growth in the size of the universities, however, and the multiplication of university staffs throughout Britain, there has almost inevitably been some falling-off in quality and a gravitation of talent to specialized institutions or to those where social prestige and amenities are greatest, most of them, as it happens, in the south of England. Scottish education seems to have fallen somewhat behind English in other directions. There is a general impression that this is so at the elementary level and perhaps also at the secondary. It is no longer true that a higher proportion of Scots than of English boys complete a secondary education; and there is more room for doubt than formerly about the relative merits of the education which they receive.

In a democratic age it is natural to lay stress on the place of the universities in training men for social leadership and for promoting social integration. It should also be one of the major functions of the universities to provide business leaders who have an adequate education to grasp and apply the latest scientific knowledge. Yet only a tiny proportion of those who take university degrees in Scotland ever find their way into Scottish industry. On the other hand, Scottish engineers and accountants enjoy a training, largely outside the universities, that enables many of them to rise to the highest posts in the management and direction of industry all over the world.

7

In medicine, the Scottish doctor occupies an equally honoured place. Perhaps one in four graduates in medicine of the Scottish universities is in employment outside Scotland; between the wars, the proportion leaving Scotland was a good deal higher. Yet in spite of the excellence of the Scottish medical service, Scotland is apparently a less healthy place to live in than the rest of the country. This shows itself both in a higher death-rate and in a higher rate of sickness. At the seasonal peak in March, 6 % of all Scottish workers are off work through sickness—about twice as many as are unemployed. The improvement in public health over the past century is perhaps the most striking single change for the better; yet it still leaves Scotland lagging a little behind a number of other countries, including England.

What is the explanation? Is it the climate, with its average of less than one hour's sunshine a day in the depth of winter? Or the notorious overcrowding of the city slums? Or just the lower standard of living corresponding to the lower level of wage-earnings? Perhaps all three contribute; and perhaps, also, some part of the explanation lies in the diet, with its high starch content and low provision for fresh vegetables. Half a century ago, one might also have pointed to the high consumption of alcohol, particularly spirits, and to the drunkenness that so astonished visitors to Glasgow. But in that half-century there has been a slump in drunkenness that has certainly transformed the statistics of crime and may well be mirrored in the health statistics too.

There are inevitably many chapters missing from this book. No account of Scotland, statistical or otherwise, could be complete without some sketch of the use to which the Scot puts his increasing leisure; of the place that he takes abroad and of external influences on life in Scotland; of Scottish art and its relation to the development of the economy of the country; and above all, of the character of the Scot and any changes that observers have detected in that character over the ages.

But it is not with such matters that this book is occupied. Its task is limited to the more measurable and pedestrian aspects of Scottish behaviour, with the march of social and economic forces rather than with the flight of the human spirit. The chapters which follow do not provide a picture of contemporary Scotland, but they contain some of the more important clues to an understanding of it.

CHAPTER 2

POPULATION GROWTH AND MOVEMENT

By D. J. ROBERTSON

THE GROWTH OF POPULATION

At the beginning of the eighteenth century Scotland had a population of a little over 1 m. against about 5·5 m. in England and Wales. During the eighteenth century population grew with almost equal rapidity in both countries, mainly because of falling mortality; by 1801 the totals had risen to 1·6 m. and 8·9 m. respectively. In the nineteenth century, the growth of population was still more rapid, but Scotland now ceased to keep pace with England and Wales. The population of Scotland grew to about 5 m. in 1951 and that of England and Wales to about 44 m. Thus Scotland's population has become five times greater than it was at the Union; but whereas in 1707 it was almost a fifth of the population of England and Wales, it is now not much above a ninth. This change in the relative size of the two populations is to be attributed not to a lower rate of natural increase in Scotland, but to the larger scale of emigration.

The rapid growth of the population of Scotland in the nineteenth century has not continued into the twentieth. In the twenty years before 1951 population rose by only 5 % and in the previous twenty years by under 2 %. The population of Scotland is not only stationary now, it has been practically stationary since 1914.

The nineteenth century also witnessed a great change in the distribution of the population—a change that has similarly been slowed down, if not indeed reversed, in the twentieth century. In 1801 the population was spread more widely over the land, but as the industrial revolution proceeded there was a growing concentration of population in the central industrial belt. The change in the balance between the industrial area lying between Clyde and Forth and the much larger areas lying to the north and south of it is brought out strikingly in Table 1, which makes use of the Registrar-General's division of Scotland into four main areas. The growth of population in each of these areas over the past 150 years is shown in Fig. 1.

The Northern division, which included nearly half the population of Scotland in 1801, has now less than a fifth. The Southern division, which once had over a tenth of the population, has now only a twentieth. In both divisions the population has risen by not much more than a third while the population

9

of Scotland has trebled; and in both the population is now lower than a century ago. On the other hand, the two Central divisions have grown remarkably, the West sevenfold, and the East fourfold, since 1801. The largely industrial Western area now includes almost half the Scottish population compared with no more than a fifth in 1801—proportions which, it will be observed, almost exactly reverse those for the Northern division over the same period. Within the West Central area the conurbation of Central Clydeside—the urbanized area centred on the city of Glasgow—has a population of 1¾ m. or one-third of the population of Scotland.

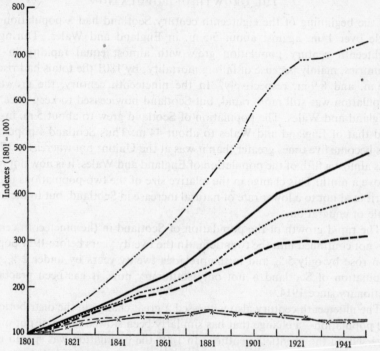

Fig. 1. Growth of population in Scotland, England and Wales, and four divisions of Scotland, 1801–1951 (1801 = 100). Scotland – – –; West Central — · · · —; East Central - - -; Southern · — · — · ; Northern — × — × —; England and Wales ——.

The changes that have taken place in the distribution of population within Scotland are shown in more detail in Table 2. By far the most rapid growth has been in Glasgow and Clydeside, followed by Edinburgh and the Lothians, and Stirling and Clackmannan. On the other hand, the population of the Highland counties is actually lower than 150 years ago, and in the Border counties and Galloway the increase has been relatively small. The most drastic fall in population has been in Sutherland, where the total in 1951 was only 59 % of the total in 1801.

If the more recent changes over the past twenty years are examined, however, a rather different pattern of growth emerges. The most rapid expansion has been in Stirling and Clackmannan, and the areas around the Forth estuary; the Highland counties and the Borders have fallen, but not heavily; and all the other regions have grown at a rate close to the average for the country as a whole.

Table 1. *Changes in distribution of population*, 1801–1951

Division*	Population of divisions at selected censuses (thousands)				Population in 1951 as percentage of 1801	Percentage distribution of population by areas	
	1801	1871	1931	1951		1801	1951
West Central	331	1,244	2,308	2,424	732	20·5	47·5
East Central	352	803	1,305	1,416	402	22	28
Southern	185	272	251	256	138	11·5	5
Northern	741	1,041	979	1,000	135	46	19·5
Scotland	1,608	3,360	4,843	5,096	317	100	100
England and Wales	8,893	22,712	35,952	43,745	492	—	—

* West Central division: Dunbarton, Ayr, Renfrew, and Lanark.
East Central division: Fife, Clackmannan, Stirling, West Lothian, Midlothian and East Lothian, and City of Dundee.
Counties to the north and west and to the south and east of these are included in the Northern and Southern divisions respectively.
SOURCE: *Census of Population.*

It would be reasonable to deduce from Table 2 that the distribution of population is now relatively stable. The rates of increase in different areas show a far narrower dispersion over the past twenty years than at any time since 1801. It is particularly remarkable that Glasgow and Clydeside have grown no faster than the average for the country as a whole. On the other hand, there has undoubtedly been a continued movement away from the more remote rural areas, partly into villages and towns in those areas. In the Highlands, for example, the landward area showed a fall of 8 % between 1931 and 1951 (in Caithness, Sutherland and Shetland, a fall of about one-sixth) while towns like Inverness, Stornoway and Fort William continued to grow.

Scotland is a highly urbanized country. True, there is only one great conurbation, while there are six in England and Wales; but the proportion of people living in conurbations (including London) is only 39 % in England and Wales while in Scotland the single conurbation of Central Clydeside contains 35 % of the population. If we look merely at cities and burghs defined by local boundaries, then 38 % of the Scottish population live in the four cities of

11

Glasgow, Edinburgh, Aberdeen and Dundee, and 54 % live in the four cities and the large burghs. If we take 'over 150,000' as equivalent to the Scottish cities and 'over 20,000' as equivalent to the large burghs, then the corresponding percentages for city- and town-dwellers in England and Wales are 29 % and 69 %. At the 1951 Census, people dwelling in urban communities of over 1000 persons totalled 83 % of the Scottish population.[1] In the Central divisions of Scotland (as given in Table 1) where three-quarters of the population live, 92 % were urban dwellers in 1951; in the Northern and Southern divisions the figures were 62 % and 52 % respectively.

Table 2. *Population of regions of Scotland, 1801–1951*

Region*	Population (thousands)				Percentage increase in population			
	1801	1871	1931	1951	1801–1871	1871–1931	1931–1951	1801–1951
Glasgow and Clydeside	343	1,259	2,326	2,444	266	85	5	613
Edinburgh and Lothians	170	407	655	707	139	61	8	315
Stirling and Clackmannan	62	122	198	225	97	62	14	263
Dundee and East	325	533	675	717	64	27	6	120
Aberdeen and North-East	221	395	444	462	79	12	4	109
South-West	107	156	141	148	46	−10	5	38
Borders	78	117	110	108	50	−6	−2	38
Crofting Counties	303	371	293	286	22	−21	−2	−6
Scotland	1,608	3,360	4,843	5,096	109	44	5	217
England and Wales	8,893	22,712	39,952	43,745	155	76	9	392

* Glasgow and Clydeside: Renfrew, Lanark, Ayr, Dunbarton and Bute.
  Edinburgh and Lothians: East Lothian, Midlothian and West Lothian.
  Dundee and East: Fife, Kinross, Perth and Angus.
  Aberdeen and North-East: Aberdeen, Banff, Moray, Kincardine and Nairn.
  South-West: Wigtown, Kirkcudbright and Dumfries.
  Borders: Peebles, Selkirk, Berwick and Roxburgh.
  Crofting counties: Orkney, Shetland, Argyll, Inverness, Ross and Cromarty, Sutherland and Caithness.
SOURCE: *Census of Population.*

Scotland has therefore a very large urban population which is especially concentrated on one great conurbation and a few large cities. There are not proportionately so many persons living in large towns (above 20,000) as in England and Wales, but the total town-dwelling population in both countries

[1] *Census of Scotland, 1951*, vol. II.

amounts to over four-fifths of all persons.[1] In 1901, 74 % of the Scottish population were living in urban areas and 26 % in rural areas; the alteration of these percentages to 83 % and 17 % in 1951 bespeaks a fairly large increase in urbanization over the last fifty years.

EMIGRATION

The Scots have a deserved reputation as wanderers and colonizers—and Scotsmen have turned up in many out-of-the-way places. The early Scottish wanderers took the sea route to the Continent as students and gentlemen adventurers. Later, the Plantation of Ulster by James VI produced a race of Scotch-Irish who were afterwards of importance in the colonization of the United States and whose descendants still live in Ulster. All through the latter half of the eighteenth century, emigration—especially from the Highlands and to a lesser extent from the Borders—was proceeding rapidly.[2] These losses continued into the nineteenth century but were partly offset by an influx of Irish labourers into the west and south-west of Scotland, beginning about 1790 and swelling rapidly towards the middle of the nineteenth century. The bulk of the Irish in Scotland in 1851 were in Glasgow and the south-west but there were some to be found in most parts of the country and a good number in Dundee.

Table 3 shows the record of net losses through migration from 1861 to 1951

Table 3. *Net loss of the Scottish population
by migration*, 1861–1951

Period	Net loss by migration (thousands)	Percentage of natural increase for period
1861–1871	117	28
1871–1881	93	20
1881–1891	217	43
1891–1901	53	11
1901–1911	254	47
1911–1921	239	66
1921–1931	392	111
1931–1951	220	44
1861–1951	1,585	43

SOURCE: *Census of Population.*

[1] No figures are available for England and Wales precisely similar to those of urban communities of 1,000 and over quoted for Scotland; but the proportion of persons in cities, boroughs and urban districts—which is probably about the closest available approximation—was 81 %.

[2] D. F. Macdonald, *Scotland's Shifting Population, 1770–1850* (Glasgow, 1937).

13

expressed as a total and as a percentage of the natural increase (i.e. the excess of births over deaths) in each period.[1]

Emigration was high almost throughout, the peak being reached in the 1920's. In that decade the net outward movement of population actually exceeded the natural increase, so that for the first time the census recorded a decline in population. In no decade was the loss by migration less than one-tenth of the natural increase and the average over the past century has been not far short of one-half.

Between 1931 and 1951 Scotland lost 220,000 persons by migration. During the same period England and Wales had a fairly substantial inward balance from migration. From 1931 to the beginning of the war the Registrar-General for Scotland consistently had cause to comment on the favourable balance of migration from countries overseas—all the more worthy of comment since it followed on a decade of heavy emigration. The inward balance from overseas, however, showed signs of declining in each year and by 1937 was very slight. Moreover, as the decade proceeded the Registrar-General found it necessary to report substantial movements to England, which doubtless helped to swell the inward balance to that country and were by the end of the period considered sufficient to offset the small inward balances to Scotland from overseas. In the post-war period—which is dealt with in some detail later—the movement overseas and to England recommenced.

From 1871 to 1951 the net number of people lost to England and Wales by migration was actually less than the number for Scotland over the same period. The total of 1·38 m. comes to only 6 % of the natural increase of England and Wales compared with a loss of 45 % for Scotland.

Emigration was accompanied by an extensive redistribution of population within Scotland. The areas that were losing population suffered both from emigration and from a movement into the central industrial belt; but the central belt itself provided a large number of emigrants. An indication of the impact of migration up to 1931 on the four main geographical divisions is provided by Table 4, which is based on calculations made by Mr J. G. Kyd, formerly Registrar-General for Scotland.

Over the sixty years from 1871 to 1931 migration from the Northern and Southern divisions was so heavy that it more than offset the increase of population due to new births; the Borders and the Highlands of Scotland had a period of absolute decline in numbers. Nearly half of the total net loss

[1] In 1855 the Office of Registrar-General for Scotland was created and the registration of births and deaths became organized. As a result it is possible after the 1861 Census to calculate the net change in the population due to migration movements over the ten-year inter-censal periods. If the natural increase of the population in the inter-censal period is added to the population at the first census and the result compared with the numbers found to be in the country at the second census, then the difference is due to the balance of emigrants and immigrants over the ten-year period.

from Scotland over these years was from the Northern division (which includes the Highlands). The two central areas continued to grow, the West Central area growing more quickly than the East Central area over the period although it lost a higher proportion of natural increase due to migration.

Table 4. *Net loss of four divisions of Scotland by migration*, 1871–1931

Division*	Net loss by migration 1871–1931 (thousands)	Percentage of natural increase for period
West Central	399	27
East Central	125	20
Southern	144	117
Northern	580	112
Scotland	1,248	46

* Divisions as in Table 2.

SOURCE: Derived from a table by J. G. Kyd in *Scotland's Changing Population* (ed. A. M. Struthers for Scottish Council of Social Service, 1947).

A rough estimate of the births and deaths over the period from 1931 to 1951 in the Borders and Crofting counties suggests that in the more outlying areas natural increase has given place to natural decrease: the new births in an ageing population are no longer able to keep pace with the deaths. The drift away from these counties is probably now smaller because there are fewer people there and fewer of an age to go. The most important internal movement in these twenty years has probably been the drift of the population in the central belt towards the east coast (towards the new coalfields) or at any rate away from Glasgow and the west.

IMMIGRATION

The chief immigrant group during the second half of the nineteenth century continued to be the Irish. From 1851 to 1881 the numbers resident in Scotland but born in Ireland increased at each census (despite inevitable losses by death in the intervening ten years), but since 1901 they have declined in each succeeding census. It seems likely that the peak of the Irish immigration had been reached by 1881 when the Irish-born in Scotland totalled 219,000. Certainly the age-distribution and length of residence of the Irish-born in Scotland in 1931 suggest strongly that the Irish-born section of the population had aged and contained a high proportion of persons who had come here by the turn of the century.[1] In the twentieth century the English have become the chief immi-

[1] In *Census of Scotland, 1931*, vol. II.

15

grant group. In 1931, for instance, 3·4 % of the population had been born in England against 2·6 % born in Ireland. During the preceding decade it is likely that as many as two or three English entered the country to every one Irishman.[1]

There are no figures of the number of immigrants into Scotland decade by decade. Some very approximate estimates of the movements of non-Scots can, however, be made for the periods 1921–31 and 1931–51 and are given in Table 5. These, while they do not give the gross movement of population, do show the net results of such movements in terms of loss of people of Scottish birth and gain of people of non-Scottish birth.

Table 5. *Net movements of Scots and non-Scots into and out of Scotland, 1921–31 and 1931–51*

	1921–31	1931–51
Net loss by migration*	392,000	220,000
Net movement inwards of non-Scots†	Nil	182,000
Therefore net movement of Scots	392,000	402,000
Inward movement of non-Scots‡	90,000	..
Therefore outward movement of non-Scots	90,000	..

* As in Table 3.

† The number of non-Scots resident in Scotland fell from 416,000 in 1921 to 347,000 in 1931. This is probably slightly in excess of the amount of fall that might be expected during this period through wastage at the current death-rates. Hence, the movements of people of other than Scottish birth have been assumed for the present purpose to be roughly self-balancing. The population of non-Scots in Scotland in 1951 was 406,000 whereas it might have been expected to fall to about 224,000 (applying current expectations of life to each age group of the 1931 non-Scots population). The difference of 182,000 may be taken as a rough estimate of the net inward movement of non-Scots.

‡ There were 85,000 non-Scots who had been resident in Scotland for less than ten years in 1931. A very rough estimate of 5,000 for deaths over the period has been allowed.

The movement of the 1920's was not entirely one-way; there was a considerable two-way movement of non-Scots and presumably a similar movement of Scots. The net loss of people of Scots births was roughly 400,000. If we could assume that this loss was felt exclusively in the younger age-groups and set it against the number of births in the decade 1901–11, it would represent a rate of loss by migration equivalent to 30 % of the generation of Scotsmen born about the turn of the century.

Between 1931 and 1951 the net loss of persons of Scots birth amounted to about 400,000. The numbers of people born outside Scotland, however, were enhanced by a net addition of about 180,000. About 100,000 of this is the net

[1] Based on information about those who had been less than ten years in the country at the 1931 Census.

addition of English-born, and about 15,000 the net addition of people born in Ireland. The Irish have therefore now been very definitely replaced as the chief immigrant group by the English. There was also a substantial net inflow of about 45,000 people born in foreign countries. During the same period the number of Scots added to the population of England and Wales was about 340,000;[1] so that for these twenty years England has gained by far the largest proportion of people of Scots birth leaving Scotland.

All these movements have resulted in the present distribution of the Scottish population by birthplace; in 1951 8 out of every 100 (406,000) of the Scottish population were born outside Scotland.[2] This includes 4·1 English-born (more than half the total); 1·6 Irish-born; 0·2 Welsh; 0·6 born in the Commonwealth; and 1·3 born in foreign countries. Among the 57,000 foreign-born residents who were not British subjects by reason of their parentage, the most numerous groups were the 11,000 from Poland; 8,000 from Germany; 7,000 from Italy; and 5,000 from territories now included in Russia. At the same date there were 560,000 Scots living in England—against 211,000 English in Scotland; but, since the English population is larger, Scots formed a lower proportion of the English population (1·4%) than English of the Scots.

MIGRATION SINCE THE WAR

The migration movements since the end of the war are sufficiently important to merit a short special section which may help to indicate the present trend in population distribution. From 1946 to the end of 1951 Scotland had a net loss from migration of 177,000 people (97,000 overseas and 79,000 to other parts of the United Kingdom).[3] Admittedly, it was a two-way movement and the net figures do not show its considerable scale. But the net figures supply the balance of the movements, and on balance the movement was substantially outward. The net loss by migration in this period amounted to 84% of the natural increase (46% through loss overseas and 38% through movement to the rest of the United Kingdom). The balance between movements out and

[1] Obtained by similar calculations to those for Table 5.
[2] *Census of Population, 1951: One Per Cent Sample Tables.*
[3] The figures used in this paragraph and in Table 6 were most kindly supplied by the Registrar-General for Scotland. They are based on a count of persons changing identity cards and ration books when shifting from one area to another (i.e. the machinery used for the National Register). This means that they include very many comings and goings and some changes of purpose. The gross figures for movement overseas represent those who intended to be away (or in this country) for three months or more. They will clearly involve much double counting of persons 'out' in one year and 'in' in the next. The net figures are therefore much more satisfactory since many errors will be cancelled out. This applies more strongly to movements between the parts of the U.K., which are recorded when they are for six weeks or more. Net figures will again be best and least likely to serious error. Movements within Scotland (shown in Table 6) possibly involving quite small distances will be the most erratic and subject to many possibilities of error.

in for England and Wales was undoubtedly much more even and the net movement was much less.

There was a net loss overseas in each year of this period. In 1946 the net loss amounted to about 17,000 but this had grown to 20,000 in 1947, 1948 and 1949 and fell again to 10,000 in 1950 and 1951. The average loss for the six-year period was about 16,000 a year. In the movement to the rest of the United Kingdom 1946 was the heaviest year by far, when there was a net loss of 40,000 people—probably a readjustment after war-time changes. This figure fell steeply and in 1948 there was an inward net movement of 6,000. Since 1948 the move south has been growing again and in 1951 it amounted to about 12,000. It may help to place these figures in perspective if they are compared with the 1920's. The average yearly loss for the ten-year period 1921–31 was 39,000. This figure compares with net losses of about 56,000 in 1946 to overseas and the rest of the United Kingdom; with 34,000 in 1947; 28,000 in 1949 and 22,000 in 1951. The loss in this post-war period has not therefore been as serious as that in the 1920's. (There has certainly been nothing to compare with the extraordinary loss overseas in 1923, estimated at about 80,000.) It has nevertheless been fairly considerable. Even in 1951, which may presumably be regarded as a normal post-war year, the net loss amounted to about 90 % of natural increase.

Moreover, young adults are the most important category of migrants. About a third of the net loss overseas in the period fell on the 25–34 age-group (though this group amounts to only about a seventh of the population) and over a fifth on the 35–44 age-group. Over four-fifths of the net loss to other parts of the United Kingdom came from the 15–34 age-group. In the movement to the south, however, there is some evidence of coming and going at different stages of life—particularly among females; there was a fairly substantial net inward movement of children, which was almost exactly offset by a similar movement southwards of people over 65. Females were more numerous than males in the net movement overseas (perhaps because of the brides who left Scotland after the war) but males were well in the majority in the net movement to other parts of the United Kingdom.

Migration did not, of course, proceed evenly from all regions of Scotland. Table 6 shows net outward movements from eight regions over a four-year post-war period, (1) overseas, (2) to England, and (3) within Scotland, as percentages of the 1946 civilian population of each area. The regions exclude the four cities, which are separately shown, and the table also contrasts the fortunes of the cities and large burghs with those of the small burghs and landward areas.

It seems that post-war overseas migration has tended to be urban rather than rural, as has the move to England. The more industrial regions seem to have lost to England more heavily than the farming and crofting regions.

In total, post-war movements appear to have operated against Glasgow and
Clydeside, to cause some redistribution of the balance of population towards
other parts of Scotland. The North-East area, probably as a result of the
problems of the fishing industry, has also lost more than other areas.

Table 6. *Percentage net movement of migrants from regions
of Scotland*, 1 *July* 1946–30 *June* 1950

Area	Civilian population 1946 (thousands)	Net movement as percentage of 1946 population*			
		To overseas	To England	Within Scotland†	Total
Regions (excluding cities):					
Clydeside	1,299	−1·7	−1·1	+0·6	−2·2
Lothians	220	−1·0	−0·9	+1·6	−0·3
Stirling and Clackmannan	212	−0·9	−1·1	+0·8	−1·2
East	511	−1·4	−1·0	+1·5	−0·9
North-East	270	−1·1	−0·4	−2·8	−4·3
South-West	143	+0·4	−1·6	−0·2	−1·4
Borders	105	−1·3	−0·4	+1·8	+0·1
Crofting counties	280	−1·0	−0·6	+1·2	−0·4
Cities:					
Glasgow	1,055	−1·6	−1·5	−1·9	−5·0
Edinburgh	459	−2·0	−0·6	+1·6	−1·0
Aberdeen	177	−2·5	−1·2	+1·8	−1·9
Dundee	169	−2·6	−0·8	+0·9	−2·5
Scotland	4,901	−1·5	−1·0	+0·2	−2·3
Cities and large burghs	2,648	−1·8	−1·2	—	−3·0
Small burghs and landward areas	2,253	−1·2	−0·9	+0·2	−1·8

* Minus sign indicates outward movements, plus sign inward movements.
† 'Within Scotland' includes movement to and from Northern Ireland, Isle of Man and
Channel Islands.
Source: Derived from figures supplied by the Registrar-General for Scotland.

SUMMARY

1. Three-quarters of the population of Scotland live in the central belt of
Scotland, a high proportion of them in the Western portion and especially
around the city of Glasgow.

2. This uneven distribution is comparatively new—a product of the last
150 years. The most striking characteristic of the change has been the decline
in the importance of the large areas to the north and south of the central belt.
The Northern area contained nearly half of the population in 1801 and now
has less than a fifth.

19

2-2

3. During the present century—and especially in the last thirty years—the population of Scotland has been much more stable, both in size and in distribution. The total population has grown only very slowly and shifts in population within the country have been much less dramatic.

4. In the process of change, of growth, and of migration, the population of Scotland has become a smaller part of the population of Great Britain. Though the Scottish population is now five times greater than it was at the time of the Union, it has decreased as a proportion of the population of Great Britain from just under a sixth to about a tenth.

5. One of the most urgent present-day Scottish problems is that of Highland and Border depopulation and the ageing of the remaining population.

6. The Scots are now an urban people. One-third of them live in a great urban area; over half live in large towns and cities; and over four-fifths live in communities of more than a thousand people.

7. Among more recent internal changes the most interesting is the tendency, during the last twenty years, for the rates of growth of the middle and eastern portions of the central belt to exceed that of the western portion. This may mark the beginning of a readjustment in the balance of the central industrial belt between east and west.

8. The Scots are a migrating people. Emigration from Scotland overseas and to England over the last 150 years has been heavy, particularly in relation to the natural increase of the population. The exodus of the 1920's more than offset the natural growth of population.

9. The most important result of this is that the record of Scotland cannot be judged merely by its internal history. The influence of Scotsmen overseas, especially perhaps on the history of the development of the English-speaking peoples, has been considerable.

10. This movement outwards has been accompanied by an inward flow of immigrants. Two nations—the Irish and English—have contributed most to this in the last 150 years. The Irish immigration, through Glasgow and the south-west, was most marked in the second half of the nineteenth century; in more recent periods, its place has been taken by immigration from England.

11. In post-war years there has been a resumption of emigration overseas and to England, which, though not as large as that of the 1920's, has been fairly heavy in relation to the rate of growth of the population.

CHAPTER 3

BIRTHS AND DEATHS

By C. E. V. LESER

Because of the loss by migration, the Scottish population has increased at a far lower rate than the population of England and Wales; this in spite of the fact that the rate of natural increase has been of a similar magnitude during the last 100 years. Indeed, the rate of natural increase appears to have been higher in Scotland than in England and Wales since the end of the first world war; during the last twenty years it has been about 5 % per decade, compared with about 4 % for England and Wales. In theory, the difference could be due to lower mortality, or higher fertility in Scotland, or to both factors combined. But in fact it is the second factor, the relatively high fertility of the Scottish population, which is entirely responsible for its relatively large rate of natural increase.

MORTALITY RATES

Mortality, far from being lower, is higher in Scotland than in England and Wales. In both countries mortality has substantially declined, particularly since the beginning of the century, but the fall has been more rapid in England and Wales. A broad indication of this tendency is given by the crude death-rate, which relates the number of deaths in any given year to the total population. Figures for both countries are given in Table 7, for three-year averages at ten-yearly intervals. The period 1940–42, which would be influenced by abnormal war-time conditions, has been replaced by 1937–39. Since men and women are subject to different mortality experiences—women tend to live longer than men—separate figures are shown for each sex.

The crude death-rates do not, however, provide a reliable indication of true mortality conditions, since they are influenced by the age-distribution of the population. To obtain comparable figures, standardized death-rates, based on a standard age-distribution, are sometimes quoted; but the results are apt to be misleading if the actual age-distribution diverges from this standard or is in course of change. It is best to use the expectation of life at birth, indicating the average number of years which a group of new-born children will live, or its reciprocal, the 'life-table death-rate', which represents the level at which the death-rate would settle if mortality remained constant with fertility at replacement level. Figures for selected years are given in Table 8.

In both countries and for both sexes, expectation of life has increased greatly, particularly since the beginning of this century, and is now more than

21

half as long again as it was eighty years ago. Conversely, mortality has steadily declined, even during the past twenty years, when the crude death-rate actually rose in England and Wales and fell hardly at all in Scotland, thus giving an entirely misleading impression of the real trend. In 1871, Scotland had a lower male mortality than England and Wales, and about the same female mortality; since then the position has changed, and the Scottish rate is now above the English rate for both sexes. The difference is, however, less marked now than it was twenty years ago.

The improvement in both countries and the difference, in favour of England

Table 7. *Deaths per thousand of the population in Scotland and in England and Wales at different dates*

Year (average)	Males		Females	
	Scotland	England and Wales	Scotland	England and Wales
1870–72	23·2	23·7	21·4	21·1
1880–82	20·5	20·9	19·0	18·6
1890–92	20·2	20·8	19·3	18·5
1900–02	18·5	18·4	17·4	16·0
1910–12	15·6	14·7	14·7	13·0
1920–22	14·8	13·3	13·6	11·6
1930–32	14·0	12·7	12·9	11·2
1937–39	13·8	12·8	12·4	11·3
1950–52	13·2	12·7	11·9	11·1

SOURCE: Registrars-General.

Table 8. *Expectation of life at birth and life-table death-rate*

	Males		Females	
	Scotland	England and Wales	Scotland	England and Wales
Expectation of life (years)				
1870–72	41·1	40·4	43·5	43·5
1900–02	45·9	45·9	49·0	49·8
1930–32	56·0	58·7	59·5	62·9
1948–50	64·1	66·3	67·8	71·0
Life table death-rate (per thousand)				
1870–72	24·3	24·8	23·0	23·0
1900–02	21·8	21·8	20·4	20·1
1930–32	17·9	17·0	16·8	15·9
1948–50	15·6	15·1	14·7	14·1

SOURCE: Registrars-General.

and Wales, between their rates of progress has been largely due to changes in infant mortality. The death of children under one year of age used to have a dominating effect upon mortality as a whole. Towards the end of the nineteenth century, about 20 % in Scotland and 25 % in England and Wales of all deaths recorded were those of infants under one year; now the proportion is reduced to little more than 5 % in Scotland and even less in England and Wales. It is best to relate infant deaths to the number of live-born children for purposes of comparison, and the resulting infant mortality rates are presented in Fig. 2.

The contrast between the nineteenth century and the present day is indeed striking. There appears to have been hardly any reduction in infant mortality

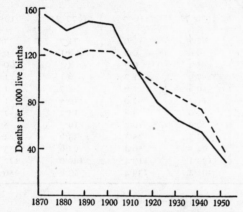

Fig. 2. Infant mortality rates in Scotland and in England and Wales, 1870–1950 (three-year averages for 1870–72, 1880–82, etc.). Scotland ‒ ‒ ‒; England and Wales ——.

during the period 1870–1900, and at the turn of the century one out of eight new-born babies in Scotland, and one out of seven in England and Wales, died before reaching its first birthday. Since then there has been a rapid and continuous improvement, and this proportion has been reduced to less than one in twenty-five in Scotland and less than one in thirty in England and Wales. Up to 1910, babies had a better chance of surviving north than south of the Border, but since then the opposite has been true. Even so, the improvement that has taken place in Scotland as well as in England and Wales since the inter-war period has been remarkable.

The fall in mortality has by no means been confined to infants, but has been equally spectacular for other age-groups. Table 9 gives specific death-rates in different age-groups for males; the female death-rates have moved in the same way.

For all age-groups under 45, mortality has been reduced to a fraction of its former level; and it is clear that apart from new-born infants, it is only in the highest age-groups that future improvements in mortality are possible to any large extent.

It is also interesting to note that in 1871, Scotland had appreciably higher mortality rates than England and Wales for males in the age-groups 5–34 while mortality was much lower for infants and slightly lower for middle-aged and old people. At present, the differential in favour of England and Wales is spread fairly evenly over all ages, except the highest ones.

Table 9. *Deaths per thousand of the population for males in different age-groups, 1870–72 and 1950*

Age-group	Scotland		England and Wales	
	1870–72	1950	1870–72	1950
0–4	62·7	10·0	71·7	7·5
5–9	9·8	0·8	8·1	0·8
10–14	5·4	0·6	4·4	0·6
15–19	7·9	1·2	6·1	1·0
20–24	10·8	1·6	8·7	1·4
25–34	11·2	2·0	10·5	1·7
35–44	14·0	3·8	14·2	2·8
45–54	20·0	10·4	19·7	8·3
55–64	32·5	25·3	33·6	22·5
65–74	64·1	56·4	67·6	53·3
75–84	139·1	119·4	146·0	122·5
85–	302·2	239·4	307·8	250·4

SOURCE: Registrars-General.

The fall in death-rates is also illustrated by the changing structure of the life tables, indicating the number of survivors at any given age out of a group of new-born babies subject to current mortality levels. Fig. 3, which compares the Scottish life tables of almost a century ago with those based on recent experience, shows how much the chance of reaching a higher age has increased. For example, fewer than one-half of all boys and girls of the age of 15 could expect to live to the age of 65; now almost two-thirds of all boys and more than two-thirds of the girls do so.

It is easy to account for the reduction in mortality, in view of the advance in medical knowledge and care, and of the improvement in social and economic conditions. But it is hardly possible to give more than a tentative explanation for the difference between the Scottish and the English death-rates. Possible factors are: a less favourable climate, inferior housing conditions, or a generally lower standard of living in Scotland. The fact that in 1871 mortality in Scotland was below the English level for infants, but above for children and young people, remains a puzzling feature.

There is some evidence that infant mortality at any rate is considerably

24

influenced by economic and social factors. There are large regional variations in infant deaths within Scotland, in favour of more residential areas, and there are large differences between different social classes; in 1949, Scottish infant mortality rates ranged from 18·5 in the highest to 62·1 per thousand in the lowest of five social classes. Some care is needed in interpreting these figures, but they tend to show that infant mortality is still capable of further reduction by improved living conditions.

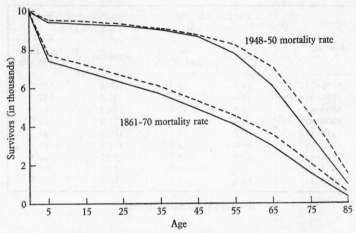

Fig. 3. Survivors at different ages out of 10,000 new-born males and females in Scotland at 1861–70 and 1948–50 mortality rates. Males ——; females – – –.

FERTILITY RATES

The general trend of fertility has been similar to that of mortality. With the exception of the most recent years, birth-rates have fallen heavily, but less so in Scotland than in England and Wales; the present higher level of fertility in Scotland more than compensates for the higher mortality and accounts for the larger rate of natural increase. Table 10 shows two alternative sets of figures indicating fertility: the 'crude birth-rate', which relates total live births to total population, and the 'general fertility rate' which relates them to the total of women aged 15–44 (or 15–49) and which gives a better indication of fertility than the crude birth-rate. Stillbirths, which only recently have come to be adequately recorded and which at present constitute no more than 2–3 % of all births, have been left out of account. It is not necessary to distinguish male and female births, the ratio of which has been more or less constant at a level of 105 to 100.

Using these rather crude measures of fertility, it would seem that until 1881 England and Wales had a slightly higher fertility than Scotland but since then the opposite has been true. The fall in the birth-rate was most marked during the thirty years 1880–1910 and again during the inter-war period, but since then there has been some recovery. The present level of fertility is somewhat above that of 1930–32, although, owing to the lower proportion of women in the reproductive age-groups, this is not showing itself in a higher birth-rate.

Table 10. *Live births per thousand of population and per thousand women aged 15–44*

Year (average)	Per thousand of population		Per thousand women aged 15–44	
	Scotland	England and Wales	Scotland	England and Wales
1870–72	34·8	35·5	149·4	153·7
1880–82	33·6	34·1	145·8	147·7
1890–92	30·8	30·8	132·5	129·7
1900–02	29·5	28·7	121·9	114·8
1910–12	25·8	24·5	107·3	98·3
1920–22	25·6	22·8	105·1	91·1
1930–32	19·1	15·8	80·1	64·3
1937–39	17·6	14·9	73·3	61·7
1950–52	17·9	15·6	80·8	71·8

SOURCE: Registrars-General.

GROSS REPRODUCTION RATES

In the general fertility rate, the influence of the age-structure of the population on births has only partially been eliminated. A better measure of fertility, based on fertility rates in individual age-groups, is the gross reproduction rate, which shows how many girl babies the average member of a group of women would give birth to, if all of the group survived until the end of child bearing age. A gross reproduction rate below one indicates that the population could not possibly reproduce itself, no matter how low mortality might be.

The calculation of gross reproduction rates is based on a classification of births by the age of the mother. This information is not generally available for Britain for years before 1938, except for 1855, in which year it has been recorded for Scotland only. The data indicate that in 1855, Scotland had a gross reproduction rate of 2·0; and the true value may well be higher, since the registration of births in that year—the first year of birth registration—appears to have been incomplete, and the data may understate the true birth figures.

For subsequent years, rough estimates only, based on general fertility rates, can be obtained. The gross reproduction rate in both countries appears to have been well above 2 in 1871 and to have fallen to about 1·1 for Scotland and 0·9 for England and Wales by 1931. For 1939, the exact figures are 1·06 for Scotland, 0·89 for England and Wales; the English population thus had a fertility which even under the most favourable mortality conditions would have been below replacement level, but this did not apply to Scotland. Since then, gross reproduction rates have risen a little; in 1950, the Scottish figure was 1·23 and the English figure 1·06.

However, even this does not tell us the whole story. About 95 % of all births are legitimate, and a large number of legitimate births may reflect one or both of two things: that a high proportion of the population are married men and women, or that a large number of children are being born to each married couple. The question thus arises how far the changes in fertility have been due to changes in nuptiality or in legitimate fertility; and similarly, which of these factors is responsible for the relatively high fertility in Scotland as compared with England and Wales.

MARRIAGE RATES

Table 11 provides information regarding the marriage habits in the two countries. It suggests that the inclination towards marriage has been consistently smaller in Scotland than in England and Wales: moreover, while it did not change very much between 1871 and 1931, it has increased considerably during the past twenty years.

Table 11. *Percentage of men and women aged 15 and over in the married state*, 1871–1951

Year	Men		Women	
	Scotland	England and Wales	Scotland	England and Wales
1871	50·2	55·9	43·9	52·2
1901	47·8	53·6	44·3	49·6
1931	52·4	59·3	47·5	53·4
1951	61·7	68·7	55·4	61·8

SOURCE: *Census of Population.*

Thus, there are at present more married men and women in both parts of Britain than there are single, widowed and divorced men and women of 15 years and over. This has never before been true as regards Scotswomen, and it has not always been true as far as either Scotsmen or Englishwomen are concerned, though it has been the normal position for Englishmen.

The recent increase in the proportion of married women is even more striking if attention is confined to the main child-bearing age-groups, which, however, now form a lower proportion of the total female population than previously. Table 12 gives the relevant details.

The difference between England and Scotland in the proportion of married women is particularly marked in the age-group 20–24 but is less noticeable in the age-groups 35–39 and over, as shown in Table 13. This means that those Scotswomen who did marry—and fewer of them did than Englishwomen—tended to marry later in life.

Table 12. *Percentage of all women in the age-group 15–44, and percentage of married women in this age-group*

Year	Women aged 15–44 as percentage of all women		Married women as percentage of all women aged 15–44	
	Scotland	England and Wales	Scotland	England and Wales
1871	44·5	45·0	42·4	49·6
1901	47·1	48·3	42·0	46·8
1931	45·9	47·2	44·0	50·1
1951	42·4	41·7	57·1	64·8

SOURCE: *Census of Population.*

Table 13. *Percentage of married women in each age-group*, 1951

Age-group	Scotland	England and Wales
15–19	3·0	4·4
20–24	38·0	48·1
25–29	69·3	77·2
30–34	76·9	83·0
35–39	79·4	83·3
40–44	75·5	81·2
Total 15–44	57·1	64·8

SOURCE: *Census of Population, 1951: One Per Cent Sample Tables.*

This shift towards the married state has been brought about by a relatively high marriage-rate in recent years. During the years 1930–32, people married at an annual rate of 13·6 per thousand of the population in Scotland and 15·6 per thousand in England and Wales. In subsequent years, the marriage-rate as defined here[1] increased slowly to 15·4 for Scotland and 17·5 for England and Wales in 1938, then jumped to a maximum of 21·2 and 22·5 respectively in 1940, and after a sharp drop, went up again to 18·9 and 18·7 respectively in 1945. For 1950–52 the average marriage rate was 16·1 in Scotland, 16·3 in England and Wales, so that the Scottish marriage-rate is considerably higher

[1] An alternative definition, which is used by the Registrar-General for Scotland, relates the number of marriages, instead of persons getting married, to the population.

than in the inter-war period and very near the still higher English rate. In terms of men (or women) available for marriage, however, the picture is a little different. In 1930–32, out of a thousand bachelors aged 15 years (strictly speaking it should be 16 years) and over, widowers and divorced men, 41·6 married annually in Scotland and 53·4 in England and Wales; for 1950–52 the corresponding figures are 59·6 and 70·9. Thus, the tendency to get married appears much greater in both countries than previously, but, as before, smaller north than south of the Border.

The changes in marriage habits provide an explanation for the recent increase in fertility but not for the previous large fall. Nor can the fertility differential between Scotland and England be accounted for by a difference in marriage habits. On the contrary, one would have expected that the lower proportion of married people in Scotland would be reflected in a relatively smaller number of births. But this is not so, and an explanation for the comparatively high Scottish birth-rate must be sought elsewhere.

TRENDS IN FERTILITY

It is obviously essential to study the changes, as well as the differences between Scotland and England, in legitimate fertility rates. Table 14 provides the necessary data and helps to correct two impressions which Table 10 tended to give. The first was that fertility used to be higher in England and Wales than in Scotland about eighty years ago; the second, that the decline in fertility has come to an end.

Table 14. *Legitimate births per thousand married women aged* 15–44

Year	Scotland	England and Wales	Scotland (England and Wales = 100)
1870–72	319	292	109
1900–02	272	236	115
1930–32	169	123	137
1950–52	134	105	128

SOURCE: Registrars-General.

Table 14 shows that even at the earlier date, Scottish married women produced more children than English married women, but the difference was not as marked then as in more recent years and was more than compensated for by the smaller proportion of married women in Scotland. The fertility differential was very large in 1931 and is still considerable.

Table 14 also shows that the long-term trend of declining legitimate fertility has by no means come to an end, though it has recently been overshadowed by an increase in marriages. It is true that there was a temporary

29

increase in legitimate fertility rates immediately after the war—between 1945 and 1947 they increased from 126 to 172 in Scotland and from 104 to 139 in England and Wales—but since then they have dropped again substantially.

Table 15. *Percentage of married women on 8 April* 1951 *who had live-born children during the preceding year, by age-group*

Age-group	Scotland	England and Wales
15–19	30·9	30·2
20–24	28·9	22·9
25–29	21·9	17·4
30–34	14·4	11·3
35–39	8·6	6·0
40–49	1·4	1·2
Total 15–49	11·4	9·0

SOURCE: *Census of Population, 1951: One Per Cent Sample Tables.*

Table 16. *Married women aged* 45–49, *by duration of marriage, and average number of children born to them,* 1951

Duration of marriage (completed years)	Married women, aged 45–49, as percentage of all durations		Average number of children per married woman	
	Scotland	England and Wales	Scotland	England and Wales
0–4	1·7	2·0	0·14	0·29
5–9	5·2	3·3	0·66	0·64
10–14	9·1	7·8	1·11	1·11
15–19	21·0	18·7	1·87	1·42
20–24	36·7	39·8	2·65	2·06
25–	26·3	28·4	3·68	2·92
All durations	100·0	100·0	2·47	2·03

SOURCE: *Census of Population, 1951: One Per Cent Sample Tables.*

The difference in current fertility between married women in Scotland and in England and Wales is very marked in most age-groups: it is small only for the age-groups 15–19 and perhaps for those aged 40 and over, as illustrated by Table 15.

The differences in completed fertility, that is to say, in total number of children born to the average married woman up to the end of her reproductive period, are equally striking. Table 16 gives an analysis of the total fertility of all married women aged 45–49—which for practical purposes can be considered as completed fertility—by duration of marriage.

There is no significant difference between the two countries in the number of children born to women 45–49 years old and married for less than fifteen years, i.e. who were at least 30 years old when they married. But the women that make the greatest contribution towards reproduction of the population are those married for at least fifteen years—all of them less than 35 years of age at their marriage—and among them Scotswomen had on the average a much higher number of children than Englishwomen.

Among all the married women of this generation, born at the beginning of the century, Scotland had a lower proportion of women married twenty years or longer than England. In spite of this, the average Scotswoman gave birth to almost 2·5 children, against little more than 2 in England and Wales. Clearly, if this experience were to continue in later generations, the population of England and Wales could not possibly reproduce itself, and it is doubtful whether the Scottish population could. For a total of two children per married woman only replaces the parents and does not make allowance for the women who do not marry or who die after marriage but before the end of their child-bearing period.

The fact has been clearly established that the fertility of married women is on the average higher in Scotland than in England and Wales, and that the difference more than compensates for the comparatively smaller number of married women in Scotland. It is not easy to find a simple explanation for these differences in social habits, though there are several possible causes of the higher fertility in Scotland. One of them is the higher proportion of the agricultural population; another, the differences in the social structure of the populations; but the differences are unlikely to account for more than a small proportion of the fertility differential.

Another and perhaps more important factor is the relatively high proportion of Roman Catholics in Scotland. This has been estimated at 14·5 %, compared with 6·4 % in England and Wales. The Roman Catholic Church discourages birth control, and there is some evidence that their teaching has not been without influence, and that the Roman Catholic element in the population has a higher fertility rate than the Protestants. The fact that burghs like Coatbridge, Airdrie and Port Glasgow—and in England, towns in the Merseyside area—which have a high proportion of Catholics have also a high fertility rate, lends some support to this view. Similarly, the attitude of the Roman Catholic Church may be responsible for some deferment of marriages in Scotland.

It is sometimes said that bad housing conditions are responsible for family limitation, but the evidence seems to contradict this; Scotland with its inferior housing has a higher fertility rate than England and Wales, and high birth-rates are found in places where there is serious overcrowding. To some extent, high fertility and high infantile mortality seem to go hand in hand, but it is

31

doubtful which is the cause and which the effect. It seems quite plausible that with a smaller family size greater care can be bestowed upon the mother and the new-born child, with a consequent reduction of infant mortality.

NET REPRODUCTION RATES

In combination with mortality, the fertility of the population determines the extent to which it is reproducing itself and whether a natural increase or decrease can be expected in the long run. A comparatively simple, though not entirely satisfactory measure is the net reproduction rate—more exactly the maternal net reproduction rate—which indicates the number of girls a group of women will give birth to during their lifetime at current fertility and mortality levels for each age-group. The net reproduction rate implies a natural increase if above one and a decrease if below one.

A rough estimate puts the Scottish net reproduction rate for the year 1855 at 1·3, which shows a definite tendency for the population to increase. The gross reproduction rate for the same year was estimated at 2·0, and the large difference between the two rates is remarkable; it indicates the high rate of wastage by death before the age of 50, and particularly in the first year of life, for women in the population. By 1939, the net reproduction rate had fallen to 0·93, that is to say, below replacement level, but since then it has risen again to 1·15 in 1950. Thus the fall in mortality has nearly made up for the fall in fertility, and the reproduction rate is little lower than a hundred years ago. For England and Wales, the effective reproduction rate, a measure similar to the net reproduction rate, but assuming a continuing improvement in mortality, amounted to 1·02 in 1949 and has fallen below 1 since then. Thus the English population appears to approach a stationary state, but the Scottish population may still have an inherent tendency towards a natural increase.

The evidence is not fully conclusive, since it rests upon the assumption that fertility rates remain unchanged, and it is not safe to assume this tacitly. True, the present marriage-rate is still high, and the number of marriages in existence is likely to remain large; but the number of children per married woman may decline still further. We can say, however, that Scotland will have a higher rate of natural increase, or a lower rate of decrease, than England and Wales for a long time to come, even if eventually the differences between the two countries may level out. In the absence of a large balance of migration across the Border, the share of Scotland in the population of Great Britain would thus tend to increase.

AGE-DISTRIBUTION

The changes in birth- and death-rates affect not only the total size of the population but also its age structure. Table 17 shows how the proportions of men and women below, at and above the main working ages have changed in Scotland, with comparable figures for England and Wales; it also shows the age-distribution that would obtain in a hypothetical 'life-table' population if 1948–50 mortality rates continued indefinitely and fertility rates were just such as to keep the population constant.

Table 17. *Age-distribution of population and life-table age-distribution*

Year	Scotland: percentage of all ages in age-group			England and Wales: percentage of all ages in age-group		
	0–14	15–64	65–	0–14	15–64	65–
Males						
1871	39·0	56·5	4·5	37·2	58·4	4·4
1901	34·8	61·2	4·0	33·5	62·3	4·2
1931	28·3	65·2	6·5	25·1	68·2	6·7
1951	26·2	64·9	8·9	23·7	67·0	9·3
Life-table 1948–50	22·2	66·3	11·5	21·7	66·2	12·1
Females						
1871	34·5	59·7	5·8	35·1	59·9	5·0
1901	32·2	62·2	5·6	31·4	63·5	5·1
1931	25·7	66·3	8·0	22·6	69·3	8·1
1951	23·1	65·8	11·1	21·0	66·6	12·4
Life-table 1948–50	21·1	64·6	14 3	20·4	63·9	15·7

SOURCE: Calculated from census data and *Annual Abstract* for 1952.

The proportion of children is seen to have steadily diminished since 1871; at first this meant a corresponding increase in size of the population of working age, but later on the main expansion took place in the number of older people. If the population became stationary at present mortality rates, the proportion of children would still go down and the proportion of old people still go up; at the same time there would be more men but fewer women of working age in Scotland.

Compared with England and Wales, Scotland has a larger number of children and fewer men—to some extent also fewer women—aged 15–64. Scotland also has fewer old people, particularly women; this difference would remain between the hypothetical stationary populations of the two countries and is therefore entirely due to the heavier mortality in Scotland.

Scotland still has a sufficiently high fertility rate to allow for a moderate natural increase in population, and the Scottish population is likely to remain slightly younger than the life-table would suggest for some time to come. In present conditions, the country benefits from the fact that a much higher proportion of the population is in the productive age-groups than in the last century. This process will not go much further but on the other hand it will not be reversed in the near future; and any fears that a shrinking section of the population may have to maintain the burden of a growing section in the non-productive ages are as yet groundless.

CHAPTER 4

MANPOWER

BY C. E. V. LESER

In the *One Per Cent Sample Tables* of the 1951 Census the gainfully occupied population of Scotland, including all employees, employers and persons working on their own account, whether in work or not, as well as members of the armed forces stationed there, is given as 2,270,100 persons or 44·5 % of the total population. The occupied population consists of 1,583,600 men and 686,500 women, forming respectively 65·0 % of the total male and 25·8 % of the total female population. These proportions are approximately the same as in 1901 but are slightly below the present proportions for England and Wales. The census figures are shown in Table 18.[1]

Table 18. *Number and proportion of males and females gainfully occupied in Scotland, 1951 and 1901, and in England and Wales, 1951*

	Both sexes	Males	Females
Scotland 1951			
Number (thousands)	2,270·1	1,583·6	686·5
Percentage of total population	44·5	65·0	25·8
Scotland 1901			
Number (thousands)	1,982·8	1,391·2	591·6
Percentage of total population	44·3	64·0	25·7
England and Wales, 1951			
Number (thousands)	20,308·4	14,078·6	6,229·8
Percentage of total population	46·4	67·1	27·4

SOURCE: *Census of Population.*

There are reasons for thinking that the census figures—at least for women—give too low a total for the occupied population, because some persons, particularly married women, do not enter in the census forms the fact that they are gainfully employed. The Ministry of Labour figures for insured employees show totals of 1,382,000 and 726,000 for men and women in 1951; and these figures point to a total for the gainfully occupied population on the same basis as in the census of about 1,530,000 men and 750,000 women. Whether one uses the census figures or the Ministry of Labour figures, however, the *proportion* of the occupied to the total population, alike for men and for women, is lower in Scotland than in England and Wales.

[1] The figures in Tables 18–24 (except Table 22) exclude members of the armed forces serving abroad.

A comparison of these proportions is necessarily crude, and too much significance should not be attached to it, since the age-structure of the population affects the potential size of the occupied population. It is, of course, the population from 15 to 64 years of age which provides most of the labour force; for the male working population, all age-groups within this range are about equally important, but for the female working population the lower age-groups make a far greater contribution than the higher ones.

Table 19. *Percentage of total population in different age-groups for Scotland, 1901 and 1951, and for England and Wales, 1951*

Age-group	Males			Females		
	Scotland		England and Wales, 1951	Scotland		England and Wales, 1951
	1901	1951		1901	1951	
0–14	34·8	26·2	23·7	32·2	23·1	21·0
15–19	10·6	7·1	6·3	9·8	6·9	6·1
20–24	9·7	7·0	6·7	9·7	7·2	6·6
25–34	15·3	14·2	14·9	15·7	14·0	14·1
35–44	11·5	14·6	15·8	11·8	14·3	15·0
45–54	8·5	13·0	13·6	8·8	13·1	13·7
55–64	5·6	9·0	9·7	6·4	10·3	11·1
65–	4·0	8·9	9·3	5·6	11·1	12·4
All ages	100·0	100·0	100·0	100·0	100·0	100·0

SOURCE: *Census of Population.*

Let us, therefore, look at the age-distribution of the Scottish population, compared with fifty years ago and with England and Wales, as given in Table 19.

The immediately obvious feature of Table 19 is the fact that the population has become older. There are relatively fewer people under 35 and relatively more aged 35 and over in Scotland than there were fifty years ago, and the change is most pronounced for children and old people. In England and Wales this process has gone even further.

The causes of this ageing process, the reduction in mortality and fertility, have been discussed elsewhere in this book and need not concern us here. The point which matters in this connexion is: What effect have these changes had on the supply of men and women for work? The answer is not as simple as one might think, nor is it as familiar as the shift towards the higher age-groups.

The fall in the proportion of children under 15 is only partly counter-balanced by a rise in the proportion of people aged 65 years and over. The male population of working age thus forms a higher proportion of the total than in 1901. This is also true for women, but the relative depletion of the age-

36

group 15–34 in favour of the ages 35–64 which do not provide so many women for gainful occupations works the other way. A more refined analysis shows that the second factor predominates, that is to say, the changes in age-structure had, on balance, an unfavourable effect on the size of the female labour force. Similarly, the age-structure of the Scottish population can be shown to make for a lower proportion of occupied males but for a slightly higher proportion of occupied females than that of the English population.

The actual figures, however, show a different picture from that which this reasoning would lead us to expect. Clearly, then, there must be powerful factors other than the age-distribution influencing the manpower totals, and within a given age-group, there must be important variations in the proportions of occupied men and women. This supposition is indeed borne out by Table 20.

Table 20. *Occupied persons as percentage of the total population in each age-group for Scotland, 1901 and 1951, and for England and Wales, 1951*

Age-group	Males			Females		
	Scotland		England and Wales, 1951	Scotland		England and Wales, 1951
	1901	1951		1901	1951	
0–14	5·7	—	—	3·8	—	—
15–19	93·8	84·9	83·8	72·6	77·9	78·5
20–24	97·8	94·1	95·4	59·6	65·8	65·5
25–34	98·8	98·0	98·1	32·2	34·4	37·4
35–44	98·5	98·3	98·8	22·3	30·0	34·9
45–54	97·3	97·8	98·0	20·7	28·8	34·6
55–64	92·3	93·5	91·7	19·9	21·5	21·4
65–	67·2	33·6	31·8	14·4	5·2	5·3
All ages	64·0	65·0	67·1	25·7	25·8	27·4

SOURCE: *Census of Population.*

The proportion of males who are occupied has been reduced to zero in the age-group 0–14, has somewhat fallen in the age-groups from 15–24 and has fallen from about two-thirds to one-third among those of 65 and over; this reflects the abolition of child labour, longer and more universal school and college training and the introduction of old-age pensions, and greater longevity after the age of retiral. There has been no significant change for other age-groups, nor is there any substantial difference from England and Wales at any age.

On the other hand, the proportion of occupied women has risen in nearly every age-group; the only exceptions are girls under 15 and women of 65 or more years. The rise is particularly marked for the ages 15–24 and 35–54. This

37

tendency for more women to go out to work now than at the beginning of the century appears the more remarkable when it is realized that during these fifty years the proportion of women who are married rose from 30·0 % to 42·6 % (changes in age-structure are only to a minor extent responsible for this apparent increase in preference for the married state). It is true, however, that the size of the average family has declined.

There are still relatively fewer occupied women in the age-groups between 25 and 54 in Scotland than in England and Wales. This is another surprising feature, since the proportion of English women who are married stands at 48·8 %, above the Scottish figure of 42·6 %; but again, the larger family size in Scotland offers some kind of explanation.

If these results are combined with those derived from Table 18, the following picture emerges:

1. Of the total male population of Scotland, a higher proportion are in the main working ages (15–64) than fifty years ago: about 65 % in 1951 compared with 61 % in 1901. But the male occupied population has not increased in size to any large extent, as the effect of this change has been largely offset by a decline in the proportion of men under 25 and over 65 years who were following an occupation; there was little scope for an increase in the proportion occupied in the intermediate age-group.

2. The size of the potential female labour force was reduced by a relative decline in the number of women aged 15–34—from about 35 % of all females in 1901 to about 28 % in 1951—which outweighed the relative increase in the age-group from 35 years onwards. But the proportion of women who went out to work increased in most age-groups, and as a result the actual labour force maintained a constant proportion to the total population.

3. In Scotland, a smaller part of the population consists of persons 15–64 years old than in England and Wales. This accounts for the comparatively low proportion of occupied males in the Scottish population.

4. Scotswomen between the ages 25 and 55 do not show the same tendency to follow a gainful occupation as do their English counterparts. It is this discrepancy, and not the difference in age-distribution, which is responsible for the relatively low number of occupied women in Scotland.

The changes which have taken place both in the age-composition of the population and in the proportion seeking work in each group have affected the age-composition of the occupied population, as well as the total numbers employed. Table 21 shows that the first of these two factors had the more powerful effect, and the occupied population has shifted a good deal towards the higher age-groups.

Of all occupied males 57 % were under 35 years of age in 1901 but only 41 % in 1951; similarly, the proportion of occupied females who were less than 35 years old has fallen from almost 75 % to 58 %. More of the men in work are over 35 nowadays than are under 35, where the reverse used to be true; and more than two-fifths instead of only a quarter of the women in work are over 35. This trend towards an older working population has gone even further in England and Wales, and the trend is likely to continue in Scotland too.

Table 21. *Age-distribution of occupied population for Scotland,* 1901 *and* 1951, *and for England and Wales,* 1951

Age-group	Number (thousands) Scotland		Percentage of all ages		
			Scotland		England and Wales, 1951
	1901	1951	1901	1951	
Males					
0–14	43·4	—	3·1	—	—
15–19	216·2	146·6	15·5	9·3	7·8
20–24	205·8	160·0	14·8	10·1	9·6
25–34	328·1	340·1	23·6	21·5	21·8
35–44	247·5	350·7	17·8	22·1	23·2
45–54	179·2	309·0	12·9	19·5	19·9
55–64	111·8	204·1	8·0	12·9	13·3
65–	59·2	73·1	4·3	4·6	4·4
All ages	1,391·2	1,583·6	100·0	100·0	100·0
Females					
0–14	28·3	—	4·8	—	—
15–19	163·9	143·9	27·7	21·0	17·4
20–24	132·8	125·9	22·4	18·3	15·8
25–34	116·6	128·2	19·7	18·7	19·2
35–44	60·6	114·0	10·3	16·6	19·1
45–54	41·7	100·5	7·0	14·6	17·4
55–64	29·2	58·6	5·0	8·6	8·7
65–	18·5	15·4	3·1	2·2	2·4
All ages	591·6	686·5	100·0	100·0	100·0

SOURCE: *Census of Population.*

The total size of the occupied population (including persons temporarily out of work) has increased steadily, hand in hand with an increase in the size of the total population. Official data are available for census years only, but an estimate of the Scottish working population over each year from 1921 to 1948, on the basis of census and Ministry of Labour data, has been made by Mr A. D. Campbell in the course of estimating the Scottish national income. The figures are not quite comparable with the census data as they include members of the armed forces serving abroad, but they provide a useful indication of the trend of the working population, and the results are presented in graphical form in Fig. 4.

39

Table 22 shows, for selected years, how the total is made up of wage-earners, managers and salaried workers (including shop assistants), and independent workers. The growth in total size of the occupied population is seen to have been accompanied by a shift from independent works to the wage- and salary-earning groups.

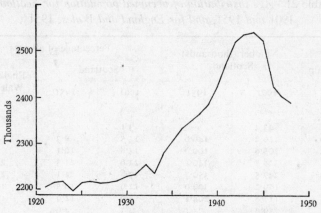

Fig. 4. Total occupied population of Scotland, 1921–48.

A more detailed occupational classification of the working population is provided in Table 23, which is based on the occupational grouping adopted for the 1951 Census; the figures for 1901 have been brought into line with those for 1951 as far as possible.

Table 22. *Occupied population of Scotland by status*, 1921–48.
In thousands

Year	Wage-earners	Managerial and salaried	Independent workers	Total
1921	1,540	534	132	2,206
1931	1,532	586	116	2,234
1939	1,655	637	94	2,386
1948	1,676	638	76	2,390

SOURCE: Estimate by A. D. Campbell.

The figures in this table refer to personal occupation and not to the industry in which a person is working; for example, carpenters engaged in building work are counted as woodworkers. Nevertheless, the industrial pattern of the country exerts a strong influence upon the occupational distribution of the population, and the changes shown here reflect to a large extent the expansion and decline of individual industries.

Table 23. *Occupational distribution of occupied population in Scotland, 1901 and 1951, and in England and Wales, 1951*

Occupation	Number (thousands)		Percentage of all occupations		
	Scotland		Scotland		England and Wales, 1951
	1901	1951	1901	1951	
Males					
Fishermen	27·5	12·5	2·0	0·8	0·1
Agricultural and forestry workers	169·1	151·8	12·2	9·6	6·8
Miners and quarriers	126·7	81·8	9·1	5·2	4·3
Metal workers	206·8	253·0	14·9	16·0	16·1
Textile workers	51·5	24·7	3·7	1·6	1·4
Leather workers, textile goods makers	45·0	20·3	3·2	1·3	1·7
Food, drink and tobacco makers	31·3	24·9	2·2	1·6	1·0
Woodworkers	73·1	54·4	5·3	3·4	3·1
Builders and decorators	95·0	125·0	6·8	7·9	8·0
Others engaged in production	96·9	184·5	7·0	11·6	11·0
Transport workers	149·3	168·5	10·7	10·6	10·0
Commercial and clerical workers	167·3	203·2	12·0	12·8	14·8
Professional workers and managers	55·7	104·9	4·0	6·6	8·1
Engaged in personal service	48·9	48·8	3·5	3·1	3·3
Miscellaneous	47·1	125·3	3·4	7·9	10·3
All occupations	1,391·2	1,583·6	100·0	100·0	100·0
Females					
Agricultural and forestry workers	40·6	14·6	6·9	2·1	1·5
Metal workers	3·0	10·6	0·5	1·5	3·4
Textile workers	123·0	56·4	20·8	8·2	5·8
Textile goods makers	75·3	36·9	12·7	5·4	7·0
Food, drink and tobacco makers	15·1	16·5	2·6	2·4	1·3
Paper and printing workers	16·2	11·6	2·7	1·7	1·4
Others engaged in production	18·5	44·8	3·1	6·5	8·7
Transport workers	7·0	16·1	1·2	2·4	2·1
Commercial and clerical workers	70·1	234·3	11·8	34·1	32·7
Professional workers	27·2	64·0	4·6	9·3	8·4
Engaged in domestic service	151·7	105·3	25·6	15·4	14·6
Engaged in other personal service	35·3	47·8	6·0	7·0	8·3
Miscellaneous	8·6	27·6	1·5	4·0	4·8
All occupations	591·6	686·5	100·0	100·0	100·0

SOURCE: *Census of Population.*

This, at any rate, is true as far as men are concerned. The way in which the male labour force is distributed over different occupations has not changed as much during the past fifty years as one might have thought. One of the chief features is the absolute and relative decline in the number of fishermen, agricultural workers, miners, textile and leather workers while, on the other hand, metal workers, professional and managerial workers and others have become numerically more important. On the whole, the changes reflect the well-known shift from primary to secondary and from secondary to tertiary industries.

When we look at the occupations of women, a rather different picture is obtained. Traditionally, the range of female occupations has been far narrower than that of male occupations. In 1901, more than a quarter of all occupied women were engaged in domestic service, the majority of them working in private households, the others in hotels, etc. Also, more than one-third were textile or clothing workers; commerce, agriculture, personal service occupations like laundry work, and the lower professions like nursing and teaching accounted for the bulk of the remainder. Of the present generation of women, far fewer do agricultural or textile work or are domestic servants, and few of the latter are now resident servants in private households. On the other hand, more than one-third of all occupied women are now shop assistants, clerks, typists, etc., and the number in the professions has also substantially increased. Generally, women have shifted from manual to non-manual occupations to a far larger extent than men.

The occupational pattern in Scotland does not differ from that in England and Wales to any marked degree, and the differences chiefly reflect the somewhat larger importance of primary production in the Scottish economy. Because the metal industries in Scotland are heavier than in England and Wales, relatively few women find employment in them. On the other hand, Scotland has a larger proportion of women and a smaller proportion of men in commercial and clerical occupations. There is no *a priori* reason why this should be so; there is apparently some difference in social habits between the two countries, traceable, perhaps, to the comparative scarcity of jobs for women in Scotland.

The industrial structure of a country or area exercises a determining influence not merely on the pattern of occupations but also on the total number of occupied women. The regional variations within England and Wales in the proportion of occupied women may serve as an illustration of this. In the north-west of England, where cotton and other light industries provide ample employment opportunities for women, 32·1 % of all females are occupied, whilst in Wales, where such opportunities are lacking, though not to the same extent as before the war, the proportion is only 19·2 %.

Similarly, there are large variations within Scotland in the degree to which women's labour is utilized; and since the proportions of occupied and un-occupied men are largely the same, these variations are also reflected in the size of the occupied population of both sexes combined. Table 24 illustrates this point from figures for the seven most populous Scottish counties (including cities and other large burghs). The proportion of occupied women, as well as of the occupied population of both sexes, is highest in Angus and lowest in Aberdeenshire. Generally speaking, a high proportion of women are gainfully occupied in textile areas, and a low proportion in mining and agricultural areas.

Table 24. *Occupied persons as percentage of total population in seven Scottish counties, 1951*

County	Males	Females	Both sexes
Aberdeen	60·6	19·2	39·1
Angus	64·1	31·3	46·9
Ayrshire	65·7	25·7	44·5
Fife	65·3	20·7	42·4
Lanark	65·0	28·9	46·4
Midlothian	65·1	29·1	45·7
Renfrew	65·1	27·4	44·9
All seven counties	64·7	27·2	45·1
Remainder of Scotland	65·7	22·0	43·1
Total Scotland	65·0	25·8	44·5

SOURCE: *Census of Population, 1951: One Per Cent Sample Tables.*

If the proportion of occupied women in Scotland was brought up to the level prevailing, on the average, in Dundee and the remainder of Angus, their number would rise to 830,000, that is to say by almost 150,000. But this is higher than was ever reached even in the war and could hardly be accepted as a realistic programme to be achieved by the establishment of more women-employing industries. In the first place, women not counted as gainfully occupied may in fact be very much occupied and not free to go out to work, particularly in agricultural areas. In the second place, there is some evidence that the female labour force in women-employing industries is to some extent recruited from outside areas by the migration of 'mobile women' to the neighbourhood of these industries. Greater industrial diversity in areas at present lacking employment opportunities for women would thus tend to level out the regional variations in the ratio of occupied to total population, but it is uncertain to what extent it would raise the level for Scotland as a whole. Nevertheless, there appears to be some under-employment of women in Scotland—rather more so than in England.

43

In addition to having a comparatively small occupied population, Scotland has been, and still is, handicapped by a relatively high incidence of unemployment. During the last thirty years, the proportion of men and women who were out of work in Scotland has been consistently higher than in Britain as a whole; although unemployment is now at a far lower level than before the war, the differential between Scotland and the remainder of Britain has not disappeared.

Fig. 5 shows the number of unemployed registered at Labour Exchanges in Scotland at half-yearly intervals since the middle of 1923. The figures on which the diagram is based are affected by small changes in the method of counting the unemployed, but only to a minor extent. The number of un-

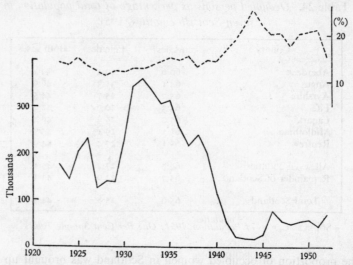

Fig. 5. Unemployment in Scotland, 1923–52. Number of persons unemployed in Scotland ——; unemployed in Scotland as percentage of unemployed in Great Britain (scale on right) – – –.

employed in Scotland was well above 100,000 throughout the inter-war period, and during the worst depression years it almost reached 400,000. During the war, unemployment practically disappeared, and since the war it has fluctuated in the neighbourhood of 60,000 persons.

The relatively high incidence of unemployment in Scotland can be gauged from the fact that, with a population and a labour force of about one-tenth that of Britain as a whole, Scotland had about one out of seven British unemployed during the inter-war period. Fig. 5 gives, in addition to the fluctuations in the total number of unemployed, the fluctuations to which this proportion has been subject. It shows that the proportion of Scottish unemployed in the total of British unemployed has actually increased since the war and is now about one in five.

44

In relation to long-term unemployment, the Scottish position appears in an even more unfavourable light. At the end of 1952 workers in Scotland who had been unemployed for at least half a year numbered 17,000 and formed about a quarter of the corresponding British total. Some of these workers appear to be practically unemployable; yet it is something of a mystery why there should not be a corresponding number of unemployables elsewhere in Britain.

Unemployment in Scotland is not now concentrated on any particular industry or occupation. It is, however, relatively high in some areas, particularly the fishing ports in the Highlands or on the east coast.

As a combined result of the larger proportion of children in the population, the higher unemployment rate and the greater extent of underemployment, only 43·1 % of the total population of Scotland were actually working in 1951, whereas in England and Wales 45·6 % of the population were working. The bearing on income per head and the standard of living is obvious. In the long run, however, the fact that Scotland has some manpower reserves may prove to be a blessing in disguise. During the inter-war period, new industries tended to be predominantly located in the South and Midlands of England. Since the war, partly because of the scarcity of labour in the South, this has ceased to be true, and the new industries that have been attracted to Scotland may well contribute towards making Scotland once again a prosperous part of Britain.

CHAPTER 5

INCOME

By A. D. CAMPBELL

A study of the Scottish economy has a firmer basis if it can be seen in its totality. For this purpose, all the activities of the community that make goods and services available for consumption or the creation of wealth must be measured and added up. Once that has been done, there is some general basis for measuring economic progress, for making comparisons with other countries, and for bringing the constituent parts of the Scottish economy into perspective.

The total obtained by adding up the value of goods and services becoming available annually is the national income. It may be considered as a sum of incomes or expenditures or outputs. If these three things are suitably defined it should make no difference which addition is made; income, expenditure and output are bound to be equal.

It is easy to see that the sum of incomes must equal the sum of outputs. The two approaches are simply different ways of enumerating the incomes received by labour and the owners of capital and land for contributions to the current production of goods and services. If incomes are added, the national income is enumerated according to the factors receiving the income; if outputs are added, the national income is enumerated according to the various industries in which the income is earned.

It is just as true that, in any period of time, income must equal expenditure. Income is generated only by spending, and all money spent must eventually become someone's income; thus the sum of expenditures on private consumption, on current government purposes and on capital formation must equal the sum of incomes.

There are, however, a number of well-known difficulties associated with these ideas and some of them may be described before going on to discuss income in Scotland.

First of all, it is necessary to find a common denominator to evaluate national income. We must always think of the national income as consisting of goods and services; but the only useful way of measuring a miscellaneous output, which includes coal, steel, beef, locomotives, ships, entertainment services and so on, is to aggregate the values of the different items in terms of money. Unfortunately, the value of money itself changes; and it is unwise to make comparisons between national incomes at different dates without taking account of changes in prices and, consequently, in the value of money.

Secondly, any income which is not paid in return for contributions to current production must be excluded from the sum of incomes. Old age pensions, health and unemployment benefits, family allowances and interest on the National Debt are not paid in return for the supply of services to current economic activity: they are obtained at the expense of other income-earners and their inclusion in the national income would cause double-counting. For example, since family allowances and interest on the National Debt are paid for out of taxation they are already counted in the incomes of taxpayers and should not also be included in the incomes of recipients.

Thirdly, national income is defined to include only the goods and services which are available to a nation, for consumption or addition to wealth, after its real capital has been maintained intact. This means that national income is measured net of depreciation and does not include currently-produced goods which are needed in order to replace capital used up in the course of production. If, for example, twenty new locomotives are produced in a year and five old locomotives have to be replaced, the value of only fifteen of the newly-produced locomotives will be included in the national income.

Finally, estimates of the national income do not normally include the value of every useful activity that is carried on, but only of the activities that command a money value in a market. The value of services rendered to oneself or one's family are conventionally excluded. Thus, if more married women come into industry and work for payment, leaving fewer unpaid housewives, the national income would show an increase, although there might well be, on a strict assessment, a net loss of welfare.

PROBLEMS OF DEFINITION AND MEASUREMENT

It is no easy task to define and measure the national income of a normal country. But Scotland is not a separate state with her own government and full political and economic sovereignty. It follows that Scotland cannot be said to have a national income in the same sense as the United Kingdom, Sweden or Eire have national incomes. In this chapter the Scottish national income is defined and measured as Scotland's share of the United Kingdom national income or the aggregate of incomes received by or attributable to individuals ordinarily resident in Scotland.

The estimation of Scotland's share of the United Kingdom national income is not a simple operation. The political integration of Scotland and the rest of the United Kingdom raises special problems in the field of public finance. Obviously the Scottish national income should include some share of the property income of the United Kingdom Government: but what is to be the size of Scotland's share? On the other hand, a share of the interest paid on the United Kingdom National Debt should be supplied by Scotland and deducted from the aggregate of Scottish incomes including National Debt interest; but there is no agreed principle defining Scotland's responsibility for the National Debt. These two problems, and similar problems in this field, may be solved by attributing the payments and receipts involved to individuals. Thus, in any year, Scotland's share of the income from central government property and her contribution to the interest on the National Debt may be taken to be the same as her share of the United Kingdom population: if Scotland has 10 % of the population of the United Kingdom then Scotland is credited with 10 % of central government property income and debited with 10 % of the interest on the National Debt. This method of division is, admittedly, an arbitrary one; but it cannot be very far, at worst, from any scheme of allocation that might be agreed politically.

The economic integration of Scotland and the rest of the United Kingdom raises difficulties in the treatment of company profits. The United Kingdom national income includes the profits, after allowance for depreciation, of all companies operating in the United Kingdom. These are the profits used for distribution as dividends and interest, for the payment of taxes and for the creation and increase of reserves. In addition, the United Kingdom national income includes some profits coming from companies operating abroad; and a proportion of the profits, earned in the United Kingdom but paid to foreigners, has to be excluded. Scotland's share of the resultant total of company profits may be determined by attributing the sums involved to individuals on the basis of their ownership of the capital of the companies. Thus, if Scotsmen own 12 % of the capital of the companies contributing to United Kingdom company profits, 12 % of the profits of these companies is included in the Scottish national income.

This treatment of profits income is not ideal. It means that the item 'company profits' in the Scottish national income neither measures nor represents the profits earned by companies *operating* in Scotland; thus 'company profits' in the Scottish national income may rise while companies in Scotland are doing badly and fall when they are prospering. But this conceptual difficulty does not tell the whole story.

Scotland's share of United Kingdom company profits cannot be estimated with precision. Estimates may be made by applying factors, reflecting the ownership of capital, to the United Kingdom totals. The use of this technique implies that Scotland's share of United Kingdom company profits is the same as her share of United Kingdom capital, excluding land and buildings. Estimates of the proportions of capital in Scottish ownership may be made from the annual records of the values of property deemed to pass on death, which are given for Scotland and for Great Britain in the 'Analyses of

Personalty' in the Inland Revenue Reports. This method of calculation gives undue weight to the successes and failures of the relatively distant past and, since a moving average of the annual figures must be used to obtain a suitable factor for any one year, damps down year-to-year fluctuations in profits. It also implies that there is no great difference in the distribution of the capital held by individuals in Scotland and in the rest of the country among different industries. No other method of division is practicable, however, and this technique has at least received an official blessing since it is implicit in one of the recommendations of the Catto *Committee on Scottish Financial and Trade Statistics.*[1]

THE SCOTTISH NATIONAL INCOME, 1924–48

The Scottish national income, defined as Scotland's share of the United Kingdom national income, is the aggregate of incomes received by or attributable to individuals ordinarily resident in Scotland. Thus the incomes of Englishmen, Americans, etc., are included in the Scottish national income if they are ordinarily resident in Scotland; but the incomes of Scotsmen ordinarily resident outwith Scotland are excluded. Since Scottish merchant seamen and members of the armed forces are normally resident in Scotland, their incomes should be included in the Scottish national income no matter where they happen to be stationed.

Estimates of the Scottish national income based on the above definition will shortly be published.[2] In the estimates the problems of public finance and company profits, and similar difficulties, are treated in the ways described in the preceding paragraphs, and the sums involved are attributed to individuals on the bases of population or ownership. The results for the years 1924–48 are shown in Table 25.

Before drawing any conclusions from the figures of Table 25 it is necessary to do two things: to issue a general warning and to correct them to allow for changes in the value of money.

Estimates of national income are never completely accurate. Even in the most advanced countries, the methods of calculation in use at the present time make it impossible to obtain complete accuracy or to give precise margins of error. The Scottish figures given in Table 25 are unlikely to be in error by as much as 10 %, and for most of the period the margin of error is probably of the order of 5 %; the results are least reliable for the years 1940–45. Despite this inaccuracy the estimates do provide an adequate background against which other magnitudes, e.g. foreign trade, the size of the housing effort, the value of agricultural output, may be examined: and, though the absolute

[1] Cmd. 8609 (1952), p. 12, para. 30. This technique, or a similar one, may be used to determine Scotland's receipts of National Debt interest.
[2] In the *Economic Journal.*

figures may not be accurate, the trends that they reveal are unlikely to be significantly in error.

The adjustment for changes in the value of money is shown in Fig. 6. In that diagram the changes that have taken place in real income per head of population are compared with the simultaneous changes in real income per head in the United Kingdom.[1] The ratio between the two is also shown.

Table 25. *The Scottish national income, 1924–48* *

Year	National income £m.	Income per head of population (£)	Year	National income £m.	Income per head of population (£)
1924	410	83	1937	440	88
1925	405	83	1938	435	86
1926	400	81	1939	490	97
1927	410	84	1940	595	118
1928	410	84	1941	710	138
1929	410	84	1942	790	153
1930	385	79	1943	850	165
1931	335	69	1944	880	170
1932	325	67	1945	860	166
1933	340	69	1946	805	156
1934	360	72	1947	870	168
1935	380	77	1948	945	182
1936	415	83	—	—	—

* No adjustment is made for stock appreciation.

A number of important conclusions may be drawn from Fig. 6.

1. There has been a large increase in income per head in Scotland since 1924, in spite of a reduction in the number of hours worked per week. The increase has been of the order of 40 %.

2. The increase in real income has been about the same as the increase for the whole United Kingdom; income per head in Scotland was about 90 % of the United Kingdom average in both 1924 and 1948. But this general conclusion conceals some important movements. First, between 1924 and 1948 the population of Scotland fell from 10·9 % to 10·4 % of the population of the United Kingdom and Scotland's share of the United Kingdom national income fell from 9·8 % to 9·3 %. Second, the boom of the war-years seems to have been the principal cause of Scotland's keeping in step with the United Kingdom. From 1924 to 1938 real income per head in Scotland increased by only 16 % compared with an increase of 20 % in the United Kingdom; and

[1] United Kingdom national income figures were based on the following estimates: 1924–37, *Studies in the National Income, 1924–1938*, ed. Sir A. L. Bowley, p. 81; 1938–48, the National Income White Papers. The London and Cambridge Economic Service Index of Retail Prices was used for deflating the figures of money income per head.

between 1944 and 1948 real income per head in Scotland fell by 9 % whereas the United Kingdom average fell by only 5 %.[1]

3. Real income per head has, throughout the period, been lower in Scotland than in the United Kingdom. The ratio of income per head in Scotland to income per head in the United Kingdom has never been higher than 94 % and fell to the low proportion of 86 % in the slump of the 1930's.

4. In addition to having a lower real income per head Scotland has had a more variable one. The wider variations, in slump and in war, correspond to some extent with the greater fluctuations of unemployment in Scotland.[2]

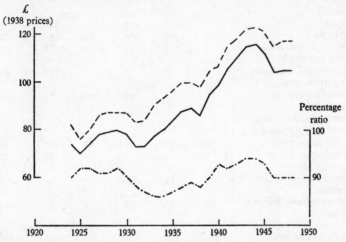

Fig. 6. Real income (in 1938 prices) per head of population in Scotland and in the United Kingdom, 1924–48. Scotland ——; United Kingdom – – –; ratio of Scottish to United Kingdom real income per head (scale on right) – · — · —.

COMPONENTS OF THE SCOTTISH NATIONAL INCOME

The pioneering studies in national income statistics aimed at providing a single total, the national income or dividend. But 'more stress is now laid on the analysis of the national income into its components and on the measurement of transactions between different parts of the economy'.[3] The principal components of the Scottish national income are shown in Table 26.

The 1948 Scottish figures are expressed as percentages of the equivalent parts of the United Kingdom national income for that year. Scotland has a large share of agricultural income, reflecting her greater specialization in agriculture, and unexpectedly large shares of company profits and net mis-

[1] It seems as though military and industrial demobilization—the reduction in the armed forces, the decline in defence orders, the release of pensioners and married women from industry—affected Scotland more severely than the country as a whole.

[2] Cf. Chapter 6, pp. 69–70.

[3] *National Income and Expenditure, 1946–1951* (H.M.S.O., London, 1952), p. 3.

4-2

cellaneous income. On the other hand, Scotland's share of United Kingdom wages is low and her share of the total of salaries is remarkably low. Similar analyses for the other years of the period reveal broadly the same picture.

Table 26. *Components of the Scottish national income*, 1924–48

Item	1924 (£ m.)	1928 (£ m.)	1932 (£ m.)	1938 (£ m.)	1948 (£ m.)	Percentage of United Kingdom, 1948
1. Wages	132	138	109	153	346	9·0
2. Salaries	65	68	65	82	155	7·0
3. Pay and allowances of the armed forces	7	7	7	8	26	10·0
4. Employers' insurance contributions	4	5	5	5	16	10·0
5. Income from agriculture*	29	28	19	21	64	12·5
6. Professional earnings						
7. Profits of sole traders and partnerships	144†	137†	91†	57	103	10·5
8. Trading profits of companies				69	174	12·0
9. Rent, excluding agriculture	14	14	17	21	24	6·0
10. Miscellaneous income (net)‡	15	13	12	19	37	11·0
11. National income§	410	410	325	435	945	9·3

* All incomes from agriculture, including wages, salaries and rent.

† Includes some National Debt interest and some profits from foreign companies; excludes some trading profits.

‡ The items included in miscellaneous income vary from year to year. The main categories are net income from abroad and the property income of government.

§ No allowance is made for stock appreciation.

Wages and company profits—items 1 and 8 of Table 26—account for 50–60 % of the Scottish national income; but whereas individual wage-earnings have been lower than in the United Kingdom, capital per head of population—the source of Scotland's share of company profits—has exceeded the United Kingdom average.[1] The first difference, which has been of the order of 5–10 %, has made for a smaller national income per head in Scotland than in the whole country, while the influence of the second difference has acted in the opposite direction. It is not easy to explain either phenomenon.

Average weekly wage-earnings are undoubtedly lower in Scotland than in England and the United Kingdom. The incomplete information available

[1] Cf. pp. 48–9. Scotland's share of company profits does not equal profits earned in Scotland.

strongly supports the conclusion that the difference is of the order of 5–10 %. It is not possible to give a comprehensive explanation of this phenomenon, but some suggestions are made in Chapter 11.

The explanation of the other phenomenon—the higher proportion of capital per head in Scotland—cannot be taken very far in this chapter. According to the values of estates passing on death, published in the Inland Revenue Reports, Scotland owns about 12 % of United Kingdom property, excluding land and buildings. Table 27 outlines the position for some of the years between 1924 and 1948.

Table 27. *Values of Scottish estates as percentages of the values of British estates*, 1924–48

Year	Nine-year moving average	Year	Nine-year moving average
1924	12·5	1938	11·9
1928	12·2	1944	12·0
1932	11·8	1948	11·8

Since Scotland's share of the United Kingdom national income is only 9–10 %, this high proportion of the value of estates, and therefore of capital per head, is something of a paradox. The inclusion of the values of land and buildings lowers the Scottish average relative to that of the United Kingdom; this is, however, only a partial answer to the problem and much remains to be explained. It seems improbable that legal rules or administrative practices are responsible for the paradox. A more important consideration may lie in the fact that the series in Table 27 suggests that Scotland's share of United Kingdom property is declining. This suggestion of a decline lends support to the idea that the Scottish estate figures reflect the prosperity of the past and not the low incomes and unemployment of the lean years of the 1920's and 1930's. A popular explanation would be that the surplus exists because the Scots live more frugally and save more of their lower incomes than do the English; but, in the absence of reliable information about savings in Scotland, this flattering suggestion cannot be confirmed.

INCOME FROM WORK AND PROPERTY

The items of Table 26 may be regrouped to show the relative importance of income from work and income from property. This is done in Table 28, in which income from wage-earnings and salaries is distinguished from property-income. Unfortunately it is not possible to obtain figures for property-income in its pure form. The category of property-income in Table 28 includes professional earnings, the profits of sole traders and partnerships and the incomes of farmers; but all of these are 'mixed incomes' received by persons whose economic activity consists of the joint provision of work and property, e.g. doctors, farmers, garage proprietors, small shop-keepers. These 'mixed incomes' come partly from work and partly from property, and it is impossible to separate the two elements.

Table 28. *Income from work and property as percentages of national income in Scotland and in the United Kingdom, 1924–48*

Year	Wages*		Salaries†		Income from property‡	
	Scotland	United Kingdom	Scotland	United Kingdom	Scotland	United Kingdom
1924	40	41	17	21	43	38
1928	41	40	17	22	42	38
1932	41	40	21	25	38	35
1938	40	39	19	24	41	37
1948	43	44	18	22	39	34

* Item 1 and parts of items 3, 4 and 5 of Table 26.
† Item 2 and parts of items 3, 4 and 5 of Table 26.
‡ Items 6, 7, 8, 9 and 10 and part of item 5 of Table 26.

Table 28 shows clearly that the distribution of income in Scotland differs from the distribution of income in the United Kingdom in two important respects: salaries form a much lower proportion of the Scottish national income than they do of the United Kingdom national income, the difference being of the order of 4 points; and income from property, including 'mixed income', constitutes a much higher proportion of national income in Scotland than in the United Kingdom, the difference again being about 4 points. Wages, on the other hand, are a little more than 40 % of national income in both Scotland and the United Kingdom.

The analysis may be carried a stage further for 1938 and 1948. In those years it is possible to divide income from property into 'mixed income' and pure property income; and the analysis shows that 'mixed income', i.e. professional earnings, income from farming and the profits of sole traders and partnerships, accounts for about 15–16 % of the Scottish national income but for only 12–13 % of the United Kingdom national income. It is interesting to note that, in those two years and probably in the others, the very low proportion of salary income in Scotland is accompanied by a fairly high proportion of 'mixed income'.

The fact that the distribution of income in Scotland differs from that of the United Kingdom in the various ways described is not surprising. The high proportion of 'mixed income' reflects, to some extent, Scotland's specialization in agriculture. Another important factor is undoubtedly the Scottish tendency, compared with England, to organize production in relatively small units:[1] this tendency reduces the number of salaried managers and clerks but increases the number of 'mixed incomes'.[2] A third factor, making for a relatively low proportion of salary income, must be the concentration in London of head office staffs, the Civil Service and the highest salaries.

Over the period 1924–48 the changes in the distribution of the Scottish national income closely follow the changes in the distribution of income in the United Kingdom. Table 28 shows that in both countries income from work has increased its share by 4 points at the expense of income from property. Most of the gain in income from work is due to the increase in the share of wages: in Scotland wages increased from 40 % of the national income in 1924 to 43 % in 1948. The Scottish increase took place, in the main, during the war. In 1924 wage-earners were 69 % of the working population and received 40 % of the national income; in 1938 the proportions were more or less the same; but between 1938 and 1948 the proportion of wage-earners in the working population increased by 1 point, whereas their share of the national income increased by 3 points—from 40 % to 43 %.

REAL INCOME PER HEAD

The difference in real income per head between Scotland and the United Kingdom must be investigated and explained. In the years from 1924 to 1948 income per head in Scotland varied from 86 % to 94 % of United Kingdom income per head, and the average over the period was 90 %. Why was real income per head lower in Scotland than in the United Kingdom?

At first sight the difference seems to be larger than is suggested by the difference in wage-earnings and in capital per head. In 1948, for example, real income per head in Scotland was 90 % of the United Kingdom average; yet Scottish wage-earnings were only 6 % less than the average for the whole country and the Scots owned as much as 11–12 % of the United Kingdom's movable capital.

The explanation for 1948 lies along the following lines. Income from work was £705 m.; of this total, the aggregate of wages was £405 m.[3] and other

[1] H. W. Singer and C. E. V. Leser, 'Industrial Productivity in England and Scotland', *Journal of the Royal Statistical Society*, vol. CXI, pt. IV (1948), p. 317.

[2] There is also evidence that Scottish industry tends to employ women where industry in England and Wales employs men. In the 1951 Census 'Managers and professional, commercial and clerical workers' were 22·9 % of the male occupied population in England and Wales and only 19·4 % in Scotland. The female proportions, excluding managers, were 41·1 % for England and Wales and 43·4 % for Scotland.

[3] Item 1 and parts of items 3, 4 and 5 of Table 26.

work incomes contributed £300 m.[1] Thus Scottish wages were only 9·1 % of the United Kingdom wage-bill of £4,430 m. and the Scottish share of other work incomes of £3,480 m. was only 8·6 %.[2]

Why did Scotland receive only 9·1 % of the United Kingdom aggregate of wages in 1948? There were three main causes: the lower level of wage-earnings; the higher level of unemployment; and the fact that Scottish wage-earners formed a smaller proportion of the total of United Kingdom wage-earners than was indicated by the population ratio of 10·4 %. These three factors combined to make the Scottish wage-bill only 9·1 % of the United Kingdom wage-bill: the deficiency due to the low level of wage-earnings was more than twice the size of the deficiency caused by the higher rate of un-employment and between one and two times greater than the deficiency due to the relatively low proportion of wage-earners.

The main causes of Scotland's low share of other incomes from work—managerial, salaried, independent and 'mixed' incomes—were the lower level of earnings and the relatively low proportion—slightly less than 10 %—of this sector of the United Kingdom working population located in Scotland. In this case the deficiency due to the low level of incomes was probably twice as large as the deficiency caused by the low proportion of people in these occupations.

Account has still to be taken of income from property, where Scotland does fairly well. In 1948 Scotland's share of United Kingdom property income was £240 m.,[3] or 10·9 %. Scotland's relatively high share of company profits was offset substantially by her relatively low shares of rents and income from abroad.

If the three parts—wages, other work incomes and income from property—are combined in a weighted average they show the Scottish national income to be only 9·3 % of the United Kingdom national income in 1948. This slice of the cake had to be shared among 10·4 % of the population of the United Kingdom. It follows that real income per head of population in Scotland was of the order of 90 % of the United Kingdom average. The factors causing this 10 % difference in income per head were, in order of importance, the lower levels of income from work, the lower proportion of occupied persons in the total population, and the higher rate of unemployment. Income from pro-perty was neutral; in 1948 it was more or less the same per head of population in Scotland and the United Kingdom.

[1] Items 2, 6 and 7 and parts of items 3, 4 and 5 of Table 26. This treatment differs from that of Table 28: 'mixed incomes' are treated here as part of income from work. The reason for the difference in treatment is that in the earlier years the methods of estimation merge 'mixed incomes' indistinguishably with income from property.

[2] The United Kingdom figures are taken from *National Income and Expenditure, 1946–1951* (H.M.S.O., London, 1952).

[3] Items 8, 9 and 10 and part—rents—of item 5 of Table 26.

A similar analysis may be made for the other years between 1924 and 1948. It is only to be expected that the relative importance of the causal factors changes in different years. In 1932, for example, unemployment was a much more important factor than it was in 1948; and, in the earlier years, the Scottish working population had a relatively smaller load of dependants on its back. This last point is of considerable importance: from 1924 to 1948 the Scottish working population increased from 45% to 46% of the total population; but in the same time the United Kingdom proportion increased significantly more, from 45·5% to 47·5%. In 1948, even if occupied persons in Scotland had earned the same incomes and had enjoyed the same level of employment as the whole United Kingdom, the difference in population structure would have caused real income per head in Scotland to be about 3% less than real income in the United Kingdom.[1]

It is appropriate, at this stage, to take account of the payment of transfer incomes and direct taxes. The net result of these operations of the central government and the national insurance funds has been favourable to Scotland, in most years from 1924 to 1948, in the sense that they have raised income per head in Scotland relative to the United Kingdom. This is only to be expected: income per head in Scotland is lower than the United Kingdom average and these operations are designed, in general, to benefit the lower income groups.

There is no possibility of discovering, with precision, the amounts of transfer incomes received and direct taxes paid by Scots: the official records are far from complete. Estimates of the sums involved in some recent years are shown in Table 29. Transfer incomes include National Debt interest,[2] national insurance benefits, pensions, family allowances and post-war credits. Direct taxes are composed of income tax and surtax, profits taxes, death duties, the 'special contribution' and one or two lesser items.[3] National insurance contributions paid by employers and employees are counted as direct taxes in this calculation. Estimates of the same nature were made for the United Kingdom so that real income per head of population in Scotland and the United Kingdom could be compared after allowing for transfer incomes and direct taxes: the results of this comparison are shown in Table 29.

The last two columns of Table 29 show clearly that Scotland gained from these fiscal operations in 1924, 1932, 1938 and 1948; in 1932, for example, real

[1] The fact that, despite the relative deterioration in the Scottish working population, income per head in Scotland was 90% of the United Kingdom average in both 1924 and 1948 suggests that Scotland was gaining in some sectors. The balance was held by a relative decline in unemployment, the increased proportion of the Scottish working population absorbed in the armed forces at uniform rates of pay, and probably a relative improvement in the level of other work incomes in Scotland.

[2] For Scotland this item involves only National Debt interest not already included in the Scottish national income.

[3] Direct taxes paid by Scotland were estimated on the lines indicated by the Catto *Committee on Scottish Financial and Trade Statistics*, Cmd. 8609 (1952).

income per head in Scotland was raised from 87 % to 90 % of the United Kingdom average. In the vast majority of years from 1924 to 1948 Scotland was relatively better off after the payment of transfer incomes and direct taxes.[1] The improvement was greater in the pre-war years than in the post-war years up to 1948. But this is only to be expected in view of the virtual disappearance of unemployment after 1939, in Scotland as well as in the United Kingdom.

Table 29. *Transfer incomes and direct taxes in Scotland, and real income per head in Scotland and in the United Kingdom, 1924–48*

Year	Transfer incomes (Scotland) (£ m.)	Direct taxes (Scotland) (£ m.)	Scottish national income *plus* transfer incomes *less* direct taxes* (£ m.)	Real income per head in Scotland as a percentage of real income in the United Kingdom	
				Unadjusted†	Adjusted
1924	55	50	415	90	93
1932	65	45	345	87	90
1938	55	55	435	88	89
1948	125	205	865	90	91

* These estimates include, as parts of the Scottish national income, the Scottish shares of undistributed company profits (after tax) and the property income of government. The original national income figures are given in Table 25.

† The unadjusted percentages are those used as the basis of Fig. 6; the adjusted percentages show the effects of transfers and direct taxes on real income per head in Scotland and the United Kingdom.

THE MOVEMENTS OF WAGES AND PROFITS

It has already been pointed out that the figures of company profits in the Scottish national income neither measure nor represent profits earned in Scotland; they are estimates of Scotland's share of United Kingdom profits. Conceptually, these estimates differ from profits earned in Scotland in two important respects: first, they exclude profits earned in Scotland paid or attributed to Englishmen or foreigners; second, they include profits earned outside Scotland paid or attributed to Scots on the basis of their ownership of the capital of the companies earning the profits.

It is impossible to construct, from existing statistical material, any estimates of the absolute amounts of profits earned in Scotland. But some indication of the movements of all profits earned in Scotland—by individuals, firms and local authorities as well as by companies—may be obtained from the figures

[1] This does not mean that the central government and the national insurance funds spent more in Scotland than they took from Scotland in revenue. Indirect taxes and many categories of government expenditure have not been brought to account.

of profits from businesses and professions assessed for income tax under Schedule D and published in the Inland Revenue Reports.

The item 'Gross Income assessed under Schedule D' may, after several adjustments, be used to provide an index of the movements of profits earned in Scotland.[1] The index does not provide a perfect picture. The major defect is that Scottish 'Gross Income' includes an unknown amount of profits earned in England and excludes an unknown amount of profits earned in Scotland. This is due to the Inland Revenue practice of allocating profits to Scotland and the rest of the United Kingdom according to the place of assessment; and the place of assessment normally depends on the location of the head office of the business concerned. It follows that the figures for England and Wales include the profits of a number of companies whose main works, and most of whose employees, are situated in Scotland. In compensation, Scottish 'Gross Income' includes some profits which really belong to England and Wales; but it is fairly certain that the gain on this account does not offset the previous loss. Thus, in using the adjusted 'Gross Income' figures as indicators of the fluctuations of profits earned in Scotland, it is implied that an Inland Revenue mixture of some profits earned in Scotland and some profits earned in England and Wales—with the profits earned in Scotland predominating—adequately represents the movements of all profits earned in Scotland.

A second difficulty, related to the first, arises if Scottish companies decide, because of amalgamation with an English company, or for many other possible reasons, to establish their head offices in London. In such instances profits formerly shown as earned in Scotland, and in fact still earned in Scotland, will now be credited to England, and the index of Scottish profits will tend to fall in a misleading fashion. Another difficulty lies in the fact that in the case of Scotland 40–50 % of 'Gross Income' is earned by individuals and firms. A substantial part of such earnings is not really profit income, e.g. the work element of 'mixed incomes', and is unlikely to fluctuate as freely as profits. The presence of this mass of non-profit income in the adjusted Schedule D figures probably damps down[2] the fluctuations of the index of profits earned in Scotland.

The movements of an index of Scottish 'Gross Income', adjusted in the manner described to represent the fluctuations of profits earned in Scotland, in the years 1924–49, are recorded in Fig. 7. The course of profits earned in

[1] The major adjustments may be described. The net receipts from profits taxes are added to the published figures of 'Gross Income' but the following items are deducted: assessments on certain interest and on the income from Dominion and foreign securities and possessions; assessments on the nationalized industries; and, in order to obtain comparable figures over the period 1924–48, assessments on agriculture and horticulture.

[2] Both absolutely and relatively to an index of United Kingdom profits compiled from the Inland Revenue figures on the same basis.

the United Kingdom, compiled on the same basis as the Scottish figures, is also shown.

The enormous increase in profits from 1924 to 1949 is clearly shown in Fig. 7: but whereas United Kingdom profits increased by about 160 %, profits earned in Scotland increased by only 140 %. And it is significant that the curve representing Scottish profits remains below the curve representing United Kingdom profits in every year after 1924. There is thus some evidence, admittedly imperfect,[1] of a relative deterioration in the Scottish position; excluding agriculture, the proportion of United Kingdom profits earned in Scotland seems to have declined.

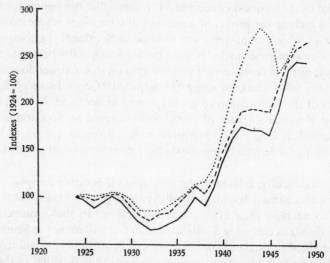

Fig. 7. Aggregates of profits and wages earned in Scotland and in the United Kingdom, 1924–49 (1924 = 100). Scotland, profits ——, wages · · · ; United Kingdom, profits – – –.

The year-to-year changes in Scottish and United Kingdom profits are normally similar in direction, but it is obvious from Fig. 7 that the changes differ in degree. Scotland suffered more severely in the depression of the 1930's. In the five years from 1930 to 1934 Scottish profits averaged 71 % of their 1924 level; but United Kingdom profits, averaging 81 %, fell much less drastically. Profits recovered from these low levels but the relative position of Scottish and United Kingdom profits, established in the slump, continued to the outbreak of war. The rapid growth of Scottish profits in the early years of the war virtually restored the 1924 position by 1941, but from that year until 1945 there appears to have been a relapse. Scotland caught up again between

[1] It is desirable to repeat the warning that, to an unknown extent, the deterioration may be administrative and not real, e.g. there may have been some movement of head offices to England.

60

1945 and 1947, only to lose ground in 1948 and 1949—the latest years for which data are available.

It is interesting and valuable to compare fluctuations in profits and the aggregate of wages. To make the comparison for Scotland, the movements of an index of Scottish wages[1] are recorded in Fig. 7.

Throughout the period 1924–48, with the exception of the war-years, Scottish wages and profits move in more or less the same way. But wages fare better than profits. The curve of wages remains significantly above the curve of profits in every year after 1924; and while the increase in the aggregate of wages is as much as 170 %, the increase in profits is only 140 %. And it is not only in the longer period that wages gained relatively to profits: in the slump of the 1930's the decline in wages was considerably less violent than the decline in profits; and in the recession of 1937–38 wages continued to rise while profits fell.

The lack of correspondence between the curves of Scottish wages and profits in the war years is due to the inclusion of part of the income of the armed forces in the aggregate of wages. Thus, in these years, a substantial part of the total of wages is not related directly to employment and profits in Scotland. If an index of Scottish wages net of all armed forces' income is prepared, it moves during the war period in very much the same way as the index of profits earned in Scotland.

SUMMARY AND CONCLUSIONS

The Scottish national income may be defined as Scotland's share of the United Kingdom national income and is the aggregate of incomes received by or attributable to individuals ordinarily resident in Scotland. Despite certain conceptual difficulties and the imperfections of the data, several conclusions may be established reasonably firmly.

Real income per head has been lower in Scotland than in the United Kingdom in every year from 1924 to 1948 and, with the exception of the war-years, the gap has shown no sign of closing.[2] In these years there has undoubtedly been a decline in the relative economic importance of Scotland in the United Kingdom: the Scottish national income was 9·9 % of the United Kingdom national income on the average of 1924–26 and only 9·4 % for the years 1946–48.

[1] Item 1 and parts of items 3 and 4 of Table 26, p. 52. Agricultural wages are excluded, but part of the earnings of the Forces is included. The index of profits does not, of course, represent the movements of dividends paid to shareholders or of distributed profits. At all times substantial proportions of the aggregate of profits have been retained by companies as reserves and to finance new developments: and, in the more recent years, most of the profits recorded have been claimed by the tax-collector.

[2] In fact the most recent trends in income and profits suggest that the gap may widen.

In most years of the period the payment of transfer incomes and direct taxes raised income per head in Scotland relative to the United Kingdom. This is only to be expected since the general intention of these fiscal operations is to benefit the lower income groups.

Income per head in Scotland would be an even lower proportion of the United Kingdom average were it not for Scotland's paradoxically high share of United Kingdom income from property—10–11 % in 1948. In contrast, Scotland's share of income from work—wages, salaries and 'mixed incomes' —was only about 9 % in 1948.

The high proportion of income from property received by and attributed to Scots is imperfectly established on the basis of the values of estates passing at death, and it is a difficult phenomenon to explain. The low proportion of income from work is due to the lower level of earnings, the higher rate of unemployment, and Scotland's relatively small share of the United Kingdom working population.

There is evidence that the distribution of the Scottish national income differs from the pattern of distribution for the whole United Kingdom. Wages take up about the same proportion in both cases; but, in the Scottish national income, salaries are a much lower proportion and 'mixed income' and income from property are higher proportions than in the United Kingdom national income. The differences in salaries and 'mixed income' are probably due to Scotland's specialization in agriculture, the concentration of the highest salaries and the Civil Service in the south of England and the Scottish tendencies to organize production in relatively small units and to use women for salaried work instead of men.

Though the pattern of distribution is different the trends appear to be the same: wages, salaries and income from property have all moved in the same manner, in Scotland and the United Kingdom, between 1924 and 1948; wages and salaries have gained at the expense of income from property.[1]

Profits earned in Scotland are not the same as property income or profits received by or attributable to individuals normally resident in Scotland; only the latter sums are included in the estimates of Scottish national income. An attempt has been made to trace the movements of profits earned in Scotland and to compare them with the aggregate of profits earned in the United Kingdom. The year-to-year fluctuations in the two totals are usually similar in direction, though they differ in degree, and there is once again evidence of a deterioration in the Scottish position in the years 1924–48. If the index of profits earned in Scotland is compared with an index of the aggregate of Scottish wages, it is clear that wages have fared better than profits in the twenty-five years up to 1948.

[1] Except in the more recent years it is impossible to separate 'mixed income' and pure property income; thus, in this comparison, income from property includes 'mixed income'.

The fact that income per head in Scotland is lower than income per head in the United Kingdom stimulates comments of contrasting nature. One view might be that the difference is not very great, and indeed surprisingly small. Far greater differences are to be found in comparisons of the different states in the United States of America or of the different administrative regions of Italy; and, closer to home, the difference between income per head in Northern Ireland and the United Kingdom is much more substantial. On the other hand, why should income per head in Scotland be more than 10 % less than income per head in England?; and why has the position failed to improve in the period 1924–48?; concern must surely be felt about the fact that Scotland suffered more severely in the trade depressions of the 1930's than did England, and about the apparent tendency to a long-period decline in the relative importance of the Scottish economy.

The problems of raising real income per head in Scotland relative to the United Kingdom level, and of halting the decline in Scotland's economic importance may be solved by using some important and obvious lines of attack emerging from the history of the period 1924–48. First, it would seem necessary to discover why, in Scotland, a lower proportion of the population is normally available for work. The high Scottish birth-rate may be a significant cause, but an arithmetical analysis of the 1951 Census results suggests that an expansion of the female working population would be possible.[1] Secondly, the situation would be improved if the Scottish share of the United Kingdom's capital formation were to exceed Scotland's current share of the United Kingdom national income. In the years 1946–48, it is probable that capital formation in Scotland was 10–11 % of domestic capital formation in the United Kingdom compared with a national income ratio of 9·4 %.[2] Thirdly, Scotland's resistance to the onslaughts of industrial depression must be increased. It is possible that industrial developments in Scotland in the last fifteen years and recent changes in world markets have made Scotland

[1] Cf. Chapter 4, pp. 42–3.

[2] Figures of domestic capital formation have been published in the Economic Surveys and the National Income White Papers. Sufficient detail has been provided to justify the preparation of estimates of Scotland's share of these totals. For the years 1946–48 investment in Scotland averaged 10·5 % of investment in the United Kingdom. The absolute figures of United Kingdom capital formation are not themselves accurate; it follows that estimates of absolute figures for Scotland must be even less accurate. Estimates of the Scottish proportion of United Kingdom domestic capital formation are also bound to be inaccurate, but not seriously so. In 1947, for example, net domestic capital formation in the United Kingdom was about £1,000 m. Some 40 % of this amount could be allocated between Scotland and the rest of the United Kingdom on the basis of published figures: in this sector Scotland's share was accurately and officially determined. The remaining 60 %, representing in the main the vitally important private industrial investment, had to be allocated on the basis of the best information available for the different branches of industry; errors in the ratio calculated for 1947 are confined to this sector and, unfortunately, may be quite large.

relatively less vulnerable in time of slump, but this proposition has still to be tested. Finally, investigations into the reasons why Scottish wage-earnings are 5–10 % below the United Kingdom average would be highly desirable. Such investigations would undoubtedly bring the inquirers face to face with the problems of industrial specialization, the size of the unit of production and the need for and the nature of new industrial development, including the renewal of existing equipment.

The formal answer to the fundamental problem of income per head in Scotland is really a very simple one: if the Scots are to be as well off as the English and if Scotland is to maintain or increase her relative economic importance, more capital and more labour must work in Scotland and the labour that does work there must be employed efficiently with up-to-date methods and machinery. Experience of emigration in the last thirty years, and current trends in Scottish population statistics, suggest that the major difficulty is in the field of capital investment. It is not enough merely to say that Scotland needs more capital investment; the industrial structure must be expanded in specific directions and existing equipment in industry must be renewed with imagination and foresight. No one can deny the importance of public investment in houses, schools, roads, etc.; but the most important sector, in this connexion, is capital development and renewal by private industry to meet the demands of the future as efficiently as possible. Real income in Scotland depends in the main on the enterprise and initiative of private industrialists, both Scottish and foreign; and, within the varying limits set by government fiscal and monetary policies and direct controls, it falls on them to make the decisions which will determine the future of the Scottish economy.

CHAPTER 6

PRODUCTION

By C. E. V. LESER

Production is generally thought of in terms of physical output, measured in quantities of goods produced. But to measure the pattern of production involves the use of a common unit: for practical purposes, either money units or units of manpower. The pattern of production can thus be measured either in terms of the value of the net output of each industry or of the number of persons employed by each industry.

In theory, it is preferable to make use of net output which gives a direct measurement of production while manpower data only provide an indirect indication. But to obtain comprehensive net output data for all goods and services produced in Scotland, so that the total adds up to the Scottish national income, would involve far more calculations and estimates than have been possible in the framework of the present study. Moreover, even for output from industry in the narrow sense (that is, excluding services of all kinds), the full results of the 1948 Census of Production were not available in time to be included in the main body of this analysis. Ample data are available, however, for the number of persons working in each industry and these are the figures analysed here. It is unlikely that the conclusions reached would be much affected if a different measure of production were used.

THE SCOTTISH PATTERN IN RELATION TO THE BRITISH

A general idea of the pattern of Scottish production can be gained from a comparison with the pattern of British production as expressed in the distribution of manpower between the main industrial groups (Table 30).

A comparison between columns 2 and 3 of Table 30 shows that there is no great difference between Scotland and Great Britain in terms of these main groups. The ratio between the two columns, given in the final column and generally referred to as the location factor, measures the divergence of the Scottish from the British industrial pattern.

It will be seen that in Scotland, as in Britain as a whole, more than half of the total employment is concentrated on the service trades, which include building, public utilities, distribution, government and other services. All these provide mainly local services, and they are of minor interest only from the point of view of industrial location, since their location factors tend to be in the neighbourhood of 1 for any region or locality (i.e. the share of an area in the service trades is generally much the same as its share in all industries and services). Somewhat over one-tenth of the Scottish working population—as against somewhat less than one-tenth for Britain as a whole—are engaged in primary production, i.e. in agriculture, forestry, fishing and mining; somewhat under three-eighths—as against over three-eighths in Britain as a whole—are in various manufacturing trades.

Table 30. *Occupied persons by broad industrial group in Scotland and in Great Britain, 1951**

Broad industrial group	Scotland		Great Britain	Col. 2/Col. 3 (Location factor)
	Number (thousands)	Percentage of total	Percentage of total	
Metal and engineering trades	358·2	16·3	17·9	0·91
Textiles, leather and clothing	174·5	8·0	8·0	0·99
Miscellaneous manufacturing	255·9	11·7	11·7	0·99
Total manufacturing	788·6	36·0	37·6	0·95
Agriculture, forestry, fishing	160·7	7·3	5·0	1·47
Mining and quarrying	97·2	4·4	3·8	1·16
Service trades	1,148·3	52·3	53·6	0·98
All industries and services	2,194·8	100·0	100·0	1·00

* Excluding persons out of work and unclassified.
SOURCE: *Census of Population, 1951: One Per Cent Sample Tables.*

Compared with England and Wales, therefore, Scotland tends to concentrate on primary rather than on industrial production. The metal trades, which are commonly thought of as a Scottish speciality, turn out to be less strongly represented in Scotland than in the rest of Britain. But on the whole, the differences between Scotland and Britain are not large; it is the similarity rather than the divergences in industrial pattern which is the striking feature of Table 30.

Before drawing any conclusions, however, it is necessary to look at the industrial pattern in more detail. For this purpose, we may divide up the figures for the total working population into the twenty-four industry groups which form the basis of the Standard Industrial Classification, as shown in Table 31.

PRODUCTION

Table 31. *Working population by industry group in Scotland and in Great Britain, 1951**

| Standard industrial classification order | Scotland | | Great Britain | Scotland as a percentage of Great Britain |
	Number (thousands)	Percentage of total	Percentage of total	
1. Agriculture, forestry, fishing	160·7	7·3	5·0	14·6
2. Mining and quarrying	97·2	4·4	3·8	11·5
3. Treatment of non-metalliferous mining products other than coal	22·4	1·0	1·5	6·9
4. Chemicals and allied trades	31·3	1·4	2·0	7·0
5. Metal manufacture	65·6	3·0	2·6	11·3
6. Engineering, shipbuilding and electrical goods	198·8	9·1	8·0	11·2
7. Vehicles	56·2	2·6	4·4	5·8
8. Metal goods not included elsewhere	27·9	1·3	2·2	5·8
9. Precision instruments, jewellery, etc.	9·7	0·5	0·7	6·3
10. Textiles	123·2	5·6	4·5	12·3
11. Leather, leather goods and fur	5·0	0·2	0·3	6·7
12. Clothing	46·3	2·1	3·1	6·7
13. Food, drink and tobacco	95·6	4·4	3·4	12·7
14. Manufactures of wood and cork	31·0	1·4	1·4	10·2
15. Paper and printing	53·8	2·5	2·3	10·6
16. Other manufacturing industries	21·8	1·0	1·2	8·4
17. Building and contracting	136·6	6·2	6·2	10·0
18. Gas, electricity and water supply	31·4	1·4	1·7	8·5
19. Transport and communication	185·1	8·4	7·8	10·8
20. Distributive trades	282·5	12·9	12·2	10·5
21. Insurance, banking and finance	40·2	1·8	2·0	9·2
22. Public administration and defence	140·9	6·4	8·0	7·9
23. Professional services	156·2	7·1	6·9	10·2
24. Miscellaneous services	175·4	8·0	8·8	9·0
All industries and services	2,194·8	100·0	100·0	9·9

* Excluding persons out of work and unclassified.
SOURCE: *Census of Population, 1951: One Per Cent Sample Tables.*

67

5-2

Table 31 reveals some differences between the Scottish and the British industrial pattern which were hidden by the broad classification. Among the metal trades, for example, Scotland has a relatively large working population in 'Metal manufacture' and in 'Engineering, shipbuilding and electrical goods' but a relatively small one in 'Vehicles', in 'Metal goods not included elsewhere', and in 'Precision instruments, jewellery, etc.'; measured by the ratio of employment in Scotland to the British total, these three groups are in fact those in which, out of all the twenty-four, the Scottish deficiency is most marked. Similarly, Scotland has a large share in 'Textiles' which is more than balanced by a small share in 'Leather, leather goods and fur' and in 'Clothing'; a large share in 'Food, drink and tobacco' but a small share in 'Treatment of non-metalliferous mining products other than coal' and in 'Chemicals and allied trades'. The industry group in which Scotland makes the largest contribution to the British total is 'Agriculture, forestry and fishing', where the Scottish labour force is nearly one-half larger than it would be if the British industrial pattern applied to Scotland. In 'Mining and quarrying', the Scottish share of manpower is also higher than in any manufacturing industry group except 'Food, drink and tobacco' and 'Textiles'.

Even so, the differences between the Scottish and the British pattern of production are not really very big. A comparison with Wales brings out the diversity of Scottish industry. Mining and metal manufacture, for example, together employ 20·1 % of the working population in Wales but only 7·4 % in Scotland and 6·4 % in Great Britain. On the other hand, textiles and other consumer-goods industries (groups 10–16) employ only 7·7 % of the working population of Wales, while the corresponding percentages for Scotland and Britain are 17·2 % and 16·2 %. There is in both cases a much closer approximation of the Scottish than of the Welsh pattern to the British. For the twenty-four industry groups shown here, the location factor varies between 0·6 and 1·5 in Scotland and between 0·3 and 3·2 in Wales—a much wider range. It can be shown that, measured by tests of this kind, the Scottish industrial pattern is closer than that of any other industrial region of comparable size to the pattern for Britain as a whole; this remains true even when individual industries instead of industry groups are considered.[1] At first sight, the skill and natural resources of Scotland, as mirrored in the industrial complex to which they have given birth, are as varied as those of the larger economy of Britain.

Such a conclusion, however, would be mistaken. The differences so far considered are not in many ways the most significant, and the real divergences between Scottish and British industry do not emerge from Table 31. These divergences can be examined from three different viewpoints: first, in terms of the preponderance of heavy industry in Scotland; second, in terms of

[1] C. E. V. Leser, *Some Aspects of the Industrial Structure of Scotland* (1951), pp. 15 ff.

differences in the rate of industrial growth and in the type of industry that has expanded most rapidly; and finally, in terms of the factory-building that has been in progress since the war.

THE PREPONDERANCE OF HEAVY INDUSTRY

The first of these divergences relates mainly to metals and engineering and is discussed in Chapter 9 (pp. 118–24), which deals with individual manufacturing industries. It will be shown there that out of nine metal industries that are concentrated much more strongly in Scotland than in England, all but one are heavy industries. In shipbuilding, marine engineering, boilers and boiler-house plant, constructional engineering, and the private manufacture of locomotives, one worker in four is in Scotland; in blast furnaces, iron foundries, and steel melting and rolling, over one worker in eight. Not only does this mean that Scotland is appreciably more dependent on this group of industries than England and Wales; it means also that those industries play a much larger part in Scotland in relation to the lighter factory trades. For example, they employ nearly four times as many workers as the clothing trades, whereas in England and Wales they employ about the same number.

This dependence on heavy industry has grown since the beginning of the century. The metal and engineering trades now account for about half the output of Scottish manufacturing industry instead of about one-third. In England and Wales, the dimensions of the change have been similar; but it has been accompanied, as it has not in Scotland, by the development of vast new industries within the group—motor vehicles, aircraft, radio and electrical apparatus.

Thus the proportion between heavy and light engineering is quite different in Scotland from what it is in England and Wales. The eight heavy industries already listed do not employ even one-fifth of all those who are engaged in the metal and engineering trades in England and Wales. In Scotland the proportion is well over two-fifths. Similarly, while in Scotland there were fewer workers in motor vehicles, aircraft and electrical engineering taken together than in shipbuilding and ship-repairing alone, in England and Wales motor vehicles and electrical engineering each employ twice as many, and aircraft at least as many, as shipbuilding and ship-repairing.

The predominance of heavy industry makes Scotland sensitive to economic depression since it is generally the production of heavy engineering products that falls off most drastically in a slump. In the early 1930's, for example, unemployment in Britain increased from 10·1 % in the comparatively prosperous years 1927–29 to 20·3 % in the worst years of the slump, 1931–33, while in Scotland the increase was from 11·4 % to 26·2 %. Scotland was rather harder hit, and one reason, but not the sole reason, was that she had specialized in some of the industries that suffered the biggest increase in unemployment. No doubt if one were to compare Scotland not with Great Britain as a whole but with the Midlands or the South of England, the difference in unemployment rates in the slump of 1932 would be much greater. But even a large difference would not constitute a demonstration that Scotland should forthwith aim at a different assortment of industries. Vulnerability to unemployment is only one among many considerations governing a desirable industrial pattern. There is, for example, the need to turn existing resources and advantages to the best account; to secure an adequate level of exports; to make an early start with new and rapidly developing industries. But, in any event, it is not necessarily true that a world recession would now follow the same course as in 1932. The slump in textiles in 1951–52 was a reminder that the comparative stability of demand for consumer-goods is not always to be counted upon. On some future occasion, it might be the turn of durable consumer-goods—which occupy a far less prominent part in the Scottish than in the British economy.

Apart from this, it would be wrong, in trying to interpret the events of the 1930's, to put all the emphasis on the collapse in the demand for ships and locomotives. The real collapse was in export markets; and it happened that there was some coincidence between the industries making capital goods and the industries making goods for export. The largest industry making capital goods, however—the building industry—exported nothing and enjoyed an almost uninterrupted expansion, combined, it is true, with high unemployment rates. Textiles, for which the demand is theoretically 'stable', were as much exposed to the depression as most industries because many of the consumers for whose requirements they catered were foreign consumers and cut their purchases severely. The highest rate of unemployment reached in the 1930's indeed, was not in any of the capital goods industries at all, but in tin-plate-making, very much an export industry, and one not carried on in Scotland.

Now it may have been true twenty years ago that Scotland supplied a high proportion of British exports: it is certainly not true now.[1] New export industries have grown up in the very areas in the Midlands and the South that were once thought of as dedicated to the home market, indeed as *the* home market. The industries like motor vehicles and radio that appeared to pass Scotland by in favour of a larger and more secure home market have been transformed into pillars of a most respectable export trade. The risk that a world recession will spread unemployment through the export trades is now at least as real in the Midlands and the South as it is in Scotland.

The predominance of heavy industry in Scotland has a significance extending beyond the vexed question of stability and vulnerability. It means, for example, a predominance of mechanical engineering over electrical and

[1] See p. 138.

chemical engineering; a comparative absence of mass production techniques; a corresponding demand for skilled men and above all for *manual* skills; a demand also for heavy metal products, particularly steel plates. It is not possible, however, to develop these points here.

INDUSTRIAL GROWTH

A second divergence between Scottish and British industry has been in the rate of industrial growth. Largely because of the absence of the newer industries from Scotland and their rapid expansion south of the border throughout the 1930's, industrial production before the war was rising more slowly in Scotland than in the rest of the country. It is not possible to measure the difference with any precision, since there are no estimates of total Scottish production in pre-war years. But it was reflected in the slower rise in the national income, in the lower rate of earnings, and in the higher unemployment percentages in Scotland. Since the war there has been more reason to expect that Scottish industrial production would keep pace with production in the rest of Great Britain; unemployment has been almost as negligible as elsewhere, and many new industries have been started. But on the other hand, there is evidence of a slower rise in productivity in Scotland; in the coal industry the divergence of trend between Scotland and the other coalfields is quite startling;[1] and in shipbuilding there has been no rise in output per man corresponding in the least to, say, the rise in the motor vehicle industry. All things considered, it would seem that in industrial production Scotland is again lagging slightly behind England and Wales.

The index of industrial production issued by the Scottish Home Department points to the same conclusion. It permits of a comparison with the United Kingdom over the period 1948–51 when production was still increasing and shows that in the majority of industries (including a number not given in Table 32) the rise was perceptibly greater in the United Kingdom than in Scotland. The most notable exceptions were building and building materials, textiles, and miscellaneous metal goods, while in the engineering and shipbuilding group the increase was apparently about the same in Scotland as in the rest of the country. The most striking divergence was in the chemical and allied trades in which a 14 % increase in Scotland fell far short of a 34 % increase in the United Kingdom. It is significant that in gas, electricity and water—a group which tends to reflect the general trend—the increase in Scotland was only 11 % compared with 24 % in the United Kingdom. For all manufacturing industries and for all industries, manufacturing and other, the index for the United Kingdom rose in 1949 and 1950 by about 1 % per annum above the index for Scotland; in 1951 both indices moved together; but in 1952 the Scottish index dipped less steeply as industrial activity fell off.

[1] See pp. 115–16.

Table 32. *Industrial production in Scotland and in the*
United Kingdom, 1948 *and* 1951 (1948 = 100)

Industry group	Scotland 1951	United Kingdom 1951
Mining and quarrying	100	108
Chemicals and allied trades	114	134
Metal manufacture	109	115
Engineering, shipbuilding and electrical goods	128	127
Vehicles	112	124
Metal goods not included elsewhere	127	113
Textiles	123	119
Clothing	107	111
Food, drink and tobacco	103	105
Building and contracting	104	101
Gas, electricity and water supply	111	124
Total: manufacturing industries	116	121
Total: all industries	112	117

SOURCE: *Monthly Digest of Statistics* and *Digest of Scottish Statistics.*

There may be a lag in industrial production now and there may have been one in pre-war years. But during the war, production must have risen faster in Scotland than in the rest of the country. It is possible to form some impression of the change between 1935 and 1948 from the results of the censuses for those years. The net output of the trades covered in both years by the Census of Production increased by 225 % in Scotland between those dates and by 207 % in Great Britain as a whole. Most of this increase was in price rather than in output; and if it were possible to value what was produced at constant prices, so as to isolate the real increase in industrial production, the degree of deflation necessary would not necessarily be the same for Scotland as for Great Britain. So far as the figures go, however, they suggest that Scotland may have caught up arrears during the war and that, over the whole period of thirteen years between 1935 and 1948, Scottish industrial production may have shown the higher rate of increase.

A very rough and speculative summary of the changes over that period is shown in Table 33. The first column of figures shows the comparative size of the contributions made by different groups of industry to the Scottish total and bears out the conclusions already drawn from the figures of employment: for example, the predominance of the metal trades followed by textiles and clothing, and food, drink and tobacco among the manufacturing industries, and by mining and building among the other 'Census' industries. The second column shows the proportion of Scottish to British production in each

72

Table 33. *The pattern of industrial production in Scotland,*
1948, *and its changes since* 1935

Standard industrial classification order	Value of net output in each industry group, Scotland, 1948		Percentage increase in value of net output, 1935–48	
	Percentage of Scottish industrial production	Percentage of total for Great Britain	Scotland	Great Britain
2. Mining and quarrying	10·3	11·9	181	194
3. Treatment of non-metalli-ferous mining products other than coal	2·3	7·2	257	171
4. Chemicals and allied trades	4·0	7·2	160	181
5. Metal manufacture	7·1	10·4	218	258
6. Engineering, shipbuilding and electrical goods	20·3	11·4	422	345
7. Vehicles	4·0	5·2	319	264
8. Metal goods not included elsewhere	2·2	4·8	459	323
9. Precision instruments, jewellery, etc.	0·5	3·7	409	254
10. Textiles	9·6	10·5	158	185
11. Leather, leather goods and fur	0·7	7·1	287	234
12. Clothing	1·7	4·1	168	148
13. Food, drink and tobacco	11·6	12·3	160	121
14. Manufactures of wood and cork	2·4	·9·9	278	203
15. Paper and printing	5·5	9·9	134	133
16. Other manufacturing industries	1·9	8·5	174	247
17. Building and contracting	11·8	10·7	302	231
18. Gas, electricity and water supply	4·1	7·6	133	128
Total industrial production	100·0	9·4	225	207

SOURCE: Estimated from *Census of Production.*

industry, ranging from a relatively high proportion for mining and the food, drink and tobacco trades to a relatively low proportion for clothing, vehicles, precision instruments and other metal goods. The average of 9·4 % is below the ratio that one would expect on a manpower basis, pointing to a lower output per head in Scotland than in the rest of Britain.

This lower output per head is of long standing. For the trades covered by the Census of Production, i.e. mainly mining, manufacturing, building, and gas, water and electricity supply, net output per head has been consistently lower in Scotland than in England and Wales since 1907. The full figures are given in Table 34.

Can this difference be explained by the divergence in industrial pattern between the two countries? Since the value of net output per head varies greatly between one industry and another, the industrial pattern obviously affects the value of output. Analysis shows, however, that this is only a partial explanation, and that England and Wales appears to enjoy, in addition to an industrial pattern slightly more favourable to a high value of output, a slight superiority in productivity. There is no simple explanation for this fact, which appears to be associated in Scotland with, amongst other things, a lesser degree of mechanization, a smaller managerial and research staff, and a comparative absence of the higher-valued products.

Table 34. *Value of net output per head for all 'Census' trades in Scotland and in England and Wales, 1907–48*

Year	Scotland (£)	England and Wales (£)	Scotland as percentage of England and Wales
1907	98	104	94
1924	206	214	96
1930	199	213	93
1935	213	225	95
1948	503	544	92

SOURCE: *Census of Production.*

A comparison of the two right-hand columns in Table 33 can only be made with great caution. The highest rates of expansion, whether due to increases in price or in output, have been in the metal groups with a range of 254–345 % for Great Britain and 218–467 % for Scotland. The lowest rates of expansion have been in gas, water and electricity supply, paper and printing, chemicals, clothing, and the food, drink and tobacco trades. Some of the lower rates of expansion clearly reflect the greater steadiness of prices (e.g. of electricity and chemicals) rather than inelasticity of output. The most striking divergences between the two columns have been the much greater increase in the metal trades in Scotland (with the exception of metal manufacture), in building and contracting and building materials, and the much smaller increase in miscellaneous manufacturing industries. It is not possible to say, however, how far these divergences reflect a genuine difference in the trend of industrial production.

Although Scottish industrial production may have tended to lag behind British production before and since the war, and although this phenomenon may be associated with the absence of some of the larger new industries from

Scotland, it is a mistake to exaggerate the lag or to imply that economic development in Scotland in pre-war years had almost ceased. The rate of industrial development can be compared with that for Britain as a whole by grouping industries according to their rate of expansion or contraction in employment between 1923 and 1947, and showing the proportion of workers falling into each group in 1947. This is done in Table 35.

Table 35. *Employed insured workers in each group of* 108 *industries, by rate of expansion or decline since* 1923, *in Scotland and in Great Britain,* 1947*

Rate of expansion or decline in Great Britain, 1923–47	Scotland		Percentage of total employment in Great Britain	Scotland as percentage of Great Britain
	Number (thousands)	Percentage of total employment		
Decline				
25 % or more	173·9	11·0	10·4	11·1
Less than 25 %	155·6	9·8	9·1	11·5
Expansion				
Less than 25 %	203·8	12·9	12·0	11·4
25 % but less than 50 %	361·2	22·8	18·6	13·0
50 % but less than 100 %	385·6	24·4	25·0	10·3
100 % but less than 200 %	178·0	11·3	13·3	9·0
200 % or more	123·2	7·8	11·6	7·1
All industries and services	1,581·3	100·0	100·0	10·6

* The figures in Table 35 are less comprehensive than the figures in Tables 30 and 31 since they are restricted to workers insured against unemployment under the old scheme.

SOURCE: *Ministry of Labour Gazette* and *Tables relating to employment and unemployment.*

The figures confirm the view that Scotland was deficient in the rapidly expanding industries. At the same time, the situation is put into its proper perspective, for it is apparent that Scotland concentrated to only a very minor extent on declining or stagnating industries. It was the industries with moderate rates of growth—25–100 %—that accounted in 1947 for almost half the total employment in Scotland as in the rest of the country. Even in the industries with faster rates of growth, the proportion of Scottish workers employed was not so very far short of the proportion for Great Britain.

NEW FACTORY BUILDING

The growth of new industry comes about in a variety of ways: through a change to new lines by existing firms; through a change in the occupation of existing factories; and through the erection of new factories. Of these, only the third is readily measurable from year to year and on this account it often occupies a disproportionate place in discussion of economic development.

New factory building between the wars was almost negligible in Scotland. In 1935, which may be taken as typical of the middle 1930's, only twenty-two new factories were built in Scotland compared with 213 in London alone. Shortly before the war, with the establishment of a number of Trading Estates, including Hillington, Glasgow, things began to change, and during the war, a large amount of new factory space came into existence in Scotland, the total disposed of to industry after 1945 reaching 5·2 m. sq. ft. or the equivalent of fifty-two medium-sized factories of 100,000 sq. ft. each. From the beginning of 1945 to the end of 1952, 536 new factories costing £22·4 m. were built in the Scottish Development Area alone and this represented about 9 % by number and 8 % by value of the total for Great Britain. So far as can be judged from these figures, Scotland, including the districts that lie outside the Development Area, has had a share of new factory building since the war fully in proportion to the comparative size of her industrial population.

If new industrial enterprise is taken to mean, not the building of new factories or extensions but new manufacturing plants, whether new businesses or branch factories and whether set up in new buildings or in old buildings, about 100 new enterprises per year have come into production in Scotland since the war. Most of these have been small, the average number of workers being between 100 and 200. About half of the new enterprises were started in existing premises and of the remainder, about four-fifths started in factories built with government assistance.[1] Many of the new enterprises—nearly a quarter—were branches of firms in England, America and elsewhere.

It is unfortunately not possible to show the industrial distribution of the new developments but the available data suggest that it conformed fairly closely to the existing broad pattern of industry. To this there are some important exceptions, notably in the large number of projects for the manufacture of electrical goods, and the small number in the food, drink and tobacco group. Within the engineering group there were also some important new developments, for example in business machinery, watches and clocks, tractors and aero-engines. The total new employment expected to result from all new industrial schemes since the war is approximately 150,000.

LONG-TERM CHANGES IN THE INDUSTRIAL PATTERN

The present pattern of production in Scotland has been the result of long developments; 100 years ago the pattern was fundamentally different. The changes which have taken place since then are brought out in Table 36.

Some caution is needed in interpreting this table, for two reasons. First, the figures shown in the census tables for 1851 and 1901 required extensive rearrangement in order to obtain figures comparable with those for 1951, and

[1] *Report of the Committee on Local Development in Scotland* (Scottish Council, 1952), p. 25.

even so they are only broadly comparable. For example, the number of persons engaged in the distribution of many commodities could not be satisfactorily segregated from those engaged in their manufacture in 1851, and the number of workers in the service trades may well be understated for that year. Secondly, the figures reflect changes in manpower only, not changes in productivity, and give no indication of the changes in output for any given industry group, nor even an accurate indication of relative changes in output between one industry group and another, since productivity trends may be very different. This applies particularly when comparing manufacturing with service trades, where productivity has probably not changed greatly; in comparing different manufacturing groups, this objection is less serious.

Table 36. *Working population of Scotland by broad industrial group, 1851–1951**

Year	Metal trades	Textiles, leather and clothing	Miscell-aneous manu-facturing	Total manu-facturing	Agri-culture, forestry, fishing	Mining and quarrying	Service trades (including building)	All industries and services
			Number (thousands)					
1851	60·8	366·4	66·2	493·4	347·6	48·1	380·8	1,269·9
1901	210·4	299·2	147·7	657·3	237·3	127·9	879·6	1,902·1
1951	358·2	174·5	255·9	788·6	160·7	97·2	1,148·3	2,194·8
			Percentage of total for all industries					
1851	4·8	28·8	5·2	38·8	27·4	3·8	30·0	100·0
1901	11·1	15·7	7·8	34·6	12·5	6·7	46·2	100·0
1951	16·3	8·0	11·7	36·0	7·3	4·4	52·3	100·0
			Percentage of total for Great Britain					
1851	10·6	16·4	11·0	14·4	15·7	14·0	11·8	13·8
1901	13·6	12·3	13·3	12·9	17·1	14·3	10·6	12·2
1951	9·1	9·9	9·9	9·5	14·6	11·5	9·7	9·9

* Excluding persons unclassified and, in 1951, persons out of work.
SOURCE: *Census of Population.*

When all this is said and done, however, some interesting points still emerge. For instance, the decline in importance of textiles, leather and clothing trades, as well as of agriculture, forestry and fishing, is strikingly brought out. In 1851, these activities kept more than half of the total labour force of Scotland occupied; since then, the numbers engaged in them have not merely failed to keep pace with the growth of the industrial population but have in fact steadily declined by over one-half in both groups, and, as a result, fewer than one-sixth of all workers are now occupied in these trades.

On the other hand, the metal industries now employ almost six times as many workers as in 1851, and other factory trades—building materials, chemicals, food, wood, paper manufactures, etc.—almost four times as many. The combined share of these groups increased steadily from 10 % in 1851 to 19 % in 1901 and 28 % in 1951. The service trades have also substantially expanded their labour force, both absolutely and relatively. The mining and quarrying industries grew rapidly during the second half of the nineteenth century but the process has since then been reversed; their labour force is still twice as large as in 1851 but their proportion to the total working population is not much higher.

All in all, primary production has lost and tertiary production has gained in importance. In spite of considerable shifts between industries, the share of secondary production (manufacturing) has remained comparatively stable.

The industrial developments which took place in England and Wales during the same period were very similar in character. But the size of both total and working population increased more rapidly there, with the result that the Scottish share of production in Great Britain fell from almost one-seventh to one-tenth, as far as we can gauge from the trend of the working population. The relative decline of Scottish production was more pronounced during the second than during the first fifty years under review. Indeed, between 1851 and 1901 Scotland obtained an increasing share in the metal trades, miscellaneous manufacturing, agriculture, etc., and mining, though this was outweighed by the more rapid decline in textiles and the slower growth of the service industries. But between 1901 and 1951, Scotland lost ground in every single industrial group, though somewhat less in the field of service trades than elsewhere.

The increase in the importance of the service trades has not, however, been by any means uniform in all the trades in this group. On the contrary, there has been a big decline in one of the trades—domestic service—between 1901 and 1951 which has run counter to the general trend. Further details are given in Table 37, which supplements the information provided by Table 36.

The word of caution which has been offered regarding the comparability of the figures from different years applies *a fortiori* to this more detailed comparison. Nevertheless, the general trend is clear. Between 1851 and 1901 the industrialization of the country was accompanied by a vast extension of transport and commercial services, and these are responsible for the largest part of the relative expansion of the service trades. But since 1901 the main factors leading in this direction were the growth in national and local government service and in the professions. These were partly counteracted by the virtual elimination of private domestic service as a major economic activity, and the shift towards the service trades as a whole is therefore much less pronounced

78

during this than in the previous period. Again, these developments were very much in line with those taking place in England and Wales at the same time.

Table 37. *Persons working in different service trades in Scotland*, 1851–1951

Year	Building, gas, water and electricity	Transport and communications	Distribution and commerce	Public administration and defence	Professional services	Domestic service	Other services	Total service trades
	Number (thousands)							
1851	67·5	47·9	67·4	16·8	27·4	118·2	35·6	380·8
1901	143·4	163·2	235·5	29·4	62·7	165·7	79·7	879·6
1951	168·0	185·1	322·7	140·9	156·2	50·6	124·8	1,148·3
	Percentage of total for all industries							
1851	5·3	3·8	5·3	1·3	2·2	9·3	2·8	30·0
1901	7·5	8·6	12·4	1·5	3·3	8·7	4·2	46·2
1951	7·7	8·4	14·7	6·4	7·1	2·3	5·7	52·3

* 1851 and 1901 including, but 1951 excluding, unemployed.
SOURCE: *Census of Population.*

THE GEOGRAPHICAL PATTERN

So far, Scotland has been treated as a single geographical unit. But it might be more realistic to analyse production by region and try to separate areas which differ in their predominant economic activity. The following pages, therefore, attempt a brief description of the distribution of industries between eight Scottish areas. These are: the 'Clyde Valley', comprising Lanark (including Glasgow), Dunbarton, Renfrew, and northern and central Ayr; the South-West, consisting of coastal and southern Ayr, Bute, Dumfries, Wigtown and Kirkcudbright; the Eastern Borders, i.e. Roxburgh, Selkirk, Peebles and Berwick; the Lothians, including Edinburgh but excluding part of West Lothian; the Forth Estuary, which covers Stirling, Clackmannan, most of Fife, Kinross and part of West Lothian; Eastern Scotland, containing Angus with Dundee, Perth and part of Fife; the North-East, i.e. Aberdeen, Kincardine, Banff, Moray and Nairn; and the Highlands and Islands, which includes Argyll but not Bute or Perth. The first of these areas has by far the largest industrial population and has therefore been subdivided, so as to show Glasgow and the remainder of the Clyde Valley separately.

A glance at the final column of Table 38 shows that the Clyde Valley contains almost half of the total industrial population of Scotland. Glasgow alone accounts for more than a quarter and for a larger total than the remainder of the Clyde Valley.[1] The areas next in importance are, in this order, the Lothians, the Forth Estuary, the East, and the North-East, which between them contain another 40 % of the insured population. The smallest of the areas distinguished here is that of the Eastern Borders, which, however, is sufficiently distinct in character to be treated separately from its neighbour areas, the South-West and the Lothians.

As one might expect, the geographical distribution of the service trades is very similar to that of all industries and services. The geographical distribution of manufacturing as a whole is also not very different, except that it emphasizes the importance of the Clyde Valley even more; more than 30 % of all manufacturing industries appear to be located in Glasgow alone, and 60 % in the whole of Clydeside. If we confine our attention to the metal trades, the percentage of industrial employment increases to over 35 % for Glasgow City and to over 70 % for the whole Clyde Valley area. In the metal trades the Forth Estuary ranks second in importance with over 9 %, followed by the Lothians and the East with over 7 % and 5 % respectively.

The concentration of industries in and around Glasgow is less marked in textiles, leather and clothing and miscellaneous manufacturing industries than in the metal trades. In the textile group, a little above one-quarter of the Scottish industrial employment is concentrated in Glasgow, and a similar proportion in the remainder of the Clyde Valley—notably in Paisley and in Ayrshire. But the East, with Dundee as its centre, is another important textile area, which contributes almost 20 % to the Scottish total; the Eastern Borders and the Forth Estuary—chiefly Fife—contribute another 15 %.

Glasgow has again the largest share—more than 30 %—of manufacturing employment in industries outside the metal and textile groups, and thus shows itself to possess a high degree of industrial diversity. In the rest of Clydeside, this is not true to the same extent, since those industries are not so well represented there; the area contains little more than one-sixth of all Scottish industries in this group and is exceeded in importance by the Lothians. The Forth Estuary, the North-East and the East have also important shares in the Scottish total.

The location of agriculture, forestry and fishing is, of course, entirely different. The insured population in these pursuits is widely scattered all over Scotland, the most important areas being the North-East, the East, the South-West and the Highlands and Islands, in which altogether two-thirds of the total number were working.

---

[1] The figures given here are based on place of work, not on residence. According to the Census of Population, 22 %—not 28 %—of the Scottish working population live in Glasgow, and the city thus provides employment for a large number of workers living outside its boundaries.

Table 38. *Distribution of insured employees (including unemployed) in each broad industrial group over eight Scottish areas, 1951*

Area	Metal trades	Textiles, leather and clothing	Miscellaneous manufacturing	Total manufacturing	Agriculture, forestry, fishing	Mining and quarrying	Service trades	All industries and services
Percentage of total for Scotland								
Glasgow City	35·6	26·0	30·5	31·9	1·3	3·8	29·9	28·0
Remainder of Clyde Valley	35·9	28·1	17·2	28·1	8·8	20·1	16·1	20·7
Clyde Valley	71·5	54·1	47·7	60·0	10·1	23·9	46·0	48·7
South West	2·2	3·2	2·9	2·6	14·0	14·6	5·7	5·3
Eastern Borders	0·4	7·8	0·7	2·1	8·0	0·1	1·6	2·0
Lothians	7·1	4·5	18·9	10·4	9·4	24·7	16·4	14·1
Forth Estuary	9·1	7·1	11·9	9·6	5·5	34·9	7·7	9·7
East	5·3	18·6	6·8	8·6	17·3	0·6	8·9	8·8
North-East	3·4	3·7	9·3	5·4	22·8	0·5	8·5	7·6
Highlands and Islands	1·0	1·0	1·8	1·3	12·9	0·7	5·2	3·8
Total Scotland	100·0	100·0	100·0	100·0	100·0	100·0	100·0	100·0
Location factor within Scotland								
Glasgow City	1·27	0·93	1·09	1·14	0·05	0·14	1·07	1·00
Remainder of Clyde Valley	1·73	1·36	0·83	1·36	0·42	0·97	0·78	1·00
Clyde Valley	1·47	1·11	0·98	1·23	0·21	0·49	0·94	1·00
South-West	0·41	0·60	0·54	0·49	2·62	2·74	1·07	1·00
Eastern Borders	0·19	3·80	0·35	1·01	3·90	0·06	0·79	1·00
Lothians	0·50	0·32	1·34	0·74	0·67	1·76	1·16	1·00
Forth Estuary	0·94	0·73	1·23	0·99	0·56	3·58	0·80	1·00
East	0·60	2·12	0·77	0·98	1·97	0·07	1·01	1·00
North-East	0·45	0·49	1·23	0·71	3·01	0·06	1·12	1·00
Highlands and Islands	0·27	0·26	0·48	0·34	3·39	0·18	1·37	1·00
Total Scotland	1·00	1·00	1·00	1·00	1·00	1·00	1·00	1·00

SOURCE: Ministry of Labour (unpublished).

Employment in mining and quarrying, on the other hand, is dominated by the location of the coalfields—other mining and quarrying being relatively unimportant—and these lie almost entirely within four of the eight areas defined here. These areas are the Forth Estuary, which contains the Fife and Clackmannan and part of the Central coalfield; the Lothians; the Clyde Valley, containing the main part of the Central coalfield; and the South-West, which takes in the South Ayr and Dumfries mines. Further details on the main coal-producing areas will be found in Chapter 8.

A different aspect of localization is considered when the location factors given in the bottom half of Table 38 are brought under review. In calculating them (by dividing each percentage by the corresponding figure in the final column), the differences in size between the areas have been eliminated, and the figures show the extent to which an industrial group is over- or under-represented in any area relatively to Scotland as a whole.

The only region which has a location factor above 1 for the metal trades is the Clyde Valley, and the location factor is even higher in the area round Glasgow than in Glasgow itself. The only other area in which the relative importance of the metal trades is nearly as high as in Scotland as a whole is the Forth Estuary. The absence of metal trades is most marked in the Eastern Borders and in the Highlands and Islands.

The textile, leather and clothing trades are most strongly concentrated in the Eastern Borders, followed by the East. They are represented in about average strength in the Clyde Valley, but in the remaining areas, particularly the Highlands and Islands and the Lothians, relatively poorly.

Of the miscellaneous factory trades, there is a good representation in the Lothians, the Forth Estuary and the North-East; examples are the rubber industry in Edinburgh; the linoleum industry in Kirkcaldy; fish preserving on the Aberdeen coast. In the South and the North of Scotland, industries of this kind are relatively scarce.

The Clyde Valley shows the greatest concentration of manufacturing as a whole, Glasgow City rather less so than the surrounding area. Other areas which have approximately an average share in manufacturing employment are the Eastern Borders, the Forth Estuary and the East. The inclusion in this category of the Eastern Borders, which one would hardly think of as an 'industrial area', may seem surprising; but the area provides employment for a large number of women in the textile trades. In terms of the value of net output or earnings, the area's share of manufacturing may be somewhat less important.

The Eastern Borders also show the greatest concentration of agriculture, forestry and fishing; next come the Highlands and Islands, the North-East, the South-West and the East. In mining and quarrying, the Forth Estuary has the highest location factor, and the next highest ones are found in the

South-West and the Lothians. By this test, most areas are either agricultural or mining areas, except the South-West which is both, and the Clyde Valley which is neither.

The location factors of the service trades do not differ much from 1, but are generally low in manufacturing areas. The high figure for the Highlands and Islands reflects, among other things, the large manpower requirements of transport and the importance of the tourist trade.

SUMMARY

1. In terms of broad industrial groups, there is no great difference between the industrial pattern in Scotland and in Great Britain as a whole; there is, however, rather more emphasis on primary production.

2. Within the metal and engineering group of industries, there is a predominance of heavy engineering in Scotland to a much greater extent than in England and Wales, and in the past this has made Scotland more vulnerable to fluctuations in employment. The newer engineering industries, which are poorly represented in Scotland, have developed large export markets, so that Scotland's share of engineering exports has diminished.

3. Industrial production both before and after the war was rising more slowly in Scotland than in the rest of the country. During the war, however, industrial production rose faster in Scotland and between 1935 and 1948 Scotland probably gained some ground.

4. Industrial productivity appears to be somewhat lower in Scotland than in the rest of the country.

5. Scotland is deficient in the rapidly-expanding industries, but, on the other hand, has not concentrated to any great extent on industries that are declining or stagnating.

6. Since the war, a large number of new factories have been built and a large number of new industries started. The total employment in all the new ventures launched since the war is expected to reach 150,000.

7. Large changes in the industrial pattern have taken place over the past hundred years; the decline in agriculture and textiles, and the rise of the metal and engineering trades and services of all kinds are the most notable.

8. Three out of every five Scottish workers in manufacturing industry work in the Clyde Valley area; one in every five works in the Lothians or in the area of the Forth Estuary. On the other hand, only one in four of the workers in agriculture, forestry and fishing works in those areas.

CHAPTER 7

AGRICULTURE

By G. F. B. HOUSTON

The land is the finest that I ever saw in my life, though I have seen every fine vale, in every county in England...it is by no means uncommon for it to produce seven English quarters of wheat upon one English acre, and forty tons of turnips upon one English acre...all in rows as straight as a line, and without a weed to be seen in any of these beautiful fields.

Oh! how you will wish to be here!...let me tell you, then, that there is neither village, nor church, nor ale-house, nor garden, nor cottage, nor flowers, nor pig, nor goose, nor common, nor green. WILLIAM COBBETT, *Tour in Scotland*

The praises of Scottish farming sung by Cobbett in 1832 were not the psalms of the converted. Although he found the level of technique in the Lothians astonishingly high, he judged the conditions of the farm workers deplorably low and any general comparisons he made of Scottish and English farming were incidental to his primary aim of showing that the Scottish farm workers were worse off than the agricultural labourers of England.

Returning to Scotland 120 years later, with prices and wages regulated by the State or semi-official authorities, Cobbett would find it less easy to contrast rural conditions north and south of the Tweed. The churches and ale-houses which he could not find may be more numerous, but at least one of the differences he noted in 1832 has remained. Rural society in much of Scotland still differs from England in that most agricultural families live, not in villages, but in houses on the farms. A generation ago this meant that the farm, not the village or parish, was the social unit in rural Scotland, but the advent of bus and bicycle has broken down the former isolation of the farming community, at least in lowland areas.

Turning to the question of agricultural techniques, there is need to show more caution in comparing Scotland with England than Cobbett may have felt was necessary after touring the Lothians. In agriculture there are greater differences within each country than across the Border; the farms of Northumberland have more in common with those of Berwickshire than the latter have with farms in Dumfriesshire; and there is no greater contrast in techniques in British agriculture than between a large farm in the Scottish lowlands and a small hill farm in the Highlands or Western Isles.

Yet Scottish farming, with all its variations, has its own distinctive features, the best of which have given it an international reputation which the farmers of many other countries, including England, may envy. The yields of many crops are higher in Scotland than in the rest of Britain. Every year high-priced Scottish pedigree livestock are shipped abroad to improve herds in Argentine, Australia, U.S.A. and other countries where Scottish-bred stock is already well established. Alternate husbandry,[1] or ley farming, which has been widely practised in Scotland for many years is still regarded as an advanced system in most European countries. Scotland's four million acres of cultivated land do not cover the most fertile soil in the world but they have made a useful contribution to world agriculture and one which cannot easily be bettered by any similar agricultural area.

THE NATIONAL FARM

Land utilization

In relation to total agricultural land, Scotland has a lower population density than the rest of Britain. This is mainly due to the large acreage of rough grazings in Scotland but if these grazings are deducted from the total area of agricultural land, giving what is known as the crops and grass acreage, Scotland is still better off than England and Wales, having almost one acre of crops and grass per person compared with just over half an acre in the rest of Britain.

Scotland not only has relatively more farm land, it also uses the land differently (Table 39). A smaller proportion of the crops and grass acreage is laid down in permanent pasture in Scotland and the arable land (i.e. crops and grass less permanent grass) is often cultivated in a 'fifty-fifty' rotation of three years temporary grass followed by three years in tillage crops. This is modified in many areas to suit local conditions, but in Scotland as a whole 47 % of the arable land was laid down in temporary grass in 1952, compared with 27 % in England and Wales. Such a system of alternate husbandry lends itself more readily to an expansion of livestock production based on home-grown fodder than the practice (more common in England) of leaving grass fields as permanent pasture. With alternate husbandry, not only do the arable crops benefit from the accumulated fertility of the grassland but new grass is more productive than old and there is an improvement both in grass and arable crops. This was recognized during the last war when there was a drive to plough up permanent pastures and to extend the system of alternate husbandry throughout Britain.

To offset any advantages afforded by the methods of husbandry, however, Scottish farms have a shorter grazing season and under some climatic

---

[1] The system in which each field has periods under arable crops alternating with periods under temporary grasses. This may be contrasted with the practice of setting aside some of the fields for arable crops and putting down the rest to permanent grassland.

conditions may find it difficult to establish fields of good grass. The results will be considered later; at present it may be noted that the large area of rough grazings backing up the arable land and the emphasis on temporary grasses should provide a good fodder base for livestock production.

The use of the tillage area (the arable less the temporary grass) remains to be considered. As Table 39 shows, a greater proportion of tillage is devoted to fodder crops[1] in Scotland than in England and Wales and the chief Scottish grain crop, oats, is mainly grown for animal fodder.[2] Apart from potatoes, there is no important crop grown chiefly for direct human consumption which is as important in Scotland as in the rest of Britain.

Table 39. *Land utilization in Great Britain, June* 1952

Utilization of total agricultural area (millions of acres)			Utilization of tillage area (thousands of acres)		
	England and Wales	Scotland		England and Wales	Scotland
Tillage area	10·1	1·7	Wheat	1,963	65
Temporary grasses	3·7	1·5	Other grains	4,632	1,111
Total arable land	13·8	3·2	Potatoes	682	172
			Sugar beet	398	10
Permanent grass	10·7	1·2	Fodder crops	1,158	352
Total crops and grass	24·5	4·4	Fruit and vegetables	756	20
Rough grazings	5·4	11·0	Other crops (including bare fallow)	527	12
Total agricultural land	29·9	15·4			
Total land area (excluding water)	37·1	19·1	Total tillage area	10,116	1,742

SOURCE: *Agricultural Returns*, June 1952.

A study of land utilization points at each stage to the main feature of Scottish farming, the emphasis on livestock production rather than crop sales. There is a similar emphasis in Britain as a whole, but it is more pronounced north of the Tweed, and there are per person almost twice as many cattle, five times as many sheep, more poultry and about the same number of pigs in Scotland as in England and Wales.

[1] 20 % in Scotland and 12 % in England and Wales. The most important fodder crops are turnips and swedes, mangolds, beans, peas, kale, cabbage, etc. for stockfeeding.

[2] About two-thirds of the oats crop remains on the 'national farm', compared with about one-third of the wheat and barley crops. Some of the value of the crops sold off the farms returns in feedingstuffs, however.

Changes in land utilization and livestock numbers since 1870

Changes in land utilization since 1870 are summarized in Fig. 8. Data for the years 1870, 1913, 1939 and 1952 have been used, and fluctuations between these years ignored. After 1913 there was a fairly steady decline in the crops and grass acreage in Britain due to the deterioration of some farm land to the

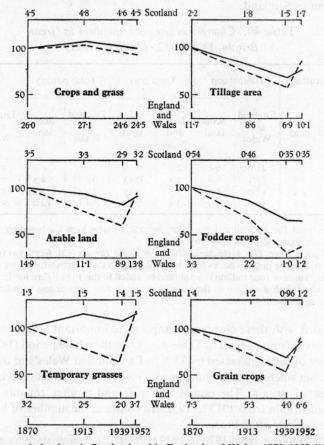

Fig. 8. Changes in land use in Scotland and in England and Wales, 1870–1952 (1870 = 100). Absolute areas (in millions of acres) are shown on horizontal scales. Scotland ———; England and Wales – – –.

level of rough grazings or its transfer to non-agricultural purposes. It would appear that the loss of farm land to agriculture in Scotland has been relatively less since 1913 than in the rest of Britain but the earlier returns are probably too unreliable to justify any comparison on this point. Changes in the use of farm land (i.e. crops and grass) can be measured with more confidence.

The most striking conclusion to be drawn from the data is that whereas the important changes in land utilization in the period 1870–1939 were relatively greater in England and Wales than in Scotland, the reversal of trends after 1939 brought land use in the two areas very close to the 1870 position, both absolutely and relative to one another. The only exception was the reduction in the acreage of fodder crops, which was much more severe in England and Wales than in Scotland.

Table 40. *Changes in livestock numbers in Great Britain*, 1870–1952. (*Million Head*)

Year	Total cattle		Total sheep		Total pigs		Total poultry		Agricultural horses*	
	England and Wales	Scotland	England and Wales	Scotland	England and Wales	Scotland	England and Wales	Scotland	England and Wales	Scotland
1870	4·4	1·0	21·6	6·8	2·0	0·16	—	—	0·83	0·14
1913	5·7	1·2	17·1	6·8	2·1	0·13	32·2†	4·5†	0·81	0·14
1939	6·8	1·4	18·0	8·0	3·5	0·25	56·4‡	7·7‡	0·55	0·10
1952	7·7	1·6	13·6	7·3	3·8	0·45	68·1	10·0	0·21	0·04

* Horses used for agricultural purposes, including mares kept for breeding. The 1870 figures exclude mares kept for breeding.

† 1908 figures from *The Agricultural Output of Great Britain* (Cd. 6277, 1912).

‡ Since 1941 some poultry flocks have been included in the returns which were omitted in earlier years. Three or four million head should be added to the 1939 figure for England and Wales and about half a million to the Scottish figure in any comparison with later years.

SOURCE: *Agricultural Statistics*.

Associated with these cropping changes were important variations in live-stock numbers (summarized in Table 40). Over the whole period (1870–1952) the number of cattle increased by 75 % in England and Wales and by 60 % in Scotland, but whereas sheep numbers also rose in Scotland they fell by a third in the rest of Britain. The numbers of pigs and poultry roughly doubled throughout Britain from 1913 to 1952. In contrast, the number of horses fell rapidly, especially after 1939.

Broadly speaking, from 1870 to 1939 there was a greater stability about the structure of agriculture in Scotland than in the rest of Britain. Two of the major changes in England, the big reduction in wheat acreage[1] and the decline in arable sheep farming, influenced Scottish agriculture to a much smaller degree. The important developments after 1939 affected the whole of Britain but they may be discussed more fruitfully in terms of agricultural output.

[1] The wheat acreage in England and Wales fell from nearly 3½ m. acres in 1870 to just over 1½ m. acres in 1913 and 1939. It was 2 m. acres in 1952. In Scotland the wheat acreage was 130,000 in 1870, 80,000 in 1939, and 65,000 in 1952.

Agricultural output

There are several definitions of agricultural output which can be used for different purposes. The gross output equals the total value of sales off farms, minus inter-farm sales, plus the value of produce consumed by the farm households, and adjusted to cover any change in the value of stocks or work in process.

The net output of agriculture, as defined by the Scottish Department of Agriculture and the Ministry of Agriculture (called simply the net output hereafter), equals the gross output less the value of feedingstuffs, live animals, and seeds imported by farmers and the costs of processing or distributing home-produced feedingstuffs; store livestock, etc. No deduction is made for purchases of non-agricultural products such as artificial fertilizers and fuel, or for repairs to machinery, and so forth.

A second definition of net output, which will be hereafter called the net product of agriculture, deducts not only imported agricultural products but also all farm purchases of non-agricultural products, and makes allowances for the depreciation of machinery, and for one or two miscellaneous items such as bank charges. The net product of agriculture (which differs slightly from the Board of Trade definition of net output) equals total agricultural income, defined as the sum accruing to the agricultural population in the form of rent, wages and farmers' profits.

Each of these outputs may be measured over a period of years at current prices or constant prices. In this chapter output at current prices is referred to simply as gross output, net output, etc., while output at constant prices will be called real gross output, real net output, etc.

Scotland's share of British output

There are official estimates of the gross output of agriculture in Scotland and Great Britain[1] for a number of years, starting in 1908. The series does not become continuous (nor very reliable) until the 1930's but the figures have been used in Table 41 as a first step in disclosing any recent trends in Scotland's share of the gross output of British agriculture.

The table suggests an apparent fall in Scotland's share of British gross output from 17 % in 1925 to 14 % in 1950/51. This is probably due in part to a change in the methods of calculating output. It is likely, for instance, that in the earlier years, when the methods were crudest, the output of meat was overestimated, thus boosting the Scottish output in relation to the British total. Changes in the method of estimating output are important for the period 1931–39 but are not likely to account for the full extent of the decline

[1] As far as possible Great Britain will be compared with Scotland. Later, United Kingdom totals have to be used.

shown in Table 41. Another possible explanation is that over most of the
period covered by the table the prices of the farm products in which Scotland
specializes did not rise as much as other farm prices in Britain. There are two
official series of agricultural price indices, one for Scotland and another for
England and Wales.[1] A comparison of the two series in Table 42 reveals that,
using 1927–29 as the base period, the general price level of agricultural
products in Scotland has invariably been several points lower than the index
for England and Wales. In the middle 1930's and the first years of the war
the divergence was quite considerable and it was only after 1947 that the gap
began to close. Price changes were therefore partly responsible for the decline
in Scotland's share of British output, at least until 1947, but do not fully
explain the overall trend from 1925 to 1950/51.

Table 41. *The gross output of British agriculture
(at current prices) 1908–1950/51*

Year	Great Britain (£ m.)	Scotland (£ m.)	Scottish output / British output (percentage)
1908	153·7	26·5	17·2
1925	282·2	48·7	17·2
1930/31	250·4	37·7	15·0
1936–39	264·0	38·1	14·4
1950/51	855·0	119·1	13·9

SOURCES: *Agricultural Statistics*. Reports on Agricultural Output (Cd. 6277, Cmd. 2815,
Cmd. 3191, Cmd. 4605, Cmd. 4496); *Scottish Agricultural Economics* (Department of
Agriculture for Scotland, H.M.S.O.).

In so far as these two explanations do not completely account for the fall
shown in Table 41, the real gross output in Scotland (i.e. output valued at
constant prices) could not have increased from 1925 to 1950/51 to the same
extent as real gross output in England and Wales. The nature of the data
prevents a direct comparison of the real gross outputs for the years 1925 and
1950/51 but it is possible to estimate trends over the period by taking it in
stages.

From 1925 to 1931 the real gross output of agriculture in England and
Wales rose by about 4 %, while in Scotland it fell by 2–3 %;[2] in the period
1931–39 real gross output in Scotland did not rise relative to real gross out-

[1] Different weights are used in the two series and are based on the relative importance
of the various commodities in the output of agriculture in each country.
[2] The estimate for England and Wales is from *The Agricultural Output of England and
Wales, 1930/31*, Cmd. 4605, p. 40. The Scottish estimate is based on a repricing by the
writer of 1925 output at 1931 prices. The extent of the fall can only be roughly estimated
but it appears certain that there was a decline.

put in England and Wales and may have fallen;[1] from 1936–39 to 1950/51 the real gross output of the *United Kingdom* rose by 19 %, in Scotland by 17 %.[2] There seems to be little doubt that over the whole period, 1925 to 1950/51, Scotland's share of the real gross output of British agriculture declined, although not to the extent suggested by Table 41.[3]

Table 42. *Index numbers of general agricultural prices,**
1927–50. (1927–29 = 100)

Year	England and Wales	Scotland	Year	England and Wales	Scotland	Year	England and Wales	Scotland
1927	99	98	1935	81	74	1943	164	148
1928	102	106	1936	83	76	1944	167	151
1929	99	96	1937	90	92	1945	172	162
1930	91	87	1938	90	83	1946	183	170
1931	83	86	1939	91	86	1947	213	188
1932	80	77	1940	126	114	1948	219	211
1933	75	67	1941	151	130	1949	229	222
1934	77	72	1942	161	146	1950	237	230

* Exchequer payments included.
SOURCE: *Agricultural Statistics.*

Output during and after the war

Output trends during and after the last war deserve special consideration. It is more convenient for this period to compare Scotland with the United Kingdom (i.e. including Northern Ireland) and Table 43 shows that from 1939 to 1950/51 there was a slight fall in Scotland's share of United Kingdom gross output (at current prices). The annual figures reveal that there was a sudden break after 1943/44, the fairly steady proportion of 13·2 % in the first six years changing to an equally steady proportion of 12·8 % over the following seven years. It is difficult to trace the cause of this change but it may have been due in the first place to the very bad season in 1944/45.

Table 43 shows the trend of gross output at current prices, but here again it is necessary to consider, for the same period, the trend of real gross output (i.e. at constant prices). Moreover, estimates of real net output[4] are available for the years 1939–50 and help to give a better picture of the expansion of

[1] Because of inadequate data it is difficult to be more precise than this.
[2] See Fig. 9.
[3] To avoid misinterpretation it is perhaps necessary to stress that Scotland's share of the *net output* of British agriculture *may* not have fallen over this period. Net output estimates are not available for the period before 1936–39; data for later years are used in the discussion which follows.
[4] It may be recalled that in the text net output according to the Department of Agriculture's definition is described simply as net output.

agriculture over this period. The data for Scotland and the United Kingdom have been used to construct Fig. 9 in which outputs in 1946/47 are taken as equal to 100.

Table 43. *The gross output of Scottish agriculture as a proportion of the United Kingdom's output (pre-war to 1950/51). (At current prices)*

Year	Scottish output (£ m.)	Scottish output / U.K. output (percentage)	Year	Scottish output (£ m.)	Scottish output / U.K. output (percentage)
1936–39			1944/45	74	12·8
(average)	38	13·3	1945/46	78	12·7
1939/40	46	13·2	1946/47	79	12·8
1940/41	58	13·2	1947/48	92	12·8
1941/42	65	13·1	1948/49	106	12·8
1942/43	75	13·3	1949/50	116	12·8
1943/44	79	13·2	1950/51	119	12·8

SOURCES: *Agricultural Statistics; Scottish Agricultural Economics; The Farm Economist* vol. VII, no. 2, p. 93.

As the general trends in gross output have been discussed already, attention will be concentrated on a comparison of real net output and real gross output after 1939.

During the war real net output throughout the United Kingdom rose more than real gross output, owing mainly to the reduction in imported feeding-stuffs, and, especially in Scotland, to the reduction in imports of store cattle from Ireland.[1] Over the same period, the real net output (and to a lesser extent the real gross output) rose proportionately more in Scotland than in the United Kingdom. The main reasons for this were the rapid increase in the volume of seed oats and seed potatoes sent from Scotland to England[2] and the much greater slump which the shortage of feedingstuffs caused in the pig and poultry output of England compared with Scotland[3] where these enter-prises were often sidelines which could be carried on with the help of home-grown feed.

After the war, or more precisely after 1943/44, the trends were different. Throughout the United Kingdom real net output followed closely the trend

[1] Retained imports of Irish store cattle in 1944–45 were 64 % of the pre-war figure. See O. J. Beilby, *Scottish Agricultural Economics*, vol. I, p. 46.

[2] In 1943–44, 443,000 tons of seed potatoes and 59,000 tons of seed oats were exported to England and Wales, compared with 75,000 tons and 24,000 tons respectively before the war. *Farm Economics*, no. 15, spring 1948.

[3] In 1943–44 pigs and poultry in the United Kingdom contributed less than 10 % of the gross output of the United Kingdom, compared with 20 % pre-war. In Scotland the cor-responding decline was from 15 to 11 %.

in real gross output, instead of outstripping it as in previous years. In the same period real net output in the United Kingdom rose slightly more than in Scotland. Production policy during the war had aimed at reducing the use of imported feed while maintaining gross output as high as possible; after the war the emphasis was on increasing gross output even if this required an equivalent or relatively greater input of imported feedingstuffs. Apparently renewed supplies of imported feed enabled English farmers to increase their output more rapidly than Scottish farmers.

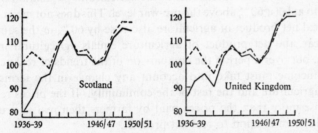

Fig. 9. Gross and net output of Scottish and of United Kingdom agriculture at constant (1945/46) prices, 1936–39 to 1950/51 (1946/47 = 100). Gross – – –; net ——.

Net product of agriculture

The definition of net output which has been given quantitative expression up till now makes no deduction for purchases from other industries. The increase of 40 % in real net output from 1936–39 to 1950/51 was partly due to an increase in the use of fertilizers, machinery, fuel, etc. As explained at the beginning of the section on agricultural output, both net output (B.O.T. definition) and net product make allowance for such purchases from outside agriculture, and estimates of these quantities would throw some light on the use agriculture has made of its additional resources.

It is a matter for regret that no official series of estimates of real agricultural net output (B.O.T. definition)[1] are published, but from data on agricultural income rough estimates can be made of the trend of real net product.

In the period 1936–39 the annual total in rent, wages and profits distributed

[1] Mr J. H. Kirk of the Ministry of Agriculture gave estimates (at current prices) of the value of net output (B.O.T. definition) for the years 1937/38 to 1943/44 in a paper to the Agricultural Economics Society in 1945 (*Journal of Proceedings of Agricultural Economics Society*, vol. VII, no. 1, June 1946). In a paper by the Department of Applied Economics, University of Cambridge (Reprint Series, no. 52), estimates (at constant prices) are given of the 'real product' of agriculture, forestry and fishing, for the years 1946–50. No separate totals are given for agriculture and the introduction states that these have been 'suppressed as confidential'. This series has been extended to cover the years 1937 and 1951 in an article in the supplement supplied by the London and Cambridge Economic Service to the *Times Review of Industry*, December 1952.

to landlords, farm workers and farmers in the United Kingdom was approximately £160 m. By 1948/49 it had risen to about £570 m. and was still roughly at this figure in 1950/51. In Scotland the relative increase was about the same, from £20 m. to £68 m., but the statistical uncertainties involved make any comparison of Scottish and United Kingdom figures of doubtful value.[1]

Adjusting these income figures on the assumption that the purchasing power of money in 1950/51 was roughly half that of 1936–39,[2] a fair statement would be that the real income of the agricultural population by 1950/51 had risen to at least 60% above the pre-war level. This does not mean, however, that the real net product of agriculture also rose by 60 % in the same period. In any year, the net product of agriculture equals agricultural income by definition, but over a period the comparison of the trends of real net product and real income must take into account any change in the terms of trade between agriculture and the rest of the community. If the prices received by farmers rise more than the prices paid by farmers then real agricultural income will rise in relation to real net product.

This is what happened from 1939 to 1950/51 when, although an accurate figure cannot be given, the real net product of agriculture probably did not rise more than 30 %[3] in comparison with an increase in real agricultural income of at least 60 %.

Translated into more general terms this means that by efficient use of resources agriculture increased by one third its contribution to the national 'pool' of goods and services and received as a reward, or incentive, a 60 % increase in its share of these goods and services. As a result the United Kingdom is now one of the few countries in which the *per capita* income of

[1] The United Kingdom figures are based on data in *The Farm Economist*, vol. VII, no. 2, pp. 92–3. The item 'rent and interest' in the original data includes interest on short-term loans and requires adjustment. Moreover, if farmers' incomes are net of depreciation then landlords' incomes (i.e. rent) should also be net of depreciation, but this point has been ignored. It is probably wise to doubt the accuracy of such income estimates but trends should not be too misleading. The Scottish estimates are by the writer based on data in the *Scottish Agricultural Economics*, and other figures on wages and rents provided by the Farm Economics Branch of the Department of Agriculture.

[2] In a written reply in the House of Commons (6 Feb. 1953) the Chancellor of the Exchequer stated that, taking 1938 as 100 the purchasing power of the £1 was 52 in 1950 and 48 in 1951.

[3] Since this chapter was prepared, estimates of what has been called here the real net product of agriculture have been published in a paper read by Mr H. T. Williams, of the Ministry of Agriculture, to the Agricultural Economics Society (July 1953). The percentage increase from 1937–39 to 1950–51 was calculated by Mr Williams at 21%, using 1945/46 prices, but at 35% using 1951/52 prices. This difference indicates some of the statistical difficulties involved in estimating trends in real agricultural output. The estimate of 30% given above has been left as a fair, if rough, approximation. It is assumed that the trend in Scotland has been similar to that in the United Kingdom. It seems unnecessary to reproduce the method of reaching the figure of 30% which is rendered obsolete by Mr Williams' paper.

the agricultural population is almost equal to the average income of the population as a whole. Scotland does not appear to be an exception to this general statement,[1] but it should be stressed that a comparison of aggregates obscures the income distribution within the industry.

Summary

From 1939 to 1950/51, after allowing for changes in prices, the real gross output of Scottish agriculture increased by 17 % but savings on imported feed and livestock led to an increase in the real net output (Department of Agriculture's definition) by 40 %.

From 1939 to 1950/51 the net product of agriculture (at constant prices) rose by about 30%, but due to a favourable change in the farmers' terms of trade, the real agricultural income (accruing to farmers, workers and land-lords) rose by at least 60%.

Comparing Scotland with the rest of the United Kingdom during the period 1925 to 1950/51 there was a decline (mainly in the early years) in Scotland's share of the gross output of United Kingdom agriculture (at current and at constant prices) and in 1950/51 it was one-eighth of the United Kingdom total.[2] Apart from this the only significant difference in trends between Scotland and the rest of the United Kingdom was the greater increase during the war in net output in Scotland, but this was cancelled out after the war.

Consumption and output

The fact that Scotland, with one-tenth of the United Kingdom population, produces one-eighth of the output of farm products suggests that it may be more 'self-sufficient' than the rest of the United Kingdom. It is not possible to measure the degree of self-sufficiency in the strict sense of the proportion of goods consumed at home which are entirely home produced; the most that can be attempted is to compare the gross home production of certain products with the home consumption of the same or similar products. In order to compare Scotland with the rest of the United Kingdom, the simplifying assumption has been made that consumption per head of the various products is the same in Scotland as in the United Kingdom. This is not strictly true (see Chapter 12) but the error is not significant and the figures given in Table 44 are in any case rounded estimates subject to considerable variation from year

[1] The number of people occupied in agriculture in Scotland is 6·5 % of the total occupied population and they receive roughly 6·5 % of the national income. Nearly 9 % of the occupied males are employed in agriculture, however, and there are slightly larger families in rural areas, so complete parity of income per head probably does not exist.

[2] In 1950–51 the value of gross output per acre of crops and grass in Scotland was £27; in England and Wales it was £30. Even excluding rough grazings, therefore, farm land in Scotland is less intensively cultivated than in the rest of Britain, largely due to the greater importance of horticultural products in England.

to year.[1] For foodstuffs as a whole the difference between Scotland and the rest of the United Kingdom is probably insignificant, but Table 44 shows that with individual products there is considerable variation.

Table 44. *Home food production (for selected products) as a percentage of home consumption*, 1950/51

Commodity	Scotland	United Kingdom
Beef	100	70
Mutton and lamb	75	30
Pigmeat	50	55
Milk products*	20	10
Wheat and flour†	5	25
Sugar (refined value)	7	25
Fruit‡	10	50
Vegetables‡	40	75

* Butter, cheese, condensed milk, etc., in liquid milk equivalent. Scotland and the United Kingdom are self-sufficient in liquid milk although in winter months milk occasionally may be sent from Scotland to England.

† In wheat equivalent.

‡ In value terms. Potatoes are omitted, the United Kingdom being more or less self-sufficient in them.

SOURCES: *Agricultural Statistics; Scottish Agricultural Economics;* Commonwealth Economic Committee, *Commodity Reports; The Farm Economist,* vol. VII, no. 2, p. 87.

Another way of making the same point in more detail is to compare the composition of agricultural output in Scotland and the United Kingdom; this is done in Table 45.[2] The Scottish emphasis on meat products and the small output of horticultural crops is again apparent. Generally speaking the United Kingdom farm output is a little more diversified than that of Scotland,[3] but this refers to the output of the 'national farm', and does not mean that farms in Scotland are more specialized than English farms. To discuss such questions it is necessary to examine the structure of the industry, the type and size of farms, etc., and this is the purpose of the next section.

[1] The figures are rough estimates, applying as far as possible to 1950/51. They are based on volume data, except in the case of fruit and vegetables. Eggs are omitted from the table as the figures are probably more unreliable than for other products. Home production of eggs in the United Kingdom is about 90 % of home consumption; the figure for Scotland is not significantly different.

[2] Figures for pre-war and 1945/46 have been included in order to indicate the main trends since 1939. The war-time switch to cropping is clear although the extent of it is understated in output data which take into account only crops sold off the farms. In Scotland, oats and potatoes have more than held their own, milk has increased in importance but meat production has declined. While fruit and vegetables remain a minor item, poultry products contribute one-eighth of the Scottish output and are now more important than sheep.

[3] This is likely to be true of any part of the United Kingdom 'national farm', compared with the whole.

Table 45. *Percentage composition of the agriculture gross output of Scotland and of the United Kingdom*

Products	Scotland			United Kingdom		
	Pre-war	1945/46	1950/51	Pre-war	1945/46	1949/50
Wheat	1·6	1·8	1·6	3·6	4·7	4·0
Barley	1·3	4·0	3·4	2·0	5·0	3·1
Oats*	4·9	7·2	5·2	1·3	1·5	0·8
Potatoes*	7·4	11·9	10·1	5·3	9·5	7·6
Sugar beet	0·3	0·6	0·4	1·8	2·6	2·2
Other crops†	0·8	0·7	0·4	1·6	2·6	1·7
Total crops	16·3	26·2	21·1	15·6	25·9	19·4
Cattle and calves*	26·2	19·4	17·0	14·6	10·4	9·5
Sheep*	11·6	8·0	9·8	5·8	3·8	4·0
Pigs	4·3	2·6	5·2	10·0	3·6	7·3
Milk and milk products	24·0	26·5	27·4	28·1	28·8	30·5
Eggs and poultry	10·4	10·3	12·9	10·7	7·6	14·0
Wool	2·3	1·7	1·9	1·1	0·7	0·7
Other livestock	0·7	0·1	0·1	1·0	0·7	0·4
Total livestock	79·5	68·6	74·3	71·3	55·0	66·4
Fruit and vegetables	3·1	4·0	3·3	11·6	16·5	12·7
Sundry output†	1·1	1·2	1·3	1·5	2·5	1·5
Total output	100·0	100·0	100·0	100·0	100·0	100·0
Value of output‡ (£ m.)	38·1	78·1	119·1	284·9	615·1	906·2

* The Scottish figures include seed oats and potatoes and store livestock sent to England.

† The basis of calculating the various miscellaneous outputs has changed and no detailed conclusions should be drawn from changes in the proportions. It is true, however, that miscellaneous receipts as a whole seem to be less important in Scotland than in the United Kingdom.

‡ At current prices, adjusted for changes in valuation of crops and livestock.

SOURCES: *Agricultural Statistics. Scottish Agricultural Economics.*

THE ECONOMIC STRUCTURE OF SCOTTISH AGRICULTURE

Early in 1952 a report on *Types of Farming in Scotland* was published by the Department of Agriculture for Scotland. Although not the first attempt at an economic classification of farms in Scotland,[1] this report made an important contribution to our knowledge of the industry. The basic statistics used are

[1] An analysis on similar lines was made of the 1927 *Agricultural Returns* but was not published. Some of the results were used by W. E. Heath in 'A New Classification of Holdings', *Scottish Journal of Agriculture*, July 1945.

not new, being derived from the 1947 *Agricultural Returns*, but the manner of presentation is different and by the use of distribution analyses by type and size groups, the report prepares the way for a more adequate picture of the structural pattern of farming.

An example of the misleading picture which may result from an uncritical use of the annual returns is the apparent existence, according to the records, of 77,500 'agricultural holdings' in Scotland, which suggests that the average size of holding (in crops and grass) is 57 acres. This cannot, however, be taken to indicate the average size of *farm*, for there are only 64,000 holdings which can be regarded as agricultural units, and of these only half have been classified by the Department of Agriculture as 'full-time' farms.[1] Since nearly 95 % of the crops and grass acreage of Scotland is found on these 32,000 farms, it would be more correct to state the average size of farm as 127 acres.

Comparing this data with what was published in the *National Farm Survey* of England and Wales, it would appear that although the size of holding in Scotland is 57 acres as against 67 acres in the rest of Britain, the size of 'full-time' farm is 127 acres in Scotland against 99 acres in England and Wales.[2]

This suggests that farms are on the whole larger in Scotland (in terms of crops and grass acreage) than in the rest of Britain, but an examination of the acreage distribution over the different size-groups shows that this too is an oversimplification. Farms over 150 acres have an average size of about 280 acres on both sides of the border, but full-time farms below 150 acres average about 70 acres in Scotland compared with 55 acres in England and Wales.

These figures probably reflect the fact that the smaller holdings which are still able to provide a return adequate to maintain a farmer and his family in England and Wales have ceased to do so in Scotland. A larger proportion of the smaller holdings in Scotland have become 'part-time' farms and this pushes up the average size of full-time farms in general.[3] Distance from the market and lack of adequate transport facilities are obvious factors in depressing the incomes of Scottish smallholders below a maintenance level.

[1] For the methods used in classifying farms as full-time, part-time, or spare-time farms see *Types of Farming in Scotland* (Department of Agriculture for Scotland, H.M.S.O.), p. 9.

[2] Such a comparison is not strictly valid, since the data for England and Wales refer to 'full-time farmers' and not to full-time farms, and the basis of classification was not the same in the two analyses. But there were not many full-time farms in England and Wales which were not occupied by full-time farmers and it is reasonable to assume that all full-time farmers in England and Wales occupied full-time farms. The different basis of classifying full-time, part-time or spare-time farms is a more difficult problem to overcome, and until a National Survey is made of all British farms, the use of the term 'full-time farm' in such comparisons has obvious disadvantages.

[3] This remains true even allowing for the qualifications made in the previous note. It is worth noting that although the Department of Agriculture found only 32,000 full-time farms in 1947, there were 42,000 people in Scotland in 1951 who returned themselves as 'farmers' in the census. This latter figure includes crofters, not returned separately in the *One Per Cent Sample Tables*.

The small dairy-farmer in England, for example, has been able to make a precarious livelihood[1] while the Scottish hill-farmer and crofter has had to take to other occupations or migrate to more rewarding farming districts.

This discussion of the average size of farms is mainly designed to show how national aggregates or averages require careful analysis if they are to help and not mislead in describing the structure of agriculture. The greater knowledge of this structure which is obtained through an economic classification of farms by type and size enables a more reliable forecast to be made of the effects of different agricultural policies.

Types of farming

The first problem of a type classification is to decide on the number of type groups and the basis of classification. In *Types of Farming in Scotland* the full-time farms are classified in ten type-groups. In Tables 46 and 47 these have been reduced to six groups: hill sheep, stock-rearing, stock-rearing and feeding, cropping, dairy, and 'others', a miscellaneous group including horticultural, intensive livestock and other farms.

The broad geographical pattern of Scottish farming is revealed by listing the main regions in which the different types of farming are predominant. The dairy farms are predominant in South-West and Central Scotland, except for small areas near urban centres where horticultural and pig and poultry farms are found. Stock-rearing and stock-rearing and feeding farms predominate in North-East and South-East Scotland, with cropping farms in between, around the Forth and Tay estuaries. Hill-sheep farms are most important in the upland areas of the mainland in the North-West and South, but on the islands stock-rearing rivals sheep farming in many areas.

Tables 46 and 47 show how the main factors of production and various crops and livestock are distributed over the different types of farms. Some interesting features of Scottish agriculture are immediately apparent.[2] The importance of dairying stands out clearly. The estimates of agricultural income (Table 47, column 8), although they must be treated with some caution, suggest that about one-third of the agricultural income of Scotland goes to dairy farms in the form of rent, wages and farmers' incomes. This large share is associated with the fact that dairy cows, more than any other form of livestock, are concentrated on a single farm type, the dairy farm. 75 % of the dairy cows are on farms of this type, while a large proportion of breeding ewes and beef cattle tend to be distributed over several types of farms. The dairy

---

[1] In many areas he has only done so by becoming a producer-retailer of milk (e.g. in Lancashire).

[2] No comparison with the rest of Britain is attempted because the basis of classifying farms is different in England and Wales.

farms, in short, can be more easily classified in a separate group; they are not, however, solely dependent on milk sales as their share in the wheat and potato acreage and sheep population is considerable.

Table 46. *Percentage distribution (by type of farm) of rough grazings, crops and grass, etc., on full-time farms in Scotland, 1947*

Types of full-time farm	Full-time farms	Rough graz-ings	Crops and grass	Cash crops		Fodder crops		Livestock		
				Wheat	Pota-toes	Tur-nips and swedes	Oats*	Dairy cows	All beef cattle	Ewes
Hill sheep	6	67	3	—	I	I	I	2	6	51
Stock-rearing	21	16	12	—	10	12	13	7	17	16
Stock-rearing and feeding	22	7	27	17	18	34	29	4	46	18
Cropping	19	I	24	64	48	29	28	5	28	4
Dairy	27	9	32	19	21	24	29	81	3	11
Others	5	—	2	—	2	—	—	I	—	—
Total	100	100	100	100	100	100	100	100	100	100
	(thou-sands)	(million acres)		(thousand acres)		(thousand acres)		(thousands)		
Total	32	9	4	79	196	294	916	320	612	2,630
Total as a percentage of all agricultural units	50	82	93	99	95	96	95	92	94	90

* Oats have been included in this table under the general heading of 'fodder crops' although this term normally does not apply to grain crops even if they are mainly used for fodder.
SOURCE: Calculated from *Types of Farming in Scotland*.

Other important features of Scottish farming illustrated by these tables are the low incomes going to stock-rearing farms and the concentration of a very large proportion of the rough grazings on hill-sheep farms, stock-rearing farms or part-time farms. Some of the implications of these features will be discussed later.

The classification of farms by product types is useful but has its difficulties and dangers. Some of them are overcome or avoided in the report, *Types of Farming in Scotland*, by grouping farms in regions as well as in product-types. Even with this refinement, however, the general picture of Scottish farming obtained is not of several clearly-defined groups of farms producing different products in different regions, but rather of a complex industry in which only a very rough grouping of enterprises according to products and/or geographical location is possible. A further distribution analysis by size of farm or business unit is required to add to our knowledge of the economic structure and functioning of the industry. In this way the ground can be prepared for an improvement of the sample studies of agriculture which have been undertaken in recent years to provide economic information for the annual price review.

Table 47. *Percentage distribution (by type of farm) of draught power, agricultural incomes, etc., on full-time farms in Scotland*

Types of full-time farms	Full-time farms (1947)	Horses (1947)	Tractors (1947)	Wages* (1949/50)	Rent* (1949/50)	Farmers' incomes* (1949/50)	Total agri-cultural income* (1949/50)
Hill sheep	6	3	2	5	7	7	6
Stock-rearing	21	17	10	9	10	8	8
Stock-rearing and feeding	22	23	26	21	21	19	20
Cropping	19	22	31	26	26	24	25
Dairy	27	33	27	33	31	37	35
Others	5	2	4	6	5	5	6
Total	100	100	100	100	100	100	100
	(thousands)			(£m.)			
Total	32	72	27	28	4·8	30	63
Total as a percentage of all agricultural units	50	91	89	99	90	95	96

* Figures for wages, rent, farmers' incomes and total agricultural incomes are estimates made by the writer, based on *Types of Farming in Scotland*, data from *Scottish Agricultural Economics*, and from the Department of Agriculture for Scotland. The income estimates should be regarded as rough approximations only.

SOURCE: *Types of Farming in Scotland*.

Analysis by size of farms

For a distribution analysis by size of unit the agricultural statistics provide scattered data over the last eighty years, but without any continuous or systematic series. The report, *Types of Farming in Scotland*, provides only limited information of this nature and recent statistics refer to holdings rather than farms. The acreage of crops and grass has had to be employed as a measure of the size of farm, although it is unsatisfactory in some respects.[1] Table 48 summarizes the most recent information available.

[1] Output, capital, or number of workers employed are other possible measures of size but cannot be used because of lack of data. If some such measure could be used, the degree of concentration in agriculture would probably be shown to be greater than in Table 48 but it is unlikely that this would invalidate the general conclusions drawn from the table as it stands.

The first point to be noted is the importance of a few thousand large farms. 9,000 holdings over 150 acres contain over half the total crops and grass acreage and farmers on these holdings receive nearly half the total net income of farmers in Scotland. These 9,000 holdings probably represent a smaller number of farmers.[1]

Table 48. *Percentage distribution (by size of holding) of holdings, crops and grass, rough grazings, tractors, workers, and agricultural income in Scotland*

Size group (acres)	Holdings (1949)	Crops and grass (1949)	Rough grazings (1931)	Tractors, all types (1952)	Workers, all groups (1931)	Agricultural income* (1949/50)
Under 50	67	15	48	20	19	20
50 and under 100	13	17	20	18	18	
100 and under 150	8	16	12	16	16	33
150 and under 300	9	30	14	28	28	27
300 and over	3	22	6	18	19	20
Total	100	100	100	100	100	100
Total	(thousands) 74·9	(thousand acres) 4,420	(thousand acres) 8,141†	(thousands) 41·3	(thousands) 112·5	(£m.) 65

* The distribution of net farm income, totalling £31 m., was similar.

† 1,360,000 acres of rough grazings were returned separately having no crops and grass area attached to them.

SOURCES: Cols. 2, 3, 5, *Agricultural Statistics* (calculated); cols. 4, 6, *The Agricultural Output of Scotland*, 1930 (calculated); col. 7, rough approximations estimated by the writer from data in *Scottish Agricultural Economics* and other information from Department of Agriculture for Scotland.

A second point arises from the distribution of the rough grazings. It will be recalled that in Table 46 almost nine-tenths of this land was found on hill sheep farms, stock-rearing farms or part-time farms. Table 48 reveals that two-thirds of the rough grazings are on holdings with less than 100 acres of crops and grass. Most of the hill grazings of Scotland are attached to farms in the less prosperous groups,[2] either by type or size. The production problem of increasing output from these grazings is therefore related to the income problem of raising the living standards on the hill farms and crofts of Scotland.

Bringing the points made in the last two paragraphs together, it may be

[1] There were 9,300 full-time farms over 150 acres in 1947 covering over 2 m. acres of crops and grass. Some of these farms were part of multiple unit businesses, thus reducing the number of farmers to perhaps 8,000.

[2] And also to farms least able to provide supplies of winter feed for hill stock.

argued that, broadly speaking, whereas an increase in output from the existing area of cultivated or improved land involves mainly a few thousand relatively large enterprises, the problem of extending the cultivated or improved land involves a much larger number of small farm enterprises. In the short run, say during war-time, an immediate increase in output can be achieved more easily from the larger than the smaller holdings. But in the long run the expansion of agricultural production in Scotland depends on finding the way to increase output from small farms as well as large, especially through the better utilization of the hill and unimproved lands attached to many small-holdings. The war-time study of Scotland's marginal farms,[1] and the setting up of the Hill Lands Commission are examples of the interest shown since 1939 in tackling aspects of this problem.

THE SOCIAL STRUCTURE OF SCOTTISH AGRICULTURE

For several centuries rural Scotland, south of the Highland line, has been divided into three classes, landlords, farmers and wage-paid workers. Apart from the larger landowners who have traditionally formed a fairly clearly defined social group, these classes have not always been easily differentiated. Under the old agriculture of the seventeenth century and earlier, the farming ladder might start from the hired man's seat 'below the salt' in a farm kitchen, reach first to a small sub-tenant's cottage with an acre or two attached and then to a farm held jointly with other tenants directly from the landlord. The agrarian revolution, dating roughly from 1750 to 1820, knocked several rungs out of any ladder which still existed[2] and by the dispossession of cottagers and engrossment of small farms led to a much sharper differentiation between tenant farmers and wage-paid workers.

Since 1820 the social structure of the country-side has remained fundamentally unchanged although a number of important modifications have taken place. The landless wage-earning class is even more clearly defined but an increase in the number of owner-occupiers has blurred the distinction between capitalist farmers and rent-receiving landlords and there has been a considerable decline in the economic importance of the landowning class. The Highlands have several distinctive features, particularly the absence of a large, landless wage-earning class of farm workers and the continuance of the crofting system under which about 17,000 smallholdings are occupied. Only a limited number of crofters, however, can be said to be mainly employed in agriculture.[3]

---

[1] 'Scotland's Marginal Farms', *General Report, Department of Agriculture for Scotland*, 1947 (H.M.S.O.).

[2] It is not implied that this 'ladder' was ever very easy to climb or reached very high.

[3] In the main crofting counties, Argyll, Inverness, Ross and Cromarty, Sutherland and Shetland, there were, in 1947, 8,320 part-time farms, 6,904 spare-time farms and 3,647 full-

Table 49 summarizes the social structure of the Scottish country-side in 1951, the number of landowners being a very rough estimate.

Table 49. *Social structure of Scottish agriculture*, 1951

1. *Owners* of agricultural land let to farmers (i.e. excluding owner-occupiers)		3,000–5,000
2. *Farmers* entirely maintained by holdings		
(i) Owner occupiers	10,000	
(ii) Tenant farmers	20,000	
Farmers chiefly but not entirely		
maintained by holdings	12,000	
	Total*	42,000
3. *Farm workers*		
Regular workers	88,000	
Casual workers	16,000	
	Total	104,000

* Excluding 13,000 other occupiers of agricultural holdings, many of whom are crofters. Other crofters are included under the general heading of farmers.

SOURCES: *Census of Population, 1951: One Per Cent Sample Tables; Agricultural Statistics; Types of Farming in Scotland.*

Land ownership

A complete picture of the ownership of agricultural land in Scotland cannot be given, for there have been no figures published since the rather unreliable 'New Domesday' survey of 1873. It is generally assumed that there are still a small number of big landlords who own a large proportion of the agricultural land but there has been a tendency recently for some of the big estates to be broken up. Associated with this development has been the increase in owner-occupancy for which figures are more readily available. From 1912 to 1948 the total acreage (in crops and grass) of holdings owned by their occupiers increased from under 500,000 to 1,500,000 acres. Moreover, as Table 50 shows, there has always been a tendency for a greater proportion of the larger holdings than of the smaller farms to be owner-occupied. Since owner-occupiers generally have been more willing to spend capital improving their farms than tenants or landlords this has tended to increase the difference in the levels of efficiency on larger as opposed to smaller farms.

Over the period in which owner-occupancy was increasing in importance the share of the agricultural income going in rents to the owners of agri-

time farms and of the last group just under half employed regular non-family labour. There are also a number of crofters in Orkney and Caithness. (See *Types of Farming in Scotland*.)

cultural land was declining. About 1850 total agricultural income was roughly divided into three equal parts, rents, wages and farmers' profits; in 1950, as indicated earlier, the respective proportions were 1:4:4. In the nineteenth century the landlords dominated the countryside, economically, socially and politically; by the middle of the twentieth century the most influential rural force in much of Lowland Scotland was the class of big capitalist farmers, often owning their farms and sometimes with interests in merchants' or dealers' businesses.

Table 50. *Proportion of agricultural holdings and acreage of crops and grass owned by occupiers in Scotland, 1912 and 1948, in size-groups*

Size-group (acres)	Percentage of holdings owner-occupied		Percentage of acres on owner-occupied holdings	
	1912	1948	1912	1948
Up to 30	6	19	7	22
30–100	8	29	8	29
100–300	8	32	8	33
Above 300	15	40	15	41
All size-groups	7	24	10	33

SOURCE: *Farm Economics* (1950), no. 20, pp. 14–16.

The farmers

From previous discussions it will be obvious that the farmers in Scotland are not a homogeneous social group: some are owners of land, others are tenants; some are employers of labour, others depend solely on their own or family labour; some receive annual incomes of several thousand pounds, others receive little if any more than a skilled farm worker.[1]

At the one extreme there are the large farmers, often owning their farms, employing several workers and in many cases occupying more than one holding. There were in 1947 1,400 multiple-unit farm businesses operating

[1] According to financial results collected by the Scottish Colleges of Agriculture from a sample of about 800 farms in the years 1948/49 to 1950/51, annual net income per farm varied as follows:

Gross rent of farms £	Average net income per farm (1948/49 to 1950/51) £
0–50	264
51–150	491
151–300	1,048
Over 300	2,093

SOURCE: *Scottish Agricultural Economics*, vols. I, II and III.

3,500 farms. In most cases these businesses had only two farms but there were fifty-seven with five or more farms each.[1] At the other extreme there are about 12,000 full-time farms which do not employ any non-family labour, and in addition there are 25,000 part-time or spare-time farms for about 12,000 of whose occupiers the income from the land was the most important part of total income.

The farm workers

The class of wage-earning farm workers in Scotland dates from the sixteenth century or earlier. Wages were originally paid in kind; in the nineteenth century the East Lothian married ploughmen still received little or no cash wages, and even in 1950 about one-tenth of the earnings of Scottish farm workers was paid in perquisites, their value being deducted from the weekly wage.[2]

This landless class of farm workers was considerably augmented during the agrarian revolution, evicted cottagers and small farmers going to work on the new large holdings, but since 1850, when there were over 200,000 farm labourers, their numbers have steadily declined and in 1950 there were just over 100,000 wage-earners in agriculture, including family and casual workers.

The *Agricultural Returns* have included questions on the employment of labour since 1921 and comparison of the figures for that year with those for 1951 shows that there have been important changes in the composition as well as the size of the farm working-class. In Scotland, as in the rest of Britain, the total number of farm workers declined by about 20 % over the period 1921–51. The decline in Scotland, however, was due entirely to the sharp fall in the number of young men workers (under 21) and of female workers. The number of adult male workers, regularly and casually employed actually increased, bringing the age composition of the farm working-class closer to that for other industries. Previously a much higher proportion of male workers were under 21 in agriculture than in other industries (30 % compared with 20 %).

Between the wars, as the 1936 report on Scottish farm workers noted,[3] young lads were recruited for agriculture as they left school, but were discharged as they grew older and demanded higher wages. This reflected on the one hand the low incomes of many farmers before 1939 and on the other the lack of opportunities for young country people to enter non-agricultural work, which was probably even more pronounced in Scotland than in England. After the second world war the problem was both to recruit young people and to retain them on the land as they grew older and attained skills on the farm or in the armed forces which enabled them to obtain employment in non-

[1] *Types of Farming in Scotland*, p. 73.
[2] *Farm Economics* (1949), no. 17, pp. 13–15.
[3] *Report of the Committee on Farm Workers in Scotland*, 1936, Department of Agriculture for Scotland, Cmd. 5217 (Edinburgh, H.M.S.O.).

farming jobs. The desire to exempt farm workers from conscription was at least partly prompted by the knowledge that many demobilized farm workers did not return to their old occupation.

The wages and earnings of Scottish farm workers are discussed fully in Chapter 11; it may be noted here that they now tend to equality with the rest of Britain although on some occasions the Scottish Agricultural Wages Board has delayed several months before granting the increase awarded to the English workers (e.g. in 1950 and 1952). In so far as general comparisons are valid, agricultural wages still tend to be lower than in other industries and this fact, coupled with the social disadvantages which living in an isolated area has for many people, would probably lead to a further drift from the land were it not for the difficulty of obtaining a town house. The 'tied house' system, which is more common in Scotland than in England, in effect ties many workers as well as houses to agriculture. Even so there has been a slight but continuous decline in recent years in the number employed in farming in Scotland.

CONCLUSION

In the last twenty-five years there have been rapid and radical changes in British agriculture. The pre-war marketing legislation and price support schemes, prompted by the depression of the early 1930's were followed after 1939 by a system of guarantees, subsidies, and controls extending throughout most of the farm economy. The Agriculture Acts of 1947 and 1948 envisaged the continuation of guaranteed farm prices and gave tenant farmers greater security of tenure, but left marketing problems for future consideration.

The first pre-war price support schemes applied to wheat and sugar, which were less important in Scotland than in England, but the direct agricultural subsidies of the war and post-war years have probably benefited Scottish farming as much as if not more than farming elsewhere. The amounts paid in direct subsidies to farmers vary from year to year, but Scotland on the average has in recent years received more than one-eighth of the United Kingdom total.[1]

The effect of guaranteed prices (and the 'food subsidies') is more difficult to estimate. It would seem that farm prices in Scotland lagged slightly behind prices in England and Wales in the twenty years following 1927–29. By this criterion, therefore, Scottish farmers have not benefited from recent policies quite so much as English farmers, but changes in farm costs would also need to be considered before any general conclusion could be drawn. It is

[1] The proportion has varied between one-fifth and one-seventh of the United Kingdom total. In 1950, for example, direct subsidies to agriculture totalled about £20 m. of which Scottish farmers received over £3 m., mainly through the grassland ploughing scheme and the hill sheep, hill cattle and calf-rearing subsidies.

unfortunately not possible to make any reliable comparison of the structure of costs in Scotland and England; the outstanding features of cost changes in recent years apply to farming throughout Britain, and include the large increase in the dependence of agriculture on purchases from other industries, especially for power resources, machines, fuel and repair services.[1]

These developments in government policy and changes in the structure of farm costs have been accompanied by a relative increase in the average income per head of the agricultural population which is now almost equal to that of the population as a whole. Scottish farming has contributed to the general progress and shared in the prosperity, but it would appear that by 1951 Scotland was producing a slightly smaller proportion of the agricultural output of Britain than it did thirty years earlier, probably due mainly to the low level of English output in the first quarter of the present century.

To sum up in a sentence, changes in agricultural policy in the twenty years following 1930 affected and benefited Scottish farming almost as much as, but not more than, farming in the rest of Britain. The most important recent developments in Scottish agriculture have been common to Britain, not peculiar to Scotland.

[1] The following table summarizes the changes in the structure of farm costs in the United Kingdom (at current prices) from 1937/38 to 1951/52.

	1937/38 £	1951/52 £	1951/52 as proportion of 1937/38 %
Labour	66	255	386
Rent and interest	43	63	147
Machinery	15	127	847
Feedingstuffs	78	180	231
Fertilizers	9	60	667
Other expenses	38	142	374
Total expenses	249	827	332
Farmers' 'net income'	59	294	498

See two articles by the Agricultural Economics Research Institute, Oxford, contributed to the *Westminster Bank Review*, August 1952 and November 1952.

CHAPTER 8

COAL-MINING

By C. E. V. LESER

The coal-mining industry has been subject to the same fluctuating fortunes in Scotland as in other parts of Great Britain. Throughout the nineteenth century the industry expanded rapidly as the source of the fuel and power on which the Industrial Revolution rested. The first world war not merely interrupted this expansion but also brought about or reinforced some long-run trends unfavourable to the industry: increasing competition from abroad or from new sources of power, and increasing economies in the use of coal. The industry was faced with a falling demand during the inter-war period; and, now that demand has received a new impetus, output is limited by manpower and other difficulties.

In Scotland, as in Britain, the peak in output was reached in 1913.[1] From a total of 42·5 m. tons in that year output fell to an average of not much over 30 m. tons between the wars. The best inter-war year was 1923, when output reached 38·5 m. tons, but from 1923 onwards the industry steadily contracted and when the second world war broke out was running at 30 m. tons per annum. In the five years 1948–52, output remained steady at between 23 and 24 m. tons. The drop from the peak in 1913 has been steeper in Scotland than in the rest of the country. Before the first world war, Scotland's share of British coal production was rising, but both the first and second world wars brought about a particularly sharp fall in Scotland and instead of over one-seventh, Scotland now produces only one-ninth of the total output of British coal. (See Fig. 10.)

Employment has shown similar fluctuations. The number of miners at work in the Scottish coal-mines fell precipitately from 147,300 in 1920 to 81,600 in 1933; and the total, after some recovery over the next five years, fell back during the war to about the same level, where it still remained in 1951. Apart from those at work, there were also, throughout the inter-war years, a large number of Scottish miners out of work, unemployment reaching a peak of 34·7 % in 1932, and falling to 14·0 % at the outbreak of war. Since the war unemployment among Scottish miners has been on a much smaller scale, never exceeding 1 % since 1947. The total number of those who earned their living in coal-mining, whether in employment or not, including salaried workers as well as wage-earners, was 91,300 in 1950.

[1] Except where otherwise stated, open-cast coal is excluded (e.g. from all figures of output).

109

The fall in output has affected mainly exports, consumption within Scotland remaining relatively steady (see Table 51).

The consumption of coal is somewhat higher than before the war, but well below the level reached before the first world war. Exports have fallen to a trickle, while production is actually less than would have been needed forty years ago for consumption in Scotland.

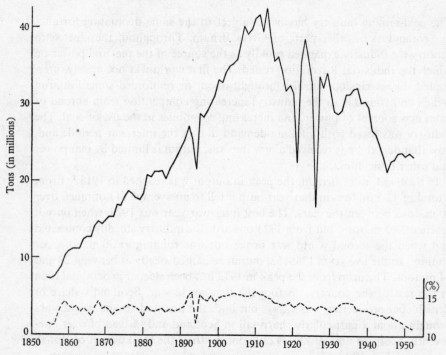

Fig. 10. Coal production in Scotland, 1854–1952. Output in millions of tons ———;
Scottish production as percentage of British output (scale on right) - - -.

The pattern of fuel consumption in Scotland does not differ greatly from the pattern for Great Britain (Table 52). More coal is used directly as a source of heat or power while less is converted into coke, gas and electricity.

The consumption of coke is markedly below the level in the rest of the country and the consumption of gas and electricity less than in proportion to population.

The pattern of fuel consumption, analysed by consumer instead of by type of fuel, is shown in Table 53.

Scotland uses rather more coal and coal-based fuel per head of population than the rest of Britain, the excess being greatest in consumption by railways

Table 51. *Consumption and production of coal in Scotland, 1913–51*
(*Million tons*)

	1913	1935	1951
Consumption	27·0	19·4	22·1*
Net exports†	15·5	11·9	1·8
Production	42·5	31·3	23·6‡

* Including consumption of open-cast coal.
† Including all bunker shipments and net movements to rest of United Kingdom.
‡ Excluding 600,000 tons of open-cast coal, and including 300,000 tons of coal added to stock.
SOURCES: Ministry of Fuel and Power *Statistical Digest*, and estimates by W. M. L. Murray.

Table 52. *Consumption of fuel and power in Scotland and in Great Britain, 1951*

	Scotland (coal or coal equiv. in m. tons)	Great Britain (coal or coal equiv. in m. tons)	Scotland as a proportion of Great Britain (percentage)
Coal (raw)	15·3	117·9	13·0
Electricity*	3·6	36·5	9·9
Coke	2·5	34·6	7·2
Gas†	1·6	18·4	8·7
Total	23·0	207·4	11·1

* Public supply undertakings only, including hydro-electric undertakings. The consumption of coal at Scottish thermal stations in 1951 was 7·5 % of British consumption.
† The consumption of coal at Scottish gasworks in 1951 was 9·5 % of British consumption.
SOURCE: Ridley report (Cmd. 8647) and Ministry of Fuel and Power.

and collieries. Apart from these two groups, there is no great divergence from the population ratio of 1:10.

Coal-mining is concentrated in four main areas: reading from west to east, these are Ayr and Dumfries; Lanark; Fife and Clackmannan; and the Lothians. The 'Lanarkshire' coalfield extends over parts of Dunbarton, Stirling and West Lothian and at one time included workings in Renfrew. The Fife and Clackmannan coalfield has in the past included mines in Kinross as well as an isolated mine at Brora in Sutherland, while the mine at Macrihanish in Argyll is included under Ayr and Dumfries, and the (now defunct) workings at Peebles are grouped with the Lothians.

All four areas are producing less coal than in 1913 but the fall has been far heavier in 'Lanarkshire' than elsewhere. A major change in the location pattern has been in progress for the past half-century (see Table 54).

The 'Lanarkshire' coalfield, once the source of two-thirds of Scottish output, now provides just over one-third. Since before the war the output of the 'Lanarkshire' pits has fallen by nearly one-half; many pits have been closed and many of the remainder have a limited life. The Fife and Clackmannan area, although still producing less coal than before the war, has almost drawn level with 'Lanarkshire' and has supplied a steadily increasing share of the Scottish total over the past seventy years. The output from Ayr and Dumfries and the Lothians has been comparatively stable since before the first world war; these two areas together now provide about the same amount of coal as the 'Lanarkshire' and Fife coalfields.

Table 53. *Consumption of fuel by main consumers*, 1951

	Scotland (coal or coal equiv. in m. tons)	Great Britain (coal or coal equiv. in m. tons)	Scotland as a proportion of Great Britain (percentage)
Households	6·6	59·7	11·1
Iron and steel	3·3	32·3	10·2
Other industries	6·1	59·4	10·3
Railways	2·2	15·7	14·0
Collieries	1·8	12·1	14·9
Public authorities	1·45	11·6	12·5
Commercial	1·25	11·9	10·5
Other	0·2	1·9	10·5
Total	23·0	204·6	11·2

* The total for Great Britain includes 1·1 m. tons of coal equivalent for water power used in generating electricity and 0·7 m. tons for oil used in gas-making. The corresponding figures in the Scottish total are 0·94 m. tons and 0·03 m. tons.
SOURCE: Ridley report and Ministry of Fuel and Power.

The change in the balance between 'Lanarkshire' and the other coalfields is likely to continue. In *Plan for Coal* the National Coal Board gives planned outputs for the various coalfields in 1961–65 which show a fall of nearly 20 % below the 1949 output in the 'Lanarkshire' area and a rise of over 50 % in the other three.[1] If the plan were to be realized, 'Lanarkshire' would produce less coal than Ayr and Dumfries and not much more than the Lothians (see Table 55).

The closing of the 'Lanarkshire' pits reflects both the exhaustion of the better seams and the high cost of mining what remains. In the Central West area, for example, costs per ton in 1951 averaged 57s. 11d. compared with

[1] The National Coal Board areas do not exactly coincide with those given in Table 54.

45s. 10d. in the Lothians and the loss per ton of saleable coal was over 6s. Figures for 1944 show that in the 'Lanarkshire' area, over 70 % of the coal came from seams less than 3 ft. thick (compared with 13 % in Fife and an average for Britain of 26 %). It is also in 'Lanarkshire' that output per head is lowest and has fallen most heavily since the beginning of the century (see Table 56).

Table 54. *Coal output in Scotland by area,* 1880–1950

Year	Ayr and Dumfries	Lanark, Dunbarton, Stirling and West Lothian	Fife and Clackmannan	Midlothian and East Lothian	Total Scottish output
(million tons)					
1880	3·2	11·8	2·2	1·1	18·3
1890	3·3	16·2	3·6	1·2	24·3
1900	4·2	21·2	5·9	1·8	33·1
1910	4·4	23·7	9·1	4·1	41·3
1920	4·0	16·9	7·0	3·6	31·5
1930	4·0	15·2	7·7	4·8	31·7
1940	4·6	13·0	7·6	4·5	29·7
1950	3·5	8·3*	7·3	4·2*	23·3
Percentage of total for Scotland					
1880	17·6	64·7	12·0	5·7	100·0
1890	13·5	67·0	14·7	4·8	100·0
1900	12·7	64·1	17·8	5·4	100·0
1910	10·8	57·3	22·0	9·9	100·0
1920	12·6	53·6	22·3	11·5	100·0
1930	12·6	48·1	24·1	15·2	100·0
1940	15·6	43·7	25·7	15·0	100·0
1950	15·2	35·4	31·4	18·0	100·0

* Published figures adjusted to secure comparability with earlier years.

SOURCES: *Reports on Mines and Quarries;* Ministry of Fuel and Power *Statistical Digest.*

The decline in coal-mining in 'Lanarkshire' has already given rise to a number of social and economic problems. First of all, there has been the social dislocation resulting from the closure of the pits. In pre-war years this mainly took the form of prolonged unemployment, and in some mining areas, such as Blantyre, there is still comparatively heavy unemployment. During and after the war, however, the closing down of the collieries generally involved the lesser dislocation of a move to another mining area or of a change to some other kind of work. There has been a good deal of movement between mining areas, but the net movement appears to have been small, since there are now fewer miners at work in each of the four main areas than before the war. The larger change that has occurred has been a movement out of the

113

mining industry altogether—a change that has been facilitated in Lanarkshire by the large number of factories built there since the war.

Although there has not, so far, been a movement of workers on any scale to the expanding coalfields, it is likely that a larger movement will be required in future. The National Coal Board may be too optimistic in assuming that it can add 50 % to the output of the Fife and Clackmannan area with an extra 1,500 men. Even if the labour requirements of coal-mining remain modest, other industries are bound to feel the cumulative effect of a displacement in coal supplies from west to east. Already nearly half Scotland's coal comes from the eastern coalfields, and over half the capital expenditure planned by the National Coal Board for the period 1950–65 is in those areas. The transport of coal to the west may involve the railways in a heavy capital outlay and will be a continuing burden on consumers in the form of high freights. Some at least of these consumers are likely to seek relief by moving to the East unless the choice is blurred by attempts to equalize fuel costs throughout Central Scotland.

Table 55. *Actual and planned output of coal in Scotland by area*, 1950 *and* 1961–65

	Ayr and Dumfries	'Lanarkshire'	Fife and Clackmannan	Lothians	Total
Output in 1950 (million tons)	4·4	7·8	7·3	3·8	23·3
Planned output, 1961–65 (million tons)	7·1	6·7	11·0	5·8	30·6
Percentage increase or decrease	+61	−14	+51	+53	+31

SOURCE: National Coal Board, *Plan for Coal* and *Annual report for 1950*.

A second type of dislocation may result from the difference in the types of coal mined in 'Lanarkshire' and elsewhere. In all areas of Scotland except 'Lanarkshire' about nine-tenths of the coal comes within classes 800 and 900 (i.e. very weakly- and non-caking bituminous coals) although these two classes form only about a quarter of total British output. 'Lanarkshire' produces all the anthracite and nearly all the good quality coking and gas coals. The fall in 'Lanarkshire' production has obliged many important consumers to obtain supplies elsewhere; and this has meant either a costly change in equipment designed for use with 'Lanarkshire' coal, or an awkward change in furnace practice (e.g. in the blending of coking coals), or importation from England and Wales, with all the additional cost in freight that this involves. Apart from any dislocation in the home market that has already been experienced or must still be reckoned with, the export market may show insufficient interest in the 'general' coals available from the east of Scotland to absorb all that the National Coal Board hopes to produce there for export.

Table 56. *Output of coal per head in Scotland by area,*
1900–09 *and* 1940–49

Area	1900–09 (tons)	1940–49 (tons)	Ratio of 1940–49 to 1900–09 (percentage)
Ayr and Dumfries	339	307	91
'Lanarkshire'	323	273	85
Fife and Clackmannan	353	329	93
Lothians	295	311	105
Scotland	329	298	91

SOURCES: *Reports on Mines and Quarries;* Ministry of Fuel and Power, *Statistical Digest.*

Table 57. *Output of coal per head in Scotland and in*
England and Wales, 1900–50

Year	Scotland (tons per man)	England and Wales (tons per man)	Scotland as a proportion of England and Wales (percentage)
1900	336	288	117
1910	315	248	127
1920	214	183	117
1930	327	254	129
1935	379	282	134
1940	344	294	117
1945	267	244	109
1950	286	294	97

SOURCES: *Reports on Mines and Quarries;* Ministry of Fuel and Power, *Statistical Digest.*

A shift of production to the newer coalfields will help to maintain productivity and reduce costs; output per head is lowest and costs are highest in 'Lanarkshire'. But the experience of the past twenty years suggests that, in spite of the shift away from 'Lanarkshire' (which has been in progress throughout the period), the Scottish coalfield as a whole is losing ground relative to the coalfields in England and Wales (see Table 57).

In 1935 output per head in Scotland was high, not only in relation to England and Wales, but also in relation to earlier years, and had climbed faster than in the rest of the country. After 1935, however, England and Wales began to overtake Scotland and by 1950 had outstripped her, not because of

8-2

any startling increase in productivity but because productivity in Scotland has fallen by a quarter since 1935.

If one takes figures of costs, the same picture emerges. The figures for the last six years show the cost of coal in Scotland coming to exceed the average cost in England and Wales and by an increasing margin. Scottish costs, from being well below the average for the country, are now well above the average and about one-third higher than in the East Midlands, the lowest cost division in Britain. The consistent profit that was earned in Scotland until 1950 gave way to a loss in 1951 and 1952.

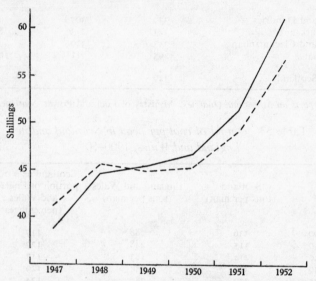

Fig. 11. Cost per ton of saleable coal in Scotland and in Great Britain, 1947–52. Scotland ———; Great Britain – – –.

Part of the explanation of this loss of ground lies in the more rapid progress in mechanization in Scotland before the war, and the loss of this lead after the war. In 1935 72 % of the Scottish output was cut by machinery compared with 50 % for Britain; in 1951 these proportions had become 86 % and 81 % respectively. Scotland also had a slight lead in 1935 in coal conveyed by machinery (48 % against 42 %) but had lost it by 1951 (80 % against 88 %). But differences in the pace of mechanization do not provide the full explanation; in coal-mining, the use of more machinery does not always bring higher output.[1]

One factor operating to keep down productivity in Scottish mines is their small average size. In 1945 only 58 % of Scottish miners (compared with

[1] Cf. *Plan for Coal*, para. 66.

83 % in Britain) were working in collieries employing 500 or more wage-earners. The average output of Scottish collieries in 1950 was 120,000 tons per annum—the lowest for any division in Britain, and far below the average for the East Midlands (420,000 tons) or the North-Eastern division (371,000 tons). In the East of Scotland collieries are larger than in the West and the average is not far below that for the country as a whole.

In spite of the adverse trend in costs and productivity in Scotland, the National Coal Board is planning to put a large part of its new sinkings in Scotland—nine out of twenty-two new deep mines and thirty-eight out of fifty-three surface mines. It does not propose, however, to make a corresponding capital outlay on major reconstructions of existing collieries and Scotland's share of the proposed capital expenditure (set out in *Plan for Coal*[1]) is not much greater than in proportion to her contribution to British coal production. To fulfil the National Coal Board's plan it will be necessary for Scottish coal production to rise faster than output in the rest of the country—no easy task, in view of the steady fall since 1935 in the ratio of Scottish to British output.

The National Coal Board's decision to embark on new sinkings in Scotland is grounded on the large reserves available in Fife and the Lothians. The deposits lying seaward of the East Fife coalfield constitute 'the largest reserves in Scotland' and 'one of the few really rich areas available for extensive exploitation in Britain'. They are in thickish seams, relatively free from sulphur, but deep and hot to work. The Lothian coalfield also has large reserves and the mining conditions are the best in Scotland. In Ayr and Dumfries the reserves are more scattered and costs are higher, but there is a large virgin field in the Mauchline area.

There is no need to examine the National Coal Board's plan in detail. It postulates an increase in output between 1949 and 1960–65 by some 7 m. tons, a *fall* in consumption by about ½ m. tons, and a rise in net exports to 9 m. tons, or nearly one-third of output. It also postulates an increase in output per head to over 400 tons per head, i.e. by about 40 %. It would be great good fortune for Scotland if all these assumptions were fulfilled; but the trends already outlined point to a less happy conclusion. In the years that have passed since *Plan for Coal* appeared, output has fallen, consumption has risen, productivity is lower than ever, and the margin between Scottish and British costs continues to widen.

[1] *Plan for Coal*, p. 42.

CHAPTER 9

MANUFACTURING INDUSTRY

By C. E. V. LESER

THE METAL AND ENGINEERING TRADES

Among manufacturing industries, those using metals are nowadays by far the largest, both in Scotland and in Great Britain. The metal trades—including all engineering, shipbuilding, vehicle manufacture and repair, instruments, precious metals, and so on—employ about one-sixth of the Scottish working population and account for nearly half the total of those engaged in manufacturing. In the rest of Great Britain the metal trades occupy an even more dominant position, nearly one worker in five finding employment in this group. The rise of the metal trades is a phenomenon of long standing.[1] In the past century, the proportion of Scottish workers engaged in them has climbed from 4·8 % to 16·3 %. Viewed in terms of physical output or of the make-up of total exports, the same change has been at work. Metal and engineering products, for example, now form 50 % of British exports where as recently as 1938 they formed no more than 38 % and in 1913, 25 %.

The Heavy Engineering Industries

As is well known, Scotland has specialized in the heavier branches of engineering, particularly in the building of ships and locomotives. The Clyde alone builds a third of the new tonnage launched from British shipyards; of the new tonnage built all over the world, no less than 15 % in 1949–51 was from Scottish yards. On the other hand, other branches of the metal and engineering trades are poorly represented or entirely absent. Scotland makes no aircraft, no passenger cars and no tinplate. Her share of total British employment in metals was 9·1 % in 1950 compared with a share of 10·1 % in industries and services of all kinds. But within the metals group there were wide departures from the average. In order to single out those departures, each of forty-three metal industries in the group has been ranked according to the proportion borne by Scottish to British employees (Table 58).

In nine industries Scotland's share of total employment was at least one-third higher than 'normal' (i.e. one-third above the ratio of total Scottish to total British workers); in ten industries, Scotland's share lay between one-third above and one-third below 'normal'; and in the remaining twenty-four

[1] See above, pp. 77–78.

118

Table 58. *Employment in the metal and engineering trades in Great Britain and in Scotland*, 1950

Industry	Great Britain (number)	Scotland Number	Scotland Percentage of Great Britain
Strongly represented			
Boilers and boiler-house plant	24,800	8,450	34·1
Marine engineering	74,600	24,780	33·2
Shipbuilding and ship repairing	203,500	52,290	25·7
'Other locomotive manufacture'	22,700	5,670	25·0
Manufacture and repair of watches and clocks	15,300	2,840	18·6
Iron and steel tubes	43,500	7,750	17·8
Constructional engineering	78,400	13,880	17·7
Iron and steel foundries	115,800	19,850	17·1
Railway locomotive shops	61,200	8,170	13·3
Total	639,800	143,680	22·5
Normally represented			
Agricultural machinery	41,500	5,020	12·1
Iron and steel melting, rolling, etc.	214,000	25,770	12·0
Blast furnaces	20,800	2,410	11·6
Wire and wire manufacture	37,200	4,310	11·6
'Other non-electrical engineering'	652,500	70,310	10·8
Bolts, nuts, screws, etc.	38,000	4,030	10·6
Motor repairing and garages	216,600	20,950	9·7
Iron and steel forgings	35,500	3,260	9·2
Steel sheets	20,100	1,620	8·1
Manufacture and repair of railway carriages, etc.	80,700	5,640	7·0
Total	1,356,900	143,320	10·6
Weakly represented			
Non-ferrous metals	99,200	6,360	6·4
Textile machinery and accessories	70,000	3,990	5·7
Ordnance and small arms	41,600	2,260	5·4
Brass manufactures	40,000	2,170	5·4
Metal industries not elsewhere specified	234,200	12,460	5·3
Scientific, surgical and photographic instruments	85,500	4,520	5·3
Batteries and accumulators	18,900	940	5·0
Manufacture and repair of aircraft	146,500	6,910	4·7
'Other electrical goods'	117,700	5,450	4·6
Machine tools	77,200	3,250	4·2
Carts, perambulators, etc.	9,300	370	4·0
Electrical machinery	169,300	5,850	3·5
Musical instruments	7,700	260	3·4
Manufacture of motor vehicles and cycles	301,600	9,700	3·2
Hollow-ware	57,300	1,750	3·0
Wireless apparatus and gramophones	82,700	2,080	2·5
Electric wires and cables	61,100	1,260	2·1
Wireless valves and electric lamps	35,000	620	1·8
Tools and cutlery	52,200	810	1·6
Jewellery, plate, and refining of precious metals	28,600	240	0·8
Stationary engines	26,100	170	0·7
Telegraph and telephone apparatus	48,400	200	0·4
Manufacture of parts and accessories for motor vehicles and aircraft	96,700	140	0·1
Tinplate	17,900	—	—
Total	1,924,700	71,760	3·7
All metal and engineering industries	3,921,400	358,760	9·1

SOURCE: *Tables relating to employment and unemployment.*

industries Scotland's share was at least one-third below 'normal'. These three groups are shown in Table 58 as 'strongly', 'normally' and 'weakly' represented.

The importance of heavy engineering emerges strikingly. Of the nine metal industries that are strongly represented in Scotland all but one can be classed as heavy, the exception being the comparatively new (and relatively small) clock- and watch-making industry. The shipbuilding group comes at the head of the list; the others include boilers, locomotive work, iron foundries, iron and steel tubes and constructional engineering. On the other hand, the lighter metal and engineering industries are prominent at the other end of the table. Electrical goods of all kinds, without exception, come at this end. So do motor vehicles, aircraft, non-ferrous metal goods, scientific instruments, and a wide range of consumer-goods from jewellery to perambulators. The intermediate class of industries which are about equally represented in Scotland and in the rest of Britain is made up of a number of branches of the iron and steel industry, such as sheets, wire and forgings, a miscellaneous group of non-electrical engineering trades, agricultural machinery, motor garages, and the manufacture and repair of railway carriages.

The heavy engineering group is dominated by shipbuilding which, with the inclusion of all the ancillary industries on which it draws, has an output greater than mining, and much greater than any other manufacturing industry. Even the steel industry, which probably ranks next in order of size, comes within the orbit of shipbuilding as a supplier of plates and as a source of material both for the engines, boilers, pumps, deck-gear, and fittings and for the derricks, steel-tubing, and so on, used by the shipyards themselves. The output of new ships from the yards in 1948 was valued at £45 m. of which £12 m. was for export. In addition, some components, including marine engines, are made for sale elsewhere and there is a fair amount of repair work, although a much higher proportion of the repair work goes to English yards. The main centre of the industry in Scotland is on the Clyde, but about one-seventh of the Scottish output (excluding work done at the Rosyth naval dockyard) comes from other areas, including Aberdeen, Dundee, Leith, Burntisland and Ardrossan.

The peak rate of production from the Scottish yards was in 1913 when the tonnage launched reached 810,000 gross registered tons. The industry—particularly the section engaged in new building—has been subject to severe fluctuations in the course of its history and at one time in 1933, output was as low as 74,000 gross registered tons, while unemployment was as high as 76 % in 1932. Since the war, however, output has been relatively steady and unemployment has never exceeded 7 %. The Scottish industry has been severely hampered during that period by shortage of steel.

The branches of engineering which are concentrated in Scotland are not only nearly all within the heavy group; they are also nearly all old. Ships and locomotives, for example, are symbols of the revolution in transport a century ago just as motor-cars and aircraft symbolize modern transport facilities. Thus it tended to be true before the war that Scotland had the sections of the industry that were ceasing to grow rather than the sections in course of rapid expansion. Since the war this has no longer been true, because, broadly speaking, the whole of the metal and engineering industries have been in process of expansion, not least some of the older industries such as steel and shipbuilding. There has also been an inflow from outside of new engineering enterprises engaged in light engineering work, notably aero-engines, watches and clocks, radio manufacturing and business machinery. It remains true, however, that light engineering is relatively insignificant.

This position has three important disadvantages. It means, first, that some of the more important growing industries have inadequate roots in Scotland; second, that line production technique, with all the planning procedures associated with it, are as yet relatively unfamiliar to Scottish managements; and third, that the impulse to technological advance that comes from the association of new industries with old is largely absent. One branch of engineering that occupies a strategic position in many of the newer industries is instrument-making, in which, in the days of Lord Kelvin, Scotland led the world. It is partly because this industry and the precision engineering that goes with it has not kept pace with progress elsewhere that many of the newer engineering industries now find difficulty in establishing themselves firmly in Scotland.

It must not be imagined that the failure of Scotland to attract some of the major new industries, such as motorcars and aircraft, is a fluke; no less than twenty-three motor vehicle factories have been started, at one time or another, in Scotland and only one (Albion Motors) remains. If the motor-vehicle industry has not taken root, it is not for lack of trying.

The steel industry

The greatest concentration of metal and engineering trades, particularly of iron and steel manufacture, is in the Glasgow area. The iron and steel industry grew up in the neighbourhood of the large deposits of blackband ironstone in Lanark, the ore being smelted with local coal in local blast furnaces. By the time the deposits became exhausted, the Clyde had developed into a large consumer of iron and steel and the industry remained in the area, switching to imported ore and making increasing use of scrap. The ample supply of local coking coals allowed it to retain some of its original locational advantages but the supply of coking coal in turn has now begun to dwindle. Nevertheless, the steel industry, which is mainly in the hands of the Colville group of companies, has continued to expand, the peak being reached in 1950

121

with an output of 2·4 m. ingot tons. The main steelworks have remained in, or on the borders of, Lanark, the largest being at Clydebridge (on the outskirts of Glasgow), in Motherwell and at Glengarnock (in North Ayr).

Most of the Scottish steelworks make use of cold metal, the only unit with any claim to be regarded as integrated being the main Colville works at Clydebridge. In 1950, for example, 2·55 m. tons of cold pig iron and steel and cast iron scrap were used, while the charge of hot metal was no more than 110,000 tons. No other steel-producing area—not even Sheffield—made so little use of hot metal. The position is changing, however, for in 1937 no hot metal was used, and by 1951 there had been an increase to 194,000 tons. A parallel change in progress is the trend towards a higher charge of pig iron per ton of steel; the famine in scrap in recent years has forced Scottish steelmakers to make themselves less dependent on imported scrap by erecting new blast furnaces.

Table 59. *Output of finished steel products in Scotland and in Great Britain, 1949–51*

Product	Average output per annum, 1949–51		Scotland as percentage of Great Britain
	Scotland (thousand tons)	Great Britain (thousand tons)	
Plates	636·4	2,090·1	30·4
Other heavy rolled products	422·5	2,618·8	16·1
Tubes, pipes and fittings	178·3	1,081·8	16·5
Castings	46·5	248·8	18·7
Light rolled products	326·1	4,465·7	7·3
Sheets	74·0	1,608·9	4·6
Wire	24·1	822·8	2·9

SOURCE: British Iron and Steel Federation, *Statistical Yearbook*.

The bulk of the output is of plates and heavy rolled products. Wrought iron and steel tubes are also prominent. On the other hand, in light rolled products, wire and above all in sheets, Scotland has a relatively small share of British production. There is also a considerable output of alloy steel, Scotland being the largest producing area after Sheffield.

No comparable figures of steel consumption in Scotland have been published. It has been estimated, however, that in the last quarter of 1950, when deliveries of finished steel from Scottish steelmakers were a little under 500,000 tons, the total consumption of steel in Scotland amounted to 289,000 tons[1] or, say, 60 % of total deliveries. This means that Scotland is a large net exporter of

[1] British Iron and Steel Federation, *Monthly Statistical Bulletin*, vol. XXVI, no. 6, June 1951.

steel, particularly heavy rolled products. The consumption of plates and heavy rolled products in Scotland may be about half the total output, and much the same ratio probably applies to steel castings, to tubes, pipes and fittings and to alloy steel. In light rolled products also, Scotland appears to have a substantial export trade. On the other hand, Scotland is a net importer of strip, tinplate, wire, and tyres, wheels and axles.

Table 60. *Consumption of steel by industry in Scotland and in the United Kingdom, at fourth quarter 1950 rates*

Industry	United Kingdom (thousand tons)	Scotland (thousand tons)	Scotland as percentage of United Kingdom
Mechanical engineering	1,356	172	13
Motors, cycles and aircraft	1,156	36	3
Constructional engineering	1,010	182	18
Shipbuilding, repairing and marine engineering	950	234	25
Railways and rolling stock	842	98	12
Hollow-ware	608	20	3
Coalmining	578	68	12
Bolts, nuts, screws, etc.	496	54	11
Metal furniture, windows, etc.	480	26	5
Electrical machinery and apparatus	458	14	3
Drop forgings	448	42	9
Iron and steel	416	56	14
Building and contracting	392	44	11
Wire manufactures	302	36	12
Agricultural machinery (excluding tractors)	196	24	12
Other British consumers and small users	708	50	7
Total	10,396	1,156	11

SOURCE: Estimates by British Iron and Steel Federation.

The British Iron and Steel Federation have published figures showing the consumption of steel by industry in the fourth quarter of 1950 and these figures bring out some of the more important differences between the metal and engineering industries of Scotland and the United Kingdom. The annual rates of consumption corresponding to the Federation's estimates are shown in Table 60.

There is a conspicuously low proportion of Scottish to British consumption in motors, cycles and aircraft, hollow-ware, metal furniture, and electrical machinery, and a conspicuously high proportion in mechanical and constructional engineering, iron and steel, and shipbuilding.

123

Centres of the metal and engineering industries

Outside the Glasgow area, the next largest concentration of metal industries (but of a different character) is in the Falkirk area. This area is the home of the Scottish ironfounding industry which produces light castings such as stoves, grates and sanitary ware. Indeed, in some of these products Scotland has the major share of the total British output. Falkirk has also an aluminium sheet-rolling mill, built during the war, partly using aluminium produced in Kinlochleven and Lochaber. It is the most important Scottish centre of non-ferrous metal manufacture which, however, is a small industry in Scotland compared with England and Wales.

Engineering is more widely dispersed than metal manufacture. Some of the smaller towns like Kilmarnock, Arbroath, Fraserburgh, Brechin and Inverness have important engineering firms, and all the large cities have an engineering industry quite apart from shipbuilding and marine engineering. In Aberdeen the emphasis is on cranes, stone-cutting and agricultural machinery, in Dundee on textile and business machinery, in Edinburgh on electrical engineering and paper-making machinery; and the Glasgow area has old established specialities like sewing machines, sugar-refining and mining machinery. Other metal trades which are largely localized in this area include old industries like locomotive, railway carriage and wagon works, and the manufacture of bolts and nuts, as well as newer industries like the manufacture of aero-engines, caravans, typewriters and clocks.

The main threat to the Scottish metal and engineering industries comes from the shortage of coking coal and the rise in fuel costs on the one side and the increasing importance of industrial research on the other. There is no real reason why Scotland need remain at a disadvantage in fuel compared with England and Wales; but the recent trend will not be easy to reverse. The building up of new industries based on advances in science may in the long run prove the more difficult problem; but unless Scotland has great good fortune she will require to look increasingly to those industries for her industrial future, not least in the field of engineering.

THE TEXTILE, LEATHER AND CLOTHING TRADES

A century ago, the textile and allied trades provided employment for far larger numbers than all other manufacturing trades put together. Although they have now been outstripped by the metal and engineering group, they still account for over one-fifth of total employment in manufacturing, both in Scotland and in Britain as a whole, and for about one-twelfth of the total working population. More important was the significance of the textile trades as employers of women. Of all women in jobs in Scotland more than one in seven was working in the textile trades; and out of 250,000 women in the factory trades as a group, no less than 110,000 were textile workers. This was a larger proportion than in England, where the engineering trades offer greater employment opportunities to women, partly owing to the different type of work and partly because of a difference in social habits. In 1950, 164,600 persons were working in the textile group of trades in Scotland, and this represented 9·5 % of the corresponding British total, not far from the proportion (10·1 %) which Scottish employment in all industries and services bore to the British total.

Of the twenty-five trades included in the group, there were seven that were strongly represented, another seven normally represented, and eleven weakly represented in Scotland, using the same terms as before to indicate the degree of divergence from the industrial pattern of Great Britain. Table 61, in which these trades are listed, shows the Scottish deficiencies to be less marked in this field than among the metal trades. For the weakly represented textile and allied industries are, in terms of the employment provided in Britain, only about half as important as the remaining (strongly and normally represented) industries in this group; whilst the metal trades weakly represented in Scotland are of about the same importance to the British economy as the other metal trades.

Among the trades which are strongly represented in Scotland, the linen and jute trades are prominent in that Scotland has the major share in the whole production of Britain, although for the linen industry this would not be true if Northern Ireland were included. In the hosiery industry—the largest trade of this group in Scotland and by far the largest in Britain as a whole— Scotland specializes on a rather narrow sector, viz. the production of knitted woollen goods like pullovers and cardigans, and in this sector it has a large share of the total British production, whilst the manufacture of socks and stockings, as well as of underwear, is almost entirely concentrated in England.

The weakly represented trades include, notably, cotton weaving, the rayon and silk trades, dressmaking and shoe manufacture. The specialization of the Scottish cotton industry on sewing-cotton accounts for the comparative deficiency in the weaving sector of the industry, which is very small. The Scottish silk industry has for a long time been small compared with England and Wales, and the newer and expanding rayon trade is also poorly represented. This provides another example for the absence of new industries in Scotland, though the statement that the country has specialized on stagnating rather than on expanding trades is generally less true for textile than for metal trades; the carpet trade, for instance, is a Scottish speciality with good expansion prospects.

The extent to which some of the clothing industries, which are not normally

125

Table 61. *Employment in textile, leather and clothing trades in Great Britain and in Scotland*, 1950

Industry	Great Britain (number)	Scotland Number	Scotland Percentage of Great Britain
Strongly represented			
Jute	17,500	17,150	98·0
Linen and soft hemp	14,000	11,140	79·6
Carpets	28,200	9,270	32·9
Rope, twine and net	15,100	3,570	23·6
Lace	13,400	2,880	21·5
Made-up textiles	22,000	3,620	16·5
Hosiery and other knitted goods	123,100	18,000	14·6
Total	233,300	65,630	28·1
Normally represented			
Repair of boots and shoes	21,700	2,670	12·3
Textile finishing, etc.	89,500	10,460	11·7
Woollen and worsted	218,700	20,870	9·5
Leather tanning and dressing and fellmongery	40,100	3,460	8·6
Tailoring	276,500	22,730	8·2
Cotton spinning, doubling, etc.	184,000	14,210	7·7
Overalls, shirts, underwear, etc.	66,900	4,780	7·1
Total	897,400	79,180	8·8
Weakly represented			
Other textile industries	25,400	1,430	5·6
Fur	9,500	520	5·5
Hats, caps and millinery	20,000	1,010	5·1
Leather goods	27,200	1,280	4·7
Rayon, nylon, etc. weaving and silk	50,100	2,210	4·4
Dressmaking	101,300	3,880	3·8
Cotton weaving, etc.	142,500	4,500	3·2
Manufacture of boots, shoes, etc.	126,200	3,030	2·4
Narrow fabrics	22,400	540	2·4
Rayon, nylon, etc. production	47,300	800	1·7
Dress industries not separately specified	36,600	590	1·6
Total	608,500	19,790	3·3
All textile, leather and clothing industries	1,739,200	164,600	9·5

SOURCE: *Tables relating to employment and unemployment.*

126

localized to any large extent, are under-represented in Scotland is striking. One would expect the number of clothing workers in Scotland to be more or less in proportion to its industrial population. This, indeed, is true of tailoring, which is the largest clothing industry and is found all over Scotland, particularly in the large cities; but other clothing industries are under-represented in Scotland and largely confined to Glasgow. Scotland has a considerable output of mackintoshes, overalls, shirts, and hats, but produces little millinery, few scarves and gloves apart from knitted ones, and no handkerchiefs. There are only a few boot and shoe factories, mainly in Glasgow and Kilmarnock, but repairs to boots and shoes appear to be more frequent in Scotland.

There is not the same tendency for textiles as for metals and engineering to be concentrated in one single area since there is generally little interrelation between different textile trades; an exception is the textile finishing trade which in Scotland tends to be located near the main cotton and jute manufacturing areas. Thus there are a number of different centres for different textile trades, like Paisley for cotton, Hawick for wool and hosiery, Kirkcaldy and Dunfermline for linen, Dundee for jute, the Newmilns area in Ayr for the small lace trade, Glasgow and Kilmarnock for carpets, etc. Some of these industries, like jute and lace, are almost entirely concentrated in one single district, but others are more widely spread over the country. For example, the woollen trade is found not only in the Borders, but also in Alloa, Aberdeen, Lewis, and other areas; similarly the linen industry is located not only in Fife but also in Dundee, Aberdeen, Greenock and elsewhere. The leather and clothing trades are generally small and widely dispersed over Scotland, although the tailoring trade is to a large extent concentrated in Glasgow.

The pattern of textile and allied industries represented in Scotland has changed considerably during the last century. Generally speaking, the decline in their labour force reflects partly an increase in productivity which was not accompanied by corresponding increases in demand, but also partly the loss of home and export markets to other countries competing in this field. These changes have not been by any means uniform in all industries, and the emphasis between different textile trades has shifted quite substantially, generally from trades with a low to trades with a high value of output per head.

A century ago cotton was the largest single textile industry in Scotland, employing about 100,000 men and women out of a total of 370,000 in this group of trades. But by the end of the century, the trade had been virtually lost to Lancashire, and while the industry actually grew in England during this period, employment in Scotland fell in terms of numbers employed to 15,000. Since then the industry has been subject to fluctuating fortunes on a similar scale to its English counterpart.

The linen and jute trades came next in importance to cotton one hundred years ago, employing about 80,000 persons in 1851, and since during the next fifty years the labour force declined by 10,000 only, the industries were of primary importance at the turn of the century, only to lose ground later on. The linen trade in Scotland is very old, originally based on home-grown flax, hand spinning and hand-loom weaving, and it became a factory trade in the industrial revolution but ultimately suffered from competition by Ireland and other countries. The jute trade came to Scotland in the nineteenth century and was originally closely linked to the Dundee linen industry, which it all but supplanted later on in the city. During the inter-war period, Dundee still depended very largely on the jute trade and suffered with its depression, but since then other industries have been established there and are competing effectively for the city's labour force, the more so as earnings in jute were relatively low.

The clothing trades, which by 1901 still employed well over 100,000 workers, have also since then experienced a very drastic reduction to less than half their former size. On the other hand, the wool textile industry has maintained a fairly steady level of employment; and, taken together with hosiery and carpet manufacture, which are of more recent origin, employment has almost doubled, increasing from about 25,000 in 1851 to almost 50,000 in 1951.

The future of the textile and allied trades is uncertain. A large expansion of this sector of the economy is unlikely; and recent events have shown that even under present conditions, the textile industries have their ups and downs, whether they be catering for the home or the export market. Some trades like jute are also vulnerable to difficulties in their raw materials supply. Nevertheless, they should remain, as a group, an important and comparatively stable element in the Scottish economy. Given the wide variety of textile trades in Scotland, there is room for a continuing shift of emphasis from one to another and a further concentration on those that can offer relatively high earnings and an expanding market.

MISCELLANEOUS FACTORY TRADES

Factory trades other than those considered in the metal and textile groups include those dealing with producer goods like chemicals and building materials, as well as consumergoods industries like the food, drink and tobacco trades, wood-working, paper and printing, and those using miscellaneous materials like rubber. Both in Scotland and in Britain as a whole, they absorb about one-eighth of the total labour force and about one-third of all factory workers. The Scottish share in the British employment total was 9·8 % in 1950, which is somewhat above the figures for the metal and textile groups but below those for non-manufacturing industries and services.

Of the nine industries in this group which are strongly represented in Scotland, three are food and two are drink trades; indeed, they include two out of the three drink industries distinguished in the Standard Industrial

Classification. The high share of Scotland in these reflects the fact that the country has a virtual monopoly of whisky production; the main products of the English wholesale bottling trade and 'other drink industries' are bottled beer, British wines, cider and spirits other than whisky. Whisky distilleries are found all over the country, though particularly in the North-East and in the Highlands, while Glasgow is a centre of whisky blending and bottling. Whisky forms now a substantial part of the Scottish export trade and is an important dollar-earner. In the brewing and malting industries, Scotland has no more than its normal share, the Scottish breweries being chiefly in Edinburgh, Glasgow, Falkirk and Alloa.

All the food industries as classified here are at least normally represented in Scotland, and those in which Scotland has a large share include baking, which is naturally dispersed, as well as biscuit manufacture, which is highly localized and chiefly concentrated in Glasgow and Edinburgh. The relatively large Scottish production appears to be associated with a relatively high consumption of these starchy foods in Scotland; whether the specific Scottish consumption habits encouraged production of these foods, or whether these habits were in fact induced by a greater range of available flour products, remains a debatable point. Other food industries are naturally linked to farming or fishing and are predominantly located in agricultural areas or near fishing ports; examples are fruit and vegetable canning in Angus, milk processing in the South-West, fish curing and canning in the Aberdeen area, which shows the largest concentration of food trades. But food industries are not confined to any particular part of Scotland: Paisley is a centre of food processing, Greenock of sugar refining, Dundee of chocolate and sweets manufacture. There are only a few minor food trades which are almost absent in Scotland; examples are cocoa manufacture and meat canning.

The tobacco industry is less well represented in Scotland. Although Glasgow was at one time, in the eighteenth century, the centre of a flourishing tobacco trade, this was a re-export and wholesale rather than a manufacturing trade. The Scottish industry, which is largely concentrated in a few big factories in Glasgow and Paisley, like those of Stephen Mitchell, specializes in pipe tobacco manufacture, although in recent years cigarette production has tended to develop in Scotland to an increasing extent.

A Scottish speciality—among the best-known after whisky—is linoleum, which is about as much associated with Kirkcaldy as jute is with Dundee. Incidentally, the two industries are linked together, since jute is one of the chief raw materials used in making linoleum, and the linoleum industry could almost be regarded as a textile trade. Scotland is responsible for over one-third of the British output of all products of this industry, which include leathercloth, etc.; if we confine our attention to linoleum proper, the Scottish share rises to almost two-thirds of the British total.

Table 62. *Employment in miscellaneous factory trades in Great Britain and in Scotland*, 1950

Industry	Great Britain (number)	Scotland Number	Scotland Percentage of Great Britain
Strongly represented			
Linoleum, leather cloth, etc.	14,700	5,570	37·9
Explosives and fireworks	37,500	12,290	32·8
'Other drink industries'	41,200	10,970	26·6
Wholesale bottling	14,500	3,290	22·7
Paper and board	77,400	15,290	19·8
Food industries not elsewhere specified	59,200	10,650	18·0
Biscuits	38,100	6,560	17·2
Bread and flour confectionery	186,100	30,100	16·2
Wood containers and baskets	23,700	3,300	13·9
Total	492,400	98,020	19·9
Normally represented			
Timber	91,100	11,370	12·5
Meat and meat products	29,700	3,510	11·8
Bricks and fireclay goods	81,000	9,070	11·2
Grain milling	40,900	4,210	10·3
Rubber	103,100	10,490	10·2
Printing and publishing of newspapers and periodicals	99,800	9,240	9·3
Furniture and upholstery	125,700	11,430	9·1
'Other printing and publishing, etc.'	239,400	21,240	8·9
Milk products	47,900	4,170	8·7
Sugar and glucose	21,200	1,770	8·4
'Other non-metalliferous mining manufacture'	76,700	6,380	8·3
Brewing and malting	94,800	7,740	8·2
Mineral oil refining	38,400	3,010	7·8
Preserving of fruit and vegetables	55,700	4,300	7·7
Manufactures of paper and board not elsewhere specified	41,300	3,120	7·6
Miscellaneous wood and cork manufactures	20,600	1,540	7·5
Cocoa, chocolate and sugar confectionery	73,600	5,420	7·4
Tobacco	47,500	3,310	7·0
Total	1,328,400	121,320	9·1
Weakly represented			
Glass containers	27,800	1,850	6·7
Chemicals and dyes	208,700	13,340	6·4
Cardboard boxes, cartons, etc.	44,600	2,620	5·9
'Other oils, greases, glue, etc.'	33,500	1,930	5·8
Paint and varnish	39,100	2,030	5·2
Pharmaceutical preparations, etc.	41,200	1,930	4·7
Shop and office fittings	19,300	880	4·6
Miscellaneous stationers goods	11,400	520	4·6
Miscellaneous manufacturing industries	64,400	2,610	4·0
Toys, games and sports' requisites	31,400	1,110	3·5
Glass (other than containers)	42,000	1,260	3·0
Brushes and brooms	15,800	450	2·8
Coke ovens and by-products	17,400	460	2·6
Soap, candles, glycerine, etc.	53,900	1,350	2·5
China and earthenware	82,000	2,010	2·5
Cement	13,300	310	2·3
Wallpaper	6,700	130	1·9
Production and printing of cinematographic films	8,400	—	—
Total	760,900	34,790	4·6
All miscellaneous industries	2,581,700	254,130	9·8

SOURCE: *Tables relating to employment and unemployment.*

The production of explosives has become another activity in which Scotland specializes, largely owing to the presence of the former Nobel and now I.C.I. works in Ayrshire near Stevenston. The country also produces a fair amount of fertilizers, notably in the Lothians and in the North-East, and of dyestuffs, chiefly in the Grangemouth area. This area is also the centre of the mineral oil refining industry which promises considerable expansion. Glasgow also has paint works and other chemical manufacturing. Nevertheless, the chemical industries as a whole are not well represented in Scotland; this applies particularly to light chemicals like pharmaceutical preparations, toilet preparations and perfumery, but the range of industrial chemicals produced in Scotland is also small.

Other important British industries which are almost absent are pottery and glass manufacture. There is no Scottish centre of china and earthenware production comparable to the English Midlands, and the industry, such as it is, specializes in sanitary ware and produces little domestic china or earthenware. The small and widely-dispersed glass industry specializes in the production of glass bottles and jars. The output of building materials, particularly cement, is also low, especially in relation to the large Scottish house-building requirements, and the dependence on scarce cement supplies from England has had unfavourable repercussions on the progress in the Scottish housing programme. An exception is bricks, in which the country is probably self-sufficient and which are chiefly manufactured in the Glasgow area and in Central Scotland.

In most of the woodworking trades, Scotland makes an important contribution to the total British output and makes good use of its natural timber resources and of its facilities for timber imports. The Scottish furniture industry is known to specialize in high-class articles rather than in utility furniture. It suffered more from the depression during the inter-war years than the English furniture industry, but since then it has recovered its position. Furniture works are found in each of the four cities, but an important centre of the industry is the Beith-Lochwinnoch district on the Ayr-Renfrew border. Other timber products in which Scotland specializes include wooden barrels and casks.

Scotland, and especially the East of Scotland, is also an important centre of paper manufacture, particularly for printing and writing paper. Publishing and printing of books as well as newspapers and periodicals, with its ancillary activities of bookbinding, engraving, etc., is naturally concentrated in the cities, and Edinburgh is particularly well known as a publishing centre.

Scotland is lagging behind in the development of plastic-goods production and in a few minor new industries, but the manufacture of rubber products promises an expanding output. Edinburgh is the main centre of the Scottish rubber industry, and the North British Rubber Company has the biggest of the few large factories in which rubber goods production is concentrated.

There is thus a wide variety of consumer-goods industries in Scotland and a corresponding variety of industrial experience and background. The food, drink and tobacco trades play a larger part than in the rest of Britain, while chemicals, building materials, and some other consumer goods are less fully represented. Few consumer-goods industries are entirely unrepresented— film production and printing is one of the exceptions—and many of those that are of long standing are still growing and adapting themselves to new market opportunities and modern techniques.

CHAPTER 10

TRADE

By W. M. L. MURRAY

In this chapter an attempt will be made to show the magnitude and composition of Scottish trade with foreign countries and to outline some of the changes that have overtaken it during the past century. Thereafter Scotland's dependence on overseas trade will be assessed, with the help of international comparisons, and some of the implications of this dependence will be analysed.

A major difficulty arises at the outset. There are no statistics of visible Scottish imports and exports, still less of the invisible items—the expenditure of tourists, shipping freights, insurance premiums and so on—that form an important fraction of total international transactions. Indeed, the Catto Committee thought that there was no practicable way of measuring Scotland's visible imports and exports. There do exist, however, figures of trade through Scottish ports and these figures have been collected and published for nearly a century. These figures throw no light on trade across the border with England and Wales and are an extremely imperfect measure of trade with countries overseas. But they provide a basis on which rough estimates of overseas trade can be built, and offer some guide both to the composition of that trade and to long-term trends in its scope and pattern.

In order to derive figures of total overseas trade (i.e. excluding trade with England and Wales) from the figures of trade through Scottish ports, a fourfold correction is theoretically necessary. To exports through Scottish ports must be added exports of Scottish produce through English ports; from these figures must be deducted English exports through Scottish ports; and on the import side, similar adjustments are required. In practice, only two of these corrections appear to be of real magnitude, the additions to Scottish imports and exports for trade channelled through English ports. This helps to simplify the problem, but only a little, for these two corrections can rarely be made directly or with any confidence. In the estimates presented below, the method used has generally been indirect, but every possible use has also been made of such scraps of direct information as were obtainable.

THE MAGNITUDE OF SCOTLAND'S FOREIGN TRADE
Imports from countries overseas

Imports from foreign countries into Scotland in 1948 amounted in value to about £190 m. (see Table 63). The known total for imports through Scottish ports in that year is £146 m., and in addition it may be estimated that some £40 m.—or about 23 % of the total—came through English ports. Of this addition some £22 m. represented refrigerated meat, fruit and vegetables, dairy produce, tea and other foodstuffs; about £15 m. represented raw materials, mainly textile fibres (nearly all the raw cotton and wool being imported via English ports); while the remainder, valued at some £9 m., was made up of a variety of manufactures.

It is not possible to give full details of how these estimates were made but a brief account of the method used is given in the note at the end of this chapter. Imports of raw materials have been calculated from the consumption recorded

Table 63. *Principal commodities imported into Scotland, 1948*

Commodity	Imported via Scottish ports (£ m.)	Imported via English ports* (£ m.)	Total imports (£ m.)
Class I			
Meat of all kinds	4·8	7·4	12·0
Fruit and vegetables	4·0	4·6	8·6
Dairy produce	8·3	3·1	11·4
Tea	2·9	2·8	5·7
Other food, drink and tobacco	43·6	4·3	47·9
Total Class I	63·6	22·2	85·6
Class II			
Raw cotton	—	2·6	2·6
Raw wool	1·0	4·5	5·5
Raw jute	7·3	1·5	8·8
Other raw materials	39·5	6·2	45·7
Total Class II	47·8	14·8	62·6
Total Class III (manufactures)	30·8	8·5	39·3
Grand Total†	146·4	43·3	189·5

* Strictly speaking, these figures represent imports through English ports for consumption in Scotland, *less* imports through Scottish ports for consumption in England; and 'total imports' represents total imports *for consumption in Scotland*. It has been assumed, however, that this adjustment can be neglected.

† Including imports in Classes IV and V and an adjustment for commodities known to have been imported via Scottish ports but not specified under any single class.

SOURCE (column 1 only): *Annual Statement of Trade*, 1948.

in the Census of Production for 1948. Imports of foodstuffs and other consumer goods have usually been estimated by assuming that imports into the United Kingdom were distributed between Scotland and the rest of the country so as to give equal consumption per head. Numerous adjustments have been made wherever there was direct evidence of a different pattern of consumption in Scotland. The final results are necessarily highly tentative but the broad picture is not likely to be very far out.

Exports to countries overseas

It is just as difficult to estimate exports from Scotland through English ports as to estimate the corresponding imports. Statistics of employment on exports furnished by the Ministry of Labour and National Service, taken in conjunction with miscellaneous information from other sources, allow rough estimates to be made, the margin of error being of the order of £5 m. in either direction.[1] These estimates put the value of Scottish exports in 1948 through English ports—notably London and Liverpool—at £35 m., or 23 % of the total of some £150 m. for exports to countries overseas. Of the total of £35 m. fully 50 % represented textile manufactures, especially cotton thread, woollen cloth, hosiery, lace, jute, and linen, while about 12 % represented Scotch whisky. The residue included a wide range of products—linoleum, machinery, chemicals, drugs, dyes, and explosives, to name but a few of the more important.

The composition of Scottish trade

The estimates of Scottish trade with overseas countries derived in this way are set out in Table 64 alongside the comparable figures for the United Kingdom. Imports amounted to some 9·4 % and exports to some 9·5 % of the United Kingdom totals; and to 1·3 % and 1·2 % respectively of world trade.

The general pattern of imports does not differ greatly from the pattern for the United Kingdom. The biggest single difference is in jute products, which are much more extensively processed in Scotland than in the rest of the United Kingdom. Of the other differences, the most interesting are the relatively low imports of non-ferrous metal manufactures, corresponding to the comparative deficiency of Scotland in the electrical trades: the high imports of paper-making materials, reflecting the importance in Scotland of the paper-making trades; and the comparatively low rate of importation of refined petroleum.

On the export side, whisky more than accounts for the big difference in the totals for 'Food, drink and tobacco'.[2] Among manufactures, Scotland comes out badly on road and rail vehicles (all the motor-cars and nearly all the

[1] For details of the method of estimation see the note at the end of this chapter.

[2] Production of whisky for maturing is very much in excess of current releases from bond of matured spirits. Provided export markets can absorb the enlarged supply, exports of Scotch whisky will ultimately be much larger than at present without any greater effort of production.

Table 64. Scotland's 'Imports' and 'Exports', 1948

	Imports			Exports		
Commodity	Value £ million (c.i.f.)	Percentage of total	Corresponding percentage for U.K.	Value £ million (f.o.b.)	Percentage of total	Corresponding percentage for U.K.
Class I. Food, drink and tobacco:	86	45	43	23	15	6
whisky (Imports: grain and flour)	23	12	10	16	11	1
dairy produce (Exports: fish, all kinds)	11	6	6	2	1	—
meat of all kinds (Exports: beer)	12	6	6	1	1	—
fruit and vegetables (Exports: refined sugar)	9	5	5	1	1	—
unrefined sugar	7	3	3			
Class II. Raw materials:	63	33	32	6	4	4
textile fibres (Exports: coal)	20	11	10	4	3	2
wood and timber	9	5	5			
paper-making materials	8	4	3			
iron ore and scrap	4	2	1			
crude petroleum	4	2	2			
oilseeds	3	2	2			
Class III. Manufactures:	39	21	24	118	79	87
refined petroleum (Exports: textiles and apparel)	8	4	6	35	23	20
jute piece-goods (Exports: machinery)	7	4	1	24	16	16
machinery (Exports: ships)	5	3	2	12	8	2
non-ferrous metal manufactures (Exports: iron and steel manufactures)	3	2	4	12	8	7
paper and cardboard (Exports: road and rail vehicles)	3	2	1	7	5	11
paper and cardboard (Exports)				4	3	1
Other imports / Other exports	2	1	1	3	2	3
Grand total	190	100	100	150	100	100

commercial vehicles being exported from England) but the difference is roughly balanced by the greater prominence of ships in the Scottish total. Textiles and paper also form a larger fraction of Scottish than of British exports, cotton thread, wool knitwear, jute manufactures, lace and carpets contributing towards the high total for textiles. Machinery and iron and steel manufactures play about the same part in Scottish as in British exports. On the other hand, a wide variety of other manufactures, such as non-ferrous metals, hardware and pottery, form a much larger fraction of British than of Scottish exports. Taking all manufactures together, they come to 87 % of the British, but only 79 % of the Scottish total.

The direction of Scottish trade

It is unfortunately quite impracticable to present any statistical account of the geographical direction of Scotland's overseas trade, the markets for her exports and the sources of her imports. Probably one would approach quite closely to the truth if one were to assume that for each commodity the market pattern for Scottish imports and exports was the same as that for British trade. This would allow for major differences in the commodity-structure of trade but not for special market connexions built up between Scotland and foreign countries in individual commodities. That Scotland does in fact draw on special sources of supply may be illustrated by reference to Table 65, which compares the sources from which Scotland and the United Kingdom drew supplies of iron ore in 1948; that Scotland supplies markets which do not coincide with those for the United Kingdom may be illustrated, as in Table 66, by the example of coal exports in 1938—a year that may be more typical of the normal geographical pattern for coal exports than any of the postwar years.

Table 65. *Sources of imported iron ore for Scotland and for the United Kingdom*, 1948

	France and French North Africa	Sweden	Newfoundland	Sierra Leone	Other countries	All sources
Scotland						
Thousand tons	270·9	259·5	246·4	120·0	45·1	941·9
Percentage of total	28·8	27·6	26·2	12·7	4·7	100·0
United Kingdom						
Thousand tons	2,258·9	2,447·8	859·1	523·1	1,033·0	7,121·9
Percentage of total	31·7	34·4	12·1	7·3	14·5	100·0

SOURCE: British Iron and Steel Federation, *Statistical Yearbook*, 1948.

Table 66. *Destination of coal exports from Scotland and from
the United Kingdom, 1938, by sea areas*

	Baltic Sea	North Sea, English Channel and Irish Sea	Mediter-ranean	North Central and South America	Other areas	All areas
Scotland						
Thousand tons	2,710	1,300	173	252	26	4,461
Percentage of total	60·7	29·1	3·9	5·6	0·7	100·0
United Kingdom						
Thousand tons	8,878	14,384	7,428	4,494	672	35,856
Percentage of total	24·8	40·1	20·7	12·5	1·9	100·0

SOURCE: Annual Report of the Secretary for Mines.

Long-term trends in Scottish trade

We may turn now to look at the development of Scottish trade over the past century, analysing the changes in its volume and composition in relation to the corresponding changes in British trade. In such an analysis we face once again the fundamental deficiencies of the available statistics, and our conclusions must necessarily be extremely tentative.

Over the last hundred years, economic trends in Scotland are inevitably affected by the greater rate of increase of population in England and Wales. Since 1851 the proportion of Scotland's population to that of Great Britain has fallen from 13·9 % to 10·4 %—that is, by 25 %. This has been reflected in a corresponding decline in the relative size both of her working population and of her overseas trade. Indeed, the fall in Scotland's share of Britain's overseas trade has probably been greater than 25 %. A century ago, imports of textile fibres and exports of textile manufactures formed a very large proportion of total imports and exports, textiles playing a far bigger part in the trade of the country than in its total industrial production. The steady decline in the relative importance of the textile trades has been more marked in Scotland than in the rest of the country,[1] and this decline has presumably been matched by a correspondingly more rapid fall in imports of textile materials and in exports of the manufactures made from them. The historical movement in the pattern of Scotland's exports is clear. From the beginning of the nineteenth century until the development of her coal and iron resources had gathered momentum in the 1840's, textile manufactures constituted the overwhelming proportion of her foreign exports. In 1820, for example, over 98 % of the employment on manufactures for export was concentrated in the textile

[1] See Table 36, p. 77.

138

trades—70 % in cotton, 24 % in linen and hemp and 4 % in wool and silk. By the middle of the century this pattern was changing rapidly in sympathy with the shift in comparative advantage from textiles to coal-mining and the developing metal trades; ultimately from a narrowly-based to a more diversified industrial structure. Though this decline of the textile trades is still continuing, the major change occurred in the second half of the nineteenth century. In the metal trades, on the other hand, the expansion relatively to other exports has been as rapid in the present century as in the last, the growth over the past generation being more at the expense of the primary industries than of the textile industries. These broad movements are to some extent mirrored in the direct export shipments from Scottish ports in the years 1868, 1907 and 1948 as shown in Table 67.

Table 67. *Analysis of export shipments through Scottish ports*, 1868, 1907 *and* 1948

Commodity	Percentage of total shipments through Scottish ports in		
	1868	1907	1948
Class I			
Food, drink and tobacco:	7·4	11·3	14·6
whisky and beer	2·6	5·1	11·3
Class II			
Raw materials:	4·3	13·3	4·0
coal	4·1	12·4	3·7
Class III			
Manufactures:	82·8	67·5	74·1
textiles	59·6	24·5	17·2
iron and steel products	17·1	32·7	45·2
Unallocated and other			
exports	5·5	7·9	7·3
Total	100·0	100·0	100·0

SOURCE: Annual *Statements of the Trade of the United Kingdom.*

To complete this discussion of long-term trends, there is shown in Fig. 12 the proportion of the value of United Kingdom imports and exports passing through Scottish ports since the beginning of this century. The downward trend in the proportion, both for imports and exports, is due to the simultaneous operation of two factors—the declining importance of Scottish trade and the increasing use of English ports. Of these, the first factor has already been commented upon; in so far as it reflects the eclipse of textile exports it exaggerates the real change that has taken place, since a large part of the trade in textiles represents no more than the re-export of imported materials. The second factor is also easily exaggerated; the falling-off in direct coal exports exclusively through Scottish ports would by itself bring about an apparent fall in the proportion of exports made through Scottish ports. Thus the trend revealed by Fig. 12 needs careful interpretation before it is used in evidence, either that Scotland is losing ground to the rest of the country as an exporter, or that increasing use is being made by Scottish exporters of English ports—true though both these propositions would appear to be.

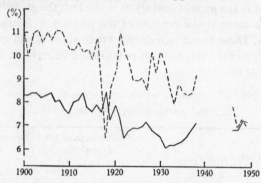

Fig. 12. Overseas trade through Scottish ports, 1900–49. Value of retained imports as percentage of total for the United Kingdom ——; value of exports as percentage of total for the United Kingdom – – –.

Scotland's dependence on foreign trade

A question of great importance is the degree to which the Scottish economy is dependent on foreign trade and is sensitive to fluctuations in world income. The conventional and probably the most useful measure of the degree of dependence on foreign trade is the ratio of trade to national income: we may either calculate the proportion of national income derived from exports or the proportion of national expenditure absorbed by imports. In Table 68 the results of this calculation for Scotland are presented along with the corresponding figures for a number of countries broadly comparable both in population and national income per head.

The conclusion to be drawn from Table 68 is that of the six countries included in it, Scotland is one of the least dependent on international trade. This conclusion ceases to apply, however, if we add Scottish imports to, and exports from, the rest of the United Kingdom, which have been omitted from the figures in Table 68. Moreover, the conventional measure of dependence on foreign trade is not altogether satisfactory; for example, a large proportion of exports may consist of imported goods, slightly worked up, and on which, therefore, few workers are employed. Nevertheless, the figures provide a salutory reminder that a high degree of dependence on other countries is common to *all* the countries listed and in no way a peculiarity of Scotland.

It would be interesting to pursue this analysis and show how the aggregate income derived from exports is distributed within the economy, both by area and by industry. Because of the difficulties involved, all that can be attempted here is a study of the distribution of industrial employment arising from exports. Such employment will, however, be highly correlated with the corresponding income, so that what is said below applies broadly to the flow of income as well as to the distribution of employment.

Table 68. *Foreign trade in relation to national income,*
and international comparison, 1948

Country	Population (thousands)	National income (£ m.)	Imports (c.i.f.) (£ m.)	Exports (f.o.b.) (£ m.)	Imports ÷ national income (percentage)	Exports ÷ national income (percentage)
Scotland	5,201	950	190	150	20	16
Australia	7,710	1,510	311	326	21	22
Denmark	4,190	810	177	141	22	17
New Zealand	1,840	360	112	123	31	34
Sweden	6,883	1,510	342	275	23	18
Switzerland	4,609	1,050	289	198	28	19

SOURCE: Calculated from figures given in *National Incomes, 1938–48* (United Nations, New York) and *International Financial Statistics*, vol. V, no. 1, 1952. For estimate of Scotland's national income, see p. 50.

The direct and indirect employment derived from overseas demand may be estimated for 1948 at about 300,000, or just under 15 % of Scotland's occupied population. Most of this employment is in industry, including agriculture and mining, but the contribution of transport, distributive and other services (which is frequently overlooked) is by no means negligible. It is too readily assumed that a country's competitive position in foreign markets rests exclusively on the productivity of its manufacturing industries, whereas in fact the efficiency of its service trades—particularly in a country engaged in processing imported materials—is of at least comparable importance.

In 1948, about 10 % of employment in primary production, distributed unevenly between agriculture, forestry, fishing and mining, was in goods for export. In coal-mining, where employment is usually highly sensitive to export requirements, the proportion in 1948 was just under 20 %, taking account not only of direct exports but also of coal used in the export industries; this proportion, however, was abnormally low in relation to pre-war experience. By contrast, only some 3 % of agricultural output entered directly or indirectly into exports, the output from Scottish farms being destined

141

almost entirely for final utilization within the United Kingdom; the only important channels through which external demand impinges on employment are the distilling of whisky and the export of wool and wool textiles. In fishing, about 9 % of the effective employment can be attributed to exports. The proportion of the herring catch exported is much higher; in 1935, two-thirds of the aggregate landings of 3 m. cwt. were exported, while in 1948, as a result of the difficulties of trading with traditional markets on the Continent, exports had declined to about one-third of a substantially unchanged total catch. This provides a notable illustration of the offsetting of a decline in foreign demand by the offer of a guaranteed market at home, the surplus catch being purchased at a fixed, lower price and converted into herring meal and oil.

Scotland's primary industries appear to be rather more dependent on overseas demand than the corresponding industries in the rest of the United Kingdom. Moreover, employment in these industries constitutes a larger proportion of total employment in Scotland than in the rest of the United Kingdom. Employment based on exports of primary produce must also, therefore, have been relatively more important in Scotland. The reverse is true of manufactures. Here the proportion employed on export work shows a smaller divergence from the United Kingdom average in one direction than the proportion for primary production shows in the other direction. Taking exports as a whole, it appears that whereas 15 % of Scottish workers are dependent on export markets, the proportion in the rest of the United Kingdom is somewhat higher.

Some light is thrown on the divergence in industrial employment on exports by the 'L' returns formerly collected by the Ministry of Labour and National Service. These returns showed, for each firm employing more than ten workers, the proportion of workers believed to be engaged on export work. As is well-known, the 'L' returns are liable to be highly misleading: the small firms excluded rarely make for export; firms making components or on sub-contract, or for merchants, may not know the ultimate destination of their products; and the percentages quoted are necessarily averages for a group of firms that may not fall neatly into a single industrial category. Nevertheless, for broad groups of industry, such as the various orders of the Standard Industrial Classification, the results are not without interest and point to some features of the Scottish economy that are very much at variance with general belief.

The Ministry of Labour statistics have been analysed in Table 69 to show the proportion of total employment derived from exports in each group of industries, and the percentage contribution, as measured by this employment, to total exports. Figures are given both for Scotland and Great Britain.

Apart from the food, drink and tobacco trades, each industrial category in Table 69 shows a lower dependence on exports for Scotland than for Great

Britain. This is a surprising result. In the immediate pre-war period (excluding perhaps the concentrated depression of the 1930's) there is little doubt that the Scottish economy contributed rather more than 10 % of the total of exports from the United Kingdom. In the post-war period, on the other hand, at least up to the year 1948, this proportion has been substantially lower; in that year, as we have seen, the figure was probably about 9·5 %. How can this performance be explained, particularly in view of the relative rise in Scotland's

Table 69. *Distribution of employment in manufacturing industry based on overseas exports, in Scotland and in Great Britain*, 1948

Standard Industrial Classification Order	Scotland			Great Britain		
	Employment (thousands)	Percentage based on exports	Percentage of total employment on exports in secondary industry	Employment in manufacturing industry (thousands)	Percentage based on exports	Percentage of total employment on exports in manufacturing industry
3. Treatment of non-metalliferous mining products other than coal	21·1	18·8	1·9	307·0	27·0	3·5
4. Chemicals and allied trades	33·8	18·7	3·0	439·5	22·0	4·1
5. Metal manufacture	63·8	33·0	10·0	519·8	36·0	8·1
6. Engineering, shipbuilding and electrical goods	195·3	38·1	35·4	1,812·9	39·3	30·4
7. Vehicles	57·1	14·9	4·0	888·2	26·7	10·1
8. Metal goods not included elsewhere	30·3	32·5	4·7	502·7	41·2	8·8
9. Precision instruments, jewellery, etc.	7·2	36·2	1·2	126·6	45·2	2·4
10. Textiles	113·1	43·0	23·4	927·7	45·0	18·1
11. Leather, leather goods and fur	5·3	23·7	0·6	77·9	27·5	0·9
12. Clothing	34·6	6·6	1·1	588·8	9·7	2·4
13. Food, drink and tobacco	91·5	11·9	5·2	692·4	5·4	1·6
14. Manufactures of wood and cork	29·4	14·3	20·0	265·7	16·7	1·9
15. Paper and printing	50·0	19·9	4·7	462·7	21·1	4·2
16. Other manufacturing industries	19·6	30·9	2·9	241·2	31·8	3·3
All manufacturing	752·1	28·0	100·0	7,853·1	29·8	100·0

SOURCE: Ministry of Labour and National Service.

143

occupied population consequent on the virtually complete absorption of the pre-war excess of unemployment?

The main explanation lies in the growth of new types of exports since the war, notably motor-cars, aircraft and electrical goods. These exports have come from industries which developed rapidly before the war but did not at that time make more than a modest contribution to exports. In response primarily to market considerations, these industries tended to cluster in the Midlands and Southern England and it was in that area that new industrial development—both in consumer and capital goods—was predominantly concentrated. Much of this development throve on the protection afforded in the home market by the tariff system established during the inter-war period, with the result that there was little inducement to enter the export market. It has only been since the war that this reservoir of potential export capacity, nearly all located south of the Border and much of it devoted to the production of durable consumer goods, has been drawn upon.

There was no similar margin in hand in Scotland except in the established industries: no new Scottish industry has emerged since the war as a major exporter. Some existing Scottish industries had sufficient capacity to spare to make a large addition to exports; some, like whisky, were able to starve the home market; but the type of industry represented by motor-cars, on which fell the main burden of the export drive, had not developed in Scotland.

It is possible that this trend has been reinforced by a differential movement in productivity. Whatever may have been true in manufacturing industry, there has undoubtedly been a serious loss of ground in the Scottish coal-mining industry,[1] so much so that had productivity moved in parallel with the United Kingdom average, the additional coal available for export from Scotland would have made an appreciable contribution to the maintenance of the pre-war status of Scotland as an exporter.

The variability of Scottish exports

Despite the expansion in exports since the war, Scotland is thus slightly less dependent on export markets than the United Kingdom as a whole and than a number of other countries of comparable size. This lesser degree of dependence, however, might still leave Scotland more sensitive to the play of world markets since, within the total for exports, there might be some that were peculiarly liable to fluctuate, or there might be an unduly narrow range and variety of products or of markets.

The degree of specialization, the first measurable characteristic, is shown in Table 70, which gives the share of the three largest commodity groups in total exports and compares the figures for Scotland with those for the five other

[1] See pp. 115–16.

countries already cited. It is clear from the table that the degree of specialization of Scottish exports is relatively weak, the three leading items adding up to 50 %, compared with over 60 % for all the other countries except Denmark. Scotland shows a rather higher degree of specialization than the rest of the United Kingdom, because of the high contribution of whisky to the total but, as whisky is a relatively stable export,[1] the difference does not imply a greater liability to fluctuation.

Table 70. *International comparison of the degree of*
specialization of Scotland's exports, 1948

Country	Percentages of leading commodities						Three leading exports as percentage of total
	(I)		(II)		(III)		
Scotland	Textiles	23	Machinery	16	Whisky	11	50
Australia	Wool	37	Wheat and flour	21	Dairy produce	8	66
Denmark	Dairy produce	37	Meat	12	Machinery	9	58
New Zealand	Dairy produce	32	Wool	31	Meat	20	83
Sweden	Wood and pulp	36	Paper	15	Machinery	12	63
Switzerland	Machinery	28	Watches and clocks	22	Textiles	12	62

SOURCE: *Year Book of International Trade Statistics*
(United Nations, New York, 1951).

As this example shows, the risk of fluctuations in employment and national income as a result of dependence on export markets is not necessarily correlated with the degree of specialization within the export total. A more important factor is the type of commodity in which the country specializes. If world income fluctuates, the amplitude of the corresponding fluctuation in demand is greater for producer goods than for durable consumer goods and greater for these in turn than for goods for immediate consumption, such as foodstuffs. From this point of view Scotland probably emerges unfavourably from the comparison with the other countries listed in Table 70. But fluctuations in the *quantity* demanded do not tell the whole story; account must be

[1] In 1937–38 and again in 1948–49, when total imports into the United States slumped—the United States being by far the largest export market for Scotch whisky—imports of whisky fell in value by about 1 % only.

taken of the reaction in supply and in the *value* of exports. The peculiarities of the supply position virtually reverse the situation; the supply of foodstuffs does not contract readily when demand falls and the *price*, therefore, drops heavily while the price of engineering products and other manufactures remains relatively steady. Scotland may suffer relatively severe variations in employment derived from exports, but her standard of living may still remain the more stable.

The scope and pattern of Britain's export trade has changed greatly since pre-war years, both because of the increase of some two-thirds in the volume of exports and as a result of the shift within the total from textiles and coal to machinery and vehicles. Scotland has shared the broad impact of this adjustment without being so deeply affected. The greater dependence on export markets that has resulted is not without its dangers to the stability of the economy, but nothing is to be gained by attempts to reduce this 'vulnerability' to precise statistical measurement. Total exports are no higher in relation to national income than in many other countries; and there is no way of settling *a priori* whether the dependence on foreign markets implied in this total would be reduced by a change in its composition. Experience suggests that the producer goods which figure so prominently in Scotland's exports are liable to severe fluctuation. But in the post-war years it has been consumer goods that have been most unstable, and if the industrial development of countries overseas continues at its present pace, capital goods may remain in firm demand. Whatever the danger that Scotland's exports may encounter a temporary failure of overseas demand, the greater danger may yet prove to be that they consist too largely of goods for which the demand has ceased to grow, and too little of the goods that are in increasing demand or which other countries have still to learn to make for themselves. In the final analysis, the adjustment of the Scottish economy to take advantage of world trends, rather than its insulation from hypothetical international fluctuations, is likely to constitute Scotland's primary economic problem in the future.

NOTE ON THE ESTIMATES OF SCOTLAND'S OVERSEAS IMPORTS AND EXPORTS PRESENTED IN TABLE 64

Imports

These have been divided for the purpose of estimation into two categories: imports for household consumption such as meat and dairy produce; and imports partly or entirely consumed by industry or subjected to processing before final utilization. Estimates of these imports in the first category rest essentially on the findings of two family budget inquiries undertaken in 1937–38 and 1949 by the Ministry of Labour and the Ministry of Food respectively. These inquiries suggest that with some exceptions the general pattern of consumption of imported produce in Scotland does not differ substantially from the pattern in the rest of the United Kingdom. (It would seem, however, that the overall consumption of imported foodstuffs in 1948 was of the order of 10 per cent. lower than a *per capita* estimate from United Kingdom figures would indicate.)

The estimation of imports in the second category is based on the fact that for the year 1948 such imports are in general recorded—implicitly or explicitly—in the statements of raw materials absorbed by specific industries which appear in the *Final Reports* of the 1948 Census of Production. In the few cases where these statements are not inclusive of all the relevant imports, or where there was difficulty in differentiating between imported and home-produced materials, independent information was usually available to provide a satisfactory solution.

The general procedure may be illustrated by the simple example of one important commodity—wheat. In 1948, official statistics show that imports of wheat into Great Britain amounted to 4,090 thousand tons; for the same year, the Census of Production records the milling of 4,086 thousand tons. After making a small adjustment for the reduction in stocks which took place, it appears that practically all of the wheat imported was absorbed by the grain milling trade. The corresponding quantity of imported wheat milled in Scotland is recorded as 415 thousand tons. As this figure more or less coincides with the quantity entering through Scottish ports (412 thousand tons) the value of these direct imports was taken as the true figure of Scotland's imports of wheat from overseas during 1948.

Exports

Estimates of Scottish exports were derived primarily from the following sources: (i) statistics of industrial employment on work for export, collected by the Ministry of Labour and National Service and supplied privately to the writer; (ii) information independently computed and published by trade associations and similar organizations; (iii) official statistics of exports through Scottish ports; and (iv) the *Final Report* of the 1948 Census of Production. These four sources will be briefly commented on in order of their importance.

The Ministry of Labour ('L') returns refer to both the direct and indirect dependence of employment on work for export. In general, therefore, we are restricted in the estimation of direct exports to those trades or industries where the indirect contribution is negligible. The principal category of exports estimated in this manner was textiles; the procedure being to apply the given employment percentage to the value of the corresponding output recorded in the Census of Production. Adjustments were made where possible to ensure on the one hand comparability of employment and output, and on the other consistency of the corresponding estimates of exports for the United Kingdom with the total officially recorded.

Published estimates of the exports of particular products or industries compiled by trade associations, etc., account for a substantial part of the total. For example, such estimates are readily available for Scottish exports of linoleum, carpets, lace, jute manufactures, sugar-making machinery and preserved fish. In a few instances, the most important being the export of whisky, exports from the United Kingdom and from Scotland practically coincide.

Official statistics of exports through Scottish ports were utilized without adjustment only in the case of coal and of newly-built ships. They were, however, also used to determine a small residual category, not amenable to other methods of estimation, by the addition of an independently calculated component to the Scottish port figures, in order to make an approximate allowance for shipment through English ports.

In the case of a few commodities, principally where an excise duty is levied on home consumption, separate statistics of sales for export are recorded in the *Final Report* of the 1948 Census of Production. The most important examples included here are beer and refined sugar, neither of which, however, is a large item in the total. The Census of Production, while indirectly very useful, is of limited direct value as a source of information on Scottish exports overseas.

CHAPTER 11

WAGES

By D. J. ROBERTSON

The term 'wages', while it is familiar to us all, is subject to several ambiguities. First, 'wages' is both the all-inclusive term for employees' earnings, and the particular designation, in contrast to 'salaries', for the earnings of those who work with their hands or are paid by the week.[1] Further, within 'wages' there are wage rates and earnings. 'The wage rate' is commonly intended to mean standard or minimum rates which are negotiated or fixed for broad categories of workers, generally for an agreed length of working time. Earnings include the 'wage rate' and all other additional payments: special rates of one kind or another, piecework payments, bonus payments, overtime, etc. These complex meanings of the word must be borne in mind in any study of wages.

A study of wages also faces the difficulty of interpreting information on wages for Great Britain as a whole. There are wage rate indices, the composition of which is designed to give a 'representative' picture of the change in wage levels. But such indices inevitably are composed of national averages for principal occupations in principal industries only (or sometimes of minima for whole industries). Beyond the few well-documented industries, there stretches an almost boundless number of wage groups distinguished by sex, by occupation, by industry, by region and by age—and the task of recording wage changes for all of them takes on the quality of a nightmare.

Material on Scotland is largely lacking. No official data on weekly earnings by industry for Scotland (or, indeed, for any other part of Great Britain) have appeared since 1906. Information on wage rates, too, is frequently either too simple to be true or too complex to be easily studied. As a result, this study must be regarded as exploratory and productive of hypotheses which later information may find to be wrong. There is enough evidence however to justify the view that a systematic collection of Scottish data on wage rates and earnings is well overdue. Official attempts to fill the gap would be most welcome and timely.

[1] The difficulty of defining the wage-earner precisely illustrates the type of ambiguity that arises. It is not strictly true that a wage is necessarily paid weekly—or that a salary is invariably paid at a different interval; nevertheless, this common distinction probably gives the right sort of mental subdivision. The main purpose here is to provide only a rough picture of the different categories rather than to give an exact division. Wages generally are more liable to fluctuation and uncertainty than salaries, which are more fixed, regular and certain in their payment. In industry, wages are generally considered as direct costs of production, while salaries are usually regarded as forming part of overhead costs. A frequent division is that between operatives on the one hand and administrative, clerical and technical staff on the other.

WAGE RATES

As a result principally of the growing power of the trade unions, there has been a marked increase in the number of nationally negotiated wage rates during the last fifty years. This tendency has been accentuated by the more recent growth in the number of Wages Councils, replacing and supplementing the old Trade Boards. It is not therefore to be expected that there will be much divergence between Scottish and United Kingdom wage rates—or at least those rates that are commonly quoted in wage rate indices and the like. The custom of fixing higher wage rates for London, is of course, fairly general throughout industry; but, taking account of the exceptions discussed below, this is not inconsistent with the view that Scottish wage rates in each industry and occupation do not differ substantially from those for Great Britain as a whole.

This is confirmed by a study of the industries making up the *Ministry of Labour Gazette* wage rate index.[1] If those industries not located in Scotland are excluded and the London differential disregarded, there are twenty-one industries out of a total of seventy-four where rates differ for Scotland. Of these twenty-one, the differences in two cases are due to different, but frequently overlapping, graded area schemes which prescribe different rates for different series of towns within each country; in three cases the published rates are higher in Scotland; in three cases they appear to be lower; and in five cases the differences are known to be of little importance. Among the twenty-one there are also some important industries where there are no national rates. These are the iron and steel group (where most prices are fixed locally, and in accordance with varying local conditions and equipment, though national sliding scales may be superimposed and all steelworkers have a national cost of living allowance) and cotton, wool, and hosiery and knitwear (where piecework is prevalent and time rates tend to be local). In the printing trades there are separate agreements for London, England and Wales, and Scotland; and, while the rates for London are higher than elsewhere, those for Scotland and the rest of England and Wales are much the same.

In the past, however, and especially prior to 1914, wage rates tended to be widely divergent and locally negotiated. The comparative levels of Scottish wage rates before they came to uniformity with those for the rest of the United Kingdom are not therefore very clear. The Wage Census conducted by the

---

[1] The industries contained in the index are given in the *Gazette* for February, 1948. Wage rates were obtained with the help of the Ministry of Labour's *Time Rates of Wages and Hours of Labour* series. In each industry the rates which are principally negotiated (whether standard or minimum—and for appropriate occupational groups and standard periods of work) were then considered in the comparison of Scotland and the rest of the United Kingdom. The Ministry regard their index as 'based on the recognized rates of wages fixed by collective agreements or statutory orders'.

Board of Trade Labour Department in 1886, reporting on a mixture of wage rates and earnings data, showed the wages of Scottish industrial workers to be generally lower than the average for the United Kingdom. To take some examples, the annual amounts paid per head in wages were lower on the average in Scotland in pig-iron manufacture, shipbuilding, brass work, saw-milling, boot and shoe manufacture, brewing, printing, bespoke tailoring, dressmaking and railway work—though the differences were not on the whole very great. Inspection of the *Time Rates of Wages* series for the beginning of the century shows that while wage rates differed regionally, the level in the industrial belt of Scotland was generally much the same as in industrial England. Wage rates were, however, only fixed for a small number of skilled occupations, so that in industries without strong trade unions and amongst unskilled workers wide differences must have persisted.

The first world war tended to lessen regional diversity. During its early stages increases in incomes were probably due principally to changes in earnings but later several factors operated on regional wage rates.[1] Very many of the increases in wage rates took the form of flat-rate changes for large areas or for all working in the same industry throughout the country. These reduced the importance of local differences relative to the total amount. The growth of munitions work and war-time controls combined to increase government intervention in the wage structure—and such intervention was not greatly concerned to preserve regional differences. Then, too, the war brought about an increase in the trade union organization of the workers—and a likelihood of consequent regularization of wage rates. The process of regularization was not complete by 1920, but continued between the wars, and national rates became increasingly common. Similar factors operating in the second world war served to complete the process in the organized industries while the Wages Councils have now ensured regularity of wage minima at least in the previously badly-organized industries.[2]

The regional differences in wage rates within Scotland have also largely diminished and disappeared. In 1900 the relationship of the four cities was clear. Glasgow and Edinburgh usually had the highest rates and, in heavy industries at least, Glasgow tended to have higher rates than Edinburgh. Dundee followed fairly closely behind these two and sometimes had the same rates; while those in Aberdeen tended to be rather lower. Agricultural wages (discussed more fully in a later section) suggest that wage rates outside the four cities followed roughly the same geographical pattern, being highest in the midland industrial belt and declining towards the north and away from the largest centres of population.

[1] Cf. A. L. Bowley, *Prices and Wages in the United Kingdom, 1914–1920* (Oxford, 1921).
[2] There is, however, some evidence of a tendency, where separate Wages Councils have been established for Scotland and England and Wales, for the former to fix slightly lower rates.

EARNINGS

The last inquiry into the average weekly earnings of workers in the various industry groups in Scotland was in 1906. It is not possible, therefore, to compare earnings then and now directly, or to provide much information, other than for a few industries, about the intervening period. In recent years, however, a quantity of evidence has appeared, especially on annual incomes in Scotland and the United Kingdom, and this will serve to indicate the present position as regards earnings.[1]

Table 71. *Average weekly earnings of men and women in a number of industries in the United Kingdom and in Scotland*, 1906

Trade groups	Men (over 21)		Women (over 18)	
	United Kingdom	Scotland	United Kingdom	Scotland
	s. d.	*s. d.*	*s. d.*	*s. d.*
Iron and steel manufacture	35 4	36 11	—	—
Engineering and boilermaking	31 11	31 3	12 6	14 7½
Shipbuilding	32 10	32 11	14 5	13 0
Wool and worsted*	25 11	25 7	13 4	15 0
Hosiery*	30 1	27 5	13 11	14 3
Carpets*	25 4	26 11	12 11	13 10
Textile finishing	26 5	25 4	11 11	9 7
Tailoring*	29 11	27 8½	12 9	13 8½
Dress, millinery, etc.*	34 11½	32 8	13 7	13 9
Grain milling	23 11	25 9	9 9	9 11
Baking and confectionery	28 10	30 10	12 6	13 6
Saw milling and cabinet-making trades	29 4½	27 8	12 5	12 7½
Printing	36 4	34 4	11 11	11 11
Building	31 6	32 0	—	—
Gas, electricity and water	30 7	29 6	—	—
Railways	26 8	21 11	—	—
Tramways and omnibus services	29 0	27 4	—	—

* The majority of the employees in these groups were women.

SOURCE: Board of Trade Earnings Enquiry, 1906.

[1] The 1906 Enquiry provided data on regional earnings within Scotland for some industries, but there is no recent information on this aspect and it has therefore been disregarded.

Average weekly earnings of men and women wage-earners in Scotland and in the United Kingdom in 1906 are given for a number of industries in Table 71.[1]

The impression gained from Table 71 accords fairly well with our background knowledge. The basic industries were still developing in Scotland at this time—and earnings were high and up to the United Kingdom average. In some other industries, however, men's earnings tended to be rather lower in Scotland. Women's earnings were higher in Scotland in almost every case shown. The iron and steel industry had high earnings for men, and so had the building and shipbuilding industries, while earnings in engineering were fairly close to the United Kingdom average. The textile and clothing industries were paying higher wages to women than the average. The lower average figure for printing was probably due to the higher London earnings incorporated in the United Kingdom average. While baking and associated trades had higher than average earnings, the service industries had lower averages than those for the United Kingdom. If we assume, on the evidence of the 1886 Wage Census, that earnings were then rather lower in Scotland, it seems safe to conclude that the prosperity of the basic industries had tended to bring the general earnings level in Scotland up to and above the United Kingdom average by 1906, although the slower powers of adjustment of the service occupations had prevented them from taking advantage of the change.

For the most recent years the main source of information is the *Ninety-Fourth Report of the Commissioners of Inland Revenue* (for the year ended 31 March 1951), which contains the first-fruits of an Income Census conducted by a sampling method for the income-tax year 1949/50.[2] The main object of this census was to bring together, into a series of tables of distribution of income, the total incomes of individuals assessed under various schedules. The number of cases and the total amounts of income assessed within each range of net income[3] are given for the United Kingdom and its four constituent countries and for each sex and marital state. Further, the tables show the contribution made to the total net incomes by the various forms of income

[1] The selection of industries for this table presented some problems. There were some where there were no regional figures. The principle underlying the selection of the others was mainly that as many different types of industries as possible should be shown—and only those fairly well represented inside and outside Scotland, and without a large concentration in Ireland which could confuse the result. While the picture is not therefore complete it is thought that the industries shown give a fair representation of it.

[2] Two complications beset many of the following figures. First, in general, Scotland has about the same proportion of females in the occupied population as Great Britain as a whole but tends to have a slightly higher proportion of females in a given industry. Secondly, the proportion of juveniles in employment is generally slightly higher in Scotland (cf. C. E. V. Leser, *Some Aspects of the Industrial Structure of Scotland* (Glasgow, 1952)). It is impossible to measure the precise effect of these complications where they occur but it is fairly certain that they do not contradict any of the conclusions drawn.

[3] I.e. Total gross income before taxation from earned income, investment income, etc.— less expenses. The census did not include net incomes of under £135 per annum.

—e.g. earned income, income from property, etc. Table 72 gives the average net income per person (obtained by dividing the total amount of income assessed by the total number of cases) for persons of each sex in each of the countries.[1] Since the total income from each source and the total number of cases in each country are also given, average annual earned income from wages and salaries is also shown.[2]

Table 72. *Average annual earnings of wage- and salary-earners and average net incomes in the countries of the United Kingdom, 1949/50*

| Country | Average earnings of wage- and salary-earners | | | | Average net income (£) |
| | All persons* (£) | Males† (£) | Females ‡ | | |
			Single women (£)	All women (£)	
Scotland	317·7	352·8	227·0	212·1	380·5
England	332·2	378·1	229·1	209·0	402·6
Wales	324·5	348·6	224·0	209·9	358·8
Northern Ireland	295·8	328·1	212·2	200·3	347·6
United Kingdom	330·0	373·5	228·5	209·1	398·1

* Earnings include income from principal employment of all wage- or salary-earners, including the earnings of married women.
† Earnings from principal employment.
‡ Earnings from principal employment of single women and widows and the earnings of married women. (Women in part-time employment earning over £135 per annum are, of course, included.)

SOURCE: *Ninety-Fourth Report of Commissioners of Inland Revenue, 1952.*

Table 72 shows that average net income in Scotland, while higher than that for Wales and Northern Ireland, was lower in 1949/50 than the average for England and for the United Kingdom as a whole. More important for our purpose, average annual earnings of employees, in Scotland were not as high as those in England for 'all persons' or for males (average earnings of males in 1949/50 in Scotland were 94 % of earnings in the United Kingdom). The average annual earnings of females in Scotland, on the other hand, were higher

[1] Income was allocated to each country according to the place of principal assessment. This means usually the place of residence and of work—so that earned income is likely to be correctly allocated from our point of view.
[2] Annual earnings data, it should be remembered, serve different purposes from weekly earnings figures—and are not a substitute. Annual figures include periods of holiday and sickness and also are affected by the changing composition of the labour force—making 'average' numbers of employees covered the best that can be given. Also, from the worker's point of view a year is a long time and can cover many changes in his circumstances.

than those for England if earnings of married women[1] are included and only slightly lower if single women only are considered—and earnings of women in Wales and Northern Ireland were similarly closer to the general average. This is somewhat puzzling: it may be, however, that the industrial structure of England is slightly more favourable to women's work than that of the other countries[2] and this may have produced a higher proportion of part-time women workers in England. The rather greater general shortage of labour in England at this time may also have resulted in greater use being made of part-time workers.

The different average levels of net incomes and of wage and salary earnings[3] in the United Kingdom and Scotland could, of course, imply very considerable differences in their distributions of income. It is only possible, however, to provide directly a percentage distribution of incomes for total net incomes (including investment income, property income, etc.), since it is on this basis that the Income Census compiles its distribution. The first two columns of Table 73 show such a percentage distribution of individuals in various ranges of net income for the United Kingdom and Scotland. The last two columns show how much of the total income falling within each range of net income is due to wages and salaries.

The first two columns of Table 73 make it clear that the lower level of average net income in Scotland in 1949/50 was not due to a substantially different type of income distribution pattern in Scotland. Both show similar 'humps' in the lower ranges and 'tails' towards the upper incomes. A larger proportion of Scottish net income appears in the lower ranges, however, and there is a more pronounced 'hump', while the 'tail' shows lower percentages of total numbers than for the United Kingdom at each level. The last columns help to indicate the contribution of wages and salaries to this result. Up to the £450 level, the proportion of the total amount of income in each range contributed by wages and salaries is higher for Scotland than for the United Kingdom, while beyond that level the proportion is lower. Incomes from wages and salaries, therefore, appear to have acted to increase the relative concentration of Scottish net incomes in the lower ranges while reducing the

[1] The Income Census did not, however, cover all cases of married women in paid employment—as given by the insurance records—and this may affect the results given for women's earnings.

[2] Cf. C. E. V. Leser, *Some Aspects of the Industrial Structure of Scotland.*

[3] It is unfortunately not possible to separate wage- and salary-earners at this point. It may be deduced from the *One Per Cent Sample Tables* in the 1951 Census, that in Scotland almost the same proportion of the occupied population were engaged in professional and technical occupations, and in commercial, financial and insurance occupations as in England and Wales; but the proportion in the clerical and typist group was lower, and also the proportion classified as administrators, directors and managers. If all these groups are taken together, the proportion in Scotland is lower than in England and Wales. This may be taken, with considerable caution, as indicating a slightly lower proportion of salaried workers in Scotland.

proportions coming within the higher ranges. Scottish wage and salary payments seem to be concentrated around a lower modal level and to have less upward spread. Further, the £200–249, £250–299, and £300–349 groups in 1949/50 would cover, for most industries, fifty-two payments of the current minimum or standard wage rates for the principal occupations—and the heavier concentration of Scottish net incomes in these groups suggests the possibility that in Scotland there were relatively fewer opportunities to supplement such wage rates by additional payments than there were in the United Kingdom as a whole. The smaller number of incomes in the upper income groups in Scotland may be regarded as offering confirmation of the idea that there are proportionately more large salary earners in England and Wales than in Scotland. The presumption that there is a large concentration of persons in the high salary ranges around the London area seems to be borne out by this table. If the 'all persons' table shown here is split up, and the categories of single males and females (which are less complex than the married group) are studied separately the general results are similar.

It will, of course, spring readily to mind that the simple explanation of the different levels in England shown by Tables 72 and 73 is the prevalence of higher wage rates and earnings in London. The Income Census does not give data for the administrative regions of England; but the Inland Revenue *Reports* contain data on the total remuneration and average number of

Table 73. *Distribution of net personal incomes before tax, in the United Kingdom and in Scotland, 1949/50*

Range of net income	Number of incomes in each income group as percentage of total number of incomes		Percentage of total net income in each income group due to wages and salaries (principal employment and wife's earnings)	
	United Kingdom	Scotland	United Kingdom	Scotland
£135–199	18·3	19·0	89·2	94·3
£200–249	14·3	15·2	90·8	94·9
£250–299	15·4	17·4	94·4	99·7
£300–349	13·0	13·9	95·0	97·1
£350–399	10·4	10·0	93·7	94·6
£400–449	7·6	6·9	92·2	93·2
£450–499	5·4	4·8	90·7	90·4
£500–599	6·3	5·0	88·0	85·1
£600–799	4·6	3·4	78·9	72·3
£800–999	1·5	1·2	62·6	53·0
£1,000 and over	3·3	3·1	33·2	24·3
All ranges	100	100	78·8	78·4

SOURCE: *Ninety-Fourth Report of the Commissioners of Inland Revenue, 1952.*

employees subject to Pay As You Earn taxation in the regions of England as well as in the four countries. This material, while not so accurate as the Income Census, allows us to compare the average annual remuneration per head in the regions of England with the corresponding average for Scotland. The Scottish average taken from the 1950/51 *Report* is lower than that for any of the English regions.[1] The lower Scottish average cannot therefore be entirely due to the effects of specially high earnings in some regions of England in raising the English average. The accuracy of this result may be judged by the fact that, if the averages for the four countries are taken from the same source, a pattern similar to that shown in Table 72 and derived from the Income Census is shown.

The conclusion to which this survey of the Income Census leads is that in 1949/50 wages and salaries in Scotland (and also net incomes from all sources) tended to be lower than those for the United Kingdom. This could arise either because the present distribution of industry gives Scotland less well-paying industries or because the earnings of Scottish workers within each industry tend to be less. The extent to which the income level of wage-earners in Scotland is affected by the distribution of industry may be tested if we assume that earnings in each industry are the same in Scotland as in the United Kingdom and at the same time study the effect on the averages for all the industries together produced by taking into account the different distribution of workers between the various industries in Scotland from that for the United Kingdom. This involves 'weighting' Ministry of Labour earnings figures in each industry by employment in Scotland in that industry to produce a 'weighted average' for Scotland. This is done for April 1951 in Table 74, for manufacturing industries only. It is evident that the present distribution of manufacturing industry is likely to lead to slightly lower average wage earnings for Scottish operatives. At the same time, the smallness of the differences shown by Table 74 (1·4 % for men and 1·8 % for women), in comparison with differences in average incomes in Scotland and England shown in other parts of this chapter, strongly suggests that a difference in industrial structure is not the only cause of lower earnings, and that differences within the same industry can be expected.

It now remains to discover directly whether within each industry the average payment is lower in Scotland than in the United Kingdom as a whole. Two sources assist in this. First, the Census of Production for 1948 produced by the Board of Trade, and secondly, Inland Revenue P.A.Y.E. statistics.

The Census of Production gives for the majority of industries separate figures for Scotland and Great Britain of average employment of operatives and the total amounts paid to operatives in 1948; and also gives an estimate

[1] It is interesting to note that on this evidence the figure for the London region is not in fact the highest of the regional figures.

Table 74. *Average weekly earnings in manufacturing industry in April* 1951

	United Kingdom (as given in the *Ministry of Labour Gazette*)*	Scotland (U.K. earnings weighted by Scottish employment)†
Men (21+)	165s.	162s. 8½d.
Women (18+)	87s. 11d.	86s. 4½d.

* I.e. Weighted by total numbers employed in United Kingdom in April, 1951.

† I.e. The *Ministry of Labour Gazette* figures of earnings for each industry weighted by the estimated numbers of employees in Scotland aged 15+ in each industry at end May, 1950 (from *Tables relating to employment and unemployment*).

of employment of administrative, clerical and technical personnel and the total amount paid to them in 1948. It is thus possible to discover from it the relative level of average annual payments to wage- and salary-earners separately in Scotland and Great Britain. The final reports distinguish 156 separate industries, each of which has appeared in a separate volume. Out of these 156 reports, 34 do not analyse the countries separately,[1] so that 122 reports contain the data required. For operatives, 99 industries have higher average annual payments for Great Britain than for Scotland; 22 have lower, and in one case the averages are the same. For salaried workers, 94 have higher averages; 26 have lower; and in two cases the averages are the same. On this evidence the conclusion that annual earnings within industries tend to be lower for Scotland than for Great Britain seems fully justified. The average remuneration per head of wage-earners in 1948 for 122 industries was £299 in Great Britain and £284 (or 95%) in Scotland; and in the case of salaried workers the average was £428 in Great Britain and £404 (or 94%) in Scotland. The results for all industries for which there are both Scottish and British figures are subdivided into broad industry groups in Table 75.

The Inland Revenue report contains a distribution, by industries for the United Kingdom, of the total amounts of pay assessed for P.A.Y.E. taxation (i.e. the total payment of wages and salaries to employees) and of the amounts of tax deducted. A similar distribution has been obtained for Scotland through the courtesy of the Board of Inland Revenue. If the tax collected in each industry is expressed as a percentage of total remuneration in that industry, then the percentage of total payment taken back in tax is lower in

[1] Details of some industries for Scotland are excluded on grounds of 'disclosure of information' relating to particular establishments. The industries for which Scottish figures are not given vary in importance and size, but usually the number of persons involved in them in Scotland is small.

Table 75. *Average annual payments of wages and salaries in* 1948, *in Scotland and in Great Britain, by industry groups*

Industry group	Average annual wage		Average annual salary	
	Scotland (£)	Great Britain (£)	Scotland (£)	Great Britain (£)
Mining, quarrying and non-metal mining products	377	365	449	453
Chemicals and allied trades	292	299	465	467
Metal manufacture	341	357	417	441
Engineering, shipbuilding and electrical goods	311	312	391	410
Vehicles, etc.	323	347	365	418
Other metal trades	262	275	418	368
Textiles, leather and clothing	192	230	435	505
Food and drink	242	260	355	411
Other manufacturing industries	258	282	424	487
Other industries giving Scottish data	266	280	380	367
All industries giving Scottish data	284	299	404	428

SOURCE: *Census of Production, 1948.*

Scotland than in the United Kingdom for almost every industry group. The individuals making up the totals for the industries will pay a lesser proportion of their incomes in tax if they have larger allowances or if they have lower incomes. The Income Tax allowances due to Scottish taxpayers for their wives, children and dependants may be deduced from the same report to come to a very slightly higher average amount than that for the United Kingdom. But a proportionately smaller amount of income is due to wives' earnings in Scotland and these are entitled to a further tax allowance. The difference in allowances between Scotland and the United Kingdom as a whole can hardly explain the lower proportion of tax to income, which must therefore be regarded as evidence of lower average earnings within each industry in Scotland.

SOME IMPORTANT INDUSTRIES
Agriculture

While wages in Scottish agriculture were not finally regulated until the Agricultural Wages (Regulation) (Scotland) Act of 1937, there are some estimates available for earlier years. Table 76 sets out information for Scotland and England for a number of years.

Table 76. *Average weekly wages of ploughmen in Scotland, 1898–1950, with indices of changes in wage levels in Scottish and English agriculture.* (1898 = 100)

Year	Scotland		England
	Average weekly wages of ploughmen	Index (1898 = 100)	Index of change in wages of ordinary male labourers (1898 = 100)
	s. d.		
1898	18 1	100	100
1902	19 5	107	104
1907	19 6	108	109
1920 (summer)	53 9	297	278
1923 (summer)	37 3	206	166
1926 (summer)	38 0	210	186
1929 (summer)	37 3	206	188
1932 (summer)	37 0	205	184
1935 (summer)	34 0	188	189
1938 (summer)	38 6	213	—
1946/47 (June–May)	92 2	509	545
1947/48 (June–May)	102 10	570	605
1948/49 (June–May)	108 1	598	622
1949/50 (June–May)	110 10	613	635

SOURCES: Figures used for 1898 and 1902 are from the First and Second Reports of Mr Wilson Fox on *Wages and Earnings of Agricultural Labourers in the United Kingdom* (Cd. 346 (1900), Cd. 2376 (1905)); those for 1907 are from the Board of Trade Earnings Enquiry. From 1920 to 1938 figures for Scotland are estimates made by Sir James Wilson and the Department of Agriculture; those used for England are estimates of rates for England and Wales prepared by the Ministry of Agriculture. Post-war figures for Scotland are from an article in *Farm Economics* (Spring 1950) by R. Bennett Jones and J. Wrigley, and those used for England from an article in *J.R. Statist. Soc.*, 1951 by H. Palca and I. G. R. Davies. Those used for 1898, 1902 and 1907 are for 'all male workers'—others are for ploughmen and ordinary male labourers respectively. All include an estimate of allowance-in-kind.

If we begin by comparing the changes which have occurred in wage levels in Scottish agriculture with those in England, two points stand out. First, there was a fairly regular tendency for Scottish wages to fall from 1925 to 1935, while English wages—which were regulated and had legal minima—remained steady. Secondly, Scottish agricultural earnings have risen along with English in the period since regulation, but not by enough to recover their former relative position. Earnings in agriculture generally were of course low when compared with other industries until recent years, and the increase since 1938 has been high relative to other industries.

Comparison of the actual amounts paid in England and Scotland is subject to two difficulties. First, the Scottish ploughman or 'horseman' is a plough-man who is, or was until the era of the tractor, responsible for stabling and caring for his own horse. The 'general worker' in Scotland was most likely to be an odd-job man (an 'orraman'). The English agricultural labourer is also generally a ploughman but had an associate (a 'horseman') to act as stableman. The agricultural labourer in England therefore has a status rather less than the Scottish ploughman but with a tendency to be superior to the Scottish general worker. Secondly, between 1920 and 1936 the figures available for England as computed by the Ministry of Agriculture probably relate more to the rates laid down by the Agricultural Boards than to the actual earnings, and may underestimate actual earnings in England. The impression that earnings in Scotland were lower in the inter-war years is confirmed by the example given in the *Report of the Committee on Farm Workers in Scotland*[1] that married ploughmen on comparable work earned from 4s. to 7s. more in neighbouring counties on the English side of the Border.

Three conclusions on the relative level of earnings in agriculture in England and Scotland can be suggested. First, average earnings were higher in Scotland before the first war. Secondly, during the inter-war period 'owing to the existence of statutory regulations the worker in England [was] protected from the severe fall in wages which his fellow worker suffered in Scotland'.[2] Thirdly, earnings in Scotland may have fallen below those in England by the middle 1930's but are probably coming towards equality again at present.

With regard to the present position, it is possible to use the figures of post-war earnings of agricultural workers, given in the two articles referred to in the sources to Table 75, to produce general averages of the earnings of agricultural workers in Scotland and England. The average for 1948/9 in Scotland is about 109s. 3d. and that for England is 109s. 10d. This justifies the view that at present earnings in the two countries on average tend to show little difference.

While the actual amount of the money estimate of payment in kind has remained fairly steady, its importance in the total wage has greatly declined. Payment in kind was much more common in Scotland than in England at 1900. The married man had a cottage supplied and with it quantities of food and milk, with possibly grazing rights and coal. Single men lived in the bothy. In the South of England at least this was much less common. Further, the different attitude was reflected in the normal six-monthly hiring fair in Scotland which contrasts with the weekly hiring of labourers in the South.

There were, until recently, considerable differences between the regions of Scotland. In 1907, for example, earnings varied between 14s. 6d. and 21s. 7d., the lower earnings generally containing a higher absolute (and relative) amount of payment in kind. Earnings were lowest in the crofting counties,

[1] Cmd. 5217 (1936).   [2] Ibid.

followed by the North-East coast and the South-West, while the midland belt had the highest. Earnings varied of course in England and Wales too, but to a lesser extent. Northern counties had the highest earnings and those in the South were low. The lowest was Oxford with 16s. 4d. Thus English wages did not fall as low as those in the most northerly crofting counties, but of twenty-three counties of the United Kingdom with averages over 20s. in 1907, sixteen were Scottish and only seven were English (mainly northern).

Wage rates fixed on other than an individual basis are a recent innovation. The Corn Production Act of 1917 to 1921 gave power to fix wage minima, but, except in the northern counties and in the South-West, actual rates were much in excess of minima. The lack of regulation in the inter-war period gave rise to two main evils 'the cases in which extremely low wages were being paid and the wide fluctuations in wages in general even on farms in the same neighbourhood'.[1] The individual fixing of wages created opportunities for exploitation and produced anomalies which finally made regulation inevitable. The Agricultural Wages (Regulation) (Scotland) Act of 1937 set up area wages boards which initially fixed rates varying from 34s. 6d. to 40s. (including all payment in kind). In the North and South-West this did raise the level of wages and it made possible a more uniform basis of wages everywhere. 'Hiring fairs' were ended by the Essential Work Order which made movement between farms more difficult, and intensified the process of raising wage rates. The Scottish Agricultural Wages Board has now a more unifying influence; wage rates fixed are now fairly uniform over the whole of Scotland and have recently come more or less into line with England, though in 1952 and 1953 the Scottish Board has fixed rates a few shillings lower than apply in England.

Coal-mining

Table 77 gives data showing for a selection of years from 1914 the average cash earnings per shift of persons employed at coal-mines in Scotland and Great Britain.

Earnings in the Scottish coalfields since 1924 have clearly been just slightly below the national average but have moved up and down in a very similar way.[2] The figures for Great Britain contain the higher earnings of the newer coalfields of Nottinghamshire, Kent, and South Yorkshire—the Scottish figures are probably quite representative of the older areas, and of those heavily engaged in the export trade.

The wage rate structure of the industry is, of course, highly complex and the actual day rates paid to workers can differ from district to district. Since 1947 there has been considerable progress towards a more simple wage

---

[1] Cmd. 5217.
[2] Data given in Table 75, however, suggest that annual wages in 1948 at least, were higher in Scotland. The Scots may therefore work longer hours.

structure but this process cannot yet be called complete. The present arrangements for a national minimum wage applicable to all districts did not come into existence until 1943, and before that date minima varied considerably from district to district and were not in any case related closely either to actual rates or actual earnings.

As to the earlier period, earnings in Scotland in 1886 (at the Wage Census) and in 1914 were about the average level for Britain. In the intervening period it may be possible to suggest—but with some hesitancy—on the basis of percentage changes in piece rates collected by the Ministry of Labour that wages in coal-mining in Scotland rose rather more than in other regions in the closing years of the nineteenth century and that the earnings figures for 1914 may represent something of a fall in the position of Scotland between 1900 and 1914.

Table 77. *Average cash earnings per manshift worked at coal-mines, in Scotland and in Great Britain*

Year	Scotland	Great Britain	Year	Scotland	Great Britain
	s. *d.*	*s.* *d.*		*s.* *d.*	*s.* *d.*
1914	6 9	6 5¾	1936	9 6½	10 0¼
1920	17 8¼	16 10¼	1940	12 7¼	13 0¼
1924	10 10¼	10 7¾	1944	20 7	21 8
1928	9 2¾	9 3½	1948	30 11	31 9
1932	8 9½	9 2	1950	33 0	34 0

SOURCES: Mines Department statistics and, later, National Coal Board.

Shipbuilding and ship-repairing

At 1900, time rates in shipbuilding in the Glasgow area (and at Leith) were about average for Great Britain as a whole. They were slightly below those for Tyneside and slightly above those for Barrow—and in the following years they moved in roughly the same way as the general average.[1] The rates for Dundee were normally rather lower than Glasgow and those for Aberdeen were somewhat lower still. A national uniform wages structure was adopted for the industry in 1929/30 and the regional differentials were to be ended by this agreement (with exceptions for two areas in England). In fact, however, the differentials for Dundee and Aberdeen lingered on for some years longer. In 1900 the rates for platers and riveters in shipyards were well below those for shipwrights in all areas. This wage rate difference had, however, about disappeared by 1914. In all areas it was customary to give rather higher rates for repair work.

[1] Rates for skilled shipbuilders in the districts are available in the *Abstracts of Labour Statistics* and there are also some figures for the earlier years in the series of articles on wages by Bowley in the *Journal of the Royal Statistical Society* around 1900.

As regards earnings, in 1906 earnings in Scotland in shipbuilding were well up to those for other parts of the United Kingdom, and were in fact generally higher than elsewhere for skilled men. Earnings on the Clyde were greater than for the rest of Scotland. By 1950, earnings in different parts of the country had tended to spread out and, while Scotland had earnings which were similar to those for the other main shipbuilding areas in the North of England, they were less than earnings in the ship-repairing areas in the South.

Through most of the period since 1900 wages in the shipbuilding industry in Scotland have corresponded fairly closely to those for the industry elsewhere. Wage rates in shipbuilding for the United Kingdom generally have moved fairly steadily in company with the general wage movements. Earnings, on the other hand, were relatively low in the early 1930's. Many of the industry's skilled men have been traditionally on payment by results schemes, and this was reflected in the development of separate piecework price lists, of which the Clyde had a well-known example.

Engineering (non-electrical)

Wage rates in the engineering industry are centred on the rates for the skilled group of fitters and for labourers—and, indeed, in recent years these have been the only rates to be nationally negotiated. The fitters' rates in the four cities of Scotland at several dates are compared with a weighted average for the United Kingdom in Table 78.

It is clear from this table that Scottish rates were very slightly below those for the United Kingdom as a whole but that the difference was not very great, at least in Glasgow and Edinburgh, and has been diminishing. In fact, with

Table 78. *Fitters' wage rates in Glasgow, Edinburgh, Aberdeen and Dundee and the national average for* 1900, 1914, 1927, 1936 *and* 1950

District	Fitters rates at				
	December 1900	October 1914	December 1927	December 1936	October 1950
	s. d.	s. d.	s. d.	s. d.	s. d.
Aberdeen	30 0	36 0	56 0	61 0	107 0
Dundee	32 0	35 0	56 10	62 0	107 0
Edinburgh	34 10	—	58 3½	63 3	107 2¾
Glasgow	36 0	38 3	58 1½	63 1½	107 1½
United Kingdom National average	—	38 11	58 1	64 1	107 0*

* The national minimum rate.

SOURCES: *Abstracts of Labour Statistics* and *Time Rates of Wages*, 1950.

the war-time growth in the money wage (which was not accompanied by a growth in the differentials) and, since the introduction of the national minimum basic rate in 1948, the difference has become quite unimportant. Wages were negotiated locally prior to the first world war but since then national wage changes have been imposed on district differentials. The rates for Dundee have been lower than those in Glasgow and Edinburgh and those for Aberdeen have generally been lower still. Wage rates for labourers have generally shown similar characteristics. At the Wage Census of 1886 similar results were shown. Wages of fitters in the central industrial area varied from 27s. 1d. to 28s. while the average for the eastern counties north of the Forth was 26s. 2d. and the United Kingdom average was 29s. 2d.

Table 79. *Average weekly earnings of adult males in engineering in Scotland and in the United Kingdom, 1906–48*[1]

Year	Average weekly earnings (shillings)	
	Scotland	United Kingdom
1906	31·3	31·9
1926 (October)	53·0	55·6
1928 (October)	58·2	60·2
1931 (October)	52·3	56·1
1938 (July)	72·0	74·4
1942 (July)	121·4	126·0
1948 (January)	124·8	131·3

The wage rate picture in engineering can be summarized as one of smallish regional differences becoming less significant with the developing national wage structure. The same does not, however, apply to earnings. Table 79 gives average weekly earnings in engineering in the United Kingdom and Scotland for seven selected years since 1906.

This table shows that, whilst wage rates in engineering in Scotland may have been coming into uniformity with the United Kingdom, earnings were not. Scottish earnings in engineering, which were only slightly lower than the United Kingdom average in 1906, fell relative to the United Kingdom for most of the inter-war period, and while recovering a little during the war, they were markedly lower than United Kingdom earnings by 1948.

[1] The figures in the table, which are derived principally from tables in K. G. J. C. Knowles and D. J. Robertson, 'Earnings in Engineering, 1926–1948 'and 'Some Notes on Engineering Earnings' *Bulletin of the Oxford University Institute of Statistics*, vol. XIII (1951) refer to all adult male workers in 1906 and 1948, and are weighted averages of fitters' and labourers' earnings in other years.

Building

Between 1900 and 1914 the hourly rates of bricklayers in the four Scottish cities were generally quite as high as in the provincial English cities, though less than those for London. The rates for masons were rather lower—especially in Aberdeen, where masons formed the bulk of the skilled building labour force. At the close of the first world war a uniform 'craftsman's' rate was established and a national grading scheme was set up for the whole of Great Britain. The Scottish cities were graded 'A'—the highest grade other than London and Liverpool (where there were special circumstances). This lasted till 1931, when Scottish employers and employees negotiated separate rates for Scotland. The craftsmen's and labourers' rates fixed for Scotland were respectively $\frac{1}{2}d$. and $\frac{1}{4}d$. above those for the equivalent English grades. The cities were still Grade A, but the lowest Scottish grade was B 3 while there were still Grade C areas in England. Areas tended to be 'up-graded' in both Scotland and England, but by 1946 all Scottish areas were Grade A while England and Wales had A 1, A 2, A 3 and B areas. The English and Scottish Grade A areas now pay the same, however, and generally alter in the same way.[1] Under normal conditions, earnings in the building industry do not appear to differ from wage rates as much as in other industries[2] and there is unlikely to be a wide divergence between earnings of similar grades in the two countries. Earnings in building in 1906 were, however, lower in Scotland than for the United Kingdom as a whole, and the shorter days in Scotland in winter are likely to mean that lower earnings than in England are usual.

Textiles and clothing

The textile industry in Scotland is of a very diverse nature. The specializations of the regions differ widely and there are many cases of very small areas with clearly individual products. Up to the present day the newer textile fabrics have, however, not been much developed in Scotland. The groups of importance where Scottish specialization is relatively greater than that for the United Kingdom as a whole are linen, jute, hosiery and knitwear, and carpets. The Scottish woollen trade, though relatively small, is also of a distinctive character. Such localized trades have produced a number of small and local trade unions and employers' associations and these have led in turn to a variety of wage rates. There have been Trade Boards and now national Wages Councils in some branches of the industry and these lay down national minima, but even so there is so much piecework that the minima are probably rarely paid.

It is not therefore possible to present a detailed picture of Scottish textile

[1] Much of this may be found in a Ministry of Works unpublished typescript *Wages, Earnings, and Negotiating Machinery in the Building Industry*, 1886–1948.

[2] Cf. K. G. J. C. Knowles and D. J. Robertson, 'Differences between the Wages of Skilled and Unskilled Workers 1880–1950', *Bulletin of the Oxford University Institute of Statistics*, vol. XIII (1951).

wage rates. Nor is it possible to show in detail how textile earnings in the past have compared with those in other parts of the United Kingdom, except to observe that in 1906 textile earnings in Scotland generally came well up to the United Kingdom average figures, except in cotton, which was by that time no longer a Scottish speciality. Evidence for the Scottish woollen trade[1] suggests, too, that the fluctuation downwards in United Kingdom textile earnings in the inter-war period also occurred in Scotland. It can be said with much more certainty, however, that the present specializations in Scottish textiles are not those which bring high earnings. If the April 1951 earnings figures for the various sectors of the textile industry in the United Kingdom are weighted by the figures of Scottish employment[2] in the different branches, and the result compared with that for the United Kingdom as a whole; then, average weekly earnings for men in the whole textile group in Scotland are 6s. lower than for the United Kingdom and those of women are 3s. 9d. lower. It seems reasonable also to assume that this has been the position for a number of years.

Table 80. *Earnings in the boot and shoe industry, in Scotland and in the United Kingdom, 1906 and 1951*

| | 1906 | | June 1951 | | | |
| | Average weekly earnings | | Average weekly earnings | | Average hourly earnings | |
	Scotland	United Kingdom	Scotland	United Kingdom	Scotland	United Kingdom
	s. d.	s. d.	s. d.	s. d.	s. d.	s. d.
Men	30 3	26 4	126 2	155 3	3 3½	3 5½
Women	12 6	12 5	93 0	91 3	2 1½	2 3

In the clothing industries similar problems occur. As regards wage rates, most sections of the industry have long been under Trade Boards and now Wages Councils. Some of these have separate councils for Scotland and the minima can diverge slightly. But, as in textiles, piecework is common and is likely to alter the effective payments. In 1906 earnings in this industry in Scotland were generally fully up to those elsewhere (and, of course, much above Ireland). The boot and shoe industry, which has uniform national minima, is the only one where detail is available for a later period,[3] and this information is set out in Table 80. Average hourly earnings in 1951 in this industry in Scotland were slightly lower than the average for the United Kingdom.

[1] Obtained from the Scottish Woollen Trade Employers' Association.
[2] Earnings figures from *Ministry of Labour Gazette*, September, 1951. Employment figures from *Tables relating to employment and unemployment*.
[3] From the earnings survey of the Incorporated Federated Associations of Boot and Shoe Manufacturers of Great Britain and Ireland.

CONCLUSIONS[1]

1. The period since 1900 has produced a uniformity in wage rates such that the standard or published rates in most industries are now nationally negotiated or agreed. Local variations in 'standard' or 'minimum' rates may generally be disregarded as unimportant.

2. Study of the earnings of Scottish workers does not, however, yield the same impression. In 1906, the basic industries, which tended to be lower paid in 1886, were well paid in Scotland relative to the United Kingdom (though service occupations tended to lag behind). The industries where information exists for the intervening period show a steady change in this relationship, and a falling of Scottish earnings below the United Kingdom level.

3. In recent years, earnings in Scotland have been below the average for the United Kingdom—or, more precisely, below the level of England. This has been specially true of men. The distributions of net incomes and of employees' earned incomes show a greater hump in the lower ranges of income for Scotland and a more attenuated 'tail'. The distribution of manufacturing industries is partly responsible for this. It is also true, however, that within industries earnings of operatives and of salaried workers tend to be lower in Scotland, and that to-day the tendency to lower earnings is spread throughout the Scottish economy. This conclusion is based on a comparison of Scottish figures with averages for England. With some regions in England Scottish earnings might compare much more favourably.

4. We have been too ready in the past to assume that wage rate movements form a sound enough basis for judgements—neglecting the area of freedom between wage rates and actual earnings. There is clearly a case for study (not least by the trade unions) of the processes by which regional differences in earnings arise and are maintained. Further, any classification of firms as being within the same industry may conceal differences in profitability and in demand for the final product which are important. In a developing group of industries the differences that can arise in the branches from the parent stem require constant investigation. This may be part of the explanation of differences in earnings within industries. This study is probably in part a reflection of a failure on the part of industry in Scotland to follow the newest and most profitable developments. Moreover, high-paying branches of industries can pull up earnings in the other industries of the region. A lack of a few high-paying industries may mean a generally low level of earnings.

[1] A rather more speculative discussion of possible reasons for the lower level of average earnings in Scotland will be found in my short article on 'Wages in Scotland', *Accountants' Magazine*, December 1952.

NOTE ON SOURCES

1. The sources for this chapter are many and various. It will be obvious that much of it is the result of correspondence with employers' associations, with trade unions and with others—to all of whom I am indebted.

2. During 1951 several articles on similar topics by Mr K. G. J. C. Knowles and myself appeared in the *Bulletin of the Oxford University Institute of Statistics*, Vol. XIII, 1951. I have drawn heavily on these in my section on individual industries. (The articles were 'Differences between the Wages of Skilled and Unskilled Workers 1880–1950' (April, 1951); 'Earnings in Engineering, 1926–1948' (June 1951); 'Some Notes on Engineering Earnings' (July 1951); and 'Earnings in Shipbuilding' (November/December 1951).)

3. Material on wage rates can be taken from several sources. While all are helpful the subject-matter is so complex that none are entirely satisfactory. The Ministry of Labour publishes three main sources:

(*a*) A monthly table on 'Changes in Rates of Wages' in the *Ministry of Labour Gazette*—containing reference to all changes reported during the month.

(*b*) An annual '*Time Rates of Wages and Hours of Labour*' series—giving the rates in most principal occupations and industries at a specific date. (There is a gap in this record between 1913 and 1946 during which only two issues appeared, in 1920 and 1929.)

(*c*) A table giving rates for a number of years in a selection of industries, occupations and regions in the *Abstracts of Labour Statistics*. (These were issued at an average interval of three years but there has been none since 1936.)

4. The main official publication on regional earnings is the 1906 Earnings Enquiry conducted by the Board of Trade (Labour Department)—the predecessor of the Ministry of Labour. There is also the Wage Census of 1886. I have found the Inland Revenue *Reports* most useful sources of earnings material, particularly the *Ninety-Fourth Report* containing the results of the recent Income Census. The 1948 Census of Production produced by the Board of Trade has also provided much valuable information.

5. Since this chapter was written two further important sources of information on regional incomes have appeared:

(*a*) The *Ninety-fifth Report of the Commissioners of Inland Revenue* (for the year ended 31 March 1952) continues the analysis of the Income Census of 1949/50 and contains an analysis of income distribution by counties.

(*b*) *Regional Variations in United Kingdom Incomes from Employment, 1948* by Phyllis Deane (*J.R. Statist. Soc.* 1953) reports preliminary results of research on this subject at the Department of Applied Economics, University of Cambridge. The results relating to Scotland are similar to those given in this chapter.

CHAPTER 12

CONSUMPTION

By D. J. ROBERTSON

The standard of living in Scotland has never been submitted to a detailed survey. The study of the conditions of life of the community that was undertaken by Charles Booth (in the 1890's) for London and by Seebohm Rowntree (on three separate occasions) for York finds no parallel in Scotland. Few private investigators have collected family budgets; and those that have been collected have almost all been incidental to some special purpose, not directed towards an analysis of the standard of living. The one outstanding exception is the Ministry of Labour's inquiry of 1937/38 which covered Scotland in common with other parts of the country.

Thus it is not possible to present an account of family expenditure at various levels of income, breaking down the total national income to show its distribution between different social groups. Nor is it possible to analyse the total expenditure of the community, item by item, with any degree of accuracy. For some particular elements in total consumption, there is fuller data: housing, for example, is discussed in Chapter 14. There is also a fair amount of statistical material on the consumption habits of Scottish families, and it is on this material that the present chapter is based.

There are always two clear ways of measuring consumption, by value and by quantity (and in the case of food by nutritional value), and such data as are available to us are not uniformly of the one type. Moreover, the normal measure of price changes as they affect the household goes under the title of a retail price index (popularly called the cost-of-living index); but it has not been the custom to build up such indices on a regional basis. It is impossible, therefore, to say, in the case of general consumption expressed in money terms, whether the quantity obtained per unit of money is the same in Scotland as in Great Britain as a whole, and vice versa. In the period from 1904 to the outbreak of the first world war some attempts were made to record the relative prices of such things as bread (and food generally) and house-room in various cities and districts; but, after the war, it seems to have been assumed—a little too readily perhaps—that the only major distinction in 'cost-of-living' was that between London and elsewhere, with the possibility of lower costs in remote country areas. It is now impossible, as a result of this neglect of the study of regional living costs, to record even the extent to which London differs from elsewhere, or the extent to which consumption in quantity terms in Scotland is hindered or helped by price differences.

Since there is no record of the total amounts consumed in Scotland by either quantity or value, we are forced to base our conclusions on how much was consumed by smaller units. The obvious units of study are the family or household—and family or household budgets (by quantity or value). Only two sources are available, and both are limited in scope to the working-class household, and in effect to the urban working-class household. They are, first, the inquiry on *The Weekly Expenditure of Working Class Households in the United Kingdom* carried through by the Ministry of Labour in 1937/38; and secondly, results obtained from the Ministry of Food's National Food Survey which collected data on *The Urban Working Class Household Diet* between 1940 and 1949. These can be supplemented to some extent by indices of changes in retail sales compiled by the Board of Trade. The rest of this chapter for the most part looks at the results obtained from these three sources.

Just before the war, in 1937/38, the Ministry of Labour collected a number of household budgets with the intention of revising the cost-of-living index. The information collected was put out in detail in typescript form after the war and included a regional analysis. Out of 8,905 budgets, 980 were collected in Scotland. The size of the Scottish households tended to be above average. There were, of course, slightly larger families in Scotland and a greater amount of over-crowding. In consequence, there were slightly more wage-earners per family in Scotland.[1] The different sizes of households and numbers of wage-earners somewhat invalidate direct comparisons of expenditure in Scotland and in the United Kingdom as a whole. This may, however, be roughly offset by taking expenditure per person in the household, and by comparing the patterns of expenditure on a percentage basis. This is done for the main heads of expenditure in Table 81.[2]

Table 81 shows up the main differences in Scottish household expenditure. The Scottish working-class household in 1937/38 spent much less per person on rent and made up for this by increased expenditure on food, clothing and 'other items'. Expenditure on fuel and light was relatively low.

There was not only a much smaller average number of rooms per household in Scotland (2·6 as against 3·9) and less spent on rent[3], but also the proportion of people buying their own houses was also very much less. Expenditure on fuel and light was presumably kept down by the small number

[1] Expenditure per household in Scotland was therefore larger though individual earnings were probably lower (cf. Chapter 11).

[2] The Ministry of Labour enquiry left out the long-term unemployed. This must give a somewhat too favourable impression of the relative position of the Scottish working-class, since a high proportion of these unemployed workers were in Scotland. (In June 1938 Scotland had 21 % of those who had been unemployed for twelve months or more in Great Britain and less than 11 % of insured workers.)

[3] The complex problems of expenditure on rents and rates, especially in the post-war period, are dealt with in Chapter 14.

171

of rooms. A higher proportion of such expenditure in Scotland was on coal; coke was little used. The expenditure on electricity was considerably less.

The percentage distribution of domestic expenditure on food in the Scottish and United Kingdom households, grouped according to the main food categories, is shown in Table 82.

Table 81. *Average weekly expenditure of working-class households, in Scotland and in the United Kingdom, 1937/38*

	Average weekly expenditure of working-class households				Expenditure per person in household	
			as percentage of total			
	Scotland	United Kingdom	Scotland	United Kingdom	Scotland	United Kingdom
	s. d.	s. d.			s. d.	s. d.
Housing and rent	8 2	10 10	9·1	12·7	2 0¼	2 10½
Food	36 11	34 1	41·1	40·1	9 2¼	9 0½
Clothing	10 7	8 1	11·8	9·5	2 6½	2 1½
Fuel and light	6 2	6 5	6·9	7·6	1 6½	1 8½
Other items	27 10	25 7	31·1	30·1	6 11¼	6 9½
Total	89 8	85 0	100·0	100·0	22 2¾	22 6¼

SOURCE: Ministry of Labour typescript, *Weekly Expenditure of Working Class Households in the United Kingdom in 1937/8.*

If their expenditure on food is considered in more detail, the Scottish households spent relatively more on bread, cakes, oatmeal and cereals, and biscuits, but used less flour. The industrial working-class in Scotland apparently did less baking, though they spent more on the cereal foods as a whole. They spent a slightly lower proportion on meats, but bought more beef and less mutton and pork, and a much higher proportion of sausages. They spent more on eggs but less on bacon. They bought more butter, margarine and jam, but less lard. They spent a higher proportion on fish, though less on 'fish and chips'. Rather less of their total food expenditure went on milk and vegetables, and on meals away from home.

The larger size of Scottish households meant that they spent more on clothing. The expenditure was fairly similarly divided between men, women and children, except that in Scotland it appears probable that the women spent rather more on clothes (proportionately) and the men less. The proportion devoted to new footwear was the same for Scotland and the United Kingdom.

The 'other items' group contains a varied assortment of goods and services. Proportions of total expenditure on 'other items' spent on most household goods were largely similar in Scotland and the United Kingdom. The proportion spent on insurance was lower in Scotland but subscriptions to trade unions were higher. Transport costs were slightly higher proportionately in Scotland. Expenditure on organized entertainment was higher in Scotland; but, while expenditure on tobacco and cigarettes was proportionately higher, that on drink was lower. If these three—entertainments, tobacco and cigarettes, and drink—are grouped with holiday expenditure, however, the proportion spent on these items in Scotland was higher than that for the United Kingdom.

Table 82. *Domestic expenditure on main food categories in Scotland and in the United Kingdom in 1937/38*

Type of food	Percentage of total expenditure on food	
	Scotland	United Kingdom
Milk, cheese and eggs	18·6	18·0
Meats	22·3	23·8
Fish*	4·0	4·1
Fats	9·6	9·9
Fruit and vegetables	11·8	12·8
Cereal foods	18·7	15·7
Sugar and preserves	5·4	4·9
Total food expenditure	100·0	100·0

* Including 'fish and chips'.
SOURCE: Ministry of Labour typescript.

It is difficult to sum up this account of the working-class budget for 1937/38. The inquiry was aimed to cover the wage-earning classes other than agricultural workers, and we can assume that the budgets from Scotland were intended to represent the same kinds of people as those from elsewhere. We find these people in Scotland living more closely together and spending less on house-room than their counterparts elsewhere. This is well enough known. We can now add that their habits in food favour more of the bread-and-jam type of diet with less milk and vegetables and more sausages than elsewhere. Further, in expenditure on personal indulgences they spend more on organized entertainment and on tobacco. Admittedly they are less inclined to spend on drink (other sources suggest that the Scot tends to drink spirits rather than large quantities of beer)[1] and they may therefore to some extent sub-

[1] The *Customs and Excise Report* for 1951 gives the consumption of spirits in Scotland as 15·6 % of the total for the United Kingdom—against a population of just over 10 %. It is generally considered (and there is some evidence to support the assumption) that the consumption of beer per head is lower in Scotland than in England. Little is known of the relative consumptions of wines.

173

stitute evenings of organized entertainment for the English custom of beer-drinking. Scottish workers (other than those in agriculture) tend to be more city-dwellers and are highly concentrated geographically into a very large conurbation in the West and a few smaller centres in the East. Taken together, these various factors tend to suggest that in 1937/38 the Scottish working-class household had expenditure habits which were more definitely urban and more determinedly in the tradition of the working-class than were found elsewhere. This, of course, probably amounts to a statement that the working-class in Scotland were poorer than average, and had not therefore tended to adjust their expenditure pattern towards the middle-class as much as their counterparts elsewhere in the United Kingdom.

Table 83. *Changes in retail sales (value) in Scotland and in Great Britain since 1937. (1937 = 100)*

Category	Country	Year						
		1939	1941	1943	1945	1947	1949	1951
Food and perish-ables*	Scotland	110	124	133	142	171	203	244
	Great Britain	109	110	116	125	154	188	228
Non food mer-chandise†	Scotland	110	127	119	142	198	259	289
	Great Britain	102	100	95	114	168	219	261
Apparel	Scotland	111	127	119	145	193	260	294
	Great Britain	104	102	94	117	160	227	271
Household goods	Scotland	110	125	101	117	218	266	303
	Great Britain	92	82	71	89	187	221	270
All merchandise	Scotland	110	125	126	141	179	221	258
	Great Britain	105	105	106	119	159	199	240

* I.e. Food, drink and tobacco.

† I.e. Apparel, household goods (furniture and furnishings, hardware, electrical and radio); music, etc.; books, etc.; jewellery and leather; chemists' goods; sports goods and cycles, etc.

SOURCE: Derived from indices of the value of retail sales published in the *Board of Trade Journal.*

Unfortunately, it is not possible to say what the pattern of consumption of households is like now, fourteen or fifteen years after the inquiry, except in the case of food. The Board of Trade, however, provides indices of retail sales of different types of commodities in Scotland and Great Britain based on samples. Technical difficulties make these indices somewhat unreliable for as long a period as from 1937. Their accuracy should, however, be sufficient to allow broad conclusions to be drawn about changes in the pattern of retail sales, and therefore in the total consumption of goods in Scotland since 1937.

The index numbers in Table 83 show the changes that have occurred in total consumption. The rearmament boom and the start of the war increased consumption in Scotland relative to other parts of Great Britain. There was some inflow of workers during the war; but more important than this, the war meant greatly increased employment in Scotland and this resulted in an increased ability to buy. With the end of the war and the departure of many incomers, the extent to which the value of sales in Scotland had grown relative to sales in Great Britain declined. The total value of sales (and of course prices) rose considerably, however, in Scotland and in Great Britain as a whole after the war. Moreover, while the rate of increase is now largely similar in Scotland and in Great Britain, the continuance of full employment has ensured that the Scottish increase over 1937 remains greater than that for Great Britain.

Total consumption in Scotland therefore appears to have become relatively greater than it was in 1937; however, the pattern of consumption, on the available evidence, has not altered greatly. Total food expenditure in Scotland has followed the trend of expenditure on all items. With the exception of the period from 1948 to 1950, when Scottish sales grew rather more rapidly, clothing sales have done likewise. The only major difference in the pattern appears to arise in household goods. Between 1938 and 1941 expenditure on furniture, furnishings, hardware and electrical goods showed a considerable rise in Scotland when it was falling elsewhere; and since 1947 sales of household goods in Scotland have continued to be relatively large. It looks as though increased income from employment, while it has preserved in general a similar pattern of expenditure changes in Scotland to that for Great Britain, has been accompanied by an increased outlay on the equipment of the home. It may be tentatively suggested that the Scot is making up for bad housing by spending rather more of his income on the better equipment of his existing house.

This completes all that can be said here about the total consumption pattern. Fortunately, more can be said about the expenditure of Scottish urban working-class households on food in 1949. The Ministry of Food began a National Food Survey in 1940 to 'check the level of consumption and expenditure on food during the war', and this is still being continued. Detailed results of these enquiries, which are now being made available, have provided valuable information on differences in food consumption patterns between regions in 1949.

The actual distribution of expenditure on the main categories of food of urban working-class households in Scotland and Great Britain in 1949 is shown in Table 84.[1]

---

[1] I am indebted to the Ministry of Food for making available the material on 1949 before the appearance of their report.

In 1949 several basic foods were rationed. As a result, expenditure per person on such foods in working-class homes could not diverge greatly in one region. If food expenditure is examined in detail expenditure on rationed meat, cooking fat, and eggs in Scotland was similar to the average for the whole country. Expenditure on bacon was higher, however, while expenditure on butter and margarine, cheese, and sugar was very slightly lower. For most of these commodities this represents a change from 1938 when Scottish working-class households spent proportionately less on meat, cooking fat and bacon and more on butter and margarine. While the expenditure on meat in 1949 was similar, however, the weight obtained per person was smaller— possibly because of a continued preference for beef instead of mutton.

Table 84. *Domestic expenditure on main food categories in Scotland and in Great Britain in 1949*

Type of food	Percentage of total expenditure on food	
	Scotland	Great Britain
Milk, cheese and eggs	16·7	17·6
Meats	20·9	19·6
Fish	6·2	6·2
Fats	4·7	5·1
Fruit and vegetables	17·6	21·5
Cereal foods	22·6	19·0
Sugar and preserves	5·8	5·0
Total food expenditure	100·0	100·0

SOURCE: Ministry of Food.

On other foods the expenditure pattern in 1949 remains as it was in 1938. In 1949 Scottish working-class households still spent considerably less than the average for Great Britain on vegetables (and also on fruit) while they bought more bread, cakes, biscuits and jam. While rationing seems to have had some effect on the consumption of foods which are rationed, for other foods the consumption pattern of working-class households in Scotland relative to other parts of Great Britain remains much as it was in 1938.

A comparison of expenditure on food in Scotland in 1949 with expenditure in 1938 shows several important changes. The proportion spent on all the rationed foods taken together has declined; the amount spent on milk has risen while that on cheese and eggs has fallen; the proportion spent on butter has declined, and that on margarine and cooking fats is greater. If Tables 84 and 82 are compared, it is seen that the expenditure on meat has fallen while that on fish has risen; the increase in the proportion of expenditure on fruit

176

and vegetables and cereal foods is noticeable.[1] Of course, many of these alterations in proportions may be ascribed directly to the food subsidy policy, which has, for example, caused much greater stability in the prices of fats than in those of fruit and vegetables.[2] It is likely, however, that the amounts of food consumed have altered in a similar way—probably, as in the case of meat, because of short supply. The Scottish diet has probably therefore followed the general tendency and become more starchy than it was in 1938.

It is unfortunate that, for lack of further information, this must conclude the connected account of the expenditure habits of the Scottish people. Some interesting sidelights can, however, be found in various sources. For instance, the tendency for the Scots to spend relatively more on entertainment is illustrated by data provided by a recent survey of the British Film Industry.[3] From this it appears that in 1951 the attendance rate at the cinema in Scotland was equivalent to thirty-eight visits per person per year against an average of twenty-nine for Great Britain as a whole. The admissions in Scotland were 13·4 % of total admissions, with a population of 10·4 % that of Great Britain. Gross takings were 11·5 % of the total. It is clear that Scots went more frequently to the cinema and spent relatively more on it—though they bought cheaper seats on the average.

[1] Comparison of Tables 84 and 82, while hampered by the reference of Table 84 to Great Britain and Table 82 to the United Kingdom, and by the possibility that, since the material was not collected by the same authorities, there may be some differences in definition and scope, should be sufficiently accurate for general purposes.

[2] The alterations in food subsidy policy since 1949 have no doubt resulted in alterations in the balance of food expenditure in both Scotland and Great Britain.

[3] *The British Film Industry*, P.E.P. Report, 1952. The data came originally from the Board of Trade.

CHAPTER 13

LOCAL GOVERNMENT

By ROBERT BAIRD

It is not possible to reduce government, central or local, entirely to quantitative terms. Budgets and votes tell a great deal about how nations are governed but there is also a great deal on which they throw no light at all. In this chapter, since its approach is rigorously quantitative, only one side of local government will be studied: the part that it plays (and has played since 1881) in the economic life of Scotland as revealed in the available statistics of revenue and expenditure.

It is necessary to stress at the outset the limitations of the material used. First of all, there is the long delay before comprehensive figures for the Scottish local authorities become available. Until the first world war, the Local Taxation Returns, prepared under an Act of 1881, provided a full and detailed abstract giving totals for all authorities and summarized accounts for each; from 1914 to 1939 this was replaced by printed and published memoranda and summaries covering only the more important totals and averages; now even this attenuated return, formerly published about one year after the close of the financial year to which it referred, is more than four years in arrears, and at the time of writing the most recent return (issued in duplicated form for limited circulation) is for 1947/48. The reader need hardly be reminded of the gulf that separates local government finance then and now: the transfer of gas and electricity undertakings to the boards of nationalized industries; the transfer of many of the major public health functions to the central government; the change in the system of block Exchequer grants in such a way that many of the better-off authorities now receive no general contribution to the rate-fund but only grants specifically earmarked for approved expenditures.

To meet this first difficulty it was necessary to resort to the laborious expedient of making abstracts of the accounts of the four principal cities (Glasgow, Edinburgh, Dundee and Aberdeen) for 1947/48 and 1950/51 so as to obtain a large enough sample to carry the story forward, however tentatively, to 1950/51. These abstracts are subject to the errors that may arise, whatever pains are taken, in reconciling four different methods of presenting accounts. What is probably more important, the figures for the four cities are not necessarily an accurate index of changes taking place in the whole of Scotland, for it cannot be assumed that by the time the various transfers of functions and changes in block grants had been completed the relationship between the totals for the cities and the rest of Scotland passed undisturbed.

A second difficulty arises whenever an effort is made to examine trends in local government expenditure over a long period. If one wishes to go back, for example, to 1881/82 (the first year for which figures are available in detail) the way back is encumbered by a series of reorganizations of the structure of local government under such Acts as those of 1885, 1889, 1894 and 1929. Since the earliest returns were by authority rather than function, and the authorities came and went with the Acts, a good deal of guesswork is needed in apportioning totals. The revenue figures were complicated in the past by the vast variety of 'assessments' which the present unified rate charges have replaced; and there is often a lack of information about revenue from specific service charges. Many *ad hoc* local government agencies that figured prominently in the Returns for 1881/82 have now disappeared from them: the Crown Agent in Edinburgh, the Board of Supervision, the Parochial Boards, the Commissioners of Supply, the Road Trustees, the Heritors, the Commissioners for Police, the occasionally mentioned Commissioners for Gas and for Water Supply, and other dimly-remembered ruins of administrative ingenuity. Gone, too, are other bodies not yet born in 1881/82—the Parish Councils and the Local Government Board, for example. Even the old-established authorities that survived reorganization exercised different functions at different times.

Thus the discontinuous changes brought about by legislation make it difficult to measure with any precision the secular growth in the powers and duties of the local authorities, which have multiplied steadily through general and special, obligatory and permissive, public and private legislation. Yet in order to give some perspective to the present state of local government finance it has seemed worth trying to show how revenue and expenditure have responded over the past two generations to that growth in powers and duties. The figures for 1947/48 and 1950/51 have been compared, therefore, with figures for 1881/82 and 1901/02 that are as far as possible on the same basis.

A third, relatively minor difficulty, is that of all the local agencies covered by the Local Taxation Returns there is one, and only one, that has not in due course been taken over by the local authorities as their powers grew. This type of agency, the port and harbour authority, is of considerable importance and at one time occupied an even more prominent part in the Returns. A body like the Clyde Navigation Trust, for example, has an annual budget of several million pounds. It is necessary either to include or exclude these undertakings and they have been included as if they all came under the orbit of some local authority.

LOCAL GOVERNMENT SERVICES

It is possible to classify local government services in different ways. For present purposes, the key distinctions are between services that do and do not bring in revenue; and between those revenue-producing services that are self-financing and pay their own way, and those that are a contingent—and almost invariably an actual—burden on the rates. On this basis local government services fall into three groups.

Self-financing services

In the heyday of municipal trading, there were several important services that the local authorities provided on a commercial footing, paying their way out of direct charges to consumers. This group included gas, electricity and transport, but transport services are now the only item of any consequence that can be included under this heading; and to judge from the current deficits of some of the transport undertakings involved, this last important instance is itself drifting a little from the heading. Markets (including slaughter-houses) are classified below as self-financing; and so are the services provided by port and harbour authorities.

Subsidized services

For the self-financing services, revenue derived mainly from consumers is expected to cover ordinary expenditure year by year and any deficit or surplus is carried forward to be cleared in later years. There are other revenue-producing services, however, on which a deficit or (in theory, at least) a surplus is carried to the rating account. Since in practice this means that part of the current cost of the service falls on the ratepayer (for we can ignore the few examples of a surplus and take a running deficit as the typical case) it seems reasonable to describe this group as 'subsidized' services. The principal services of this kind have been housing and water supply; of these two, water supply was fifty years ago by far the more important, but is now completely dwarfed by housing.

Free services

There are, finally, the purely 'rating' services, which are financed mainly from rates and grants (supplemented by other items, which may include an element of service charges). Such services are, broadly speaking, free to the consumer although the ratepayer and taxpayer might regard them as anything but costless. For present purposes they may be called 'free' services to distinguish them from the services that are less heavily subsidized from public funds. They form a long list, but only those (such as education, police, roads and so on) that have involved at one time or another an expenditure significant in relation to the total have been specifically mentioned below.

180

ORDINARY REVENUE AND EXPENDITURE OF SCOTTISH LOCAL AUTHORITIES

On the basis of the above classification, the development of local government revenue and expenditure can now be examined. The years selected for purposes of comparison have been 1881/82, 1901/02, 1947/48 and 1950/51. The growth in total revenue and expenditure is set out in Table 85.

Table 85. *Total ordinary revenue and expenditure of Scottish local authorities and undertakings,* 1881/82 *to* 1950/51 (£ m.)

Year	Expenditure	Revenue	Surplus or deficit
1881/82	4·81*	4·45*	−0·36
1901/02	12·47	12·69	+0·22
1947/48	115·71	115·19	−0·52
1947/48†	57·34	56·53	−0·81
1950/51†	46·37	45·85	−0·51

* Not including an amount of £1·03 m. raised by the Parochial Authorities under the Education Acts and presumably transferred to the Scottish Education Department.
† Four cities only.

The impression conveyed by Table 85 is of an extremely rapid expansion in local government expenditure, and this has undoubtedly occurred. The value of money in 1947/48, however, was probably less than one-third of its value in 1881/82 and the population was over one-third higher. Instead of a twenty-fold expansion, therefore, the expansion in real terms and per head of population between those years was probably not more than about fivefold. A second impression, derived from the figures for the four cities, is that there was a drop in local government expenditure after 1947/48. Such a drop, however, was no more than the automatic result of the nationalization of the cities' gas and electricity undertakings, and did not reflect some violent change of policy. On the contrary, there is every indication that the upward movement in expenditure has proceeded, uninterrupted except by this major surrender of functions.

In 1947/48 the national income of Scotland was about £900 m. while the ordinary expenditure of Scottish local authorities amounted to £116 m. By 1950/51 local government expenditure was somewhat less; but the proportion which it bore to the national income of the country must certainly have remained in excess of 10 %.

It will be noticed that in three of the four years shown in Table 85, revenue fell short of expenditure. The sources of this revenue are shown in Table 86.

Rates have provided a steadily diminishing proportion of the total, while government grants have risen from only 6 % in 1881/82 to over one-third in 1947/48. By 1947/48, grants had actually become a more important source of revenue than rates, and in spite of the steep increase in the poundage of rates levied since that year it is probable that this is still true.[1] Table 86 does not bring out the full significance of the contribution now made to local finance by government grants and this is a subject to which we shall return presently.

Table 86. *Sources of ordinary revenue of Scottish local authorities and undertakings,* 1881/82 *to* 1950/51

Year	Rates		Grants		Service charges and miscellaneous income		Total £ m.
	£ m.	Percentage	£ m.	Percentage	£ m.	Percentage	
1881/82	2·64	59·3	0·27	6·1	1·53	34·6	4·45
1901/02	5·28	41·6	2·06	16·3	5·35	42·1	12·69
1947/48	32·22	28·0	38·83	33·7	44·14	38·3	115·19
1947/48*	14·33	25·4	12·51	22·1	29·69	52·5	56·53
1950/51*	14·59	31·8	11·71	25·5	19·55	42·7	45·85

* Four cities only.

The expenditure of the local authorities is analysed in Table 87 in terms of the three groups of services already discussed.

The self-financing services have lost in importance and the 'subsidized' services have grown but, on the whole, the proportions have remained relatively stable. Like Table 86, however, this table is too general to give an adequate impression of the changes that have occurred. In Table 88 figures are given for individual revenue-producing services, showing both the expenditure on them and the revenue from sources other than rates and grants, and distinguishing self-financing from 'subsidized' services.

[1] The poundage of rates (i.e. the average amount of rates collected per £ of rateable value) was 11s. 3d. in 1938/39 and remained more or less constant until the end of the war. Thereafter it increased to 14s. 9d. in 1947/48, fluctuated around 13s. 6d. in the next three years and rose sharply from 13s. 9d. in 1950/51 to 18s. 0d. in 1952/53. Revenue from rates showed similar fluctuations:

Years ended 15 May	Poundage of rates s. d.		Total receipts from rates (£ m.)
1939	11	3	22·4
1945	12	1	25·1
1948	14	9	32·2
1949	13	8	29·8
1950	13	5	30·3
1951	13	9	31·9
1952	15	5	36·7
1953	18	0	44·2

SOURCE: *Returns of rates in Scotland,* 1951/52 *and* 1952/53 (Scottish Home Department, 1953).

No figures for 1881/82 are given for self-financing services because, although some such services must have existed (e.g. markets, bazaars, etc.), the Returns give no details, the one self-balancing account included for that year being 'Ports and harbours'.[1] In 1901/02, self-balancing expenditure had jumped to £4 m., of which gas accounted for nearly half, and ports and harbours and transport for most of the remainder. By 1947/48, the total had grown to about £30 m., with gas still the largest item, followed by transport and electricity. A few years later still, two of these three had passed from the control of the local authorities.

Table 87. *Forms of ordinary expenditure by Scottish local authorities and undertakings, 1901/02 to 1950/51*

Year	Self-financing services		'Subsidized' services		'Free' services	
	£ m.	Percentage	£ m.	Percentage	£ m.	Percentage
1901/02	3·9	32·0	1·1	8·5	7·5	59·5
1947/48	29·6	25·6	17·1	14·8	69·1	59·6
1947/48*	20·9	36·4	5·7	10·0	30·7	53·6
1950/51*	10·8	23·2	7·2	15·6	28·3	61·2

* Four cities only.

Meanwhile the surplus shown by most of the self-financing services in 1901/02 had become a general deficit in 1947/48: all without exception were 'in the red'.[2] Transport, which survived nationalization, had the largest deficit and by 1950/51 it had become bigger still. In that year the four cities were spending about 25 % more on transport than in 1947/48 and had a deficit of almost £900,000.

The 'subsidized' services, as might be expected, involved relatively little expenditure in 1881/82 or even in 1901/02, water being the only item of any real consequence. From just over £300,000 in 1881/82, the total grew to over £17 m. in 1947/48 and has continued to grow since. This vast increase and the radical change in the pattern of expenditure that has accompanied it are alike due to the emergence of housing as one of the principal responsibilities of the local authorities. The £30,000 found for Artisans' Dwellings in 1881/82 had reached the considerable total of £12·5 m. by 1947/48—almost three-quarters of the total for 'subsidized' services and the biggest single item of current local expenditure apart from education. This item of expenditure is, of course,

[1] In point of fact, this account was running a deficit equivalent to almost one-third of expenditure. It accounted for 20 % of the grand total of ordinary local expenditure in that year—a remarkably high proportion.
[2] Gas to the extent of £4,500 only.

Table 88. *Ordinary expenditure and revenue of Scottish local authorities: revenue producing services*, 1901/02 *to* 1950/51

(a) *Self-financing services.* (£ m.)

	1901/02 All authorities		1947/48 All authorities		1950/51 Four cities only	
	Expenditure	Revenue	Expenditure	Revenue	Expenditure	Revenue
Gas	1·76	1·85	10·86	10·86	—	—
Electricity	0·28	0·28	7·03	6·80	—	—
Transport	0·74	0·77	8·50	8·25	10·59	9·70
Markets, etc.	0·16	0·10	0·37	0·34	0·19	0·16
Ports and harbours	0·96	0·98	2·82	2·78	—	—
Total*	3·91	4·01	29·58	29·03	10·78	9·86

* Including £15,000 for telephones in 1901/02. In 1881/82 total expenditure on 'Ports and harbours' came to £0·97 m. and total revenue to £0·67 m. and the accounts show no expenditure under the other headings. Specific grants to cover any of the expenditure shown can be ignored, the total in 1947/48 being £40,000.

(b) *'Subsidized' services.* (£ m.)

	1881/82 All authorities		1901/02 All authorities		1947/48 All authorities		1950/51 Four cities only	
	Expenditure	Revenue	Expenditure	Revenue	Expenditure	Revenue	Expenditure	Revenue
Housing	0·03	—	0·12	—	12·51	6·56	5·08	2·90
Water	0·26	—	0·82	0·37	3·32	1·51	1·41	0·93
Baths, etc.	—	—	0·06	0·03	0·75	0·35	0·71	0·33
Burial	0·02	—	0·06	0·02	0·48	0·14	0·04	0·02
Total	0·31	—	1·06	0·42	17·06	8·56	7·24	4·18
Revenue from rates*	0·31		0·64		4·90		1·72	
Revenue from specific grants	—		—		3·60		1·34	

* Including water rates.

exclusive of any *capital* expenditure on new houses and represents only the current outlay in repairs and maintenance, interest charges and so on.

Finally, there is shown in Table 89 the expenditure of local authorities on 'free' services, the cost of which falls wholly or almost wholly on the rates or on government grants. Throughout the fifty years covered by Table 89 education has been easily the biggest item of expenditure and it has formed an increasing proportion of the total, both for 'free' services and for all services. Public assistance, once a large item, has now disappeared and health services have been curtailed through the transfer to the central government of responsibilities formerly borne by local authorities. Health services, however, remain second in importance only to education. Of the remaining services, those involving the largest expenditure are roads, police, and parks; all of these have grown in the past fifty years at a rate comparable with the total for 'free' services as a group.

Table 89. *Ordinary expenditure and revenue of Scottish local authories: 'free' services*, 1901/02 *to* 1950/51

	1901/02 All authorities		1947/48 All authorities		1950/51 Four cities only	
	£ m.	Percentage	£ m.	Percentage	£ m.	Percentage
Expenditure:						
Public assistance	1·18		5·26		—	
Education	2·34		28·20		13·15	
Health, etc.	1·01		12·39		5·24	
Lunacy, etc.	0·11		3·30		0·04	
Roads	0·96		6·86		1·58	
Police	0·56		4·62		2·82	
Parks	0·14		1·45		0·96	
Miscellaneous	1·20		6·99		4·55	
Total	7·50		69·07		28·34	
Revenue:						
Charges, etc.	0·92	12·3	6·60	9·5	5·51	19·4
Specific grants	1·58	21·0	25·94	37·6	9·73	34·3
Rates and general grants	5·00	66·7	36·53	52·9	13·10	46·3
Total	7·50	100·0	69·07	100·0	28·34	100·0

From this hasty review it is clear that the financial responsibilities that really matter are transport, housing, and education, which together accounted for 62 % of the expenditure of the four cities in 1950/51, while health services, police and roads accounted for a further 21 %. But to an increasing extent the responsibilities are passing from the local authorities. Transport services are limited on one hand by the continuing limitations imposed by the government on capital expenditure and on the other by the apparently chronic deficits of the local undertakings. Fares are subject to government control, costs are at the mercy of inflationary forces, and the local authorities, finding the task of keeping the two in step almost beyond them, tend to adjust the amount and standard of service supplied in order to set a limit to their losses. As for housing, the struggle to keep the deficit within bounds is just as unremitting, if a great deal less effectual. The local authorities are torn between the rise in the capital cost of new houses and their anxiety to keep down rents. Faced with a housing shortage and a housing deficit, they show an almost uniform distaste for raising rents and postpone such an act until forces other than the will of the majority of councillors can be blamed for the direction of events. Strangely enough, rents, unlike fares, can be raised without seeking the agreement of the central government; while on the other hand, local authorities enjoy less discretion in varying the standard of accommodation than of transport service.

Neither in the case of transport nor of housing does it appear that local authorities enjoy complete freedom in the discharge of their responsibilities, or that they shoulder these responsibilities with any show of firmness, or that the present division of responsibility between the local authorities and the central government is likely to prove a stable one. Transport policy and housing policy are now national matters, however much the central government may depend on the local authorities in their execution, whatever local variations remain in the energy and boldness with which the authorities approach their task, and whatever the range of deficits that appear as it proceeds.

The 'free' services are also increasingly dependent on policies laid down from above and this dependence is evident in the larger proportion of the cost that now falls on the central government. Figures have already been given (in Table 86) of the sources of revenue of the local authorities and these show the growing importance of government grants, and the striking fall that has taken place in the proportion of current expenditure financed out of rates. In 1881/82 grants formed about one-tenth of revenue from rates; in 1947/48 they exceeded revenue from rates by over 20 %.

The full measure of the change appears more strikingly if self-financing services are left out of account and the comparative importance of rates and grants towards the financing of other services is analysed. For this purpose it is convenient to take the deficit on each service, after counting in revenue from specific government grants, charges on consumers, fees, rents, etc., and split this deficit between rates and block grants in a uniform proportion, this proportion being the ratio of the totals of incomes from rates and block grants to one another. The actual proportions used are shown in Table 90.

When these proportions are applied to the deficits on 'subsidized' and 'free' services, and the proportion of these expenditures already covered by specific government grants is added back, some interesting conclusions emerge (see Table 91). The purely rating services, which we have labelled 'free' services, are seen to have been financed in 1947/48 to the extent of more than 50 %

Table 90. *Revenue of Scottish local authorities from rates and government block grants, 1901/02 to 1950/51*

	1901/02		1947/48		1950/51*	
	£ m.	Percentage	£ m.	Percentage	£ m.	Percentage
Revenue from rates	5·28	91·7	32·22	77·7	14·59	95·8
Revenue from block grants	0·48	8·3	9·24	22·3	0·64	4·2
	5·76	100·0	41·46	100·0	15·23	100·0

* Four cities only.

Table 91. *Percentage contribution of central and local government in Scotland to cost of 'subsidized' and 'free' services, 1901/02 to 1950/51*

	1901–02	1947–48	1950–51*
'Subsidized' services			
Rate-borne	57·7	20·5	22·7
Grant-borne	5·8	29·3	19·5
Other	36·5	50·2	57·8
'Free' services			
Rate-borne	60·6	37·8	44·3
Grant-borne	27·1	52·7	36·3
Other	12·3	9·5	19·4

* Four cities only.

by the central government. Between 1901/02 and 1947/48 the *proportionate* contribution of government grants had almost doubled while the share of rates had fallen from over 60 % to less than 40 %. These services, which have consistently accounted for three-fifths of local government expenditure, are traditionally the eminent domain of local self-government; but, as matters stand now, rates have ceased to be the main source of finance and have almost come to be local subventions in aid of Imperial services. Nor should the figures for 1950/51 be interpreted as indicating a movement towards greater dependence on rates. The new Exchequer Equalization Grant formulae have cut the four cities off almost completely from block grants as a source of income; but in the majority of other Scottish local authorities, rating services are probably still more than half financed out of grant income.

In the other group of services—in practice, housing and water supply—the rise in the share of expenditure falling on government grants has been even more spectacular—from under 6 % in 1901/02 to nearly 30 % in 1947/48. The fall in the rate-borne share of expenditure has also been striking—from 58 %

187

to 20 %. To some extent this corresponds to the growing importance of housing subsidies provided by the central government. But it is also in part a reflection of the decline in water supply relatively to housing, water supply being normally financed largely from rates while housing is not.

The figures analysed so far convey a general picture of local government activities and finance for Scotland as a whole, but do not, except for the four cities, give any indication how individual authorities are placed. This is too large a subject to be treated here, but an extreme example, the county of Sutherland, will show how far dependence on government grants has gone. Sutherland has a population of 14,000 living in an area more than twice as large as Lanarkshire. Out of a total ordinary expenditure of £367,000 in 1950/51, 89 % came from government grants while receipts from rates averaged only £3 per head.[1] Several other counties were in much the same position.

CAPITAL EXPENDITURE

The rise in the capital expenditure of Scottish local authorities has been more striking than the rise in their ordinary expenditure. In 1881/82, if one may judge from the sums borrowed in that year, expenditure on capital account was not much over £1 m.[2] Most of this, apart from what was spent on road and harbour works, was incurred by the burghs for waterworks, public buildings, and so on; and almost as fast as fresh debts were contracted for these purposes, existing debt was retired. By the beginning of the century, capital expenditure had passed £4 m. per annum, and the objects of this expenditure had widened with the growth of municipal trading. Gas, electricity, transport and water each took about £500,000, the only other items of any size being ports and harbours, telephones, schools and hospitals (see Table 92). Almost exactly half the total capital expenditure was undertaken by the twelve separate local authorities whose functions were later taken over by the councils of the four cities.

The year 1901/02 was probably the high watermark in local government capital expenditure prior to the first world war. By how much the total for that year has now been surpassed is evident from Table 92. Even if we assume

[1] I am indebted to the Scottish Home Department for these (unpublished) estimates and also for figures showing that the proportion of ordinary expenditure covered by grants varied between 78 % and 89 % in Sutherland and between 72 % and 82 % in Shetland in the years 1949/50 to 1951/52. It would appear from *Return of Rates in Scotland, 1951/52 and 1952/53* that receipts from rates in 1952/53 amounted to £54,600 in Sutherland and £47,800 in Shetland; ordinary expenditure in each county was in the neighbourhood of £500,000.

[2] The only available figures are for expenditure out of loans, excluding temporary loans to cover deficits on ordinary account. The total for 1881/82 was £1·31 m. and of this total, £0·21 m. was raised by port and harbour authorities and £0·96 m. by the burghs. Since repayment of loans came to £0·86 m. (none of it by the port and harbour authorities) *net* borrowing was less than £500,000.

Table 92. *Capital expenditure of Scottish local authorities and undertakings*, 1901/02 *to* 1950/51. (£ m.)

	1901/02 All authorities	1947/48 All authorities	1947/48 Four cities only	1950/51 Four cities only
Self-financing services				
Gas	0·54	0·95	0·49	—
Electricity	0·49	1·60	1·13	—
Transport	0·47	0·06*	0·19*	1·30
Ports and harbours	0·31	0·13	—	—
Miscellaneous†	0·13	0·08	0·06	0·03
Total	1·94	2·82	1·87	1·33
Percentage of grand total	46·4	8·2	17·0	8·6
'Subsidized' services				
Housing	0·09	26·65	7·18	10·88
Water	0·50	1·36	0·56	0·57
Baths, burial, etc.	0·09	0·03	—	—
Total	0·68	28·04	7·74	11·45
Percentage of grand total	16·2	81·2	70·1	73·8
'Free' services				
Education	0·44	0·86	0·53	1·88
Health, etc.	0·42	1·79	0·59	0·10
Roads	0·14	0·34	0·06	—
Miscellaneous‡	0·57	0·67	0·24	0·76
Total	1·57	3·66	1·42	2·74
Percentage of grand total	37·4	10·6	12·9	17·6
Grand total for all authorities	4·19§	34·52	11·03	15·52

* It has proved impossible to reconcile the capital expenditure of the four cities with that of all local authorities on transport in 1947/48.
† Mainly: 'Telephones' in 1901/02 and 'Common good' in 1947/48 and 1950/51.
‡ Including 'Public assistance', 'Mental deficiency', 'Police', 'Parks' and all other items.
§ The grand total for four cities only was £2·12 m.

that money has fallen in value to one-third in the past fifty years, capital expenditure is now at least three times as great in real terms. Assuming that it bore the same ratio in 1950/51 as in 1947/48 to the capital expenditure of the four cities, i.e. just over 3:1, it must have risen to over £48 m. and may be put at approximately £50 m. For Scotland as a whole, capital expenditure must be of the order of £200 m. so that the local authorities now account for about one-quarter of the total. If this expenditure is looked at from the other side, as a draft on the nation's savings, it assumes even greater importance. For much of the capital expenditure of industry is in replacement of existing assets and is financed out of depreciation allowances: but this does not hold true to anything like the same extent of the capital expenditure of local authorities.

189

Apart from the change in the scale of this expenditure, there has been a complete change in its composition. By 1947/48 everything had come to take a back seat to housing. Over three-quarters of the total in that year went on this single item. The only other services to absorb more than 2 % each of the total were public health, electricity, water, gas and education in that order. On transport, harbours, asylums and police stations less was spent than in 1901/02. No complete figures for years after 1947/48 are available, but it is possible to form some impression of recent trends from the figures for the four cities. These show an increase in transport and education, both in absolute terms and in their share of the total. For housing, it is possible to make an independent estimate of capital expenditure, the data for 1950/51 pointing to a total of no less than £30 m.—about as much as the total capital expenditure of all Scottish local authorities as recently as 1947/48.

One consequence of the increased importance of housing has been a change in the balance between the four cities and other local authorities. In 1901/02, the two were roughly equal. Now, with the transfer of various municipal undertakings to the State and the increase in the building of council houses in all areas, the capital expenditure of the local authorities outside the cities is growing relatively to the total.

There has also been a rise in the ratio of capital expenditure to ordinary expenditure. This ratio was about 27 % in 1881/82, 34 % in 1901/02, just under 30 % in 1947/48 and perhaps about 46 % in 1950/51. Simultaneously with this more rapid rise in capital expenditure there has been a great expansion in outstanding debt and in the loan charges that arise from this debt. This expansion is still in progress; and it is instructive to reckon what the position will be in, say, ten years' time if the existing scale and pattern of capital expenditure is maintained.

Outstanding debt

Before attempting this, we may examine the growth of the debt over the past seventy years. In 1881/82 the total was £17·6 m., of which £7·6 m. came under the heading of 'ports and harbours' and was not strictly local government debt. Of the remainder, £8·9 m. had been incurred by the burghs and £1·1 m. by the parishes and *ad hoc* road authorities.

By 1901/02, there had been an astonishing increase. If ports and harbours are left out, total local government debt rose in twenty years from £10 m. to £43 m.—and this at a time when prices were stable or falling. Most of this debt represented outlay on public utilities of various kinds—water, gas, electricity and transport. But there were also large items for schools, hospitals, parks, etc.; and housing was already beginning to be a significant claimant for capital, the housing debt standing just short of £2m.

Fifty years later, the housing debt stood at well over £200 m. and was increasing at the rate of about £30 m. a year. In 1947/48, for which full figures are available, housing accounted for two-thirds of the total debt and no other item was even one-tenth as big. Debt on account of gas, ports and harbours, waterworks and parks, was hardly any greater than in 1901/2; transport debt was far less; and of the other items, only electricity, roads, health services and baths had more than doubled.

Table 93. *Capital debt of Scottish local authorities*, 1901/02 *to* 1950/51 (£ m.)

	1901/02 All authorities	1947/48 All authorities	1947/48 Four cities only	1950/51 Four cities only
Self-financing services				
Gas	6·00	6·41	3·63	3·08
Electricity	2·42	9·70	6·03	4·79
Transport	3·58	0·59	0·59	3·91
Ports and harbours	11·10	13·81	—	—
Markets, etc.	0·27	0·21	0·12	0·09
Miscellaneous*	0·17	0·71	0·49	0·34
Total	23·54	31·44	10·86	12·22
Percentage of grand total	*43·3*	*13·4*	*12·6*	*10·7*
'Subsidized' services				
Housing	1·97	151·98	51·98	76·21
Water	11·34	13·17	4·33	5·01
Baths, burial, etc.	0·47	0·81	0·12	0·10
Total	13·78	165·96	56·43	81·32
Percentage of grand total	*25·3*	*71·5*	*65·3*	*71·2*
'Free' services				
Education	5·08	9·21	4·56	7·59
Health, etc.	2·79	11·53	4·68	5·36
Roads	1·43	5·77	3·51	3·20
Miscellaneous†	7·58	8·41	6·32	4·55
Total	16·88	34·93	19·07	20·70
Percentage of grand total	*31·4*	*15·1*	*22·1*	*18·1*
Grand total for all authorities	54·20	232·33	86·36	114·24

* Made up of 'Telephones' in 1901/02 and 'Common good' in 1947/48 and 1950/51.
† Including 'Public assistance', 'Mental deficiency', 'Police', 'Parks' and all other items.

After 1947/48 the transfer of services from local to national agencies reduced both the assets and liabilities of the local authorities; but the transfer had not proceeded far enough by 1951 to take the corresponding outstanding debt out of the books of the cities. The figures for 1950/51 in Table 93, therefore, include services whose ownership and operation were no longer the responsibility of the local authorities.

If the figures for the four cities are used in order to estimate national totals, the same caveat applies. Such an estimate can be made by assuming that the

191

ratio between the capital debt of the four cities and of all authorities, which came to 37 % in 1947/48, was the same or slightly lower in 1950/51. On this basis, the outstanding debt of all Scottish local authorities in 1950/51 was about £320 m. Similarly, the total housing debt may have been about £225 m.[1] This represents fully 70 % of all outstanding debt (including debt on services that have been nationalized) and over £40 per head of the Scottish population. The interest payable on the housing debt is rapidly becoming one of the main items of ordinary expenditure and will shortly exceed the whole amount of the expenditure of local authorities at the beginning of the century.

If we look ten years ahead, the size of the debt of local authorities seems likely to double or nearly double. The current rate of capital expenditure is £50 m. per annum and the rate of loan repayment out of sinking funds is comparatively small. Even when allowance is made for some shrinkage in the debt on account of services taken over by the State, the total may well go on increasing at, say, £30 m. per annum and so reach by 1961 a total of over £600 m. Of this total, it is almost certain that at least three-quarters would be for housing—that is, the housing debt in 1961 may be no less than three times as large as in 1948.

[1] The ratio for all debt fell from 38 % in 1945/46 to just over 37 % in 1947/48 and has been assumed above to have fallen further to 36 %. The ratio for housing debt stood at 38 % in May 1946, and was just over 35 % in May 1948. It has been taken at 34 % in 1951 in the estimate given above.

CHAPTER 14

HOUSING

By ROBERT BAIRD

Scottish housing has for long had an unenviable reputation and, rightly or wrongly, the Glasgow slums have widely been regarded as without equal in Western Europe. No other part of Britain has been the subject of a Royal Commission on Housing during the present century or been so comprehensively indicted as Scotland was in 1918 for the 'unspeakably filthy privy-middens in many of the mining areas, badly constructed, incurably damp labourers' cottages on farms, whole townships unfit for human occupation in the crofting counties and islands... gross overcrowding and huddling of the sexes together in the congested industrial villages and towns, occupation of one-room houses by large families, groups of lightless and unventilated houses in the older burghs, clotted masses of slums in the great cities... farmed-out houses, model lodging-houses, congested back-lands, and ancient closes'.[1]

Yet it was of Edinburgh, not Glasgow, that Defoe exclaimed: 'in no city in the world do so many people live in so little room'; and it was Glasgow, not Edinburgh, that he thought 'the cleanest and beautifullest and best built City in Britain, London excepted'. Not much more than a century later another observer was to write that he 'did not believe until he visited the wynds of Glasgow that so large an amount of filth, crime, misery and disease existed on one spot in any civilized country'. A century later still, in 1952, the City Architect of Glasgow was complaining that the net residential density for over half the houses in the city was ninety-five dwellings to the acre, and was busy planning for the rehousing elsewhere of half the entire population.[2] The industrialization of the eighteenth and nineteenth centuries may have left its hall-mark stamped more indelibly upon housing in Scotland than elsewhere, but within the past twenty years there have been improvements as remarkable in Scotland as in the rest of Great Britain. A population that has hardly altered since 1931 had 230,000 more houses and nearly a million more rooms by 1951; the one-roomed houses in which over a quarter of the population once crowded together were well on the way to extinction; the worst of the slums were rapidly being pulled down.

[1] *Report of the Royal Commission on Housing in Scotland* (1918), Cd. 8731, p. 346.
[2] *Glasgow's Housing Needs*, report by City Architect (Mr A. G. Jury), August 1952.

Housing standards

Until after the first world war, houses in Scotland, in town or country, were almost invariably built of stone. They had high-ceilinged rooms of a generous cubic capacity, and external walls from 18 in. to 2 ft. and more in thickness, built with great care and a high standard of craftsmanship, to stand against cold winds and weathers for a century or more. The cavity brick wall which is now a standard (even a traditional) specification was regarded with suspicion, and as late as 1918 representations were made to the Royal Commission that it was not suited to Scottish conditions and would literally fail to stand up to the winds in exposed areas. The traditional Scottish house was built to last; and non-traditional materials, designs, specifications and building practice which seemed to endanger durability have always had a hard struggle for acceptance. Even now, much of the post-1945 non-traditional practice, introduced to economize scarce materials and labour, is being supplanted by the post-1918 'non-traditional' methods which are regarded as the minimum trustworthy. Stone is coming into favour again, and so are tenements and flats after a long spell in the wilderness.

In the nineteenth century the typical houses in the rural areas and small burghs, and to a lesser extent in the large burghs and cities, were the one-room and room-and-kitchen cottages, few of them with a piped water supply or internal sanitary and domestic appliances. In the rural areas, and particularly in the small non-industrialized towns where it was standard building practice, there were also two-storied cottages with or without attics, many of them originally built for occupation by a single household, some of them 'double-flatted' with an external stair for use by the household living in the top storey, and most of them subdivided in the latter part of the century into several tenancies under pressure of scarcity of house-room. Sanitary arrangements, if they existed at all, were generally grossly inadequate, shared by several households, and sited in the most inconvenient and unhealthy part of the building. In the industrial towns and the great cities, apart from surviving samples of the various cottage type and two-storied houses, there were the tenement and terrace houses that had once been occupied by the fairly well-to-do, and were now subdivided to house many more families than they had been built for and many more than they could cope with on any standard of public or private health and comfort. Sanitary arrangements were primitive and had been so even for the few households originally catered for.

Last, but by no means least, there were the tenements that had been built as tenements, the nineteenth-century's distinctive contribution to town housing in Scotland for the poor, the skilled craftsman, the middle-class and the comparatively rich alike—the 'flats' which, with all their enormous drawbacks, have yet so many attractions for the Scots town-dweller that they seem to have come to stay. These tenements were typically of four stories, but were often of more. The worst of them were the mid-century back-lands, built in the back-courts, gardens or yards of houses already fronting on a main thoroughfare, and abutting on narrow closes leading to the street from which they were all but hidden. Such houses, which excluded most of the light and air, soon became plague-spots and were destined to become the object of slum-clearance and demolition activities for years to come.

At the other extreme, the best of the Victorian tenements had two flats on each landing, with perhaps six entering from the common stair and the two ground-floor flats forming main-door houses. These flats had three, four and more rooms and kitchen with a bathroom, water closet and hot-water system, and a 'built-off' scullery. They were built in the 'better class' districts of the towns and their rents put them out of reach of even the well-paid highly-skilled workmen. Then there were middling quality tenements occupied by what the Royal Commission described as 'the superior artisan class' and the 'good artisan class' of tenants. These had either three houses on each landing (nine or twelve per common stair), each of two rooms and kitchen with a bath-room, or four houses on each landing (sixteen to twenty per common stair), each with a room and kitchen and a water-closet, or in some cases a bathroom.

Nearly all these tenements could and did eke out their sleeping accommodation with 'box beds' or 'bed recesses' or 'bed closets'—all amounting to the same thing but variously described according to whether the family, the lodger, or the servant slept there. All but the worst of them, which were unfortunately only too numerous, were provided with the minimum of sanitary equipment that we now consider essential to public health.

It was on the erection of tenement houses that building in the latter part of the nineteenth century and the first years of the twentieth was concentrated; and it was these houses, as the Royal Commission observed, that were largely responsible for the marked improvements over that period in average sanitary conditions, if not in density of occupation, in the towns of Scotland. During the inter-war period, there was a marked change in the type of building erected. The tenement was completely out of favour except for some rehousing and slum-clearance schemes and for rebuilding on cleared expensive sites in the towns. Privately-built houses for sale to owner-occupiers were usually of the detached or semi-detached bungalow or small villa types. Local authority houses for letting were principally four-flatted two-storey cottages, small two-storied terrace blocks of 'front-door' houses, or semi-detached small villas. Outer shells were mainly of brick (the cavity wall) and sanitary and domestic fittings were invariably good enough to be immune from any likely improvement in standards during the lifetime of the house.

Since 1945 a much larger proportion of the new houses in Scotland than in England and Wales have been non-traditional in material or design and the new houses have been larger and better equipped than those put up by Scottish local authorities before the war though still smaller, on the average, than the post-war English council houses. The various kinds of non-traditional outer shells—of poured concrete, concrete blocks, prefabricated slabs and panels, timber, aluminium, steel and other materials—that were so extensively used after the war are now giving way to the cavity brick wall, though a great deal of non-traditional design, material, building practice and fittings remain in the internal structures. Pressure on building space, shortage of house-room together with the requirements of town plans have in some cases—particularly in Glasgow—led to the resumption of the building of flats in tenement blocks.

THE CONTRAST WITH ENGLAND AND WALES

Whatever the gulf between housing conditions in Scotland and in the industrial areas of the rest of Britain, it is not sufficiently remarkable to the ordinary observer to make statistical tests of the difference superfluous. The first such test that one can use is the degree of overcrowding. There can be no fixed measure of over-crowding. Public standards are constantly being raised. The standard most commonly adopted has been 'more than two persons per room'; the Royal Commission in 1918 in its first calculations of housing needs made use with some reluctance of the comparatively low standard of 'more than three persons per room'; the Registrar General for England and Wales at that time used 'more than two persons per room'; the Housing Act of 1935 laid down a complicated formula which remains the statutory definition although no day has ever been appointed for its enforcement;[1] and the Scottish Housing Advisory Committee in 1944 recommended a higher standard, permitting two persons to each room except the first (which was not to be counted at all). This last standard has been accepted by local authorities in Scotland in fixing standards of occupancy for new houses and has influenced the size of the houses that they have built. It is, however, a standard that it would be quite impossible to enforce generally in Scotland for many years.

The surveys undertaken under the 1935 Act (and the corresponding Act for Scotland) showed that by the standard adopted nearly one house in four was overcrowded in Scotland compared with one in twenty-six in England and Wales. It is not possible to apply the same standard for other years; but if the simpler and slightly more stringent formula of more than two persons per room is used, it would appear that, in spite of a considerable improvement over the past twenty years, overcrowding is still much worse in Scotland than in England and Wales.

In 1951 there were nearly as many people living more than two to a room

[1] The general effect of the formula was to allow 2 persons in the one-roomed house, and from 1½ to 2 persons per room in larger houses, children under one year not being counted and those of one to ten years being counted as half an adult.

in Scotland as there were in England and Wales, where the population was about nine times as great. The proportion of the Scottish population living in those conditions had, however, fallen steadily from about 60 % a hundred years ago to 45 % before the first world war and 15·5 % in 1951; and there is every reason to expect a substantial further improvement by the next census.

Percentage of population living more than two to a room		
	Scotland	England and Wales
1931	35·0	6·9
1951	15·5	2·2

Overcrowding is not equally bad in all parts of Scotland but is almost uniformly worse than in England and Wales. The highest rates are reached in Glasgow; in some wards such as Hutchesontown, Dalmarnock, Gorbals and Cowcaddens, not far short of half the population still live at a density of over two to a room. The percentage living more than two to a room in Glasgow has fallen, however, from 42·3 % to 24·4 % in twenty years, and it is a re-markable fact that out of thirty-seven Glasgow wards, only Hutchesontown and Dalmarnock are now above the average for the whole city in 1931. Rates of over-crowding similar to Glasgow's are common in the industrial towns such as Motherwell, Coatbridge and Paisley, but in the other large cities the rate of overcrowding is only about half Glasgow's, and in some of the county towns and rural areas it is a good deal lower still.

A second test of density of occupation, permitting comparisons with England and Wales over a long period of years, is the average number of persons to each dwelling-room. The figures are given in Table 94.

By this test also, housing standards are well below those of England and

Table 94. *Density of occupation in Scotland and in England and Wales, 1871–1951*

Year	Scotland			England and Wales
	Persons per house	Rooms per house	Persons per room	Persons per room
1871	—	—	1·69	—
1891	4·90	3·03	1·62	—
1911	4·55	3·14	1·45	0·95
1931	4·08	3·21	1·27	0·83
1951	3·53	3·37	1·04	0·73

SOURCE: *Census of Population.*

197

Wales; in 1951 Scotland had failed to reach a standard of occupancy already reached in England and Wales forty years earlier. This is, however, putting matters in the least favourable light. The rooms in the traditional Scottish house built before 1920 are slightly larger, certainly as regards height and probably also as regards area, than in the average English house.[1] It is probably also more common for the kitchen to be equipped for use as a living room. These are no more than qualifications and do not detract from the undoubted lag revealed by the figures. What is of more significance is the acceleration in the rate of improvement since the first world war. In the forty years from 1871 to 1911 the density of occupation improved by 14 %, and in the succeeding forty years by 28 %. But this contrast does not, as one might suppose, reflect a greater effort of house-building in the later period. On the contrary, nearly as many rooms were added in the first as in the second period, (1,185,000 compared with 1,483,000) and by a smaller and poorer population. The really significant change was the more gradual increase in population: nearly five times as many persons were added to the population between 1871 and 1911 as were added between 1911 and 1951.

The contrast between Scotland and England and Wales is only fully appreciated when the figures are looked at in detail. In only one of the six English conurbations does the average density of occupation rise above 0·8 persons per room and in that one (Tyneside) the average is 0·88. On the other hand, in Clydeside the average is 1·23, and in one Glasgow ward in three it is 1·50 or over, the peak being reached in Hutchesontown with 1·82.

A third test is provided by the size of house occupied by the majority of the population. In Scotland a far higher proportion than in England and Wales live in houses of one room ('single ends') or two rooms ('but and bens'). In 1951 the proportions were 26 % and 2·6 % respectively and there were actually more people living in these small houses in Scotland than there were in the whole of England and Wales. The 'single ends' have been consistently more overcrowded than any other size of house and their ultimate elimination is now an accepted aim of policy.[2] Very few have been built during the present century, but in 1911 they formed 12·8 % and in 1951 still accounted for 5·7 % of the total stock of houses. Houses of two rooms were until recently more numerous than any other size of house in Scotland but are now outnumbered by houses of three rooms. In Glasgow, however, they still predominate and together with houses of one room make up nearly half the total for the city. Forty years ago, at the 1911 Census, they accounted for no less than two-thirds of all houses in Glasgow.

[1] 50 % in cubic capacity and 20 % in floor area (Cd. 8731, p. 44). Houses built since 1920 have approximated more closely to the normal English measurements.

[2] The most vivid and effective attack on the 'single end' was written as far back as 1888 by J. B. Russell, *Life in One Room* (included in *Public Health Administration in Glasgow*, 1905).

Table 95. *Size of dwelling-houses in Scotland and in*
England and Wales, 1951

Number of rooms in house	Number of houses in		Percentage of houses	
	Scotland (thousands)	England and Wales (thousands)	Scotland	England and Wales
I	76·9	84·4	5·7	o·8
2	362·5	424·9	26·3	3·6
3	422·2	1298·9	30·6	10·9
4	293·0	3369·3	21·2	28·2
5	104·4	4246·6	7·6	35·5
6 or more	119·0	2509·8	8·6	21·0
All sizes	1378·0	11933·8	100·0	100·0

SOURCE: *Census of Population* 1951: *One Per Cent Sample Tables.*

Table 96. *Households in Scotland and in England and Wales*
with no piped water, etc., 1951

Households lacking	Scotland		England and Wales	
	Number (thousands)	Percentage	Number (thousands)	Percentage
Piped water	75·1	5·2	735·4	5·7
Kitchen sink	77·3	5·4	827·9	6·4
Water-closet	86·5	6·0	1,028·0	7·9
Fixed bath	626·5	43·6	4,809·2	36·8
Cooking stove	71·5	5·0	262·6	2·0
All households	1,438·0	—	13,043·5	—

SOURCE: *Census of Population*, 1951: *One Per Cent Sample Tables.*

The predominance of small houses in Scotland emerges strikingly from Table 95. Only 37·4 % of Scottish houses have more than three rooms, while in England and Wales the proportion is 84·7 %. The proportion of new houses built in Scotland with four or more apartments has also been below the corresponding proportion for England and Wales. For Scotland the proportion shows a steady drop throughout the post-war period. Of the 68,500 houses approved between January 1946 and September 1948, 94 % were of four apartments or more; thereafter, the proportion fell progressively from 87 % in 1948/49 to 64 % in 1949/50, 44 % in 1950/51, and 42·5 % in 1951/52 (*Hansard*, 24 February 1953, Written Answers, cols. 207–8).

Finally, one may use the data in the 1951 Census on housing arrangements. Nearly half the Scottish households (43·6 %) were without a fixed bath; about

199

one in sixteen (6·0 %) lacked a water-closet and a slightly smaller proportion a piped water supply and a kitchen sink; apart from those households that were without a water-closet, nearly one in three shared one (Table 96).

It is clear from Table 96 that these proportions did not all compare unfavourably with those for England and Wales. The one arrangement for which the comparison is plainly unfavourable to Scotland is the cooking stove; and the fixed bath is rather more frequently lacking from Scottish houses. If the comparison is put on a different footing, however, and the proportion of households *without exclusive use* of these household arrangements is analysed, Scotland emerges rather less creditably (Table 97). In particular, a much higher proportion of Scottish families share a water-closet, and only two families in three have the exclusive use of one.

Table 97. *Percentage of households in Scotland and in England and Wales without exclusive use of household arrangements*

Households lacking exclusive use of	Scotland	England and Wales
Piped water	12	17
Kitchen sink	12	13
Water-closet	35	21
Fixed bath	49	45
Cooking stove	11	7

SOURCE: *Census of Population,* 1951: *One Per Cent Sample Tables.*

It is the more striking that the figures in Table 97 are less favourable to Scotland than those in Table 96 because apparently a far higher proportion of families share a house in England and Wales. The proportion there in 1951 was 15·1 % while in Scotland it was only 7·7 %. Thus many of the households shown in Table 97 as sharing arrangements in England and Wales do so because they share a house while in Scotland far more families do so because the household arrangements shared by neighbours are external to the houses themselves.

The reasons for the contrast

All this evidence of lower housing standards in Scotland than in England and Wales inevitably raises the question of cause. The divergence is not due to the greater wealth of England, since the divergence was wider in the days when Scotland was probably as rich as, or richer than, her neighbour. Nor is it associated with a more rapid increase in population—population rose more slowly in Scotland. An explanation may be sought in one of three directions: the greater cost of providing house-room in Scotland; a lower demand for house-room and a greater reluctance to pay for it; or the effects of the Scottish system of rating and valuation, operating in conjunction with the Rent Restriction Acts.

The first of these explanations is difficult to test since there are no figures for exactly comparable houses in different parts of Britain. The stone houses built in Scotland prior to 1914 do at least look more costly than houses built for similar tenants in England. In Glasgow, their cost in the fifty years before 1914 varied between about £65 and £100 per room, so that the average house of two or three rooms cost some £200; this was exclusive of all interior fitments, plumbing and so on, but many working-class houses in Scotland at that time were built without a piped water supply and sanitary and domestic appliances. No corresponding figures appear to exist for England and Wales. Since the average size of house was certainly larger, it was probably also more costly. It would be surprising if the older brick houses characteristic of the average English town were built at a cost less than £200.

Table 98. *Average tender prices for council houses in Scotland and in England and Wales*, 1922–47

Year	Scotland	England and Wales
	Four-apartment house	Three-bedroom house
	£	£
1922	559	378
1935	325	293
1939*	473	(under 400)
1947	1,293	1,170

* For Scotland, average to end of August; for England and Wales, estimate for 'immediately before the war'.

SOURCES: *Scottish Building Costs* (Report of the Laidlaw Committee, 1948). *The Cost of Housebuilding* (Report of the Girdwood Committee, 1948).

For the inter-war years, there are no figures showing the final cost per house in either country but it is possible to make a comparison between average tender prices for four-apartment council houses in Scotland and three-bedroom council houses in England and Wales. These figures (Table 98) are strictly comparable, and they point to a level of building costs in Scotland rather higher—perhaps 10 % higher—than in England and Wales. This tends to inflate the rent charged for given accommodation and hence to limit the demand for house-room in comparison with England and Wales.

There is not much doubt, however, that the second explanation of the difference in housing standards is far and away the most important. Scottish families have long been accustomed to a standard of housing far below the standard for families in similar circumstances in England. The size-distribution of Scottish houses shown in Table 95 is not the outcome of some perverse wish to perpetuate overcrowding on the part of those who built or who own the houses; it reflects the preference of many Scottish families for small houses. Many forces have gone to the creation of such a preference. There is, first, the force of tradition and inertia; those who have been brought up in a house of two or three rooms often feel no great urge to move to one of four or five rooms, and when they do, may be at a loss to make full use of the additional space. There is too the strong conservative disinclination to make the change to a new environment and pattern of life which very often the bigger house would involve. There are, in addition, economic factors pressing in the same direction; to move to a larger house means extra rent, rates, furniture, and fuel. It is not too much to say, therefore, that much of the over-crowding in Scotland is attributable to the householders' own preferences.

This may seem a paradoxical proposition when householders are in fact clamouring for more house-room and, by implication, for less overcrowding. But the present shortage is not the simple result of a desire on the part of householders for larger houses; it is caused by a number of circumstances of which housing subsidies are perhaps the most important. And there is no evidence that the number of houses that would put an end to the present shortage would also reduce overcrowding to the point already reached in England and Wales. It is not even true that the size of the new houses built is decided by their prospective tenants; it is fixed on the recommendation of the central government by the local authorities who build them and fixed by reference to what the tenants are thought to need, not to the free choice that tenants might make if they could pick and choose between houses of different sizes all equally heavily subsidized.

The *customary* standard of housing has certainly risen much nearer to the level in England since the first world war, but there is no doubt about the difference in standards before then. The demand for houses throughout Britain was hardly at all inhibited at the time of the 1911 Census by any physical shortage. In Glasgow, for example, more than one house in ten stood empty, and in other Scottish towns the average was not much lower. Some 6,000 houses in Glasgow of three rooms or more which had been occupied a few years previously, and were occupied again before the war was over, stood empty in 1911. Householders there who felt themselves over-crowded in a house of two rooms could have moved without difficulty in 1911 to one of three rooms. The extra rent would have been of the order of 1s. per week—no impossible burden for working-class households with an average income of about £2 per week. Moreover, the building industry stood ready to take advantage of any demand for new houses that would relieve the deep and prolonged depression that had overtaken it. Yet there was no such movement and no such demand; the proportion of houses of three or four rooms that stood empty was just about as high as the proportion of smaller houses. At the same time the census revealed that 53·3 % of the stock of houses in Scotland were of one or two rooms, while in England and Wales the proportion was no more than 11·5 %.

The fact is that Scottish families, then as now, paid a smaller proportion of their income in rent. In 1911 the Inhabited House Duty statistics showed that a far higher proportion of Scottish than of English houses were of less than £10 gross annual value (58 % compared with 37 %). Since the Scottish assessments included owners' rates while the English assessments excluded all rates, the true difference was even larger. If one takes houses of under £20 gross annual value as coinciding roughly with working-class houses, the average for the gross annual value comes to £10·1 for England and £8·6 for Scotland. Allowing for the inclusion of a larger proportion of the total stock of Scottish houses in this calculation and of the inflation of the gross annual value by owners' rates in Scotland, we are not likely to be far out if we put the rent paid by the average Scottish working-class family in 1911 at 75–80 % of the rent paid by a similar family in England and Wales. It may also be estimated that the income of the average wage-earning household at that time was about £2 per week,[1] so that in Scotland about 8 % of family income went on rent, and in England and Wales 10 %.

Table 99. *Houses of gross annual value under £60 in Scotland and in England and Wales*, 1911

Gross annual value	Scotland		England and Wales	
	Number (thousands)	Percentage	Number (thousands)	Percentage
Exempt from duty				
Under £10	576	58	2,664	37
£10–£15	183	18	1,921	26
£15–£20	92	9	869	12
Total	851	86	5,454	75
Charged to duty				
£20–£60	124	12	1,563	21
£60 and over	17	2	274	4
All houses	992	100	7,291	100

SOURCE: *Annual Report of Commissioners of Inland Revenue*, 1912.

[1] There were just over 9 m. families in Great Britain, of whom about 80 % were wage-earning, and the wage-bill was a little under £750 m. per annum. This gives a family wage-income of approximately £2 per week and this average can be applied both to Scotland and to England and Wales as there was no great difference between the two (above, p. 153). The number of wage-earners was about twice the number of wage-earning families, i.e. there were, on the average, two wage-earners in each working-class family.

The evidence suggests that this difference persisted throughout the inter-war period. The household budgets collected by the Ministry of Labour in 1937/38 showed that the average weekly expenditure on rent and rates by a Scottish working-class household was 8s. 2d. while the British average was 10s. 10d. In terms of total household expenditure, the Scottish proportion was 9·1 % on rent and rates compared with 12·7 % for Great Britain.[1] A further calculation, based on fuller details of these budgets, shows that while in England and Wales average net rents (excluding all rates) varied from £14·9 in Wales to £27·8 in London, in Scotland the limits were £9·4 in the Highlands and £13·5 in Glasgow. There is no doubt, therefore, that, after deduction of rates, the average Scottish tenant in 1937/38 was paying much less in rent than his neighbour in the south.

It would be difficult to argue from these figures that all that stood between Scotland and the level of housing customary in England was a physical shortage of houses. Given rent-control and the shortage of houses, one cannot, it is true, argue from what was in fact spent on rent to the underlying demand for house-room; it is at least conceivable that the lower expenditure on rent in Scotland was only a sign of more drastic rent-control. But it is no more than conceivable, and on the face of things it is highly improbable.

There remains the third point of difference that may help to account for the backward state of Scottish housing, namely the system of rating and valuation, taken in conjunction with the Rent Restriction Acts. In Scotland rates are not paid exclusively by the tenant, as in England, but are divided between land-lord and tenant, the landlord paying owner's rates out of what he receives from his tenant, who remains responsible for occupier's rates.[2] Owner's rates, moreover, are levied on a gross annual value which includes owner's rates, so that any increase in owner's rates would operate twice over to increase the rate payment made by the landlord if he raised the rent to the tenant. In the circum-stances ruling before the first world war, the difference in the rating system was probably of little importance: given the amount to be raised in rates, it did not matter much in the long run whether the money was collected from the landlord (and recouped by him in the form of extra rent) or direct from the tenant. But the Rent Restriction Act in 1920 altered matters. The contractual rent[3] of a controlled house (i.e. one with a rateable value under £45) was pegged at

---

[1] Since the average number of rooms per household was 2·6 in Scotland and 3·9 in England and Wales, the average payment per room was 3s. 9d. and 3s. 4d. respectively. This difference may be partly attributable to the difference in building costs referred to above but has probably more to do with differences in local rates and in the rating systems in the two countries.

[2] Although in the case of 'small dwellings' (i.e. dwellings of less than £26. 5s. rateable value), the tenant pays his occupier's rates to the landlord along with his rent.

[3] That is, the payment received by the landlord excluding any occupier's rates such as might be paid to him by a tenant of a 'small dwelling'. In Scotland, the terms 'contractual rent' and 'assessed rent' are interchangeable.

140 % of the 1914 contractual rent plus any increase in owner's rates between 1914 and 1920. Any subsequent increase in occupier's rates fell on the tenant, but not any increase in owner's rates, which had to be met by the landlord out of the fixed contractual rent. Thus, as owner's rates rose, the net return to the landlord from his property fell, and he had a diminishing incentive to maintain and improve it.

As housing conditions improved in the 1930's, some of the restrictions were gradually relaxed, but most houses with a rateable value under £35 had not been decontrolled even in 1939. Controlled rents then stood, as they had done since 1920, at about 50 % above the 1914 level. With the outbreak of war the restrictions were reimposed, this time on houses with a rateable value under £90 and so covering nearly all the rented houses in Scotland, except those built and owned by local authorities. There has been no relaxation since. The owner of a rent-controlled house in Scotland tends, in consequence of the restrictions, to bear a rating burden which an English landlord escapes. The magnitude of this additional burden may be estimated roughly by comparing the average level of owner's rates in Scotland in a pre-war year—say, 1937/38— and in 1951/52. For those years the averages were 4s. 4d. and 6s. 4d. respectively.[1] The difference of 2s. in the £ represents 10 % of the contractual rent and a higher proportion on the rent, net of all costs, left to the landlord. On a new house built shortly before the war this last proportion would be about 20 % and on an older house would be still higher. When other factors, such as increases in taxation and in the cost of repairs, were already operating to reduce the return on house-property—sometimes to a very low or even negative figure—this additional burden has obviously been an extremely serious one.

Yet it can have had only a limited influence on housing conditions in Scotland. The situation in 1914 had little or nothing to do with the peculiarities of Scottish rating. Between the wars the number of new houses built in Scotland (337,000) was less, but not very much less, per head of population than the number built in England and Wales (4,194,000).[2] It would be no great exaggeration to say that what private enterprise did not build, the local authorities did, so that a much larger proportion of inter-war building in Scotland was on local government account—67 % compared with 25 % in England and Wales. At the very most, an additional 100,000 houses might have been built in the inter-war period had the rating system affected the private landlord in Scotland in the same way as in England and Wales. After 1945 building by private enterprise was so restricted that even if private land-

---

[1] For 1937/38 calculated independently; for 1951/52 estimate for cities, large burghs, counties (except Sutherland), small burghs with a population over 8,000 as given in *Rating Review*, 1951, published by the Scottish branch of the Institute of Municipal Treasurers and Accountants.

[2] Houses completed between March 1919 and March 1940.

lords had wished to build large numbers of houses for rent, they would not have been granted licences or, if they had, would have forced the local authorities to cut their programmes more or less correspondingly. Thus the main influence of the difference in rating systems has been on the maintenance and improvement of existing houses rather than on new building. If landlords had had a greater incentive to maintain their property, the mass of the population might perhaps be living in houses in a rather better state of repair; but it is doubtful whether overcrowding would be perceptibly less, even if the dilapidation of Scottish houses of an otherwise adequate standard has enforced a somewhat higher rate of demolition and abandonment of such houses than in the rest of the country.[1]

If one looks forward and not backwards, however, the Scottish rating system begins to have a different significance. It operates not only to transfer the function of building houses to let from private enterprise to public authorities but also to give the tenant cheaper house-room than he could rent under the English system of rating. The Scottish landlord, viewed in comparison with the English, is penalized; the Scottish tenant, by the same standard, is subsidized. Thus even if the housing shortage has not been greatly affected from the side of supply because of the load on the building industry, it is affected from the side of demand. The lower the rent, the more house-room tenants feel they can afford and the more difficult it is for newcomers to find a house. From this point of view, rent restriction, reinforced by the rating system, has operated in the same general direction as housing subsidies. Scotland provides a more extreme illustration of forces that have also been at work in England and Wales.

The position in Scotland at the end of 1952 can be best brought out by taking the example of Glasgow. For working-class houses already built the average rents in 1906/07, 1937/38, and 1952/53 were approximately as shown in Table 100. The figure for 1906/07 applies to all houses with rents below £20 (gross of owners' rates), the figures for the other two years to all houses below £30. This means that a diminishing proportion of the total stock of houses is

[1] Between 1 January 1946 and 31 January 1953, 268 tenement properties in Glasgow comprising 3,569 houses were offered free by their owners to the City Council. By January 1953 owners of a further sixty-seven tenement properties comprising 1,086 houses had intimated to the City Assessor that they had ceased to collect rents and it is certain that many more had ceased to do so without giving any such intimation. In 1952, 705 houses in fifty-one properties were condemned as dangerous on Dean of Guild Court Warrants, and the Works department would have made this figure much higher if the policy of conserving as many houses as possible had not been so stringent. This same policy had radically reduced the annual number of certificates of 'unfitness' issued by the city Medical Officer of Health. These had amounted to 631 in the six years from 1945 to 1950. Altogether 2,953 houses in the city were condemned as unfit by the Medical Officer of Health or dangerous by the Master of Works between 1945 and 1950 and this was equivalent to 21 % of the number of houses built by the city in that period.

covered but in view of the large amount of demolition of old property, the extension of the city boundaries, and the erection of new and bigger houses, the figures err, if at all, in comparing houses that were on the average steadily improving. It is striking to find, therefore, that while the gross rent paid by the tenant (inclusive of rates) was 93 % higher in 1937/38 than in 1906/07, the amount retained by the landlord was only 25 % higher. By 1952/53 these proportions had become 132 % and 17 %. The tenant, faced with higher occupier's rates, was paying about 20 % more in gross rent than in 1937/38 but the landlord's average net rent was less in amount than before the war. If one assumes that the value of money in 1952/53 was about one-third of its value in 1906/07, the tenant is getting house-room at about 60 % below parity with other items in the cost of living, while the landlord's income, net only of rates, is in real terms just under 40 % of its 1906/07 level.

Table 100. *Rent and rates in Glasgow, 1906–53*

Year	Limit of contractual rent of houses included in the table	Percentage of all Glasgow houses included	Average contractual rent	Occupier's rates	Owner's rates
	(£)		£ s. d.	£ s. d.	£ s. d.
1906–07	20	85	9 18 6	1 19 8	1 0 8
1937–38	30	80	16 6 0	6 14 6	5 3 3
1952–53	30	78	17 5 0	10 8 5	6 16 10

SOURCE: Calculations from figures supplied by Glasgow City Assessor's Department. The average contractual rent for 1952/53 is a near-estimate.

If next one takes a new council house of four apartments, it is interesting to examine the degree to which, given current housing policies, the tenant enjoys a subsidy from public funds. These policies may have changed by the time this book appears, but in 1952 this is how things would have worked out. First of all, the average final cost of a four-apartment local authority house was estimated to be £1,911 at March 1952.[1] A private landlord, letting such a house, would require to charge at least £150 in rent and the tenant would probably have to pay £215 or more, inclusive of rates. In point of fact, the average amount charged by local authorities for such a house was no more than £33 and the sum paid by the tenant, inclusive of rates, came to only £47. 17s. If the local authority had put itself in the position of a private landlord and charged accordingly without any element of subsidy, central or local,

[1] This was the average for traditional and non-traditional houses as submitted in the course of subsidy review discussions in 1952 by the Local Authorities Associations in Scotland.

the tenant would have paid 4½ times what he was in fact being asked to pay. Even allowing for the central grant of £42. 5s. and the statutory local subsidy of £14. 5s. he would still have to pay 3½ times his present gross rent.

These are startling figures. They are obtained on the following assumptions:

(i) Loan charges (£88. 10s.) are assessed on a loan at 4¼%, repayable in sixty years. These are more favourable terms than a private landlord could hope for.

(ii) Maintenance is taken at the statutory minimum of £8 per annum— a quite derisory figure in relation to the probable cost of maintenance over the life of a house costing over £1,900.

(iii) An allowance of £3 is made for management expenses.

(iv) Owner's rates are taken at an average of 6s. 8d. in the £, and occupier's rates at 9s. in the £. These figures are probably close to the average for all Scottish local authorities in 1952.

Thus the total gross rent works out at:

					£	s.
Annual charges	...	...	...	...	99	10
Owners' rates	...	...	...	...	49	15
Occupiers' rates	...	...	...	...	67	3
					216	8

These figures can be put rather differently to show how the actual payment made by the tenant of such a new house would fall short of the full cost:

				£	s.
Rent paid by the tenant	...	...	...	33	0
Rates paid by the tenant	...	...	...	14	17
Actual payment by the tenant	...	...	...	47	17
Statutory subsidy from central government	...			42	5
Statutory subsidy from local authority		...		14	5
Charges not collected	...	...	...	...	10	0
Rates not collected	...	...	...	...	102	1
Total	...	...	...	...	...	216	8

Thus the largest element of subsidy consists of neither the contribution made by the central government nor the statutory contribution made by the local authority out of the rates, but the rates that a private landlord (and his tenant) would require to pay, which do not feature at all in the accounts of the local authority.

This is how the situation appears from the point of view of a private landlord; if it continues, the private landlord will inevitably become extinct. From the point of view of a local authority, the situation looks rather different; the

208

local authority shoulders the same costs as a private landlord when it builds a new house but, unlike a private landlord, it draws rates as well as rent towards these costs. On a four-apartment house, it will be out of pocket only to the extent of the difference between the annual charges on the house (£99. 10s.) and the sum of what is paid by the tenant (£47. 17s.) and by the central government (£42. 5s.): in other words, by £9. 8s. This is actually less than the statutory subsidy which it is empowered to provide.[1] Were this all, there would be no reason for alarm. But the local authority has also to provide the various services incidental to the occupancy of the new house— the very services that cause it to levy rates. To have less than nothing to contribute to the rating account represents both an injustice to other rate-payers and a sure source of deficit on those other services.

By how much it would be necessary to raise the rent of a new council house to prevent it from becoming a net burden on other ratepayers, it is difficult to say. Conditions vary from one area to another. But if one were to assume that the average new house should contribute the moderate sum of £20 per annum towards rating services,[2] in addition to clearing the statutory subsidy of £14. 5s., it would be necessary to charge the tenant, in rent and rates, not £47. 17s. but £77. 5s. This would represent an increase of just over 60%. Such an increase, even if it did not cause the housing shortage to disappear overnight, would involve serious discrimination in relation to other tenants, both of existing council houses and of rent-restricted houses. It is impossible, for this reason, to separate the financial problems involved in new house-building from those involved in balancing Housing Revenue Accounts and from the wider problems arising out of rent restriction.

On these, little need be said here. But it is evident that what will ultimately oblige the local authorities to take action will be, not the deficit on new houses, but the progressively larger total deficit over a long period of years in their Housing Accounts. Glasgow alone had an annual deficit of £1·1 m. on housing account in 1952/53. Indeed, a not insubstantial part of the full economic cost to the tenant of a new house is made up of rates necessary to meet the deficit on existing council houses. Now there is little likelihood that housing deficits will be covered by any large increase in central government subsidies,[3] so that the unstable financial balance established so far by trans-ferring annual deficits to rating account will become progressively more un-stable as the proportion of houses built and owned by rating authorities

---

[1] Without, however, being given any additional sources of revenue from which to finance the subsidy.

[2] In 1952/53 the average Glasgow house (which was old and had less than three apartments) contributed a little over £17 in rates (see Table 100).

[3] The 1952 increase barely covered the increase in interest charges by the Public Works Loan Board and the 1946 Act contained provisions only for review *downwards* if the expected fall in building costs occurred.

increases. Failing other reliefs, a general increase in rents and a redistribution of rate burdens consequent thereon seem to be unavoidable.

It may be asked whether a 60 % increase in the payments made in rent and rates by the tenants of existing council houses would be sufficient to bring Housing Accounts back into balance. If the current annual deficit, excluding all income from rates, is of the order of £5 m.—as seems probable—the answer is that it would do rather more than wipe out the deficit. In 1951 the 365,523 houses owned by Scottish local authorities were let at an average contractual rent of just under £24 per annum[1] and the average amount paid by the tenant inclusive of rates was about £35. An increase of 60 % in rent and rates would, therefore, swell local authority revenues by some £7·7 m. Part of this, however, would undoubtedly be needed in order to provide rebates in established cases of hardship. It may be reasonably near the truth, to put the increase in average rents necessary to bring Housing Accounts into balance at 40 % and the increase in the rent of new houses necessary to maintain that balance at 60 %. If some relaxation of the rent restriction policies were simultaneously introduced (and this would seem to be necessary even if only to bring the rents of council houses and equivalent private houses more into line) this would automatically reduce the magnitude of the adjustment in the gross rents of council houses necessary to procure financial stability.[2]

An increase of 40 %, however drastic, would still leave rents relatively low in comparison with other elements in the cost of living. How much hardship it would create would depend on the relation between the new level of gross rent and average household earnings. In 1937/38 the family budgets collected by the Ministry of Labour gave an average for working-class household expenditure of £231 for Scotland and £223 for Great Britain. With fewer workers unemployed, increased social benefits and average weekly earnings nearly three times as high as in 1938, the average income of a Scottish working-class household must have become between $2\frac{1}{2}$ and 3 times as great by 1953.[3] An average gross rent of £49 (£35 × 140 %) would thus represent from 7 % to 9 % of average household earnings. This does not seem an impossible proportion to ask for a good standard of housing accommodation. It includes, of course, payment for all rating services other than housing; and if the net rent alone is taken the proportion is not more than 4 % to 5 %.

However local authorities deal with the financial problems that are rapidly building up, four things are clear. The first is that no private landlord can now

---

[1] *Rents of houses owned by local authorities in Scotland, 1951* (Cmd. 8654, 1952).

[2] The adjustment would presumably be made by way of a general reduction in the poundage of rates.

[3] In spite of a possible reduction in average size of household and perhaps therefore in the average number of earners per household in Scotland. The comparatively large household earnings in 1937/38 were dependent on a large average number of earners per household.

afford to build houses to let. Secondly, although over 1 m. of Scotland's 1·4 m. houses are in private ownership, there is very little incentive to landlords to maintain their property if it is let at a controlled rent—far less incentive than in England and Wales. Thirdly, the Scottish rating system involves a stiff tax on existing house-property, and this tax is bound to rise progressively the smaller the proportion of privately-owned property left to pay owners' rates and the larger the building programmes on which local authorities embark. Fourthly, the current method of combating Scotland's housing shortage relies almost exclusively on the building of new houses to be let at rents which bear little relation to the economic cost. Thus on the one hand the bulk of the existing stock of houses is neglected and all the limelight is thrown on the small annual increment (currently about 2 %) in the stock; and on the other the capital for lack of which development is frustrated in almost every other sphere is lavished unstintingly on housing. Nothing makes greater demands on capital in relation to its immediate contribution to welfare than does housing; nothing can do more to prejudice Scotland's economic prospects than the use of capital for any but the most urgent purposes; yet the housing programme has been given priority over all other investment requirements. So grave a decision, which has undoubtedly the backing of public opinion, might seem reasonable if there were evidence that tenants could be found for the new houses who were prepared to pay something more than one-half of the full economic rent. But at the time of writing it appears to be settled policy that such evidence must on no account be sought.

CHAPTER 15

HEALTH

By T. T. PATERSON

The main index of health is ill-health or morbidity, but unfortunately, with one minor reservation, no comprehensive figures of morbidity exist. A second, but less satisfactory, index which provides comparative figures over a long period, is mortality. If, in any age-group, fewer people die than previously, people in that age-group are presumably healthier to the extent that they are more capable of resisting mortal diseases. In fact, mortality has fallen in all age-groups; as a result, the Scotsman's expectation of life at birth has risen from 41 years in 1871 to 64 in 1949, and the process continues.

It may be objected that in these days sick people do not die so readily as before because they are molly-coddled by the expert therapeutic skills of the general practitioners and the care of hospital staffs: that the Scotsman is no healthier than he was, but is kept by science and government from dying earlier. How far the improvement in life expectation is due to vastly better medical service, especially in the fields of preventive medicine and epidemiology, or to socio-economic factors such as higher real incomes, more and better food, and improved housing conditions, it is difficult, wellnigh impossible, to say; all these factors play a part. Nevertheless, if the mortal diseases of younger age-groups are more and more held in check or eradicated, the population is healthier by that much, whether the morbid diseases decrease or not.[1] Notifications of diseases are hardly valid figures for comparison of one period with another, since the skills in diagnosis have altered so rapidly over the years.

MORTALITY

The death-rates attributable to most diseases have been declining over many years, and at about the same rate of change as in England and Wales (see Fig. 13). Deaths from typhoid fever, typhus, smallpox, scarlet fever and diphtheria have practically disappeared, and those from measles and whooping-

---

[1] 'Constant hereditary environment being assumed, the health of the child is determined by the environmental conditions existing during the years 0–15, and...the health of the man is determined preponderatingly by the physical constitution which the child has built up. All the figures are consistent with the hypothesis that the death-rates of the adolescent and adult depend on the constitution acquired during the first fifteen years or so of life and...the latter has undergone a very substantial improvement, presumably as the result of the general raising of the standard of life and the amelioration of social conditions.' 'The reduction (in the death-rate) has been most marked at ages under 45 years' (*Report of the Committee on Scottish Health Services*, Department of Health for Scotland, 1936, pp. 47–8).

cough can be counted on the fingers of one hand. Such infectious diseases affect mainly children and the younger age-groups, and the decline has been marked almost wholly in these groups.

Tuberculosis is another disease which affects mainly younger people; respiratory tuberculosis causes more deaths in the middle age-groups, and other forms of tuberculosis in infants and young folk below the age of 20.

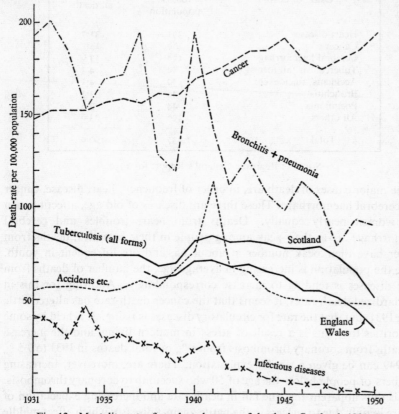

Fig. 13. Mortality rates for selected causes of deaths in Scotland, 1931–50.

Among men the highest mortality for pulmonary tuberculosis is between the ages of 45 and 65, and among women between 15 and 35. For other forms of tuberculosis the death-rate is highest among children of both sexes below five, decreasing with age.

The fall in the death-rate from all forms of tuberculosis continues an improvement begun in the middle of last century when about 400 in every 100,000 of the population died from that disease. It dropped to half that rate before the first world war, to about 70 before the second world war, and was

31 per 100,000 in 1952. The death-rates from pneumonia and bronchitis, which affect the younger age-groups in the main, are nearly half what they were in the early 1930's. Infant mortality is also declining rapidly.

Table 101. *Causes of death in Scotland*, 1950

Cause of death	Death-rate per 100,000 population	Percentage of all deaths
Heart disease	391	31·7
Cancer	188	15·7
Cerebral haemorrhage	168	13·6
Tuberculosis (all forms)	54	4·3
Accidents, suicide, etc.	50	4·1
Bronchitis	46	3·5
Pneumonia	44	3·5
All others	296	23·6
Total	1,237	100·0

SOURCE: Registrar-General's Report for 1950.

The major causes of death are, in order of frequency: heart disease, cancer and cerebral haemorrhage. These three are diseases of old age, affecting men and women nearly equally. Deaths from heart troubles and cerebral haemorrhage are at their peak among people in their seventies; deaths from cancer have their peak number at about 65, and are infrequent in youth. Since the population is increasing in average age, the number of deaths from these diseases is tending to increase correspondingly. Allowing for this in standardized death-rates, it seems that the cancer death-rate has altered little since 1931, but that the rate for circulatory diseases is rising. It is held by some authorities that this is a result of stress in modern living, and the increase in deaths from coronary thrombosis from 1 % of total deaths in 1931 to 9·5 % in 1949 can be given a similar explanation. There are, moreover, increasing numbers of people below the age of 50 who succumb to coronary thrombosis.

It is thus apparent that the fall in death-rate and increasing expectation of life are mainly due to success in the battle against diseases which affect middle age, youth and infancy, and is thus a measure, to some extent, of the improvement in health in these groups.

There is a noteworthy exception in this general improvement. The death-rate from accidents, suicides and the like, as distinct from disease, is not improving. Infancy and middle age are more subject to death from such causes, and deaths also occur more frequently among men and boys, thus accounting for part of the disparity in the death-rates of the sexes in the earlier years of life, as well as for some of the difference in expectation of life.[1]

[1] The death-rate in 1950 was 36 per 100,000 for males and 28 per 100,000 for females.

214

Comparative mortality

The incidence of mortal disease varies according to the distribution of the population in urban and rural areas. Infectious diseases, pneumonia, bronchitis and pulmonary tuberculosis are most deadly in urban areas. The diseases of old age do not show this urban excess—as would be expected.

Table 102. *Urban-rural distribution of death-rates in Scotland*, 1950

Disease	Death-rate per 100,000 population in 1950		
	Large burghs	Small burghs	Landward areas
Heart disease	353	429	362
Cancer	184	200	167
Cerebral haemorrhage	163	196	160
Tuberculosis (all forms)	56	35	36
Bronchitis	44	40	29
Pneumonia	37	33	33

SOURCE: Registrar-General's Report for 1950.

There are also certain areas of Scotland where death from tuberculosis is particularly prevalent (see Fig. 14). The variation between one area and another is broadly similar to that for the years 1911–13 and 1931–33, taken as samples of previous periods. A few smaller counties such as Selkirk and Peebles have shown a rise in the pulmonary tuberculosis death-rate, offset by others such as Berwick, showing a large fall. Broadly speaking, the highest death-rates from pulmonary tuberculosis are to be found in the large cities, excepting Edinburgh; secondly, there is a greater concentration of high rates in West-Central Scotland and the Northern Highlands, and of low rates in the East-Central and Border counties. One could say that there is a preponderance of higher tuberculosis death-rates in the West and North, and of lower in the East and South. This is possibly the result of climate and socio-economic factors.

The high infant mortality of Scotland has been the subject of the Orr Report from the Department of Health for Scotland.[1] It relates to the period prior to 1941 but its findings are still relevant (see also Chapter 3, Fig. 2). The former high infant mortality is declining but it is declining almost as fast in most other countries. The West-Central region of Scotland shows the highest infant mortality of any region in Britain. Infant mortality is lower in rural than in urban areas but, even so, the predominantly rural areas of South-West and North-East Scotland are as bad as, or worse than, the mining villages

[1] *Infant Mortality in Scotland*, 1947.

of the small industrial towns of the Lowlands and of North-east England. The rate for Scotland as a whole is no better than that found among the poorer working-classes of England and Wales. Edinburgh is the only one of the large cities which compares favourably with any city of England; Glasgow is the worst in Britain. Climate seems to bear no relation to infant mortality, but there is a statistically significant correlation between infant mortality and overcrowding, which is much higher in Scotland. There may also be a correlation with unemployment, and there is a marked correlation with social class as defined by occupation and income.[1]

The crude death-rates for cancer and for various infectious diseases such as typhoid, paratyphoid and scarlet fever, puerperal fever, diphtheria and poliomyelitis, are much alike in Scotland, England and Wales. But the Registrar-General for Scotland has shown that, after allowing for differences in the age-composition of both countries, Scotsmen succumb to all kinds of diseases (except bronchitis and pneumonia), more readily than Englishmen (see Fig. 14). Even the death-rate from accidents is higher. The noteworthy difference in the tuberculosis death-rate has not yet been explained by the medical authorities.

Though tuberculosis death-rate is higher in Scotland the percentage of notified cases dying is noticeably smaller than in England and Wales. The same applies in comparing deaths from, and notified cases of infectious diseases. Therefore the higher tuberculosis death-rate is clearly no fault of the Scottish medical service. It is further permissible to suggest from this observation that, because of Scottish doctors' interest in the disease, there is earlier diagnosis of the condition. In England, out of every six cases resulting in death, one is not notified before death.

MORBIDITY

Information on sickness in the post-war years is meagre. The Ministry of National Insurance has not yet begun to publish data other than on numbers claiming sickness and injury benefits, and weekly averages of numbers off work.[2] By far the best morbidity statistics available are contained in the seven annual reports on *Incapacitating sickness in the insured population of Scotland*, issued by the Scottish Department of Health for the years 1931–37.[3] Most of the information given below is culled from these reports and relates only to the insured population.

[1] P. L. McKinlay, 'Social class differences in causes of infant mortality', *Health Bulletin, Dept. of Health for Scotland*, vol. x, 1952, p. 78.

[2] The Registrar General for England and Wales has relied on a Social Survey from 1946 to 1950 but the sample was small and not representative of the insured population. There are no Scottish figures of this kind for the same period.

[3] As far as is known to the writer, such statistics on national morbidity are unequalled anywhere.

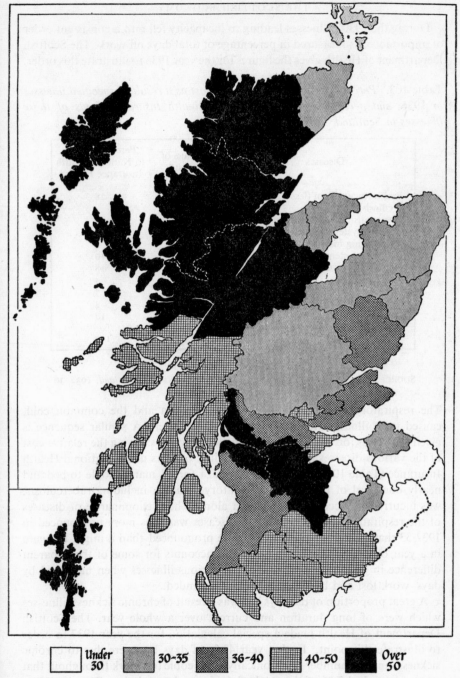

Fig. 14. Variations by county, excluding the four cities, in tuberculosis death-rates
per 100,000 population in Scotland, 1946–49.

Under 30   30-35   36-40   40-50   Over 50

During the 1930's illnesses leading to incapacity fell into a consistent order of importance, as measured in percentage of total days off work. The Scottish Department of Health gives the figures for the year 1936 to illustrate this order.

Table 103. *Percentage of total days' work lost as a result of specified illnesses in 1936, and percentage cost to National Health Insurance funds of those illnesses in Scotland, 1932/33*

Diseases	Percentage of days lost*	Percentage cost to National Health Insurance Funds†
Respiratory system (less tuber- culosis)	12·8	28
Rheumatism	12·5	13
Nervous system and sense organs (including insanity)	10·8	7
Digestive system	10·6	10
Circulatory system	8·4	8
Accidents	8·2	5
Neurosis	7·7	7
Tuberculosis (all forms)	5·2	4
All other	23·8	18
Total	100·0	100

* 1936.   †1932/33.
SOURCE: *Incapacitating sickness in the insured population of Scotland*, 1932–36.

The respiratory diseases, which include influenza and the common cold, caused most illness, with rheumatism next in order. A similar sequence is given by figures for 1932/33 (the only available year) showing the relative cost of the various diseases in sickness and injury benefits under National Health Insurance (Table 103). In 1932/33 influenza forced many people to bed and nearly one-third of the cost of respiratory troubles, including tuberculosis, was incurred on account of influenza alone. The predominance of diseases of the respiratory system over other diseases was thus more pronounced in 1932/33 than in 1936 (although not more pronounced than it might be again in a year of influenza epidemic) and this accounts for some of the apparent difference in relative importance of the various illnesses when measured by days' work lost and by sickness benefits expended.

A great proportion of the days lost was a result of chronic sickness, illnesses which were of long duration and current over a whole year. The Scottish Department of Health made a special calculation for the year 1937 in order to illustrate this point. In that year 42 % of days lost were due to chronic sickness, and the number of chronically sick people (off work throughout that year), was only 1·7 % of the total of the insured population. That is to say, one person in each sixty of the insured population accounted for two-fifths of the total days lost.

The relative frequency, measured by number of cases, of the major reasons for chronic incapacity in Scotland in a typical year, 1936, is shown in Table 104. Here, too, rheumatism and diseases of the respiratory system were very prominent, but insanity was the most striking single cause and, in terms of hospital services, by far the most important. Those cases of chronic sickness which terminated in 1936 were estimated to have had an average duration of 179 weeks for men and 188 weeks for women.

Table 104. *Major reasons for chronic incapacity in Scotland, 1936*

Diseases	Percentage of total number of cases
Insanity	21·2
Rheumatism	12·6
Respiratory system (less tuberculosis)	11·8
Circulatory system	11·4
Tuberculosis	11·2
Neurosis	6·9
Accidents	3·4
All other	21·5
Total	100·0

SOURCE: *Incapacitating sickness in the insured population of Scotland, 1936.*

Leaving aside the 1·7 % of chronic sick, it was found that 23·5 % of the insured population were incapacitated one or more times. The average length of period off work was 22·7 days, and the average number of times off work 1·2. The rest of the insured population, nearly three-quarters, were not off work owing to sickness in 1936.

Age and sex

In terms of days off work, the older a man got the more he was sick. For men over 55 years the rate was six times greater than at ages below 25. However, the actual number of cases showed no striking increase with age—there was, indeed, a tendency towards a greater absolute number of cases in the age-group 30–40. Among women, the number of cases was high between 20 and 30 years of age, but dropped to its lowest between 35 and 40.

The growing incidence of sickness with age emerges clearly from figures for 1932–33 showing the cost to the National Health Insurance funds, in sickness and injury benefits, of incapacity at various ages. Because of the importance of the respiratory diseases, which affect younger people, half the cost of sickness and injury benefits in 1932/33 went on persons under 35, the peak

219

age-group being 20–25. But the cost *per head* (see Fig. 15) showed one peak in the 30–35 group and a great rise in the cost of sickness in the over-60 group.

The sex differences in sickness rates, for the quinquennium 1931–35, are shown in Table 105. Women were more prone to be sick, and were longer off work than men (married women especially so).

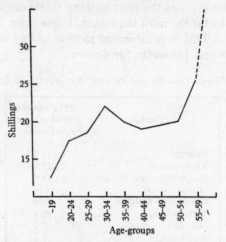

Fig. 15. Cost per head at various ages of incapacitating sickness to National Health Insurance Funds, 1932/33.

Table 105. *Sickness rates of insured population by sex (including chronic cases and cases of injury), 1931–35*

	Both sexes	Males	Females
Cases per 100 insured population per annum	21·4	20·9	22·3
Average days off work per case due to incapacity	46·7	44·8	50·1
Average days off per insured person per annum	10·0	9·4	11·2

SOURCE: *Incapacitating sickness in the insured population of Scotland*, 1936.

Men were off work more often for rheumatism, accidents, bronchitis, pneumonia, gastric and duodenal ulcers, gastritis, cerebral haemorrhage and influenza. Women showed appreciably more frequent absence for neurosis, anaemia, infectious diseases, tonsillitis and appendicitis. Men recovered more quickly than women from cerebral haemorrhage, influenza and rheumatism; and women more quickly than men from anaemia and neurosis.

The sexes differed in the rates for chronic sickness; and also by age. For both sexes in the age-group under 35, the order of frequency was the same, with tuberculosis and nervous disease (mainly insanity) much the highest. In the next age-group (35–55), insanity became the most frequent disease. Tuberculosis dropped progressively with age and its place was taken by rheumatism. Heart diseases took third place in the over-55 group in both sexes. The bronchitis-pneumonia cases increased with age, and the neuroses declined.

Occupational differences

For men workers, the rate of sickness in mining was by far the highest, followed by that in textiles and paper-making. Men in transport and in the food and drink industries came next, closely followed by workers in the metal trades and agriculture and fishing. The building trades operatives and wood-workers were next, then those in commerce (clerks, warehousemen, shop assistants). The rate was lowest for men in domestic service of all kinds (cooks, waiters, chauffeurs, etc). The order of occupational frequency for chronically sick men was the same.

The women workers in transport and domestic occupations (waitresses, cooks, maids) were most frequently ill, and coming close behind were women in coal-mining, textiles, and agriculture and fishing. The commercial workers (typists, clerks, shop assistants) were next in the order of frequency, and lastly those in the building trades, manufacture of food and drink, and the metal trades. The majority of chronically sick women came from four of the first five occupational groups given above, the exception being transport, which supplied comparatively few cases, though providing a majority of women sick for short periods. It may be that this occupation (mostly conductresses on vehicles), provided some resistance to the major chronic diseases of the circulatory system, tuberculosis and rheumatism.

Among miners, who showed the highest incidence of cases, occupational sicknesses, injuries and inflammatory skin conditions were much in excess. Among male agricultural workers and fishermen the incidence of tuberculosis, neurasthenia and anaemia was much less than among other men, but there was a wide difference between the lowest rate in the Lothians and the highest in the Highlands and Islands (see below). Such a variation implied that there were other factors besides occupation affecting these workers.

Regional differences

For ease of consideration the Scottish Department of Health has divided Scotland into four regions, Highlands and Islands, North-East, Industrial Belt, and the Borders. Excluding the four large cities it can be said that:

1. The *incidence*, cases per 1,000 of insured population, was least in the Highlands and Islands, increasing in the order of North-East, Borders and Industrial Belt—for both men and women and also for chronic sickness.

2. The *days of incapacity per person* were least in the Highlands and Islands,

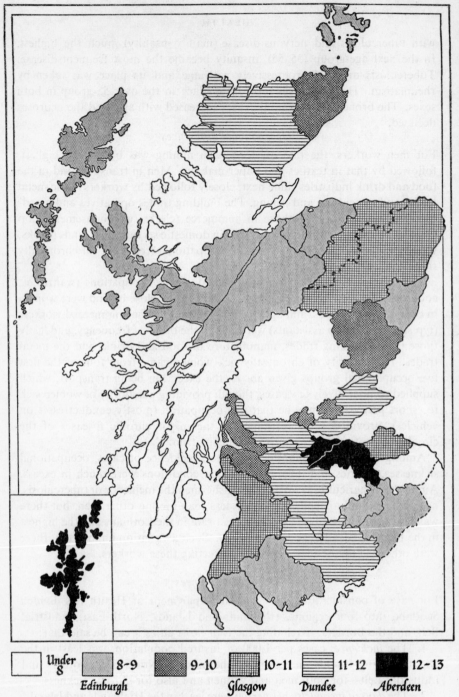

Fig. 16. Variations by county, excluding the four cities, in days of incapacity per insured person per annum in Scotland, 1931–36.

Legend:
Under 8 | 8-9 | 9-10 | 10-11 | 11-12 | 12-13
Edinburgh | Glasgow | Dundee | Aberdeen

increasing in the order of the Borders, North-East and the Industrial Belt—
for women the Borders was lower than the Highlands and Islands.

3. The *average duration* of the incapacity was least in the Borders and
Industrial Belt, and highest in the Highlands and Islands (see Fig. 16).

The outstanding peculiarity was the low incidence, high average duration
and, in spite of the latter, low incapacity per person of morbidity in the Highlands and Islands. A Department of Health study concluded that this
peculiarity was due to the prevalence of long-term sickness, mainly tuberculosis, anaemia, rheumatism, and some neurotic conditions.[1] The high
average duration of incapacity in the North-East was mainly due to joint-
rheumatism and arthritic conditions for both men and women, and a heavy
rate for diseases of the nervous and circulatory systems. It is tempting to
suggest that the high rheumatism rate is partly conditioned by climate.

Claims to sickness and injury benefit

There is no published information which can provide an accurate comparison
of Scottish and British morbidity. Data on absences from work and new claims
for sickness benefit as the result of disease give only a rough picture.

Table 106. *New claims to sickness and injury benefits and absences from work
as a result of sickness and injury in Scotland and in Great Britain*, 1951

	Sickness		Injury	
	Scotland	Great Britain	Scotland	Great Britain
Numbers employed	2·11 m.	20·75 m.	2·11 m.	20·75 m.
New claims during 1951	0·80 m.	7·55 m.	88,000	764,000
Proportion of new claimants to total employed	*37·9 %*	*36·4 %*	*42·1 %*	*36·7 %*
Average number absent from work in 1951	108,100	906,300	7,500	58,200
Proportion of persons absent to total employed	*5·1 %*	*4·4 %*	*0·4 %*	*0·3 %*
Days off per new claimant	49	44	31	28

SOURCE: *Monthly Digest of Statistics.*

The figures for the year 1951 given in Table 106 are comparable to those
for 1949 and 1950. Apparently there was a slight tendency for the Scotsman
to be more often off work long enough to claim sickness benefit. At any rate,
more new claims to sickness benefit were lodged than was strictly in proportion to the size of the working population, and a higher proportion of
Scottish workers were off work at any one time. The Scottish worker was also
away from work for a slightly longer period than the average British worker.

[1] *Incapacitating sickness*, 1934.

223

It is in keeping with the higher figures of mortality from accidents in Scotland that claims for benefit from injury should also be higher. It will be seen from Table 106 that there was a larger excess of such claims in Scotland than of claims in respect of illness. The number of days' work lost through injury was fully 25 % higher in Scotland than in Britain as a whole. It seems likely that not only does the Scotsman succumb from diseases more readily than the average British worker but he is also more often sick and injured.

THE COST OF ILL-HEALTH

The cost of ill-health can be measured as the sum of
  (a) the value of the days' work lost;
  (b) the amounts disbursed as sickness and injury benefits from national insurance; and
  (c) the amounts spent on hospital and other medical treatment.
Within each of these amounts the proportions attributable to various diseases differ in relative importance.

In Table 105 the loss of output is put at 10 days off work per insured persons per annum in the quinquennium 1931–35—or, say, 4 % of output. In Table 106, a rather higher figure is reached: on the average, 5·1 % of all insured workers are off work through sickness at any one time and 0·4 % are off work through injury. On this basis, we may put the loss to the community under the first head at about 5·5 % of the national income, i.e. about £50 m. in 1951.

The cost of death is concealed in the undertakers' account books. The cost of sickness and injury benefits to National Insurance funds in 1951 was £10 m. This total can be divided among the main illnesses on the basis of pre-war experience:[1] it may be estimated roughly that £2 m. represented the cost of diseases of the respiratory system (excluding tuberculosis), £1 m. the cost of rheumatism, £4 m. the cost of all other diseases, £1·6 m. the cost of injuries and a further £1·6 m. the cost of administration.

There remains expenditure under the National Health Service. Taking first hospital services, the total net expenditure in 1951 on beds and in-patients (excluding specialist and unstaffed beds) was close on £20 m., an average of about £1 per day being the cost of maintaining a patient in hospital. Over and above this was the treatment of nearly 1·7 m. out-patients, each attending on the average five times.

The majority of cases of chronic sickness require hospital treatment. It is not surprising, therefore, to find that insanity (see Table 104) is by far the most costly single group of diseases in terms of hospital beds required and their total running expenses. In 1951, out of about 52,000 occupied hospital beds, 45 % were given over to patients with mental disorders, and just under

---

[1] See above, p. 218.

10 % to sufferers from tuberculosis. (These proportions are much the same in England and Wales.) Of the total net expenditure in staffing of beds and treatment of in-patients mental diseases accounted for about 25 % and tuberculosis about 7 %.

The total cost of hospital services in 1951 may be summarized as follows:

						£ m.
In-patients						
Mental disorders	...	...	...	...	...	4·9
Tuberculosis	...	...,	...	...	...	1·4
All other	...	...	...	...	...	13·7
Out patients						
Treatment	...	...	...	...	...	2·0
Specialist and ancillary services		...	...	...	...	8·5
Total ...	...	...	...	...	...	30·5

Total expenditure on hospital and general medical services in Scotland and in England and Wales in 1951 is shown in Table 107. Since gross expenditure in Scotland was 12·9 % of expenditure in England and Wales, while for population the corresponding proportion is 11·7 %, expenditure per head of population was higher in Scotland. The expenditure in Scotland was about £9. 14s. per person per annum, and about £8. 18s. in England. The data on the relative amounts on such services before the inception of the National Health Service are scarce, and no conclusions can be drawn from them.

Thus Scotland's total bill for ill-health comes to over £100 m.—£50 m. each for loss of output and for health services and a further £10 m. for sickness and injury benefits. It is not possible to say definitely whether this total represents

Table 107. *Gross expenditure on National Health Service in Scotland and in England and Wales,* 1951

	Scotland (£ m.)	England and Wales (£ m.)	Scotland/ England and Wales (percentage)
Hospital services	30·5	229·2	13·3
General medical services	5·4	42·1	12·8
Prescriptions	4·1	34·8	11·8
Dental services	5·2	40·3	12·9
Eye services	2·3	19·6	11·8
Local authority health services	1·2	15·6	7·7
Supplies	0·4	3·1	12·9
Superannuation	0·3	5·7	8·1
Total	49·4	388·4	12·9

SOURCE: *Annual Abstract of Statistics.*

a larger or smaller slice of the national income than in the past; all the indications are that it is larger, not because there is more ill-health, but because sickness is better cared for. It is also not possible to say how much the community gains from the greater longevity and the longer working life of the average citizen that are in part the fruit of better medical attention, or to assess the greater well-being that Scotsmen may enjoy as consumers or the greater activity that they may be able to support as producers.

SUMMARY

1. There has been a continuing, all-round improvement in Scotland's health as measured by the crude death-rate. Deaths due to accidents and the like are not decreasing.

2. The apparent increases in death-rates due to heart disease and cancer (diseases of old age) are a result of greater longevity, itself the result of lower death-rates in the younger age-groups.

3. The same improvements in death-rates are to be found in England, and are most likely to be due to advancing medical science and improving conditions of life.

4. Scotland remains relatively less healthy than England; expectation of life is shorter and death-causing diseases are more frequent; what evidence there is on morbidity suggests that the Scotsman is more often sick and more liable to accident.

5. Nevertheless, the figures for tuberculosis and infectious diseases show that Scotland's medical service, at least in these fields, is, if anything, superior to England's. This superiority existed before the inception of the National Health Service.

6. The inferiority in general health may account for the larger Scottish expenditure per person on medical services.

7. The most expensive diseases are the respiratory, which include the common cold and influenza. But mental disorders take up a large percentage (45 %) of the hospital beds available, and hence of the energies of doctors and nurses.

8. The total bill for ill-health is probably in excess of £100 m., made up as to about £50 m. by loss of output, £10 m. by sickness and injury benefits, and a further £50 m. by health services.

CHAPTER 16

CRIME

By JOHN MACK

The criminal statistics of Scotland have been tabulated on a broadly comparable basis since 1868, with progressive alterations, tending towards greater precision, in 1897, in 1925 and in recent years. As a result it is possible to detect certain broad changes in criminal behaviour and in social habits over the whole period, and to draw some more precise conclusions over the last twenty-five years or so.[1] It is important not to read too much into the figures. Criminal statistics are affected by variations between police districts in method and accuracy of recording; by the increase in police detective efficiency, and in public confidence in the police, since the last century; by such profound changes in social climate as that evidenced in the growth of concern for the young offender in the last two generations; and by national differences in legal structure and tradition. The Scots are statistically more wicked than the English, but this may reflect only the greater effectiveness of the Scottish system of public prosecution in bringing petty offenders to account.

The statistics record every offence against the law of the land which comes to the attention of the police, from the most serious to the most trivial. The distinction between 'crimes' and 'offences'[2]—the analogous distinction in England and Wales is between 'indictable offences' and 'non-indictable offences'—corresponds to the common-sense distinction between crimes and nuisances. It is discussed by Gloag and Henderson as follows:

Judicial opinion and writers of text-books have sometimes distinguished 'offences' from 'crimes' in the sense that an offence is some act or omission not wrongful *per se*, but prohibited by some statute and for which a money penalty is imposed. The leading modern Scots text-book treats as crimes only those offences for the suppression of which the judge has power to pronounce sentence of death or deprivation of liberty without pecuniary penalty.[3]

'Offences' may be of minor interest to the criminologist, but they yield much knowledge to the student of social history. They are far more numerous

---

[1] See Appendix, 'Yardsticks of Crime', p. 243.

[2] 'Crimes' are listed under Classes I–VI, and 'Offences'—the full title is 'Miscellaneous Offences'—constitute Class VII, in the official Classified List of Crimes and Offences. The list is published in *Criminal Statistics, Scotland*, 1951, pp. 19–22 and more fully in *Criminal Statistics, Scotland*, 1946, pp. 48–63.

[3] W. M. Gloag and R. C. Henderson, *Introduction to the Law of Scotland* (Edinburgh, 1946), p. 635.

than crimes and consequently affect far more individuals. 'They concern manners rather than morals, but manners make the man.'[1]

OFFENCES

Judged by the trend of offences Scottish manners have improved in the last fifty years. Table 108 shows a steady decline since 1900 in the volume and incidence of offences. The apparent exception to this downward movement in the ten years 1934–44 is explained for the 1935–39 period by a change in recording method in 1936,[2] and for the 1939–44 period by the creation of new categories of offences against war legislation, for example infringements of black-out regulations.

Table 108.[3] *Annual average of persons proceeded against in Scotland for crimes and offences, 1871–1951*

Period	Crimes		Offences	
	Annual average	Rate per 1000 population	Annual average	Rate per 1,000 population
1871–1880	25,197	7·1	117,109	33·0
1881–1890	20,498	5·3	116,567	30·0
1891–1900	20,829	4·9	146,926	34·6
1900–1904	25,961	5·7	149,911	33·0
1905–1909	26,043	5·6	145,220	31·0
1910–1914	25,607	5·6	136,243	26·7
1915–1919	21,210	4·4	90,288	18·7
1920–1924	22,273	4·4	94,504	19·4
1925–1929	21,956	4·5	96,544	19·9
1930–1934	20,547	4·2	81,462	16·6
1935–1939	22,328	4·6	108,402	22·1
1940–1944	26,471	5·6	103,466	21·9
1945–1949	24,747	4·9	77,789	15·5
1950	23,492	4·6	85,562	16·6
1951	25,871	5·1	87,143	17·0

The change in the composition of the total of offences, as indicated in Table 109, is equally notable. In the two decades before the first world war the time-honoured combination of drunkenness and breach of the peace (mostly petty assaults and boisterous conduct) ran at an annual average of well over 100,000, three-quarters of the total of offences. In the five years ending 1951 the annual average is 26,000, about one-third of the total of offences.

The rate per 1000 of the population has dropped from 21·5 in 1913 to 5·2

---

[1] S. K. Ruck, *Penal Reform in England* (London, 1940), p. 142. This distinction is only broadly true. Offences such as prostitution concern morals rather than manners.

[2] See p. 231, below, and Appendix, § 1 (c).

[3] Unless otherwise stated, all statistics included in Tables 108–13 are derived from the annual series of *Criminal Statistics, Scotland* and *Criminal Statistics, England and Wales*.

in 1947–51. The volume and incidence of drunkenness taken by itself has fallen even more sharply. This downward trend has been slightly reversed since 1949, a development not shown in the table: the drunkenness figure has risen from 8,226 in that year to 9,930 in 1951: but this last total is still just over one-half of the 1938 figure and one-fifth of the 1913 figure.

Table 109. *Persons proceeded against in Scotland: composition of total of offences*, 1913–51

Nature of offence	1913	1938	1940–44 (annual average)	1947–51 (annual average)
Drunkenness	49,860	17,446	13,926	8,455
Breach of the peace	51,874	22,154	16,189	18,145
Total	101,734	39,600	30,115	26,600
Rate per 1,000 *population*	*21·5*	*7·9*	*5·7*	*5·2*
Offences against Road Acts (including 'Drunk in charge')	7,950 (—)	48,150 (754)	18,557 (474)	32,633 (707)
Offences against Education Acts	1,263	230	1,382	1,543
Offences against Police Acts	19,187	12,210	9,397	9,933
Offences against War Legislation	—	—	26,613	2,047
Other offences	17,309	15,280	17,402	11,582
Total all offences	147,443	115,470	103,466	84,338
Rate per 1,000 *population*	*31·2*	*23·1*	*19·6*	*16·4*

The vacuum left by the shrinking army of drunks and disorderlies has been partly filled by careless drivers. The numbers of offenders against the Road Acts rose from just under 8,000 in 1913 to more than 47,000 in 1938. The second world war sent cars off the road, but the 30,000 decline in Road Acts offences was almost made up for by nearly 27,000 offences against war legislation. Now traffic offences are mounting again. Offences against the Education Acts have never been numerous—the pre-1914 figure of over 1,200 persons proceeded against had dwindled to 230 in 1938—but the numbers rose to 1,700 in the war-years and remained at over 1,400 until 1950. The latest annual return—1951—is 1,300. Since these offences concern parents who fail to ensure their children's regular attendance at school, this later development probably indicates a reaction, now beginning to weaken, against the raising of the school-leaving age.

CRIMES[1]

The trend of Scottish crimes is harder to interpret. The figures of persons proceeded against (Table 108, column 2) show a certain constancy. In the decades before 1914 a rate of between five and six per thousand of the total

[1] See Appendix, §1.

population was maintained: this fell in the course of the 1914–18 war to a slightly lower rate of between four and five per thousand which has been maintained for the 1920's to the present day. The level rose during the years of the second world war but subsided again in the late 1940's. But the figures of all crimes known to the police tell a different story. These, which seldom rose above 40,000 in the whole period 1870–1925, have mounted in the past twenty-five years from 33,070 in 1925 to 58,976 in 1938 and 83,008 in 1951, this last being the second highest figure ever recorded; the highest was in 1945, when 86,075 crimes were made known to the police. The rates per thousand of the total population are 6·8 in 1925, 11·8 in 1938, and 16·2 in 1951. The gap between crimes known to the police and crimes in which one or more persons were apprehended etc., the latter being the official measure of crimes cleared, has correspondingly widened: the percentage of crimes cleared falling from 53 % in 1913 to 41 % in 1951.[1] There is no similar gap nor divergence in the case of offences: the percentage of offences cleared is consistently in the region of 95–100 %. But the crimes barometer, the barometer of public morals as distinct from manners, gives these two conflicting readings. By the first, the number of persons proceeded against, the long-term trend is downward and the movement in recent years is one of return to the level of 1938 after the disturbance caused by the war. By the second, the number of crimes known to the police, there has been since the 1920's a steady and continuing increase in criminal behaviour *and* in the evasive skill of the criminals.

Which reading are we to adopt? Some expert opinion favours the latter. But it must be used with great caution. A similar remarkable increase in crimes known to the police has taken place in England and Wales in the last twenty years: and in this case it can be partly explained by the adoption of more accurate methods of recording petty crimes against property, which make up the bulk of all crimes. In the Metropolitan Police District (Greater London) a book-keeping reorganization in 1932, involving the abolition of the 'Suspected Stolen' book, and compelling the station officers in each division to deal with all cases reported either as crimes or as 'property lost', sent the total of crimes known to the police up from 26,192 in 1931 to 82,846 in 1932: 5 % of the increase being real and the rest statistical.[2] A similar tightening up has been made since then by police forces throughout England and Wales, being expedited by the explicit recommendations to this effect in the *Report of the Departmental Committee on Detective Work and Procedure*.[3] There is no similar reported instance of a major change in Scottish police

[1] This fall in the percentage of 'crimes cleared' is apparent only, as is shown by the breakdown of the respective totals into the various classes of crimes on p. 233 below.

[2] Ruck, op. cit. p. 16: and *Report of the Commissioner of Police of the Metropolis* for the year 1932 (Cmd. 4294), pp. 16–17.

[3] London, 1939, paras. 20–28.

procedure affecting the recording of crimes. A minor change was made in Scotland in 1936,[1] but its immediate effect is perceivable mainly in the totals of offences known to the police, and of offences cleared, each of which increased by about 30,000 in that year; crimes known to the police were affected not at all, although crimes cleared were increased to some extent, doubtless by the inclusion of petty property crimes formerly disregarded.

No other change has been reported in Scotland. But the figures from the different police districts show pronounced variations, some recording a low figure of crimes known to the police and a correspondingly high percentage of crimes cleared, others showing the reverse. Thus, in 1951, the city of Dundee reported 10·4 crimes known per 1,000 of the population and 61·8 % of crimes cleared. Aberdeen, a city of equal size, had a rate of 22·3 crimes known per 1,000 of the population and 42·8 % crimes cleared. The figures for Edinburgh were 22·2 and 26·4 %. Even more striking variations are found in the large burghs. Ayr registered 27·5 crimes per 1,000 with 29·5 % cleared. Kilmarnock, a nearby town of equal size, recorded 8·7 crimes per 1,000 with 84·3 %. Similar contrasts are offered by Airdrie and Coatbridge on the one hand (9·4 % and 60·8 %: 8·3 % and 79·7 %) and Paisley and Greenock on the other (22·1 % and 36·4 %: 41·4 % and 23·1 %). These differences clearly reflect differences between systems of recording—in respect, for example, of order of magnitude of crimes recorded—rather than differences in criminal performance.

These discrepancies cast considerable doubt on the value of the figures of crimes known to the police, as compared with the figures of persons proceeded against, which are less affected by recording systems. But we may agree generally with S. K. Ruck that

it is as well to bear each set of figures in mind in studying the other, and the general conclusion to be drawn from both is that crime has been gradually increasing in this country since 1918....The increasing divergence between the curves of crimes detected and of persons tried is very noticeable, but this is rather to be attributed to an increase in the statistical honesty of the police than to a decline in their detective efficiency since the middle of the last century.[2]

This last point, that the increasing divergence between crimes detected and persons tried is no indication of any decrease in police efficiency, is supported by the following breakdown of the total crimes figure into the several types of crimes.

Crimes against person and property

'Crimes' are distributed under six main heads in the classified list of crimes and offences. The great bulk of all crimes are crimes against property—Classes II, III and IV—constituting 95 % of the total in 1951. Moreover, the

---

[1] See Appendix, §1 (c).   [2] Op. cit. pp. 16–17.

huge increase in the total of crimes known to the police since the 1920's is entirely an increase in these classes. As Table 110 shows, 'Crimes against the Person', Class I have fallen from 5,775 in 1897 to 2,756 in 1951.

Table 110. *Crimes in Scotland, 1897–1951*

Class of crime		1897	1913	1925	1938	1951
I. Crimes against the person	(a)	5,775	5,002	3,001	3,643	2,756
	(b)	5,625	4,724	2,531	3,230	2,199
	(c)	97	94	84	89	80
II. Crimes against property	(a)	3,205	4,641	6,618	14,909	27,901
with violence (house-	(b)	941	1,482	1,601	4,698	7,984
breaking and robbery)	(c)	29	32	24	32	29
III. Crimes against property	(a)	19,184	24,280	19,990	33,789	44,695
without violence	(b)	10,063	10,786	9,371	15,268	19,976
(mainly theft)	(c)	52	44	47	45	45
IV. Malicious injuries to	(a)	4,188	3,528	2,511	5,483	6,539
property (mainly	(b)	2,888	2,332	1,509	3,198	2,949
'malicious mischief')	(c)	69	66	60	58	45
All crimes (Classes I–VI)	(a)	32,632	38,569	33,070	58,976	83,008
	(b)	19,750	20,295	15,609	26,976	33,719
	(c)	61	53	47	46	41

(a) Numbers known to the police.
(b) Numbers in which one or more persons apprehended, etc.
(c) Percentage of crimes cleared.

'Crimes against Property with Violence'[1] (Class II) mainly house-breaking, have risen dramatically: the increase between 1897 and 1951 is almost nine-fold, from 3,205 to 27,901. 'Crimes against Property without Violence' (Class III) have risen less steeply to a higher total of 44,695, being mainly composed of the simplest and most prevalent crime, namely, theft. 'Malicious Injuries to Property' (Class IV) are mostly the work of juveniles, and of children of ten to eleven at that; the numbers are comparatively moderate and the increase comparatively gradual. The remaining two classes of crime, 'Forgery and Crimes against Currency' and 'Other Crimes', need not be detailed. The only item of any magnitude under the latter heading is 'Indecent Exposure', and it runs to under 1,000 cases annually reported and less than 300 appearances in court. For the rest, while these categories include such varied and picturesque crimes as coining, treason, rioting, poaching by night, and piracy, these occur in such comparatively small numbers as to be statistically indiscernible.

[1] Meaning, in the case of house-breaking, violence against property, i.e. breaking in. Robbery, involving violence against the person robbed, is discussed below along with other crimes of personal violence.

It is to be noted that there has been no major alteration in the proportion of crimes cleared except in the less numerous categories I and IV. The percentage remains high, at 80 %, in Class I, 'Crimes against the Person'. The pre-1914 figures of well above 90 % are reminiscent of that simpler and ruder period. In those days the police had a more compelling way with them, and the number of prisoners proceeded against frequently exceeded the number of Class I crimes known to the police. The fall in the proportion cleared of 'Malicious Injuries to Property' (Class IV) is steep, from 66 % in 1913 to 45 % in 1951. But in the two major categories there is little or no change whatever. The percentage of crimes cleared in Class II, 'Crimes against Property with Violence', was 29 % in 1897 and 29 % in 1951. In Class III, 'Crimes against Property without Violence', it was 44 % in 1913 and 45 % in 1951. There appears here to be a major discrepancy in the record. The proportion of crimes cleared in respect of all six classes taken together has fallen, as we saw on p. 230 above, from 53 % in 1913 to 41 % in 1951; but there has been no such fall in the corresponding percentages of the two classes which contain seven-eighths of the total. The discrepancy is apparent only. Both calculations are correct. What has happened is that the crimes where a low proportion of criminals are normally detected have shown the largest rate of increase and the average for all crimes has thus fallen without any significant change in the proportion of crimes detected.

When we take into account the swelling of the figures of 'crimes known' by the more minute recording of recent decades, it becomes evident that these figures conceal a steady improvement in the effectiveness of police detective methods. This conclusion is strengthened by a study of the facts behind the figures. The rise of the big department store, the growth of new suburban residential areas, the growing tendency in the past fifty years for shopkeepers and owners of public houses to live away from their business premises, the increase in working-class prosperity and in thievable articles in the vulnerable tenement house—all these developments make things progressively more difficult for the police. The detective skill of the police has at least kept pace, as is shown by the constant level of the percentage cleared. But even if the proportion detected remains the same, the sheer volume of crimes uncleared, the 'dark figure' of undetected crimes, is mounting steadily.

To sum up provisionally about crimes against property. It does not appear from the statistics that Scotland is becoming decisively more criminal in any serious sense; but it does appear that the national moral minimum over a wide area of society is lower than it was. If the barometer of offences shows a gentler social climate, the crimes barometer shows a looser social climate, a more easy-going and irresponsible way of living than held in former years. This provisional conclusion will be reinforced when we come to examine the changes in the age-structure of persons charged with crimes.

233

Crimes of personal violence

Crimes against the person make up, as we have seen, less than 5 % of all crimes, and appear to be decreasing over the last fifty years. But those crimes against the person which involve violence, and crimes of a sexual nature, demand special scrutiny.

The chief and capital crime of murder is too infrequent, too individual, and too complex, to permit of easy arithmetical generalization. But for what it is worth, it can be chronicled that the average number of murders known to be committed annually has not varied greatly over the past eighty years, being generally more than ten and less than twenty. The trend, such as it is, is downward, from four murders per million of the population in the late nineteenth century to three murders per million population in recent decades.[1] The annual

Table 111. *Crimes against the person in Scotland, including all crimes of personal violence*, 1897–1951

Class of crime		1897	1913	1925	1938	1948	1949	1950	1951
I. Murder	(a)	17	10	17	15	14	14	21	9
	(b)	14	8	12	10	6	8	17	7
II. Assaults, etc.	(a)	6,186	3,461	1,736	1,823	514	446	437	736
	(b)	5,359	3,420	1,722	1,632	454	253	247	414
III. Sexual crimes involving vio- lence	(a)	102	345	473	466	421	338	308	323
	(b)	113	254	200	96	104	85	95	115
IV. Robbery	(a)	134	135	38	114	353	325	346	305
	(b)	237	83	23	12	88	74	79	89
V. All crimes of violence (I–IV inclusive)	(a)	6,439	3,951	2,284	2,418	1,302	1,123	1,112	1,373
	(b)	5,723	3,765	1,957	1,750	562	420	438	625
VI. All sexual crimes (including III above)	(a)	242	776	830	1,168	1,381	1,375	1,441	1,599
	(b)	230	648	523	457	490	509	550	600

(a) Known to the police.   (b) Persons proceeded against.

Key: II. Assaults, etc.: 2, 3, 4, 5, in classified list (Attempts to Murder, Culpable Homicide, Assaults, Intimidation and Molestation).

III. Sexual Crimes involving violence: 11, 12, 13 in list (Rape, Assault with Intent to Ravish, Indecent Assault).

VI. All Sexual Crimes: as in III, plus 9, 10, 14 and 15 in list (Incest, Unnatural Crimes, Lewd and Libidinous Practices, and Procuration, etc.).

[1] The incidence of murders in England and Wales is apparently slightly higher (3·8 to 3·1 per million in 1930–50 on an annual average). But in Scotland the figures refer to acts of murder: in England and Wales the figures refer to the number of people murdered. If this were adjusted there would be little or no difference between the murder-rates.

average in the five years from 1947 to 1951 was in absolute number fifteen, and in rate per million of the population, three. Of the twenty-four persons proceeded against for murder in 1950 and 1951 twenty-two were called for trial. The charge was withdrawn in one case, one case found not proven, three persons were found not guilty, seven were found insane, and ten were sentenced to death: of these last, seven were reprieved.

Table 111 gives details of the various groups of crimes for various years since 1913 including each of the four years 1948–51. 'Assaults, etc.' comprise assaults, attempts to murder, culpable homicide, and intimidation and molestation—the last three amounting to very few in any one year. Both the long-term and the recent movement of this group of crimes is downwards, the sole exception being in 1951. But the figures since 1938 have been considerably affected by recording changes. The decrease from 1,823 in 1938 to 514 in 1948 is partly due to a down-grading of minor assaults by husbands on wives to the category of breach of the peace—an 'offence' not a 'crime'. The sudden rise from 437 in 1950 to 736 in 1951 is contrariwise due to a substantial extent to an up-grading of some other types of assault from breach of the peace to criminal assault by one or more local decisions. Throughout these changes, it may be noted, the proportion cleared remains high at 85%.

Crimes of a sexual nature show a striking difference from the other crimes against the person, in that the long- and short-term trend is steadily upwards. The increase is, however, in sexual immorality rather than in violence. Crimes of sexual violence, numbering one in five of the present total, show no increase on 1913, rapes having decreased from 27 to 18. 'Lewd and Libidinous Practices' have, however, increased thirteenfold, from 71 to 964, and now constitute three-fifths of the total.

Robbery, technically a crime against property, is substantially a crime of personal violence. The number of robberies is very small relative to the total of crimes, being just over 300 in 1951. But this figure is nearly three times greater than in pre-war years, and the crime itself, including as it does those violent assaults on unprotected citizens and notably on women which are now causing public concern, is important out of all proportion to its numbers.

A further source of concern is that robbery by its very nature is hard to detect. The proportion cleared was 43% in 1938, 22% in 1948–50, and 27% in 1951.

Geographical distribution of crimes

Turning to places and people in relation to crime, we find that, as always, the bulk of crimes are committed in the cities and towns; that, as always, the great majority of criminals are of the male sex, and this male preponderance is increasing; and that in the juvenile sector, the proportion of persons under 17 years of age proceeded against or against whom crimes are proved, has expanded greatly in the last generation, this last being a new and unprecedented development.

The incidence of crime increases with density of population. The four cities, containing 38 % of the population, had 58 % of all crimes known to the police in 1951. The number of crimes per thousand of the population in that year was 24·8 in the four cities (22·5 in 1950); 19·2 in the ten large burghs with separate police forces (13 in 1950); and 9·4 in the nineteen county or joint police areas (8·8 in 1950). The corresponding figures for offences show by contrast an even distribution—19·9, 20·7 and 19·7 respectively in 1951.

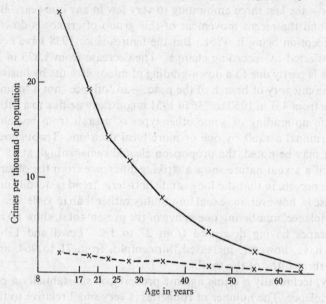

Fig. 17. Criminal charges proved in Scotland in 1951, by age of criminal.
Males ——— ; females - - -.

Sex and age distribution of criminals

The exact proportion of males to females of all ages against whom crimes were proved in recent years is just under nine to one: the percentage of male persons so classified being 89·2, 89·6, and 89·7 in the years 1949, 1950 and 1951. A broad comparison with previous years is possible in terms of 'persons proceeded against'; here the male-female ratio was 5:1 in 1913, 6:1 in 1925, and 8:1 in 1938. This decline in female criminality—it is also a drop in the *total* of female persons charged—is matched by an even greater decline in the female quota of 'offences', the male-female ratio rising from 4:1 in 1913 to 12:1 in 1951. Thefts constitute the bulk of female crimes.

As Fig. 17 shows, the incidence of crime among males is highest in the juvenile age-group,[1] the under-17's, and falls with each succeeding age-group. The same is true in 1951 for females, though it should be noted that in 1949 and 1950, and probably in most previous years the incidence was highest in the 17–20 age-group. Restating the male-female ratio in terms of the incidences in each age-group, we get the 1951 proportion of nine to one for all ages: nearly eleven to one in the 17–20 age-group; thirteen to one in the juvenile sector; and five to one from the ages of 30–60. The proportion of women committed to prison is now very low. There was one woman prisoner in 1900 to every three male prisoners; today the proportion is one in twenty.

Table 112. *Criminal charges proved in Scotland, 1938–51*

	1938	1947	1948	1949	1950	1951
Juvenile crimes	8,133	8,235	10,308	8,949	9,749	10,419
Index	100	101·3	126·7	110·0	119·8	128·2
Adult crimes	11,888	12,255	13,157	11,542	11,785	13,417
Index	100	103·1	110·7	97·1	99·1	112·9

The increase in juvenile delinquency

The outstanding development in the field of crime in Scotland in the last generation is the expansion of the juvenile sector. In 1925 the under-17's made up an estimated 30 % of all persons against whom crimes were proved; this had risen to 41 % in 1938 and to the astonishing figure of 44 % in 1951. In the inter-war years the increase in all crimes from 1929, the lowest point in the 1920's to 1938, was entirely an increase in juvenile crime. All persons proceeded against rose from 19,520 to 22,148, an increase of 2,628: the number of juveniles proceeded against rose from 5,475 (under 16) to 8,558 (under 17) an increase of 3,083, of whom not more than 400 would be accounted for by the raising of the age-limit in 1932. In the post-war years the same is broadly true. As Table 112 shows the number of crimes proved against adults fell below pre-war level in 1949 and 1950 although crimes proved against juveniles are well above pre-war level.

It is somewhat reassuring that the increase in persons proceeded against in Scotland, comparing 1929 and 1951, is almost entirely an increase in juvenile crime, and that the juvenile increase has not so far (if we suspend judgement on the 1951 adult increase) been reflected in the adult figures. But even if the persistence of juvenile crime at its present level were to remain permanently unaccompanied by any increase in crimes proved against adults, it is in itself a sign of deterioration in moral standards and in parental care.

[1] Details are given in a new table commenced in the 1949 *Criminal Statistics, Scotland* (Table 8 in 1949 and 1950; Table 7 in 1951).

It is, of course, probable that some of the juvenile increase is unreal. Many middle-aged persons will remember being summarily and unofficially cuffed by the policeman or by the nearest adult for matters which today might land their offspring in the juvenile court. The institution in 1908 of this more suitable tribunal, and its further improvement in 1932 and 1937, has disposed public, parents, and police to make much more use of the official procedures than they did in the past. But it is also true that the Scottish police take special steps through the informal procedure of the 'police warning'[1] to warn many children and their parents for petty crimes which are thus kept 'off the record'. It is also to be suspected that the Scottish police are more reluctant than most to bring young females into court. The proportion of girl to boy offenders is one to fourteen in Scotland, one to eleven in England and Wales, and one to four in U.S.A. (where the juvenile court is a chancery and not a criminal court).[2] This suggests that the Scottish figures of juvenile crime might well be higher. And even if the increase in the 1930's is to be regarded as mainly unreal the increase in 1951 as compared with 1938 is real enough.

A comparison with the statistical trend in England and Wales will help to focus the Scottish situation. The number of juveniles found guilty of indictable offences in England and Wales was 28,116 in 1938 and 47,473 in 1951, an increase of 69 %: the corresponding Scottish increase is 28 % (Table 112). In the same period, the number of adults found guilty in England and Wales also increased by 69 %, from 50,347 to 85,344: the corresponding Scottish figure is 13 %. In short, the increase in juvenile crime in England and Wales since 1938 is $2\frac{1}{2}$ times the increase in Scotland in the same period, and has been accompanied, as the smaller increase in Scotland has not, by an equally massive increase in adult crime. As we shall see in a moment, Scotland compares unfavourably with her Southern neighbours on a direct estimate of incidences or crime-rates. But it is more satisfactory, when comparing two different systems of criminal administration, to base the comparison on the statistical movements within the two systems over a period. On this basis the figures suggest that the post-war state of crime, both adult and juvenile, is decidedly less serious in Scotland than it is in England and Wales.

Meantime it remains to be noted that about 99 % of juvenile crimes are crimes against property, three out of ten being classed as house-breaking, nearly five out of ten theft, and two out of ten malicious injuries to property, mostly malicious michief. Fully half of the latter are committed by children

---

[1] See *Police Warnings: Report by the Scottish Advisory Council on the Treatment and Rehabilitation of Offenders* (Scottish Home Department, 1945).

[2] Calculated for Scotland and England and Wales, on the annual average for the five years 1946–50 inclusive; given for U.S.A. in *Juvenile Court Statistics, 1946–1949*, p. 4. (Children's Bureau Statistical Series, no. 2, 1951, Federated Security Agency, Washington).

of 11 and under. Juvenile crimes of violence against the person have varied little since the war, and constitute a small proportion of the total of such crimes (see Table 113).

Table 113. *Crimes of violence in Scotland:
charges proved, 1946–51*

	1946	1947	1948	1949	1950	1951
All crimes of violence	505	555	526	329	341	493
Juvenile crimes of violence	49	36	49	28	45	65

SOURCE: *Hansard*, 18 November 1952, col. 1571.

Comparison of Scotland with England and Wales

It has long been known to students of statistics, if not to the general public, that the Scots excel their neighbours south of the Border not only in church- and university-going but also in crime. The crime-rate in Scotland is, or has been until recently, markedly higher than the crime-rate in England and Wales. Why is this? Many Scottish men of law are apt to ascribe this superiority, following William Roughead,[1] to the genial temperament of the Lowland Scot, and notably to his quality of smouldering perversity in the face of con- stituted authority. But a study of the figures reveals that even if the Scot paddles more lustily in the waters of iniquity he sticks with native caution to the shallows. The statistical-criminal pre-eminence of Scotland is maintained, in so far as it is still maintained, only in the totals and in the less serious categories of officially recorded crime. Even taking the total figure the gap has narrowed considerably since 1938. In that year all crimes known to the police in Scotland[2] numbered eleven per thousand of the total population: the rate in England and Wales was seven per thousand. In 1951 the Scottish-rate had increased from eleven to fourteen per thousand of the population: but the rate in England had moved up from seven to fourteen.

These all-in totals are not strictly comparable, as is indicated below.[3] It is more satisfactory to make the comparison in respect of the different categories of crime—crimes of violence, crimes of a sexual nature, crimes against property, and the smaller group of more serious crimes against property.

[1] In *The Seamy Side* (1938) that incomparable archivist of murder deplores the lament- able scarcity of material adapted to his purpose and confidently hopes that his fellow Scots 'will see to it that in future they keep me so supplied with the natural and kindly products of our common country that I shall not again be, in a literary sense, expatriated' (p. x).
[2] The Scottish figures have been recalculated to omit Class IV Crimes ('Malicious Injuries to Property') so as to give a fairer comparison with the figures for England and Wales (see Appendix, §3).
[3] See Appendix, §3.

239

In crimes of violence, generally and rightly regarded as the most serious type of crime, what difference there is now favours Scotland. In 1938 this was not so. In that year 'assaults, etc.' in Scotland were six times as frequent as 'woundings, etc.' in England and Wales: 365[1] 'assaults, etc.' made known to the police in Scotland per million population compared with 64 'woundings, etc.' per million population in England and Wales. The very high Scottish figure we have already ascribed to the Scottish practice, now discontinued, of recording minor domestic mêlées as criminal assaults. In 1951, on a more approximately equivalent scale of comparison, the respective rates per million were 144 in Scotland and 146 in England and Wales.

Crimes of a sexual nature—a small proportion only being crimes of violence—were twice as frequent in Scotland in 1938 as in England and Wales, numbering 260 per million as compared with 113 per million. But by 1951 the positions were reversed, although the incidence has increased in both cases—313 in Scotland and 324 in England and Wales per million of the population.

Robbery is the sole exception to the rule that the Scots now hold the statistical lead only in the less serious crimes. Small as was the Scottish incidence of known robberies in 1951—60 per million of the population—it is more than three times that of England and Wales, 20 per million. It may be that the recording system in the English police districts excludes a large number of minor matters which are in Scotland recorded as robberies.

The much more numerous categories of crimes against property still retain the traditional pattern. It is fast disappearing in the most prolific category of all. In the case of thefts (larcenies in England) the English rate for crimes known to the police in 1951, and the rate of persons tried, or proceeded against, was only slightly less than the Scottish, although in 1938 it was very much less. Not so in house-breaking. The incidence of all house-breakings known to the police is more than twice as high in Scotland as in England in 1938 (2,958 to 1,193 per million) and remains more than twice as high in 1951 (5,395 to 2,519 per million). The incidence of persons charged follows the same pattern (713 to 276 in 1938, and 1,116 to 586 in 1951, per million). But if we divide house-breakings (which include shop-breaking and factory-breaking and all other kinds of breakings and enterings) into 'less serious' and 'more serious' the case is altered. Let us consider for example, only those more substantial crimes which earned for their perpetrators a spell in prison or a period of Borstal training. For 1938 we have English figures of all sentences above three months and Scottish figures only of sentences of three months and above. The comparison is therefore imperfect and strongly

---

[1] All of the figures in this paragraph refer to crimes known to the police expressed as a rate per million of the *total* population. (*Criminal Statistics, England and Wales*, 1951, Table E, pp. 17–18, gives a rate per million of the population of 8 years and over).

favours England and Wales. Nevertheless, the respective rates per million population were 55 in England and Wales and 60 in Scotland. For 1951, by courtesy of the Scottish Home Department, a direct comparison is possible in terms of sentences for house-breaking of above six months. The rates per million population were 112 in England and Wales and 68 in Scotland. This is not a conclusive argument—corrective training was operating in England and Wales by 1951, involving longer sentences—but it goes to confirm other evidences that the disparity between the two national incidences for all house-breakings, past and present, exist only in the larger sector of the smaller fry.

Why should this be so? An obvious answer is that there are in fact more petty house-breakers to the square mile in Scotland, particularly among the under-17's. Another possibility is that the Scottish police have over the past century been disposed to rope in a greater proportion of petty offenders than have the police south of Tweed, and that the distinctive Scottish office of Procurator-Fiscal, or public prosecutor, has operated to secure a greater number of prosecutions. On this latter hypothesis the closing of the gap between the two countries in recent years may be due as much to a tightening up of the recording of crimes in England and Wales as to an actual increase in minor crimes against property.

Disposal

The 113,014 persons proceeded against for crimes and offences in Scotland in 1951, a year which shows the same pattern of disposals as in previous years, were dealt with as shown in Table 114.

It does not fall within the scope of this chapter to discuss long-term penal changes, but two points may be mentioned. The first is the marked decrease over the past fifty years in the number of persons committed to prison, from over 50,000 at the turn of the century to 8,762[1] in 1951. The fall in the proportion of women prisoners, from 23·2 % in 1900 to 4·6 % in 1951 (the lowest figure on record) has already been noted. The decrease is largely in short-sentence prisoners, mostly drunks of both sexes imprisoned in lieu of payment of fine. As a result the average sentence is much longer, being now about eighty-six days, and the daily average population has fallen only a little, from 2,698 in 1900 to 1,851 in 1951. The remarkable post-war rise in the daily average population of prisons in England and Wales, from 10,000 in the pre-war period to 25,000 in early 1952, has no parallel in Scotland; the 1951 daily average population is about one-fifth higher than the 1,543 of 1938. This follows naturally from the contrasting trends in adult crime already described.

The second point of interest is the comparative reluctance of the Scottish courts to consider probation (by which is meant probation with supervision) as a method of dealing with adult offenders. Thus the 3,649 persons put on

---

[1] This total of 8,762 includes 2,821 imprisoned in default of payment of fine.

probation in 1951 included 3,052 under-17's, 401 in the 17–20 age-group and 196 only of those of 21 and over. This accent on juvenile probation, which has been obvious since 1931, when probation was made a full-time service, is in some ways a natural consequence of the drift of Scottish crime. But it appears that as the main provisions of the Criminal Justice Act (Scotland) of 1949 come into force the practice of adult probation in Scotland is being extended.

Table 114. *Persons proceeded against in Scotland: disposal of cases*, 1951

| | All persons proceeded against | Not tried or acquitted | Charges proved | | | | | | |
| | | | Without finding of guilt | | With finding of guilt | | | | |
			Absolute discharge, etc.	Pro-bation	Prison including Borstal	Ap-proved school	Remand home	Fine	Admon-ished, etc.
Crimes Juvenile	11,083	664	1,310	2,977	39*	553	322	2,330	2,888
Adult	14,788	1,487	176	492	3,986†	—	—	7,464	1,503
Total	25,871	2,151	1,486	3,469	4,025	553	322	9,794	4,391
Offences Juvenile	7,293	376	430	75	2	14	24	4,030	2,342
Adult	79,850	10,655	298	105	1,851	—	—	60,779	6,186
Total	87,143	11,031	728	180	1,853	14	24	64,809	8,528

* Two sent to prison. † Including one death sentence.

CONCLUSION

The main findings of this study of Scottish criminal statistics may be summarized briefly. The pavements of Scottish cities are no longer thronged with the crowds of drunks and disorderlies of the pre-1914 era, but the highways are much more dangerous to life and limb. That is the main reading of the 'barometer of offences'. The 'crimes barometer' records only one major change. The level of adult crime does not change; the increase in the last twenty years in detected offenders is almost entirely an increase in youthful offenders. The trend of violent crime is by and large a downward trend. The comparison of long-term movements of crime within Scotland with those within England and Wales—the only valid method of comparison between different systems of criminal administration—yields a different and less disquieting picture in Scotland. The comparison of the respective national incidences or rates of crime in so far as it can legitimately be drawn, shows that the ancient Scottish supremacy in this unhonoured field is now being lost, and never amounted to much except on a purely arithmetical assessment. The only alarming feature in the Scottish situation is the rapid growth of the dark figure of undetected crimes. So far as can be judged the inferential increase in criminal behaviour is an increase only in minor crimes. But the gradual moral deterioration which this implies may be a worse omen for Scotland than would a period of outbreak of a smaller number of much more serious crimes.

APPENDIX
Yardsticks of crime

1. For long-term trends the best measures in order of reliability are:

(a) Number of 'persons proceeded against'. This has the double advantage that it is available for every year since 1868, and that the most reliable police figures are those of persons and those taken nearest the point of arrest.

(b) Number of 'crimes and offences known to the police'. This also has been kept since 1868. As explained in the text there is reason to believe that it has been kept more accurately in recent decades.

(c) Number of 'crimes and offences in which one or more persons were apprehended, cited, warned, etc., or traced'. This number, calculated as a percentage of 'crimes, etc., known to the police', gives the percentage of 'crimes, etc., cleared'. This is sometimes regarded as a measure of police efficiency, but it is unsatisfactory in this respect for a variety of reasons (see pp. 230–1 above). In 1936 a change in recording practice was made in an attempt to secure uniformity between police districts. Previously only 'crimes and offences in which a person or persons were apprehended or cited', had been recorded. The addition of '...persons...warned, etc., and traced' increased this total considerably and automatically brought it well above the total of 'persons proceeded against' for 1936 and all subsequent years, with the consequences noted on p. 231.

2. For more recent years a more accurate measure of persons dealt with is available in the number of 'charges proved'. This cuts out all those cases which are dropped at an early stage, or in which the persons proceeded against are cleared of the charge after trial. In Scotland a charge may be proved without finding of guilt, so that 'charges proved' subdivides into 'persons against whom charge proved but not found guilty' and 'persons found guilty' (or 'convicted'). It is a source of confusion that the *Annual Abstract of Statistics* should reproduce without explanation the Scottish figures of 'persons convicted or found guilty' (*Abstract* No. 89, Tables 72–3). This suggests a direct comparison with the figure for England and Wales of 'persons found guilty' (ibid. Tables 65–7). But the Scottish equivalent for the English 'persons found guilty' is 'charges proved'.

Where possible in this chapter 'charges proved' have been quoted.

3. The *totals* of 'crimes' in Scotland and of 'indictable offences' in England and Wales in any one year are not strictly comparable. The Scottish list is the more comprehensive. It includes, under Class IV, all cases of 'malicious mischief'. But the majority of such cases occurring in England and Wales are classified as 'non-indictable offences' under the title of 'malicious damage'. In addition the English

list has in some special tables a class of 'non-indictable offences akin to indictable offences' which have a strong family resemblance to several Scottish 'crimes'. Pending the production of a conversion formula which will yield a more accurate comparison—it is understood that the Departments concerned are exploring this possibility—the best rule is to omit Class IV in the Scottish list, making no alterations in the English figures. The resulting rough comparison is as good as can be obtained at present. For a more detailed comparative study of recent years see A. M. Struthers's admirable *Measuring Bad Behaviour* (National Council of Social Service, 1950).

[The writing of this chapter was materially helped by information and advice from Mr W. D. Watson, Mr J. Utterson and Mr W. Hewitson Brown, Scottish Home Department; Mr T. S. Lodge, Home Office; and Mr Robert MacDonald, Procurator-Fiscal in Glasgow and Lecturer in Evidence and Procedure in the University of Glasgow; to all of these thanks and acknowledgments are gratefully rendered.]

CHAPTER 17

EDUCATION

By JOHN HIGHET

Scottish education is marked, administratively, by a simple, unified and planned structure; and philosophically, by a preference for the 'book-learning' type of education, continuity between primary and secondary education, and emphasis on equality of opportunity.

These features are of long standing. Many authorities assert that Scotland was the first nation in Europe in which an integrated system of education was established; and the archetype of Scottish education goes back to the *First Book of Discipline* of 1561 with its plan for a school in every parish and for 'high schools' in the large towns, so that education might be available for all who could benefit by it, irrespective of social class or financial resources. For long retarded by various factors, this ideal has now come near to complete fulfilment in current educational organization and practice.

In the past, comparison between Scottish and English education would have shown marked differences in administration and in aim and ideals, most of them favourable to the smaller nation. To give but one example, whereas the English Act of 1870 restricted grants to elementary education, the Scottish Act of 1872 gave the School Boards of the time power to levy rates for the upkeep not merely of elementary schools but of schools providing mainly secondary education. With the passing of the Education Act of 1944 the contrasts have become less distinct and fundamental. While the Scottish Act of 1945 constituted little more than another step in a gradual progression, the 1944 Act brought about what were by comparison radical changes in English education. Some of its major innovations were already contained in Scottish statutes and were, even if in imperfect form, part of Scottish educational practice. The influence has not, however, been all one way, and if there is less emphasis now in Scotland on book-learning, and greater willingness to experiment in methods, in content of curriculum and in extra-curricular activities, much of this change is due to English as well as overseas developments.

Nevertheless, interesting differences remain, among them the fact that the Scottish educational structure is still a more completely national system than is that of England and Wales. A brief description of this national system and a discussion of its more important aspects accordingly forms the bulk of this chapter. Other sections deal with further education, finance, and the universities.

245

THE NATIONAL SCHOOL SYSTEM

Education is compulsory for all children able to profit by it between the ages of 5 and 15, and is available up to the age of 18 and over in the senior secondary schools and for some children between 2 and 5 in nursery schools. For the first stage of his educational career—normally for a period of seven years— the child attends primary school, from which he passes, about the age of 12, to the secondary school. There are two types of secondary school—the junior secondary, designed mainly for those not likely to remain at school after the leaving age, and providing courses of three years' duration; and the senior secondary, offering courses of five or six years' duration designed for those intending to remain at school to take the Scottish Leaving Certificate, normally at the age of 17. Some schools are exclusively either junior or senior secondary, and some, commonly called 'omnibus' or 'comprehensive' schools, accept all the post-primary pupils in their area regardless of school-leaving intentions, and provide the whole range of secondary education. At present no Leaving Certificate based on an external examination is awarded to pupils leaving school at 15; instead, all leavers receive a School Leaving Record showing *inter alia* the subjects of the course and the proficiency gained in each.[1]

In all, there are just over 3,000 schools within the public educational system. The great majority of them are non-fee-paying day schools under the management of education committees exercising powers delegated by local authorities under the Education (Scotland) Act, 1946, and answerable formally through the local authorities to the Scottish Education Department. These schools may be called 'state schools'. This term should be applied also to the few schools under the control of local education authorities at which moderate fees are charged, but which in other respects are similar to those just described. Thirdly, there is a group of fee-paying schools which, although they are not to be described as state schools, are still within the national system in that they are grant-aided schools having administrative relationships of varying degrees of closeness with the education committee in their area. At 31 March 1951, there were just under 794,000 pupils on the registers of the schools in these three categories. Within the national system also are twenty-five Approved Schools with about 1,600 pupils on their rolls, while about the same number of pupils receive education from Education Authorities elsewhere than at school.

Outside the public educational framework (although subject to inspection by the Department) there are about 200 schools, officially designated 'independent schools'—schools which are under private management, are mostly

---

[1] Some Local Education Authorities award a Junior School Certificate, based on class work, after three full years' secondary education.

boarding or part-day and part-boarding schools, have no administrative relationships with Local Education Authorities, and are not grant-aided.[1] At the end of March 1951 there were just over 21,000 pupils on their registers. Thus 97·4 % of children receiving education in Scotland in 1951 were pupils of schools within the national system.

Table 115. *Pupils at schools within and outside the public educational systems of Scotland and of England and Wales*, 1951

Scotland (31 March 1951)			England and Wales (January 1951)		
Type of school	Number receiving education (thousands)	Percentage of total	Type of school	Number receiving education* (thousands)	Percentage of total
Public and other grant-aided schools	794·0	97·0	Grant-aided schools maintained by Local Education Authorities	5,800·0	94·9
Other places of education	3·2	0·4	Direct grant schools	96·0	1·6
Schools within public education system	797·2	97·4	Schools within public education system	5,895·0	96·5
Independent schools	21·0	2·6	Other schools 're-cognized as efficient'	220·0	3·6
Total	818·2	100·0	Total	6,115·0	100·0

* As reported to the Ministry of Education.

SOURCES: *Education in Scotland in 1951* (Scottish Education Dept.); *Education in 1951* (Ministry of Education).

How does this compare with the situation in England and Wales? Pupil-numbers as provided in the two official reports—that of the Scottish Education Department and that of the Ministry of Education—are shown in Table 115, but the figures are not strictly comparable. The reason for this is that the Ministry figures include only those independent schools which have been inspected and recognized as efficient and which report annually to the Ministry. By the close of 1951 there were approximately 4,000 schools either

[1] Perhaps the best-known of the independent schools are those which, by the double standard of membership of the Headmasters' Conference and being wholly or partly boarding, can be regarded as 'Public Schools' in the English middle-class sense of the term, viz. Fettes, Glenalmond, Loretto, Merchiston Castle, Gordonstoun, Edinburgh Academy, Glasgow Academy, Robert Gordon's College and George Watson's Boys' College. One or two other schools, such as Dollar Academy, are also sometimes included among Scottish 'Public Schools'. Board and tuition fees vary from about £150 to about £320 per annum, and fees for day boys (at the schools which admit non-boarders) vary from £36 to £120 per annum.

visited and still to be recognized, or still to be visited. The Ministry's figures do not, therefore, embrace all children receiving education in England and Wales, and there is no central source from which figures concerning these 'non-recognized' independent schools could be obtained. In Scotland, on the other hand, inspection of independent schools was completed in 1951, so that the Department's figures cover all—or all but the merest fraction of—Scottish children receiving education.[1]

It follows, therefore, that of the total in fact receiving education in England and Wales, the percentages at Local Education Authority schools and at direct grant schools were somewhat less than the 94·9 % and the 1·6 % shown in Table 115, while the percentage at schools outside the state system was correspondingly higher than 3·6 %.[2] Education in Scotland is, therefore, rather more completely a preserve of the state educational organization than it is south of the Border.

Of the estimated total population of compulsory school age, 98·3 % were receiving education at public or private schools in Scotland in March 1951. No English and Welsh figure is available for strict comparison, but the number of pupils of compulsory school age reported to the Ministry as receiving education forms 95·3 % of the estimated population within these age limits. It is most unlikely that the proportion of children of school age who were not attending school was nearly three times as high in England and Wales as in Scotland; and the contrast between the percentages just quoted may be one more indication of the greater importance of independent schools in England and Wales.

The age-distribution of the 21,000 pupils attending independent schools in Scotland is shown in Table 116. There is a more even spread over the three selected age-groups than in the state schools, but in no age-group do these pupils form more than 2 % of the total population. They bear a much higher relation to state school pupils under 5¼ and over 15¼ than to pupils within the compulsory age-limits, the proportion varying from over 15 % for the youngest and nearly 8 % for the oldest to only 2 % for the intermediate age-group. For every senior secondary pupil at an independent school in Scotland there are twelve in schools within the public system. This compares broadly with about 1 in 5 in England and Wales; or with an even lower ratio if full account could be taken of independent schools for which no figures are available.

[1] The Department recognizes that there may be a few small schools in existence of which it is unaware, but the number of pupils concerned is likely to be very small. There is, again, no source from which data relating to such schools could be obtained.

[2] For the purpose of this comparison 'direct grant' schools in England and Wales have been classified as within the public educational system. It is true that they are semi-independent; on the other hand, Local Education Authority representatives sit on their governing boards, and about half the places at these schools must be given to pupils chosen by the Local Education Authorities, these pupils either paying no fees at all or fees graded according to their parents' income.

Table 116. *Pupils at schools within and outside the public educational system in Scotland, by age-group, March* 1951

| Type of school | Pupils in age-group* | | | | | |
| | 2 to under 5¼ | | 5¼ to under 15¼ | | 15¼ to approx. 18† | |
	Number (thousands)	Percentage of estimated population in age-group‡	Number (thousands)	Percentage of estimated population in age-group‡	Number (thousands)	Percentage of estimated population in age-group‡
Schools in public system	18·6	6·3	753·8	96·3	24·8	8·7
Independent schools	3·4	1·1	15·6	2·0	2·0	0·7
Total	22·0	7·5	769·4	98·3	26·9	9·5
England and Wales§	181·6	7·7	5,651·8	95·3	275·6	12·5

* In *Education in Scotland in 1951* the Scottish Education Department gives figures for 31 March 1951, in columns headed 'Born in 1945', etc., and the age-groups have had to be adapted to these figures.

† Including a few over 18.

‡ In nearest age-group for which figures are available.

§ For England and Wales the figures relate to January 1951; the age-groups are 2 to under 5, 5 to under 15, and 15 to 18 (including a few over 18); and the numbers are of pupils reported to the Ministry to be receiving education (i.e. they exclude some at non-recognized independent schools).

SOURCES: *Education in Scotland in 1951*; *Education in 1951*; *Census of Population, 1951: One Per Cent Sample Tables*; Registrar-General's estimates as at 31 December 1950.

Although it might seem from Table 116 that nursery schools play about the same part in Scotland as in England and Wales, the figures for the younger children are not comparable, since those for Scotland include some children of school age. There is, however, a marked difference between the two countries in the proportion of pupils attending school at ages above 15. Of those aged 15–18, 1 in 8 was still at school in England and Wales while in Scotland the proportion appears to have been under 1 in 10. The 1951 Census provides further evidence of this contrast. Of those occupied persons who were under 20 in 1951 and had left school, 15·6 % had done so in England and Wales after reaching the age of 16, but only 7·1 % in Scotland. For those aged 20–24 the proportions were rather higher but little closer to one another —18·0 % compared with 11·1 %. On the other hand, a much higher proportion of Scotsmen than of Englishmen had left school at 15.

This conclusion is not at all in keeping with popular belief. It is generally thought that, since a higher proportion of Scotsmen go to a university, the average Scotsman also stays longer at school than the average Englishman. It will, indeed, be seen from Table 117 that a higher proportion of Scotsmen than of Englishmen completed their education at age 20 or over; and it is probable that once the decision not to leave at 15 has been taken, Scottish pupils are more likely to complete a secondary course or go on to a university, whereas in England there is a relatively greater exodus at 16 and 17. It will also be seen, however, that the younger the group taken, the more pronounced is the tendency for English pupils to complete their education at a later age than their Scottish contemporaries. For example, taking young and old together, 7·9 % of the occupied population in England and Wales left school at 16 compared with 4·8 % in Scotland; for the generation under 20, however, these figures become 11·8 % and 5·5 %, a comparison suggesting that Scotland has made a good deal less progress than England.

Table 117. *Percentage of occupied population (in three age sections) finally leaving an educational establishment at various ages in Scotland and in England and Wales*

Age in 1951	Percentage finally leaving at age									
	Under 15		15		16		17–19		20 and over	
	Scot-land	Eng-land and Wales	Scot-land	Eng-land and Wales	Scot-land	Eng-land and Wales	Scot-land	Eng-land and Wales	Scot-land	Eng-land and Wales
Under 20	31·7	31·8	61·2	52·5	5·5	11·8	1·6	3·8	—	—
20–24	72·1	70·0	14·5	10·0	5·8	11·0	5·3	7·0	2·2	2·2
All ages	73·6	73·1	15·3	11·7	4·8	7·9	3·6	4·8	2·7	2·4

SOURCE: *Census of Population, 1951: One Per Cent Sample Tables.*

The main factors producing this contrast in school-leaving practice in Scotland and in England and Wales would seem to be the different ages at which school-leaving certificates could in the past and can now be taken in the two countries, greater economic pressure in Scotland towards early employment, the different occupational pattern[1] and the higher esteem in which university education has traditionally been held in Scotland.

It is also possible to gauge from Table 117 the effects of the increase in the school-leaving age to 15, since most of those under 20 in 1951 were under 15 when the measure came into force in 1947. Over 73 % of the occupied population, both in England and Wales and in Scotland, left school before reaching the age of 15; but for those still under 20 in 1951 the proportion was below 32 % and is presumably considerably lower now.

[1] Cf. Chapter 18, pp. 268–9.

FEE-PAYING SCHOOLS WITHIN THE PUBLIC SYSTEM

In addition to the 21,000 pupils who attend independent schools there are a number who attend fee-paying schools within the public system. This number is not known but is unlikely to be large. What evidence there is suggests that the demand for the available places in these schools, which in some areas began to manifest itself some years before the war, has become even heavier in the post-war period. Middle-class parents who fifteen to twenty years ago would have felt assured that their children would receive at a good non-fee-paying state school an education that would seriously challenge that provided at both local authority fee-schools and at many independent schools, and that the children would there be 'mixing' in the main with others of their own social level, now seem to be equally convinced that socially and educationally most state schools have deteriorated. Since many who take this view are parents of relatively moderate means, this has led to intensified pressure on the inexpensive fee-charging schools under the management of education authorities or in administrative relationships with them—schools which, in most cases, have a very high educational standing.[1]

In respect of the cities at least (and more especially, perhaps, of Glasgow) there is unquestionably some ground for the belief that the majority of non-fee-paying state schools now draw on pupils from much more varied social backgrounds. Movements of population, the building of new housing schemes without adequate school facilities and the consequent placing of children from mainly working-class homes in schools in other areas which at one time had a predominantly middle-class register, changes in the social standing of some middle-class 'residential' areas in which are sited the state schools formerly accorded at least an intermediate status—these are among the factors that have brought about changes in the social composition of the pupil body at many non-fee-paying state schools. In addition, some authorities operate a zoning arrangement whereby, on the one hand, children of the middle-class remnant in declining areas have no choice of a non-fee-paying school other than the one in the vicinity of their home, and, on the other hand, children from districts of a somewhat humble status may, for reasons of pressure on accommodation due to restrictions on building extensions, be assigned to schools in a nearby district of a more elevated status.

[1] The fees charged per session at the five High Schools under the management of Glasgow Education Committee, for example, range from £5. 17s. to £18. 9s. for primary classes and from £10. 7s. to £23. 2s. for secondary, the High School for Boys charging the highest in each case. These compare with £36 for the younger classes of day boys and £81 for the senior classes at Glasgow Academy, and from £33 to £60 for primary classes and from £60 to £72 for senior classes at Kelvinside Academy, while at three schools for girls the primary fees rise from £31. 10s. (at Park) to £59. 17s. (at Park and Westbourne) and the secondary from £53. 11s. (at Laurel Bank) to £66 (at Park). Compare also p. 247, n. 1 for the general range of fees paid by day boys at Scottish Public Schools.

It is probable that there is substance also in the belief that educational standards are falling in many of the non-fee-paying state schools in whose classrooms at one time sat men who have reached the highest levels in a wide field of professional and public service. The above developments tend to take a high proportion of the top intelligence levels away from the non-fee-paying state schools, while in schools housing the overflows from environments un-favourable to full application, the greater 'scatter' of aptitudes acts as a retarding influence on the more able of the middle-class remnant still on their registers. Moreover, conditions in local authority fee-paying schools allow of a greater provision than can be made in most 'free' state schools of the type of extra-classroom communal activity which has come to be recognized as playing an important part in the education of the whole person.

While there can be no doubt that social snobbery of a kind is not the exclusive property of parents—mothers especially—whose children are at expensive fee-paying schools, but is shown also to some extent by parents paying moderate education authority fees, it is clearly an over-simplification to regard the increasing middle-class attraction to fee-paying authority schools as deriving wholly from social class interests. It is in part, and probably in the main, an indication of a concern for the educational well-being, as the parents see it, of the children: and that not simply in the narrower, 'book-learning' sense of the term 'educational'. Whichever of these motives is the pre-dominant one, whether or not the parents who have taken or tried to take this step away from the non-fee-paying state schools have done so with reluctance, there is discernible in this situation the beginning of a break, both educationally and socially, with an honourable tradition in Scottish education.

TEACHERS AND CLASSES

During and since the war much has been heard of a shortage of teachers and of various difficulties resulting from the raising of the school-leaving age. In some schools, for example, it was not possible to accept pupils until they had reached 6 years of age. The number of teachers, however, has more than kept pace with the number of pupils. In 1951 the average number of pupils per certificated teacher in public and grant-aided schools in Scotland was 24·3. This was the lowest number not only for any post-war year but for any year since records were first kept. In 1914, for example, the average was 42·5; in 1936 it was 28. In 1948, despite an increase in the school roll consequent on the raising of the leaving age, the average fell from 26 to 25·5. During the three following years the school roll remained fairly constant at just over 790,000, but the staff continued to increase.

In some areas, however—among them the most populous in the country—the ratio of pupils to staff is appreciably above the national level. If the 911 uncertificated teachers are added to the number of certificated teachers, bringing the total of full-time teachers to 33,540, the ratio for Scotland in 1951 becomes 23·7.[1] Seven city and county education areas had ratios above this level: Dunbarton (28·6), Renfrew (26·6), Lanark (26·2), Glasgow (25·9), Dumfries (25·3), West Lothian (25·1) and Fife (24·8). These contain 1,008 of the 3,171 schools (31·8 %) and 423,408 out of the total school roll of 793,996 (53·3 %) within the public organization.

Excluding secondary practical classes, there were 24,074 classes in the public system in 1951. Of that number, 1,986 or 8·2 % had rolls above the maximum sizes for various categories of classes, as laid down by the Schools (Scotland) Code, 1950, namely: in a primary class, 45 (reduced from the previous maximum of 50); in a secondary class of the first, second or third year, 40; in a secondary class beyond the third year, 30; and for various kinds of special classes, a range of from 10 to 30. Of these 1,986 oversize classes, 1,466 were primary (8·8 % of total primary classes), 404 secondary (5·9 % of total), and 116 special classes (18·7 % of total).

Here again an examination of education areas reveals an uneven picture. Five areas show percentages of oversize to total classes above the national average of 8·2 %. Dunbarton heads the list with 30·7 %, followed by Dumfries with 14·7 %, Renfrew with 13·1 %, Glasgow with 12·5 %, and Lanark with 12 %. These five areas contain 25·2 % of all Scottish public and grant-aided schools, and 45 % of the pupils at these schools.

The decreasing ratio of pupils to staff does not altogether bear out the common impression of an acute shortage of staff. Yet it has been estimated that there is a deficiency of about 2,300 teachers which will rise to nearly 3,300 by 1957;[2] and that by that date there will only be two teachers qualified to teach mathematics in secondary schools for every three posts in that category, filled and unfilled. The deficiency in science teachers is expected to rise to over one-fifth of the available posts. Figures obtained from an inquiry sent recently to the four Scottish Training Colleges show that the total number of Honours graduates in mathematics completing training courses in 1952 was 9, compared with 14 in 1951. The number in science in 1952 was 29,

[1] 'Uncertificated' means 'not holding a Scottish certificate'; it does not necessarily mean 'unqualified'. Of these 911, 88 were graduates, 128 were trained teachers (although not in Scotland) and 350 were skilled in the practical subject they were teaching; 771 held regular teaching posts and will require to be replaced by certificated teachers.

[2] *Supply of Teachers in Scotland: Second Report of the Departmental Committee*, Cmd. 8721, pp. 21 and 23. The shortage of teachers in recent years has been held in check not only by special recruitment and training schemes, but by the return to the profession of about 200 retired teachers and by the return or continuance of nearly 1,200 certificated married women teachers not seeking long-term employment (out of just over 4,400 married women teachers in employment in October 1951). Of the married women teachers, about 400 are thought to wish immediate replacement. The rest of the estimated deficiency of just over 2,300 as at October 1951, is made up of 681 to fill vacancies, 771 to replace uncertificated teachers, and 300 to constitute a reserve for relief purposes.

compared with 35 the year before. The grand total for mathematics and science (including those who had trained in both subjects) was 44 in 1952 as against 53 in 1951.[1]

The persisting staff shortage is not, however, symptomatic of a large-scale spurning of the teaching profession. There has, it is true, been a drop from the peak of 2,470 commencing training in 1947 to 1,972 in 1950/51. Even so, the number annually obtaining recognition as teachers since 1946 has been well above the average for the years 1933–39 of approximately 1,380; and the post-war average (1946–51) is approximately 2,180. In spite of slight reductions in the output of the Training Centres in 1949/50 and in 1950/51, the total number of teachers, certificated and uncertificated, employed within the public education system in Scotland has risen steadily to reach the record figure of 33,540 in October 1951 (see Table 118).

Table 118. *Students in training and number of certificated and uncertificated teachers in the Scottish public educational system, 1938–52*

Session	Number commencing training in	Number in training on 1 November	Number who successfully completed training in	Estimated total number of full-time teachers (certificated and uncertificated) in October
1938/39	1,558	2,946	1,306	29,061*
1946/47	2,470	4,065	2,042	—
1947/48	2,208	4,225	2,209	—
1948/49	2,137	4,183	2,279	31,200
1949/50	2,095	3,967	2,173	32,050
1950/51	1,972	3,777	2,193	32,850
1951/52	—	3,633	—	33,540

* Certificated only, March 1938.
SOURCE: Annual *Reports of Scottish Education Department*.

Further, although the Departmental Committee expect the supply of teachers to fall from just under 2,000 in 1952/53 to 1,700 in 1956/57, it would still, at that lower figure, be above the immediate pre-war average. While, then, it is true that teachers are not coming forward in sufficient numbers to meet new needs arising from occupation of new school buildings, the increase in the school population, and other factors on the demand side, there is little ground for maintaining that the explanation of this situation is the simple one that young people are less attracted to teaching than they were before 1939. Indeed, the Departmental Committee suggest that Scotland is approaching an educational era 'when its teacher-supply problem is just part of

[1] These figures were given by Mr Harry Bell, rector of Dollar Academy, in an address in Glasgow (reported in the *Glasgow Herald*, 28 November 1952).

the more general problem of limited man-power and woman-power, particularly of highly educated man-power and woman-power'. Nor is it sufficient to explain the particular shortage of mathematics and science teachers in terms of enticement to other fields, for the shortage of mathematicians and scientists is not, according to the Committee, confined to the teaching profession. 'From our perusal of reports issued by bodies who have been dealing with recruitment and staffing in other professions, we see that the shortage of persons with qualifications in mathematics and science is widespread.'[1]

Table 119. *Certificated teachers employed in the public educational system (including further education) in Scotland, 1929, 1938 and 1951: analysis by sex and graduate qualification, with comparative figures for England and Wales, 1951*

Year	Total teachers	Men teachers as percentage of total	Graduates		
			Men graduates as percentage of all men teachers	Women graduates as percentage of all women teachers	All graduates as percentage of of all teachers
Scotland:					
1929	27,251	25·3	57·5	19·7	29·2
1938	29,061	29·5	70·2	31·3	42·8
1951	33,205	32·8	67·8	33·4	44·8
England and Wales					
1951	237,069	40·5	27·2	12·0	18·2

SOURCES: Annual *Reports of Scottish Education Department* and *Report of Ministry of Education*, 1951.

Two further questions arise, both concerning the composition of the teaching profession: Is it attracting a smaller proportion of graduates? And is it becoming more of a women's profession? Detailed figures concerning the total teaching staff are available for only one post-war year, 1951, but analysis of these and of the relevant information for pre-war years back to 1929 shows that both questions are to be answered in the negative. There were more graduates, both absolutely and relatively, and proportionately fewer women, among teachers in 1951 than for any year between 1929 and the outbreak of the war. Moreover, 1951 shows a return to the position obtaining in 1929 of an almost exactly equal division of total graduates. Not only were there

[1] *Supply of Teachers in Scotland: Second Report of the Departmental Committee*, Cmd. 8721, pp. 19–20.

proportionately fewer women among teachers in 1951, but the proportion of women graduates to all women teachers was the highest that year since 1929. It will also be seen from Table 119 that, both for men and for women, the proportion of graduate teachers was between two and three times as high as in England and Wales.

Of all women teachers employed in schools within the public system in 1951, 14,441 or 64·8 % were teaching in primary departments and 5,647 or 25·3 % in secondary departments. Of the latter number, 3,488 or 61·8 % were graduates, and of these only 610 held the Special Certificate while a further 562 held the General and Special Certificate. Most women graduates teaching in secondary departments, then, held the General Certificate with an Article 39 qualification, entitling them to teach in the younger secondary classes.[1] While no exact figure is obtainable, it appears that a number of Article 39 teachers, especially of science and mathematics, are being asked to teach senior secondary classes as an emergency measure. The bulk of non-graduate women teachers in secondary departments (and this applies also to men non-graduates in secondary departments) were teaching 'technical' subjects. Of primary teachers 64 % were women non-graduates. Further, women formed almost 59 % of graduate General Certificate teachers and 92 % of non-graduate General Certificate teachers; and 42·5 % of Special Certificate teachers.

FURTHER EDUCATION

As defined by the Education (Scotland) Act, 1946, 'Further Education' comprises voluntary part-time and full-time courses of instruction, and voluntary leisure-time occupation in organized cultural training and recreative activities, for persons over school age.[2] Administratively, further education is regarded as falling into two main types, formal and informal. Our concern here is with the formal section, comprising on the one hand various forms of occupational or vocational education pursued at Central Institutions or through Education Committee Continuation Classes;[3] and, on the other, the

[1] The General Certificate recognizes the holder as qualified to teach primary school subjects. Holders of the General Certificate are usually referred to as 'Chapter III' or 'Chapter IV' teachers, the reference being to the Chapters of the Regulations under which they are certificated. Chapter III (or IV) teachers, whether graduates or not, may obtain an endorsement under Article 39 of the Regulations which qualifies them to teach in secondary departments. The Special Certificate recognizes the holder (referred to as a 'Chapter V' teacher) as qualified to teach secondary school subjects in which he holds a university degree with first or second class honours.

[2] The Act also provided for compulsory full-time and part-time courses of instruction in junior colleges for young persons between the ages of 15 and 18, but this provision is not yet in operation. Some employers, however, have made attendance at appropriate day continuation classes a compulsory part of their apprenticeship and other training schemes.

[3] There are thirteen central institutions in Scotland. In addition to the Royal Technical College, Glasgow, the Heriot-Watt College, Edinburgh, Robert Gordon's Technical College,

more liberal or cultural education pursued by persons over 18 years of age, partly in the appropriate type of continuation class and partly in classes organized by University Extra-Mural Departments or Committees in association with Education Committees and by the Workers' Educational Association.

The beginnings in Britain of what is now termed 'further education' are to be found not, as appears to be commonly supposed, in England and Wales, but in Scotland: Birkbeck's evening lectures in the first years of the nineteenth century, and the founding of the Glasgow Mechanics Institute shortly after, were pioneer activities not without influence across the border.[1] A promising start, however, appears to have been followed by a period of inertia or at best of intermittent and unco-ordinated attempts at expansion, in contrast to steady advance in England and Wales.

One reason for this contrast is to be found in England's much greater educational deficiencies during a large part of the period which saw spectacular growth in further education in that country.[2] The urge to make up for inadequate schooling and post-school instruction, which formed so large a part of the drive behind further education developments in England, was accordingly less compelling in Scotland.

Taking the whole field of further education into account, just over 2,200,000 students attended all establishments providing further education courses in England and Wales in 1950/51. The broadly comparable figure for Scotland appears to be about 272,000—rather surprisingly, a higher total in relation to population than that for England and Wales. While differences in classification make exact comparison impossible, inspection of the relevant statistics suggests that it is the relatively greater numbers in part-time day and evening continuation classes that account for the comparatively higher Scottish total; certainly the comparison is much less favourable to Scotland in such branches as day-release and adult education.

Although it would now appear to be past its peak, there has been in all branches of further education in Scotland a marked post-war expansion in enrolments—an expansion which would doubtless have been even greater but for accommodation, financial and other difficulties. The number of day-time students in central institutions has risen from 7,067 in 1929 to 13,210 in 1950. The 1951 total for all courses, including part-time and correspondence courses,

Aberdeen, the Dundee Institute of Art and Technology, and three other technical colleges, the group includes colleges of art, music, commerce and domestic science. The three agricultural colleges in Scotland are under the administration of the Department of Agriculture.

[1] Cf. *Further Education, a Report of the Advisory Council on Education in Scotland*, Cmd. 8454 (1952), pp. 9–10.

[2] Almost ninety years ago, according to the Argyll Commission, 1 in every 140 of the Scottish population was on the roll of a burgh school, academy, or other secondary school, compared with 1 in 1,300 in England; and at that time Scotland had, as indeed she still has, more University students per head of the population.

was 31,669. Very nearly 44 % of students enrolled in all courses in 1950/51 were in science and technology courses (including engineering, naval architecture, applied chemistry and applied physics and metallurgy); about 16 % were in commercial and professional courses (including, for example, librarianship and management); 19 % were in domestic science and catering courses; 15 % were in art courses (including, for example, architecture and town and country planning); 5 % were in music courses (including drama); and 1·5 % were in courses described as general.

The total enrolment in continuation classes was 163,605 in 1939, compared with 267,047 in 1951 or, if short courses are excluded, 227,878. The number enrolled in full-time classes was 3,337. Of the full-time students, almost half were pursuing pre-apprenticeship courses in building and engineering, and about one-fifth were taking pre-nursing courses, while of the part-time enrolments about 38 % were in courses in 'General Subjects' (including languages and the social sciences), about 35 % in subjects related to commerce and industry, and the rest in domestic and miscellaneous subjects.

The number of day-release students in 1950/51, about 15,000, showed a 50 % increase on the figure for the previous year. In spite of this recent jump in numbers, Scottish industry is a much less enthusiastic supporter of day-release than its counterpart in the South—in England and Wales the number released by employers in 1950/51 was just over 281,000, including students at art establishments.

Attendance at adult education classes is also lower in Scotland.[1] From the record figure of 15,096 in 1949 the number dropped in 1951 to 12,740.[2] In relation to population, attendance in England and Wales, at 162,850, was about 1½ times what it was in Scotland. One reason for this difference may be that in Scotland organizations providing facilities for non-residential adult education are not in receipt of direct government grants as are their counterparts in the South. The universities are financially assisted by the education authorities in their areas which have recognized them as their agents in this field; and harmonious relations with the authorities notwithstanding, this is not as satisfactory an arrangement as would be receipt of a single grant from one source.[3] A second reason may be that more potential

[1] We are here concerned with enrolments in evening classes providing tutorial, one-year, informal and other courses, but passing reference should be made to the related field of residential courses. At Newbattle Abbey, Scotland's only residential college for adult education, there were twenty-one students in 1950/51, of whom fourteen were in attendance for the whole session. In addition, a number of week-end and summer schools are held each year under the auspices of the universities, the Workers' Educational Association, and other bodies.

[2] This drop coincided with a raising of fees.

[3] Under the new Further Education (Voluntary Associations) (Scotland) Grant Regulations, 1952, however, bodies such as the universities and the Workers' Educational Association may apply for grants towards expenses of organization and administration.

students in Scotland are either at university or are graduates, and are therefore less attracted to adult education classes; and a third that the Englishman with his greater sociability is more likely than the Scot to be attracted to an evening class at least initially as providing an opportunity for social intercourse.

FINANCE

Although there are certain education grants which are paid directly from moneys voted by parliament, for example, Treasury grants to the Scottish universities and grants for Approved Schools, the greater part of Exchequer grants for education in Scotland (the General Aid Grant) comes through the Education (Scotland) Fund. The General Aid Grant has been mounting steadily from its level of £7·4 m. in 1938/39 to £24·4 m. in 1950/51, in which year it accounted for about 86 % of the Fund's receipts of £28·4 m. For the year 1951/52 the receipts of the Fund were estimated at £30·7 m., of which the General Aid Grant accounted for an estimated figure of £26·1 m. For a number of years the main items of the Fund's expenditure have been grants to education authorities, teachers' pensions, and grants to central institutions. In session 1950/51 these amounted, respectively, to £22·4 m., £2·3 m. and £0·6 m.

Grants from the Fund in turn comprise the bulk of the income of education authorities. In 1936/37 this source supplied 52 % of the Authorities' income, and in 1951/52 an estimated 62 %. School fees have accounted for the merest fraction, ranging from 1·4 % in 1936/37 down to 0·6 % in 1951/52. Apart from Scottish Education Department Grants through the Fund, the only substantial source of authorities' income is Consolidated Rates and Grants under the Local Government (Scotland) Acts, 1929 and 1948. In 1936/37 this source supplied £6·2 m. or 46 % of income; in 1947/48, £9·1 m. or 32 %; in 1950/51, £10·7 m. or 31 %; and in 1951/52 an estimated £12·9 m. or 32 %. The actual contribution made in recent years by local rates by themselves is not readily accessible, but the figure for 1950/51 is 26 %, other grants under the 1948 Local Government Act contributing approximately 5 %.

By far the greatest single item on the expenditure side is teachers' salaries (including retiring allowances, National Insurance and superannuation contributions). In 1936/37 this item amounted to £8·8 m. or 65·4 % of total expenditure, while in 1950/51 the amount had doubled to £17·9 m., although the proportion of total expenditure had fallen to 51·5 %. The next largest items in 1950/51 were repairs and maintenance (11·6 %) and school meals and milk (10·5 %). Administration expenses accounted for almost exactly the same proportion, 3 %, in 1950/51 as in 1936/37; and bursaries, scholarships and allowances also came to just over 3 % of expenditure.

EDUCATION COSTS PER PUPIL

In 1950/51 all heads of education authorities' expenditure amounted to £34·8 m., of which a little over £22 m. was met by Scottish Education Department grants. The Department's report for that year gives a partial analysis of this total into expenditure on primary and secondary schools together and on further education. Heads such as administration, school meals, medical inspection and treatment, and the repayment of loan and interest charges on school buildings apply to all stages of education and cannot be analysed even as between the schools and further education. If, however, we take those items which can be subdivided in this way, we find that a total of £24·5 m. was spent on primary and secondary education in respect of educational staff (salaries, superannuation and other expenditure); maintenance of schools (books, etc.; furniture and equipment; rent, rates, taxes, insurance, etc.; repairs, fuel, light, cleaning, etc.; and other expenditure); and provision of transport, board and lodging, bursaries, etc. This sum works out at about £31 per pupil on the public system registers. If, however, we include expenditure on school milk and meals and on the School Health Service, as presumably applying in the main to primary and secondary schools, the total becomes £28·7 m. and the cost per pupil approximately £36. It must be emphasized that these are not merely estimates but are, unavoidably, minimum estimates.

BURSARIES AND SCHOLARSHIPS

An important influence on post-secondary education in Scotland has been the number of bursaries and scholarships provided either by private endowment or, more recently, by the local authorities. The Carnegie Trust has played a notable part in helping poorer students to take a university degree as well as in financing post-graduate study and research. Bursaries derived from other private benefactions, now greatly diminished in real value by inflation, have been awarded by the four universities on the results of a special bursary examination on entrance; scholarships, awarded to graduates either after a special examination or on their performance in the degree examinations, have helped to maintain a link between the more distinguished Scottish graduates and the Universities of Oxford and Cambridge.

Until recently public funds have played a subordinate part. Before the war, the education authorities awarded bursaries—mainly to intending teachers—totalling just short of £200,000. This sum, and the number of awards made, has increased greatly: in 1950/51 a total of £1·06 m. was contributed by the Scottish education authorities to the support of 23,439 students whose parents were assumed to contribute a further £326,000 towards the cost of their education. Of the total contributed by education authorities, £427,000 was to 4,795 full-time university students, the remaining awards being to students at schools, central institutions and training colleges, or undertaking further education. There has been a gradual decline in the amount contributed per award (the average in 1947/48 being £55·5 compared with £45·4 in 1950/51), and a simultaneous rise in the amount to be met by parents (from £9·1 to £13·9 over the same period). For full-time university students the average award is £89 per annum and this, too, has shown a tendency to fall over the past few years.

In addition to these bursaries a small number are usually awarded out of the Education (Scotland) Fund to supplement open scholarships won by Scottish scholars at English universities. Most of these beneficiaries are graduates of Scottish universities holding these supplemental allowances at Oxford and Cambridge. In 1950/51, fifty-seven allowances were awarded, amounting to £10,803 or about £190 per allowance.

Before the war, a rather larger proportion of Scottish than of English university students received financial assistance from public funds, the proportions being 45·7 % and 38·5 % respectively. Wales, with 58·8 %, had a higher proportion than either in receipt of assistance. By 1950/51, Scotland had the lowest proportion of the three. Although 63·1 % of all full-time students were being financially assisted in that year, the proportion had risen in England to 73·8 % and in Wales to 85·9 %.

Whereas in England and Wales financial support for students is provided through state as well as local authority scholarships, in Scotland the responsibility for providing bursaries and scholarships rests exclusively on the local authorities. This responsibility is fairly adequately discharged up to the graduate level, but for the graduate, the Scottish local authorities do little or nothing. They seem quite unaware both of the importance of financing post-graduate study and of their duty to do so. As a result, post-graduate research in arts is dependent almost exclusively on private funds such as the Carnegie Trust, while research in science—the bulk of it in pure science—is financed largely by the Department of Scientific and Industrial Research. No figures are readily accessible for the Scottish universities as a whole, but at Glasgow University in 1950/51 forty-six students were in receipt of grants from D.S.I.R. The number undertaking research for a higher degree in technology, whether financed by D.S.I.R. or otherwise, was, however, only four. There were seventeen students undertaking research for an advanced degree in arts.

THE UNIVERSITIES

The Scottish universities have shared with those of Britain as a whole a substantial post-war increase in the number of full-time students. In Scotland, after a steady advance, the post-war peak of 16,987 was reached in 1948/49. In 1950/51 there was a fall to 16,001, and since the supply of students largely financed by Further Education and Training Grants is now virtually exhausted it is likely that the downward trend will continue. The peak for Wales was reached in 1949/50, when the total was 5,284. This fell slightly, to 5,133, in 1950/51. In England, however, the experience has been different. There the post-war numbers have risen steadily to a peak of 64,180 in 1950/51. Table 120 shows the growth over the past twenty years in absolute numbers and in terms of percentage increase.

Table 120. *Growth in student numbers in Britain*, 1930–50

Country	Student numbers (full time)			Percentage increase, 1950/51 on 1930/31
	1930/31	1938/39	1950/51	
Scotland	11,150	10,034	16,001	43·5
England	33,569	37,189	64,180	91·2
Wales	2,868	2,779	5,133	79
Great Britain	47,587	50,002	85,314	79·3

SOURCE: *Returns from Universities and University Colleges* (University Grants Committee).

Notwithstanding the much greater proportionate increase in student totals in England and Wales, Scotland has still, relative to population, the largest student community of the three countries. In 1950/51 she had one full-time student for every 318 of the population, compared with 1 in 641 in England, 1 in 505 in Wales, and 1 in 572 for Britain as a whole. Apart from a few years when Scotland gave place to Wales, most of the past twenty years (excluding the war years) show Scotland with the highest proportion of women students of the three countries. In 1950/51 the percentages of the student totals in the three countries who were women were: Scotland 24·9; England 22·1; Wales 26·5.

If we compare the distribution of students over faculties (as classified by the University Grants Committee) in the three sessions, 1931/32, 1937/38 and 1950/51, we find that the distribution of men students in Scotland shows proportionately more in medicine (including dentistry) and arts (except in 1950/51) and less in pure science and technology (again with the exception of 1950/51) than in England. The decline in the arts faculty and the expansion of technology have been more pronounced, however, in Scotland than in England and Wales in recent years, the latter change being due in part to the incorporation of outside institutions. Women students, once heavily concentrated in the arts faculty, have shown a continuing tendency to turn to other faculties. Details of the distribution of men and women students over the six faculties are provided in Table 121.

An analysis of those obtaining first degrees in the British universities shows that the institution of the ordinary (or pass) degree bulks much more largely in Scottish academic life than in the rest of Great Britain. Only 24·2 % of those who took a first degree at a Scottish university in 1931/32 obtained an honours degree, compared with 64·6 % in England. In 1950/51 the proportion had risen in Scotland to 31·1 % but was still less than half the corresponding English proportion of 66·0 %. Part of the difference arises because of the slightly larger proportion of women graduates in Scotland and the greater tendency for women, particularly in Scotland, to take an ordinary degree.

Table 121. *Percentage distribution of students by sex and faculty in Britain, 1931/32, 1937/38 and 1950/51*

Faculty	Men			Women		
	Scotland	England	Wales	Scotland	England	Wales
Arts*						
1931/32	45·0	41·5	53·9	62·3	69·0	72·2
1937/38	39·5	38·7	54·7	65·3	64·2	66·8
1950/51	31·9	38·2	41·3	62·3	62·6	69·2
Pure Science						
1931/32	11·1	18·3	25·1	7·6	18·3	21·7
1937/38	11·3	16·1	22·6	11·2	17·9	17·6
1950/51	14·3	21·9	31·9	13·8	17·6	19·4
Medicine (including dentistry)						
1931/32	31·0	25·2	9·5	9·5	10·8	4·3
1937/38	35·8	30·3	9·3	22·4	15·7	11·9
1950/51	27·0	20·7	6·3	20·5	16·2	7·9
Technology						
1931/32	10·1	13·4	7·4	0·2	0·9	0·1
1937/38	11·2	13·1	7·6	0·4	1·0	—
1950/51	19·4	15·2	12·0	1·2	1·1	0·2
Agriculture and forestry						
1931/32	2·8	1·7	4·1	0·4	1·0	1·7
1937/38	2·1	1·9	5·8	0·7	1·2	3·7
1950/51	4·0	2·9	8·5	1·1	2·0	3·4
Veterinary Science						
1931/32	—	—	—	—	—	—
1937/38	—	—	—	—	—	—
1950/51	3·4	1·2	—	1·1	0·3	—

* Including theology, fine art, law, music, commerce, economics and education.
Source: *Returns from Universities and University Colleges* (University Grants Committee).

Another feature of the Scottish universities—a feature which distinguishes them from Oxford and Cambridge—is their dependence on lectures rather than tutorials and seminars. This may be economical in staff but is generally a less satisfactory method of instruction. In the past twenty years lectures have been increasingly supplemented by other teaching which brings staff and students into more personal contact and this change has been facilitated by a steady growth in full-time staff (see Table 122).

The staffs of the four universities have more than doubled since before the war and now bear the same relationship to the size of the student population as in other parts of Britain. In view of the lower percentage of honours students, this development appears to leave Scotland in at least as advantageous a position as England and Wales. This expansion in staff has been brought about largely by increased parliamentary grants, and the increase in these grants has in turn increased the financial dependence of the universities on public funds. Before the war, less than 40 % of the income of the Scottish universities came from government grants, but by 1950/51 the proportion had mounted to 68·6 %—a rather higher proportion than the 64·9 % applicable to the British universities taken together.

Table 122. *Growth in numbers of full-time staff, and staff-student ratio, 1931–50*

Country	Number of full-time staff			Percentage increase, 1950 on 1931	Percentage increase, 1950 on 1938	Number of full-time students per member of full-time staff		
	1931/32	1938/39	1950/51			1931/32	1938/39	1950/51
Scotland	651	718	1,570	141	119	17	14	10
England	2,611	2,905	6,465	148	122	13	13	10
Wales	328	371	568	73	53	10	7	9
Great Britain	3,590	3,994	8,603	140	115	14	13	10

SOURCE: *Returns from Universities and University Colleges* (University Grants Committee).

Both by tradition and in actual fact, the Scottish universities draw more students from poor families than do the English.[1] There are no figures showing the social origin of undergraduates, but the University Grants Committee publishes the percentage of new students coming from homes within the United Kingdom who began their education in a public elementary school. In the last pre-war year, the percentage for Scotland was 65·7 % and for England 38·6 %; in 1950/51 the corresponding percentages were 88·2 % and 58·6 %. The Scottish percentage remained well above the English.[2]

So we return to earlier points of contrast. The Scottish universities draw on a wider social range of students than the English; but they concentrate less on honours degrees and their post-graduate degrees are more narrowly

[1] For a full analysis concerning Glasgow, see A. Collier, 'Social origins of a sample of entrants to Glasgow University', *Sociological Review*, vol. XXX (1938), pp. 161, 262.
[2] The percentage for Wales, however, was 92 both in 1938/39 and in 1950/51.

confined to pure science. Moreover, the proportion of the population that continues its education to the age of 20 is small and not appreciably higher than in England; while the proportion that leaves school at the first opportunity is extremely high and a good deal higher than in England. The passion for education may still burn fiercely north of the Border; but it is far more doubtful than it was fifty years ago whether superior zeal is matched by superior opportunities or exertions.

[Acknowledgment is due to the following for reading either the whole or part of an early draft of this chapter and for sending in comments and items of information: Dr Norman T. Walker, Reader in Education, Aberdeen University; Mr A. G. Phemister, Deputy Director of Education, Glasgow; and Mr David Lees, Rector of the High School of Glasgow. Assistance was also given by Dr David S. Anderson, Director, the Royal Technical College, Glasgow; Mr William McClelland, Executive Officer, Central Executive Committee, the National Committee for the Training of Teachers; and Mr W. R. Richardson, Director of Establishments and Organization, Ministry of Education.]

CHAPTER 18

RECRUITMENT AND TRAINING OF YOUNG WORKERS FOR INDUSTRY AND COMMERCE

By JAMES CUNNISON

The main flow of recruits to industry and commerce consists of young people who have just left school. At 1 March 1951 the number of boys and girls receiving education in Scotland was approximately 818,200, made up as follows:

In schools within the public educational system ...	797,200
In 'independent' schools	21,000
Total	818,200

Of the number in the first group, who form the major section of school children, 70,640 left school in the twelve months ended 31 July 1951. These consisted of three categories: 57,250[1] who left at the minimum statutory leaving age; 6,290[1] who left after completing a five-year secondary course at least; and 7,100[2] who stayed on at school beyond the minimum leaving age but left before completing the five-year secondary course. Of the number attending independent schools there are no figures to show how many leave school annually; but a rough estimate for 1950/51 suggests that the number may be put at approximately 2,000. The total number leaving all schools in Scotland in 1950/51 was therefore about 72,650.

With few exceptions these young persons, whether they come from public authority schools or from independent schools, sooner or later take a job and begin to contribute to the work of the community in industry, commerce, services or professions. Some go straight from school to a paid job, becoming insured workers. As will be seen from Table 123, the number who did so in the twelve months ended 31 August 1951 was 68,700. Others postpone their entry into a gainful occupation, and proceed from school to further education or training in universities, 'Central Institutions' (technical, commercial and other colleges), or full-time continuation classes; or in one of the many private offices and schools which train for such work as shorthand and

[1] *Education in Scotland, 1951*, Report of the Scottish Education Department, App. 26, p. 117.
[2] Figure supplied by the Scottish Education Department.

266

typing. The third category, small under present-day conditions, consists of those who take no paid job but stay at home or give voluntary service, or leave the country.

The number in the second category cannot be exactly ascertained. While it is known, for instance, that approximately 3,000 students enrolled for full-time university courses for the first time at the beginning of session 1951/52, not all of these can be taken into the present reckoning because some had held a paid job between leaving school and entering the university, and are therefore already included in the 68,700 in the first category. Others again did not belong to the 1950/51 group of Scottish school-leavers, having left school earlier, or having come from outwith Scotland. Again about 2,000 students entered teachers' training colleges in Scotland at the beginning of session 1951/52, but about half of these were graduates and belonged to an earlier school-leaving year, and others may already have held a paid job. Similar considerations apply to the numbers enrolling in 'Central Institutions' and full-time continuation classes. It may be hazarded that the number of 1950/51 Scottish school-leavers who proceeded to further education in public institutions without having held a paid job did not exceed 3,000; while the number of similar trainees in private establishments is indeterminate.

Our main concern is with the 68,700 who passed immediately from school to a job. Table 123 shows for Scotland, for the twelve months ended 31 August 1951, the number of young persons to whom insurance cards were issued at the time of their first entry into employment, and their distribution throughout industry. The distribution, it is to be noted, is an industrial, not an occupational one; the figures entered under each industry include all young people under 18 whose first job was in the industry, irrespective of their personal occupation.

The 35,100 boys and 33,600 girls covered by Table 123 were the main source but not the only one for the recruitment of Scottish industry in the year in question. They represent 3·3 % of the total number of employees in Scotland in May 1951. For Great Britain as a whole the new entrants under 18 represented only 2·6 % of the total number of employees in Great Britain in May 1951. The higher Scottish percentage is a reflection of the higher birth-rate in Scotland fifteen to eighteen years ago.

Boy entrants represented 2·5 % of total male employees in Scotland in May 1951, girl entrants 4·6 % of female employees. The higher figure for girls is due to the greater wastage of female employees, whose industrial life is much shorter than that of men. Both Scottish percentages were higher than the corresponding British percentages (which were 2 % and 3·8 % respectively), but in nearly the same proportion.

A high proportion of Scottish children (88 %) started work under 16. The percentage for Great Britain was less than 82 %. There are two possible explanations of the difference. It may be that in Scotland there is a greater representation of the kind of firm which can and does make use of the services of very young labour, and that children leave school earlier in consequence; or that, partly no doubt by necessity, Scottish children leave school early, and thus provide a supply of young labour of which industries avail themselves. The connexion is probably two-way. The fact that in this respect

Table 123.* *Juvenile new entrants into insurable employment in Scotland from* 1 *September* 1950 *to* 31 *August* 1951

Industrial group	Boys		Girls	
	Aged 15 and under 16 years	Aged 16 and under 18 years	Aged 15 and under 16 years	Aged 16 and under 18 years
Agriculture, forestry, fishing	3,277	490	470	159
Mining and quarrying	1,738	95	143	24
Metal manufacture	868	87	224	31
Engineering, shipbuilding, etc.	3,824	605	925	107
Vehicles	1,479	140	277	50
Metal goods	704	49	241	31
Precision instruments, jewellery, etc.	145	23	85	8
Chemicals, etc.	179	58	354	60
Textiles	1,348	87	4,185	171
Leather, leather goods and fur	99	9	59	1
Clothing	510	50	2,713	113
Food, drink and tobacco	1,724	118	2,044	173
Manufactures of wood and cork	1,181	100	178	24
Paper and printing	773	88	1,529	92
Other manufacturing industries	186	19	226	33
Building and contracting	2,904	388	335	67
Gas, electricity and water supply	71	15	61	14
Transport and communications	1,276	362	372	127
Distributive trades	6,853	419	10,007	713
Insurance, banking and finance	177	231	474	338
Public administration and defence	276	187	379	354
Professional services	363	352	1,412	840
Entertainment and sport	189	28	208	43
Miscellaneous services	903	91	2,641	459
Total	31,047	4,091	29,542	4,032

* Except where otherwise indicated, the statistical tables in this chapter are based on information supplied by the Scottish Headquarters of the Ministry of Labour, or on material collected in a survey of 1,313 Glasgow boys who left school (at 14) in January 1947, and whose industrial careers were followed up to January 1950. The main results of that survey were published in *The Young Wage-Earner*, by T. Ferguson and J. Cunnison (1951).

Scotland contrasts with the London and South-Eastern Region, where the percentage is only 75 %, suggests that employment opportunity is a factor. In London entrants into financial, governmental and professional services are proportionately more numerous than in the rest of the country, and entry into such services tends to be at 16 or 17 rather than 15. On the other hand, in the Northern Region of England, where employment opportunities more nearly resemble those of Scotland, the proportion of 15-year-old entrants to industry is nearly the same as in Scotland, namely 88 %.

Table 124. *Percentage of first entrants into different industrial groups in Scotland at 15 and at 16–18*

Industrial group	Boys			Girls		
	15	16 and under 18	Total under 18	15	16 and under 18	Total under 18
Agriculture, forestry, fishing	10·6	12·0	10·7	1·6	3·9	1·9
Mining and quarrying	5·6	2·3	5·2	0·5	0·6	0·5
Metal manufacturers, engineering, shipbuilding, etc.	22·6	22·1	22·5	5·9	5·6	5·8
Other manufactures	19·3	12·9	18·7	38·3	16·6	35·6
Building and contracting	9·6	9·9	9·6	1·3	2·0	1·4
Transport and communications	4·1	8·9	4·7	1·2	3·2	1·6
Distributive trades	22·1	10·2	20·7	33·9	17·8	31·9
Public administration, professional services, commerce, finance, entertainment	3·2	19·5	5·1	8·4	39·2	12·1
Other services	2·9	2·2	2·8	8·9	11·1	9·2
Total	100	100	100	100	100	100
Total number of entrants	31,047	4,091	35,138	29,542	4,032	33,574

There is little difference between boys and girls in this matter of age of entrance into industry. Of the former the Scottish percentage that entered under 16 years of age was 88·3, of the latter 88·0. Comparative equality holds for Great Britain as a whole, and also for most regions of Great Britain, except Wales and the London and South-Eastern District, where more boys than girls start work under 16. For the former the proportions are: boys, 81 %, girls, 77 %; for the latter, boys, 76 %, girls, 74 %.

The age at which young people first enter industry makes a considerable difference to their industrial distribution. The difference can be seen in Table 123, but is shown more clearly in Table 124, which condenses the industry groups and gives the entrants into each group as a percentage of total entrants.

In Table 124 three industrial groups stand out as having a strong attraction for boy entrants under 16, the distributive trades, the metal, engineering and shipbuilding trades, and 'other manufactures',[1] in that order, absorbing respectively 22·6 %, 22·1 % and 19·3 % of these young entrants. For boys who entered industry when over 16, metal manufactures continued to be attractive, but the distributive trades and 'other manufactures' had to a great degree lost their appeal; they absorbed a far smaller proportion of those over 16 than of those under 16. On the other hand, there were two groups of services which absorbed a small percentage of the under-16 boy entrants, but a greatly increased percentage of the over-16 entrants. The outstanding case is the group including public administration, commerce, finance, which accounted for only 3·2 % of the boys entering employment under 16, but for 19·5 % of those entering employment over 16; the other is the transport group in which the corresponding percentages were 4·1 % and 8·9 %. Finally, the percentages entering agriculture, forestry, fishing, building and 'other services' are much the same whether under 16 or over.

There were similar differences in the case of girls. Two groups of industry between them took in nearly three-quarters of all the 15-year-old girl entrants —'other manufactures' which took 38·3 %, and the distributive trades, which took 33·9 %. By contrast, these two industries employed only one-third of the girls who entered industry at 16 or over. The greatest appeal to these older girl entrants was made by the group of services covering commerce, finance, public administration and the professions, which took 39·2 % of the girls of 16 and over, against only 8·4 % of those under 16.

This being so, it is not surprising to find that there were considerable differences between the industrial distribution of first entrants into industry and the general pattern of industry in Scotland, as reflected in the industrial classification of the 2,052,000 Scottish employees in 1950. These differences are brought out in Table 125, which shows in the first column the total number of employees in each industrial group in 1950, in the second column the total number of first entrants under 18 years of age in the year 1950/51, similarly classified, and in the third column the number of first entrants per 1,000 total employees in each.

The last line of column 3 of Table 125 shows that over the whole of Scottish industry new entrants in 1950/51 numbered 33 for every 1,000 employees. If the 1950 pattern of Scottish industry, as reflected in the number of employees in each industrial group, is to be maintained without subsequent redistribution each number in this column would be 33. But divergence from that number rather than approximation to it is the striking feature of the

---

[1] 'Other manufactures' include all manufactures except the metal industries. Among them the most attractive to the youngest boys are the food, drink and tobacco trades, textiles, and manufactures of wood and cork.

table. This means that there must take place considerable movement into some industries and out of others. Industries like the distributive trades, and 'other manufactures' will have to shed many workers; while transport, the commercial, financial and similar services, and building, will have to acquire workers. Agriculture, forestry, fishing, 'other services' and metal manufacturing are the only groups to and from which large-scale movements will not be necessary in order that the present relative position may be maintained.

Table 125. *Distribution of employees and of first entrants (under 18 years of age) by industrial groups in Scotland, 1950/51*

Industrial group	Total employees (thousands)	First entrants under 18 (thousands)	First entrants per 1,000 employees
Agriculture, forestry, fishing	117·9	4·4	37
Mining and quarrying	119·7	2·0	17
Metal manufactures	358·9	9·9	27
Other manufactures	397·8	18·5	47
Building, etc.	173·7	3·9	22
Transport	195·0	2·1	11
Distributive trades	234·7	18·0	77
Services: finance, public administration, professional	307·6	5·8	19
Other services	147·6	4·1	28
All industries	2,052·9	68·7	33

Such movements do take place on a large scale. The necessary data are not available to show their extent on the national level; but the point can be illustrated from the results of the survey of 1,313 Glasgow boys already referred to.[1] Of these 1,313 boys, only 10 % were still at the age of 17 in the job which they had entered at 14. On the average, the boys changed their jobs once a year during the three-year period. The net effect of these changes of job on the industrial distribution of the boys is shown in Table 126, which gives for each industry group the numbers at 14 years of age, and the numbers of the same boys at 17. The industry groups are arranged in two sections, the first consisting of those which lost boys over the three-year period and the second those which gained.

In Table 126, column 1 shows the number of the boys in the survey group who were in each industry at age 14, column 2 the number in each industry at 17. If each of the numbers in column 1 has a value of 100, column 3 shows the relative number in each industry at 17. It will be seen that over the three-year period the distributive trades lost most heavily, but heavy losses were also sustained by the clothing industry. At the other end of the scale, vehicle

[1] See p. 268n.

271

manufacture, 'other metal goods', building and contracting and 'other manufactures' attracted many boys from other industries and employed many more of the boys at 17 than they had at 14. Engineering, shipbuilding, etc. is the outstanding case of an industry in which the number of the boys employed remained almost steady over the three-year period.

Table 126. *Distribution by industrial groups of* 1,313 *Glasgow boys, at* 14 *and at* 17 *years of age*

Industrial group	At 14 years	At 17 years	Column 2 as percentage of column 1
Decreases			
Distributive trades	370	131	36
Clothing	81	38	47
Textiles	26	17	65
Insurance, banking, professions	15	10	67
Miscellaneous services	59	40	68
Paper, printing, etc.	55	44	80
Metal manufactures	35	28	80
Engineering, shipbuilding, etc.	272	251	92
Increases			
Precision instruments	15	16	107
Wood, cork	58	66	113
Mining, quarrying	8	10	125
Agriculture, forestry, fishing	14	18	129
Transport	65	109	168
Leather	20	35	175
Food, drink	66	116	176
Other manufactures	22	40	182
Building, contracting, etc.	93	213	229
Other metal goods	22	60	273
Vehicles	17	48	282
Armed Forces, Merchant Navy, etc.	—	23	—
All industries	1,313	1,313	100

Whether the shifting of juvenile employees between occupations and industries is or is not to be deplored depends largely on the circumstances that give rise to it. It may arise from the immaturity of the young wage-earner, ignorant of what he wants to do and of the nature and prospects of different occupations, who tends therefore to be influenced in his choice by immediate earnings, the pressure of parents or friends, or the accident of advertised vacancies; and who, being dissatisfied with his first experience, moves from job to job without any very definite purpose in view. On the other hand, he may know quite clearly what he wants to do but be handicapped by lack of local opportunity, or unable to start a training or apprenticeship for his chosen work because he is too young. Such a boy may fill in the gap with a number of temporary jobs. So far as the latter circumstance operates, any advance in the school-leaving age should make for greater stability, and so far as the former operates, a developed and efficient service, such as the new Youth Employment Service may become, could do much by advice and guidance to eliminate false starts. But under existing circumstances industries and firms which employ young people in makeshift jobs, irrespective of their later prospects, prove attractive and give occasion for much shifting. Of the types of job which are least enduring, and the industries in which they are most frequently to be found, some indication is given in the following paragraphs.

Table 127. *Distribution of* 1,313 *Glasgow boys, at* 14 *and at* 17 *years of age, in different types of occupation*

Types of occupation	Number of boys employed		Column 2 as percentage of column 1
	At 14 years	At 17 years	
Decreases			
Message-running	512	82	16
Handy boys, odd jobs, etc.	75	27	36
Office, clerical	128	46	36
Store-keeping, packing, despatch	94	57	61
Labouring, shop assisting	418	346	83
Increases			
Van and motor-drivers and assistants	50	117	234
In training for skilled work	36	638	1772
All occupations	1,313	1,313	100

The distribution of young workers which has been examined in the foregoing paragraphs is their distribution among *industries*—textiles, metal manufactures, transport, etc. But much of the shifting between industries results from the different types of *occupation* they offer, some being acceptable only by the youngest school-leavers while others are suitable for older juveniles or for adults. The Glasgow survey already referred to provides data for an examination of the distribution of the 1,313 boys among different types of occupation, at two stages in their career, at 14 and at 17 years of age. The analysis is set out in Table 127.

So far as the Glasgow sample can be taken as representative, the kind of jobs that suffer the severest casualties as boys pass from 14 to 17 years of age are the message-running, hoist-attending and office-boy jobs. The degree to which such jobs existed, in this same sample, in different industries is shown in Table 128, which in the first column gives the total number of boys of 14 in each industry, and in the second column shows the percentage of those who were in the 'dead-end' jobs mentioned.

Table 128. *Distribution of* 1,313 *Glasgow boys, at* 14 *years of age, in different industrial groups, and percentage in 'dead-end' jobs*

Industrial group	Number of boys employed at 14	'Dead-end' jobs	
		Number	Percentage
Professional, financial and commercial services	15	15	100
Distributive trades	370	281	76
Transport and communication	65	46	71
Miscellaneous services	59	31	53
Agriculture, forestry, fishing	14	7	50
Other manufactures	328	155	47
Metal manufactures	361	144	40
Building and contracting	93	34	37
Mining	8	1	12
All industries	1,313	715	54

The opportunities offered by certain industries in the form of non-enduring occupations lie at the back of much juvenile job-changing. While in the long run the result may be undesirable, these opportunities do, in existing circumstances, meet a need in the case of young people who have not made up their minds or who cannot start training for their chosen work till later. Even at 14, and more so at the existing school-leaving age of 15, boys have generally some idea of the kind of work they would like to do. Of the 1,313 boys in the Glasgow survey group, about 80 %, before leaving school at 14, had expressed a preference—though in most cases it was in general terms only—for manual or non-manual work, or for skilled or unskilled work. This schoolboy preference, however, is often unstable, and liking may change with age or as other opportunities offer. Thus, before leaving school, 732 of these boys expressed a preference for skilled manual work; and at 17 years of age, 607 were in training for such work. But of the 607, only 376 were among those who had indicated this choice; the other 231 had elected otherwise, or had expressed no preference. And there were similar divergences in other directions between expressed preference and attainment.

Entrance to skilled manual work is still mainly by way of 'apprenticeship', although the name rarely implies nowadays the strict legally indentured apprenticeship of a former time. Some apprenticeship contracts are indentured, most are not; some are in writing, some verbal; some carry penalties for breach, some do not. But all apprenticeships imply a more or less systematic training, generally in the workshop, covering a number of years (five is usual) and leading to skilled status. Modern modifications include pre-apprenticeship training, in special institutions, of six months or a year, or more. A less exigent form of training is the 'learnership', generally shorter in duration (though still covering a number of years); it is common in 'Wage Council' trades, where 'learners' for a strictly limited number of years may be paid less than the general minimum time rate.

Table 129. *Age of commencement of apprenticeships of Glasgow boys, by industrial groups*

Industrial group	Apprenticeships commencing at age			
	14	15	16/17	Total
Metal manufacture, engineering, shipbuilding, etc.	7	37	271	315
Other manufactures	14	27	98	139
Building and contracting	13	41	138	192
Distributive trades	2	10	7	19
Services, professional and other	—	4	9	13
Others	—	3	8	11
All industries	36	122	531	689

In the absence of figures for the whole of Scotland, some indication of the pattern of training in an industrial area may be gained from the Glasgow survey. Of the 1,313 boys in the survey who started work at 14 years (in 1947), 607 were, at the age of 17, serving an apprenticeship or other systematic training for a skilled trade covering a number of years. Thirty-one others were undergoing a recognized training for various kinds of non-manual work. In addition, fifty-one boys had started an apprenticeship at some time during the three years, which was later broken and neither resumed nor followed by another. The 638 boys with unbroken apprenticeships made up 48 % of all the boys in the sample.

The most usual age of commencement of apprenticeship was 16 years. Of the 689 apprenticeships (which include the fifty-one that were broken), thirty-six began at 14 years, 122 at 15 and 531 at 16 (including a small number at 17). By large groups of industries the age distribution for the commencement of training is shown in Table 129.

Table 129 shows that a very large proportion of all apprenticeships (46 %) occurred in the metal group of industries, and a large proportion in building (28 %) and that these two groups along with 'other manufactures' account for 94 % of all apprenticeships. The engineering, shipbuilding and electrical industries had 215 out of the total of 689, and about 180 of them commenced at 16 years of age. In the building trades also, 16 was the prevalent starting age. In the distributive trades, where the number of apprenticeships was small, 50 % of them began at 15.

18-2

Table 130 shows that about two-thirds of all training agreements were verbal apprenticeship agreements and about a quarter written apprenticeship agreements.[1] The metal manufactures and building had the greatest proportion of agreements in the written form.

Table 130. *Forms of training agreement of Glasgow boys, by industrial groups*

Industrial group	Not stated	Apprenticeship		Learner-ship	Total
		Written	Verbal or indefinite		
Metal manufacture, engineering, shipbuilding, etc.	5	91	208	11	315
Other manufactures	3	21	99	16	139
Building and contracting	5	51	128	8	192
Distributive trades	—	—	14	5	19
Services	—	2	8	3	13
Others	2	—	8	1	11
All industries	15	165	465	44	689

In spite of the vast increase in the use of machinery, industry has still need for a great variety of special skills, in traditional crafts, in new industrial occupations and in technical occupations, all of which demand periods of progressive training for which the apprenticeship system has proved its value. There are, indeed, indications that the proportion of young people training for occupations which may properly be termed skilled, may be increasing rather than diminishing. The Balfour Committee on Industry and Trade estimated in 1926 that something like 25 % of boys entering industry could hope to have a skilled occupation. In 1951 the Ministry of Labour showed that among boys 36 % of the first entrants into industry under 18 in 1950/51 became apprenticed to a skilled craft or articled to a profession.[2] In the survey of Glasgow boys already cited, the boys who at 17 were in course of training for a skilled trade or responsible non-manual work formed 48 % of all the boys in the group. This last figure is not, indeed, strictly comparable with the others, being based solely on the experience of an industrial and commercial city, which offers a variety of occupational opportunities, and has a large representation of industries like engineering and shipbuilding in which apprenticeships are traditional. In such a centre it is perhaps to be expected

[1] These proportions compare with those disclosed for Scotland by the Ministry of Labour *Report on Apprenticeship and Training, 1925–26*, which were: indentured, 16·1 %, verbal, 77·3 %, learners, 6·6 %.
[2] *Ministry of Labour Gazette*, August 1951, p. 305.

that a higher percentage of young wage-earners will reach skilled status than in the country as a whole. Yet this survey provides other evidence of the upward trend in the proportion of skilled workers, in a comparison between the occupational status of the boys and their fathers.

The survey, following the industrial careers of 1,313 boys up to the age of 17, showed the occupational status the boys had reached at that age. In the case of 1,127 of them the fathers' occupational status was known as well. Of these 1,127 fathers, 283 were skilled manual workers; of the sons of these 1,127 fathers, 541 were in training for skilled trades. Analysis establishes the comparative figures set out in Table 131 for the whole of this group of fathers and sons.

Table 131. *Occupational status of fathers and sons in Glasgow sample*

Occupational status	Fathers	Sons
Manual		
Skilled	283	541
Semi-skilled	302	121
Unskilled	385	189
Non-manual	157	276
Total	1,127	1,127

This result suggests an increase in the proportion of skilled to less skilled workers in the course of one generation which is greater than might have been expected. It is true that over the generations such terms as 'skilled' and 'unskilled' change their meaning: but in this case the same definitions were applied in the determination of the occupational status of fathers and sons, and it may be taken that like was compared with like. The result may indeed exaggerate the rise in the proportion of skilled workers; at 17 a boy's apprenticeship is not completed, and it is possible that he may not stay the course but give up his training and descend to a lower grade of occupation. Yet casualties on the scale necessary to reduce the number of skilled sons to the number of skilled fathers are unlikely.

These comparisons suggest another conclusion of some importance: that in Glasgow, with its wide spread of industrial and occupational opportunity, the status of the father has less influence on that of the son and still less on his ambitions than has been assumed, or even than might naturally be expected. There have in the past been obvious reasons why the son should follow the father's trade: he was familiarized with it in his home life; local conditions frequently offered few alternatives; the father's income was related to his status and in turn affected that of his family, directly because of cost of training and indirectly through the schooling he could afford his sons. But these considerations have become less weighty: the wages for skilled and for unskilled work have become less widely differentiated; schooling and training have become less burdensome; and occupational isolation (as of miners in mining villages) is breaking down. At any rate the survey showed that there was no correlation between the occupational grade of the fathers and the grade which the boys, at 14, expressed their desire to enter; the same percentage—56 %—of the sons of skilled, of semi-skilled and of unskilled fathers all gave their preference as for skilled work. Nor was there any strong correlation between the fathers' status and the status the sons were in process of attaining at 17; approximately half of the sons of skilled, of semi-skilled, and of non-manual workers were all in training for skilled work at that age. The only exception was that a larger percentage of the sons of unskilled fathers than of other grades of fathers were unskilled at 17.

The need for guidance and advice to young persons entering industry has long been recognized; and for many years Juvenile Advisory Committees in Scotland, working under the Ministry of Labour, existed for the purpose. Under the National Youth Employment Service set up by the Employment and Training Act of 1948, it was open to local education authorities in Scotland for the first time to assume responsibility for the local operation of the service, and twelve authorities out of the thirty-five now do so—nine county councils and three town councils. In the rest of Scotland, the service is still operated by the Ministry of Labour.

The general aim of the service is to ensure that the best use is made of the varied aptitudes of young people. To this end it advises them at the school-leaving stage and endeavours to place them in suitable employment. It encourages the training of young workers by stimulating industries, nationally and locally, to formulate schemes of training, and by giving grants to suitable young applicants to enable them to take a course of training for a skilled occupation away from home if local facilities are not available. It keeps in touch with young workers and helps them over the difficulties of their early working years. And it seeks to provide a service of information about the nature and prospects of different occupations by the publication of a series of *Choice of Career* booklets and by other means.

The service in its present form is still too young for a proper assessment of its prospects. The only official statistics of its work, published in the first *Report of the National Youth Employment Council*, for 1947–50, are already some years out of date. One of its functions, however, the placing of young people in suitable employment, had already been carried on for many years, through the Ministry of Labour, by its predecessor, the National Advisory Committee for Juvenile Employment (Scotland). It is therefore of some interest to note the number of young persons under 18 years of age placed in their first situations by the Youth Employment Service. These are shown, in Table 132, for three periods in 1950, 1951 and 1952.

Table 132. *Placings of young people in first employment by the National Youth Employment Service in Scotland, 1950–52*

(Figures in italics show placings in first employment as percentage of total first entries into employment.)

Period	Boys		Girls		Total
	Under 16	Over 16	Under 16	Over 16	
1 January 1950 to 31 December 1950	9,826 *32*	885 *18*	10,108 *34*	751 *15*	21,570 *30*
1 January 1951 to 31 January 1952 (thirteen months)	12,015 *32*	1,091 *18*	12,430 *36*	911 *15*	26,447 *31*
1 February 1952 to 30 September 1952 (eight months)	7,149 *34*	758 *20*	7,812 *37*	728 *19*	16,447 *33*

SOURCE: Figures supplied by Ministry of Labour Scottish Headquarters, Edinburgh.

In the three periods shown in Table 132, the National Youth Employment Service placed about one-third of the young people in their first job after leaving school, and there has been a slight increase in the percentage of placings since 1950 (from 30 % to 33 %). They have placed a slightly larger percentage of girls than of boys, and a much greater percentage of those under 16 years of age than of those over 16.[1] The majority of first jobs, however, are still found by the efforts of the young people themselves and of their friends and relations.

[1] It is obligatory on school authorities to supply the Ministry of Labour with school-leaving reports in respect of all boys and girls who leave at the statutory minimum leaving age, but not in respect of older school-leavers.

279

CHAPTER 19

TRADE UNIONS

By J. D. M. BELL

INTRODUCTION

In their celebrated history,[1] the Webbs define a trade union as 'a continuous association of wage-earners for the purpose of maintaining or improving the conditions of their working lives'. Today that definition appears incomplete. Not only have the functions of trade unions broadened to include, notably, a growing concern with the status of the worker as a 'citizen of industry', but powerful organizations of salary-earners now take their place in the trade union movement alongside those of the wage-earners. These and similar developments have led more recent writers[2] to emphasize the nature of trade unions as 'vocational associations', a term which draws attention to the resemblances between them and the associations of professional men. It was under the heading of 'Occupational Associations' that A. M. Carr-Saunders and D. Caradoc Jones dealt with trade unions in their volume on *The Social Structure of England and Wales*.

The category of 'vocational associations', however, includes too much for our purpose. The emphasis in the activity of trade unions is upon the status and remuneration of their members, and the distinction between them and those associations and institutes whose prime, or only, concern is with the techniques of particular professions or occupations is clear enough. But in between there is much debatable territory. The British Medical Association, for example, is much concerned with the techniques of medicine and with professional standards, but it also takes a live interest in questions of status and remuneration. Yet one would hesitate to include it as a trade union. Where, then, is the line to be drawn?

The most workable definition of trade unions would appear to be that used by the Ministry of Labour. This includes 'all organizations of employees— including those of salaried and professional workers, as well as those of manual wage-earners—which are known to include among their functions that of negotiating with employers with the object of regulating the conditions of employment of their members'.[3] It is not sufficient for an association to

---

[1] Sidney and Beatrice Webb, *The History of Trade Unionism, 1666–1920* (1920 edition), p. 1.
[2] E.g. W. Milne-Bailey in his *Trade Unions and the State* (1934).
[3] *Ministry of Labour Gazette*, November 1951, p. 419. The definition has since been revised to read, at the end, 'with the object of regulating conditions of employment' (*Ministry of Labour Gazette*, November 1952, p. 375).

concern itself with the conditions of employment of its members; it must also employ to that end the method of negotiating with employers. By that test the British Medical Association is excluded, but the Educational Institute of Scotland, to give a borderline case, comes within the definition.

Even so, the line of demarcation is somewhat arbitrarily drawn. An association whose members generally have no employer in the usual sense may find itself sporadically and incidentally drawn into negotiations with employers on behalf of specially-situated sections of its membership. To make the definition workable, some conception of *habitual* negotiations with employers would seem to be implied. On the other hand, some organizations may satisfy even this further test without the bias of their activities being directed towards the exercise of this particular function. It is inevitable that the Ministry of Labour will, in practice, exclude organizations which do from time to time, in special cases, negotiate with employers, and will include others which exist primarily for some other purpose (as benefit societies, for instance).

Such difficulties will, however, arise on any definition. The one selected has the convenience of being used in compiling the statistics of the membership of trade unions in the United Kingdom which appear annually in the *Ministry of Labour Gazette*. By the use of the same definition in a statistical treatment of trade union membership in Scotland, comparability with the United Kingdom figures can be maintained, and this procedure is facilitated by the publication from time to time of directories which list those organizations regarded by the Ministry as trade unions.

THE GROWTH OF TRADE UNION MEMBERSHIP IN SCOTLAND

The Ministry, unfortunately, does not collect separate statistics of trade union membership for Scotland. Such information as is available comes from the efforts of individual inquirers. Three inquiries, at convenient intervals, have been made in the last sixty years. Sidney and Beatrice Webb, as part of their far-reaching investigations into the trade unionism of the late nineteenth century, conducted a 'census' of trade unionists in the United Kingdom with the end of 1892 as the selected date. The results were published in *The History of Trade Unionism*, and contain separate figures for Scotland. It was largely under the stimulus of the Webbs' researches that the Labour Department of the Board of Trade (as it was then) was encouraged to extend its own inquiries and to produce really comprehensive statistics of trade union membership in the United Kingdom for each year from 1892 onwards.

In 1924 the Scottish Trades Union Congress undertook a survey of trade union membership in Scotland, the results of which were embodied in a report presented to the 1925 Congress. Finally, the present writer carried out a Scottish trade union 'census' for 1947, the report of which was published in

1950 for the Department of Social and Economic Research of Glasgow University under the title, *The Strength of Trade Unionism in Scotland.*

The 1947 survey, for reasons already explained, was confined to those trade unions which are recognized by the Ministry of Labour as such. Within that category (to keep the project manageable), it was limited to those unions with 5,000 or more members in the United Kingdom plus any smaller organizations which either affiliate to the S.T.U.C. or, if unaffiliated, have a membership largely confined to Scotland. The 125 unions so included yielded a total membership of 881,202. An alternative estimate, based on the assumption that unions with 5,000 or more members all told account for the same proportion of Scottish as of United Kingdom trade unionists, gave a total of 908,982. The truth probably lies somewhere between the two and the good round figure of 900,000 is likely to be near the mark.

Table 133. *Estimated numbers of trade unionists in Scotland and in the United Kingdom in* 1892, 1924 *and* 1947

	Scotland		United Kingdom*		Trade unionists in Scotland as a percentage of those in the U.K.
Date	Estimated numbers of trade unionists (thousands)	Trade unionists per 100 of the population	Estimated numbers of trade unionists (thousands)	Trade unionists per 100 of the population	
1892	147	3·7	1,576	4·6	9·3
1924	536	11·0	5,544	12·6	9·7
1947	900	17·7	9,145	18·2	9·8

* Great Britain and Northern Ireland only at each date.

SOURCES: S. and B. Webb, op. cit.; J. D. M. Bell, op. cit.; *Report to Scottish T.U.C.*, 1925; *Census of Population*, 1951; *Ministry of Labour Gazette*, October 1937 and November 1951.

The two earlier surveys employed the Webbs' definition of a trade union,[1] but it is impossible now to say precisely how they applied it in particular cases. The Webbs themselves give some hints. They included every union with 1,000 or more members and many which were even smaller, but they excluded organizations of non-manual workers, the clerks and the shop assistants as well as the teachers, and those which were essentially benefit societies. The 1924 survey, on the other hand, interpreted the term 'wage-earners' as including also all salaried employees, and attempted to cover all unions operating in Scotland, no matter how small. With the reservations which these differences of definition and interpretation impose, Table 133 shows the trade union membership in Scotland at each of our three dates and compares it with the size of the total population. Corresponding statistics for the United

[1] See above, p. 280.

Kingdom are also given and these are based throughout on the Ministry of Labour's figures. They are, therefore, more strictly comparable one with another than are those for Scotland.

The proportion of the strength of the whole British trade union movement which Scotland represents is here shown to have remained remarkably stable. There is an apparent slight increase, but the relative imperfections of the Scottish figures make its precise significance difficult to assess. If, on the other hand, the degree of trade union organization in Scotland is still, at 17·7 % of the population, lower than that found south of the Border, the relative gap has apparently narrowed with each successive survey. Scotland, moreover, would appear to have reduced the leeway more rapidly since 1924, an impression which is somewhat fortified when allowance is made for the omission by the Webbs of the non-manual workers' unions, though this is not likely to have been a serious matter in 1892.[1]

Moreover, the Ministry of Labour figures include all the members, at home and overseas, of unions with headquarters in the United Kingdom, a circumstance which is unlikely to be wholly offset by the corresponding exclusion of members of foreign (including Irish Republic) trade unions resident in this country. Allowance for this factor, of minor importance though it is, would suggest that there is very little difference between the densities of trade unionism in Scotland and in the rest of the United Kingdom. But the comparison, it should be noted, is not directly with England and Wales, which will still retain some lead over Scotland, the Northern Ireland density almost certainly falling below the general average.

Though tolerably reliable in indicating comparisons and trends, trade union membership statistics should not be taken too literally. Any attempt at enumerating the members in a given area almost inevitably involves a measure of double-counting. Especially as one approaches the 'professional association' fringe of trade unionism does one find membership by the same individual of more than one union a not infrequent occurrence, and even amongst manual workers it is by no means unknown. Perhaps it is particularly common for members of those organizations which are primarily benefit societies to be found joining other unions for purposes of 'trade protection'. It is impossible to say how serious this duplication is; the reader can only be warned of its existence when assessing the evidence of Table 133, that rather more than 1 in 6 of the total population of Scotland belongs to a trade union as compared with more than 1 in 30 sixty years ago.

---

[1] The Webbs' estimate of the total number of trade unionists in the United Kingdom (including the modern Irish Republic) at the end of 1892 was 1,507,026. The revised Ministry of Labour figure (including non-manual workers' unions) is 1,576,000. This refers to Great Britain and Northern Ireland only, but all Irish members of United Kingdom unions are in fact included.

A more useful indication of the overall strength of trade unionism in Scotland than is afforded by a comparison with the total population is that which gives trade union membership as a percentage of the total number of employees. The Webbs, writing in the days before Unemployment Insurance and with their attention concentrated on the members of the adult male manual working-class, could only estimate roughly that, in the United Kingdom, about 1 in 5 of these was a member of a trade union. The 1924 survey, using an estimate (derived from the 1921 Census) of the total number of workers in Scotland over 16 years of age exclusive of domestic servants, calculated that 35·6 % were members of trade unions. If, instead, we employ the figure for the number of workers insured against unemployment at that date, we obtain a trade union percentage of 41·1 %.

Today we are much more fortunate in having at our disposal the statistics of employees insured under the National Insurance Acts, which came into operation in July 1948.[1] If the number of trade union members at the end of 1947 is expressed as a percentage of the number of insured employees at mid-1948 the figures obtained are 43·0 % for Scotland and 43·9 % for the United Kingdom. The Scottish figure is thus higher than that for 1924, despite the fact that the comprehensive character of the new National Insurance statistics means that they cover many areas of employment where trade unionism is notoriously weak. Perhaps a more precise measure of the progress made since 1924 is provided if we base our calculations on the numbers of employees insured in mid-1947 under the old Unemployment Insurance schemes.[2] The 'trade union proportion' now becomes more than half—54·3 % for Scotland and 58·1 % for the United Kingdom.

If this proportion were true of each and every class of worker, trade unions would be much less influential bodies than they are. Within the bounds of particular categories of employees, the proportion is, however, a good deal higher. Women workers, for example, are notoriously less well organized than men and the same is true of juveniles. On the basis of its estimate of the number of workers in Scotland over 16 years of age, the 1924 survey gave the degree of organization among women as only 21·3 % compared with 40·2 % among men. The 1947 survey did not enumerate female membership separately. In that year, however, out of a total membership of 728,841 affiliated to the Scottish Trades Union Congress, 131,957 were women. On the assumption that, of the total trade union membership in Scotland, the same proportion were women, their numbers would have been about 163,000. The numbers of trade union members in the two sexes, expressed as percentages of the numbers of employees insured under the old schemes at mid-1947, would have been 64·0 % for men and 32·2 % for women. The proportion of Scottish

[1] See *Ministry of Labour Gazette*, March 1951.
[2] *Ministry of Labour Gazette*, December 1947.

trade unionists who are women has risen, between 1924 and 1947, from 14·6 % to about 18·1 %, but over the whole range of employment of the two sexes the chances of a woman worker joining a trade union are still, on the average, about half those of a man.

THE INDUSTRIAL DISTRIBUTION OF TRADE UNION MEMBERSHIP

By industry as by sex there is considerable variation in the degree of organization attained. The relevant statistics are presented in Table 134, but here, even more than with the other tables in this chapter, care in interpretation is needed. The chief difficulty is that trade union and industrial 'boundary lines' by no means coincide, with the consequence that the thousands of workers in the engineering, building and other industries who are members of one or other of the big general unions do not appear in their proper industrial categories. And this, though the most serious, is not the only imperfection caused by the same fundamental difficulty.

Moreover, only the 881,202 trade unionists actually enumerated in the 1947 survey could be assigned to their appropriate industrial groups. There were, it is legitimate to assume, about another 20,000 or so who could not be included in Table 134, and, while they form a small proportion of the total of Scottish trade union members, their absence may considerably affect the results for individual groups. Particularly is there reason to suppose that the numbers in the coal-mining and water transport groups have been understated.

With all its limitations, the table indicates how uneven the spread of trade unionism has been as between one industry and another. Among the coal-miners and the railwaymen organization in most grades will, in fact, be well-nigh complete, and the same is nowadays true also of the dockers. A decisive majority of the craftsmen in the metal trades, of the printers and the boot and shoe operatives, of the civil servants and, probably also, of some sections of the teachers and the builders and woodworkers belong to their trade unions. At the other extreme, of the workers in banking and insurance, commerce and distribution, and (apparently) the pottery and glass industries not more than about 1 in 5 is a member of a trade union. To these poorly-organized industries can certainly be added also some of the minor manufacturing industries, agriculture, and various branches of unskilled labour, all of which hide within one or other of our two heterogeneous groups, 'Other transport, agriculture and general labour' and 'Miscellaneous groups'.

As in England and Wales, the largest single group is that of the transport and general workers (to which, in Scotland, agriculture must be added). Its membership is, admittedly, scattered over a wide variety of occupations and industries, but organized as it is largely by only two unions, the Transport and General Workers' Union and the National Union of General and Municipal Workers, it represents, nevertheless, a considerable concentration

285

Table 134. *The industrial distribution of trade union membership in Scotland, compared with that of insured employees*

Industrial group*	Number of trade union members at the end of 1947	Percentage of total	Number of insured workers at the end of June 1948	Trade union membership as a percentage of the number of insured workers
Coal-mining	65,370	7·4	91,440	71·5
Pottery and glass	773	0·1	5,070	15·2
Metals, machines and conveyances	178,929	20·3	350,620†	51·0
Textiles	31,247	3·5	114,890	27·2
Boot and shoe (manufacture and repair)	3,435	0·4	5,690	60·4
Tailoring and other clothing	10,106	1·2	29,630	34·1
Printing and paper	27,389	3·1	50,430	54·3
Building, contracting and woodworking	76,563	8·7	184,760	41·4
Railway service	65,122	7·4	79,940	81·5
Water transport	4,054	0·5	19,780†	20·5
Other transport, agriculture and general labour‡	211,729	24·0 }	655,630	38·4
Miscellaneous groups§	39,880	4·5		
Commerce and distribution	51,251	5·8	256,140†	20·0
Banking and insurance	7,206	0·8	31,150	23·1
National government‖	43,216	4·9	55,980	77·2
Local government	28,847	3·3	70,470	40·9
Teaching	28,674	3·3	57,450	49·9
Entertainments and sport	7,411	0·8	19,740	37·5
All groups	881,202	100·0	2,095,300¶	42·1

* The total membership of each union has been included in the group with which the majority of the members are believed to be connected. The figures for the industrial groups are exclusive of certain large unions, the membership of which is spread over a variety of industries and is included under 'other transport, agriculture and general labour' or 'Commerce and distribution'.

† Some rearrangement has been effected in the industrial classification adopted in the *Tables relating to employment and unemployment in Great Britain*, in an attempt to relate more nearly the industrial and trade union 'boundary lines'.

‡ This is a combination of two groups, 'Agriculture' and 'Other transport and general labour', which appear separately in the Ministry of Labour's returns for the United Kingdom. They are here treated as a single aggregate because, in Scotland, trade union organization among agricultural workers is entirely the province of the Transport and General Workers' Union.

§ Includes mining and quarrying (other than coal-mining); manufacturing industries not separately specified; organizations of clerks, chemists, foremen, etc., when not classifiable by industry.

‖ Government industrial employees are not included here, but are assigned to the appropriate industrial group.

¶ This total exceeds the sum of the individual group-totals because of the inclusion of some groups of unemployed workers not easily classifiable by industry.

SOURCES: J. D. M. Bell, op. cit.; *Tables relating to employment and unemployment*.

286

of trade union power. This group, the metal workers, the builders and wood-workers, the miners and the railwaymen together account for more than two-thirds of Scottish trade unionists. Nevertheless, and despite the low degree of organization which often obtains elsewhere, the tendency in the last sixty years has been for the habit of trade union organization to spread to an ever greater variety of industries and services. In 1892 the Webbs gave special mention to the fact that in Scotland almost one-third of the trade unionists were in the engineering and metal trades alone (as against one-sixth in England and Wales). The miners and the builders, at the same date, accounted for nearly another third. Even among some of today's most highly-organized groups of workers—the railwaymen, the teachers and the civil servants, for example—trade union membership was then of rare occurrence. The Webbs found only 1,500 members for their category of 'Railway traffic workers'!

In Table 135 the industrial distribution of the Scottish membership of trade unions in 1947 is compared with that of the United Kingdom member-

Table 135. *The industrial distribution of trade union membership and employment in Scotland compared with that in the United Kingdom,* 1947

Industrial group	Number of trade union members in Scotland as a percentage of those in the United Kingdom	Number of insured employees in Scotland as a percentage of those in the United Kingdom
Commerce and distribution	14·4	10·4
Building, woodworking, etc.	12·9	10·9
Printing and paper	11·1	10·7
Metals, machines and conveyances	10·9	9·3
Railway service	10·3	11·2
Teaching	10·0	12·0
Entertainments and sport	9·0	7·9
Other transport, agriculture, general labour and miscellaneous groups	9·0	11·0
Coal-mining	8·5	11·5
Textiles	8·2	11·3
Local government	7·7	9·0
Banking and insurance	7·6	7·3
Tailoring and other clothing	6·9	5·8
National government	6·8	5·4
Water transport	3·9	12·6
Boot and shoe	3·5	3·8
Pottery and glass	2·3	3·5
All groups	9·7*	10·0

* The total membership of trade unions in Scotland is here taken as 881,202.

SOURCES: J. D. M. Bell, op. cit.; *Ministry of Labour Gazette*, February 1949; *Tables relating to employment and unemployment.*

287

ship. The various industrial groups are listed according to the relative importance of the Scottish element among their trade unionists. The placings will clearly depend not only upon the density of trade union organization achieved in Scotland as against the United Kingdom but also upon differences in industrial structure. For this reason, the final column of the table compares the distribution of insured employees in the two units.

The Scottish trade union figures are less complete than those for the United Kingdom, and this may affect seriously the performance of individual groups. This applies particularly, perhaps, to 'Coal-mining' and to 'Water transport'. The degree of organization in Scotland in these two groups may, even so, be genuinely lower than in the rest of the United Kingdom, and this is likely to be true, also, of textiles and of pottery and glass. Trade unionism appears to be stronger in Scotland than elsewhere among metal workers, tailors and clothing workers, printers and paper workers and builders and woodworkers, and among employees in commerce and distribution, banking and insurance, the entertainments industry and national government service. On the railways, in local government service, in the boot and shoe industry, and (more doubtfully) among the teachers there is no significant discrepancy between the Scottish and the more general figures. With the vast army of general workers and their allies, the level of organization in Scotland is perhaps lower in some sectors, but the omnibus character of the unions involved makes it difficult to read very much into the statistics.

THE REGIONAL DISTRIBUTION

The considerable variations which we have seen to exist in the levels of trade union organization in different groups of industries and services contribute to the uneven geographical spread of trade unionism. The Webbs did not publish separate figures for the various regions of Scotland, but something can be gathered from their statement that 'nearly all' of their 147,000 Scottish trade unionists were to be found 'in the narrow industrial belt between the Clyde and the Forth, two-thirds of the total, indeed, belonging to Glasgow and the neighbouring industrial centres', while the Highlands were 'practically devoid of Trade Unionism'.[1] The survey undertaken for the Scottish Trades Union Congress in 1924, however, included a comprehensive regional analysis of the figures, and this is compared in Table 136 with my own results for 1947.

The 1947 survey was only able to give a regional analysis of the membership of those unions which were willing to supply branch or district figures, in fact rather more than one-third of the total. The estimates in Table 136 are based on the assumption that the geographical distribution of the whole membership

[1] S. and B. Webb, *The History of Trade Unionism* (1920 edition), pp. 425–6.

Table 136. *Geographical distribution of trade union membership in Scotland,* 1924 *and* 1947

Region	1924		1947		1947 member-ship as a percentage of 1924 member-ship
	Number of members (thousands)	Percentage of total in Scotland	Estimated number of members (thousands)	Percentage of total in Scotland	
City of Glasgow	133	24·7	259	28·4	195
City of Edinburgh	47	8·7	89	9·8	191
City of Dundee	34	6·3	53	5·8	157
City of Aberdeen	20	3·7	41	4·5	204
Ayr			51	5·6	
Lanark	129	24·1	76	8·3	161
Renfrew			81	8·9	
Lothians	40	7·4	25	2·8	63
Fife, Clackmannan and Kinross	48	8·9	51	5·6	108
Dunbarton	35	6·6	50	5·5	256
Stirling			41	4·5	
South-eastern Borders*	11	2·0	9	1·0	81
Dumfries and Galloway	5	0·9	12	1·4	245
Perth	16	2·9	11	1·2	183
Angus			18	2·0	
Highlands and Islands†	10	1·9	22	2·4	221
North-East‡	10	1·9	21	2·3	206
Total	536	100·0	909	100·0	169

* The counties of Berwick, Peebles, Roxburgh and Selkirk.
† The counties of Argyll, Bute, Caithness, Inverness, Orkney, Ross and Cromarty, Sutherland and Shetland.
‡ The counties of Aberdeen, Banff, Kincardine, Moray and Nairn.
SOURCES: J. D. M. Bell, op. cit.; *Report to Scottish T.U.C.*, 1925.

in Scotland (taken as 908,982) was the same as that of the 325,813 whose distribution was known. The effect will clearly be to understate the membership in those areas where many of the workers belong to highly localized unions not included in the sample, and to overstate it where the localized unions have been included. The most serious omissions, from this point of view, are those of the miners, the iron and steel workers, and the textile workers of the Borders; on the other hand, the shipbuilders, the metal-working trades and certain other groups of textile workers are perhaps over-represented. The consequences for the regional analysis will be to underestimate trade union strength in Lanark, notably, and also in Fife, the Lothians, the Eastern Border counties, and perhaps Ayr; over-representation is likely for Renfrew, Dunbarton and Angus. These considerations severely limit the usefulness of the 1947 figures, but at least the weaknesses are known and allowances for them can be made.

The regional analysis for 1947 was on a basis of individual counties or cities: the 1924 survey employed rather wider regional units, and this less ambitious approach has, with a few modifications, been adopted. The main conclusion to be drawn is that the geographical concentration of trade union members within Scotland which was noted by the Webbs is still very marked; the secondary conclusion is that it is, nevertheless, diminishing. It is difficult to say precisely what area was intended by that 'narrow, industrial belt between the Clyde and the Forth' within which the Webbs found 'nearly all' Scotland's trade unionists to be located. If, however, we take the cities of Glasgow and Edinburgh with the counties of Ayr, Lanark, Renfrew, the Lothians, Fife, Clackmannan, Kinross, Dunbarton and Stirling as constituting the 'central industrial region' of Scotland, we find that they contained in 1924, 80·4 % of the Scottish total, and in 1947, 79·4 %. The proportions are indeed high, but are scarcely equivalent to 'nearly all'. Again, the city of Glasgow today contains nearly 30 % of the total, but if we were to add the whole of the counties of Ayr, Renfrew, Dunbarton, Lanark and Stirling, we would still not reach that two-thirds proportion which the Webbs claimed for 'Glasgow and the neighbouring industrial centres'.

Of the trade unionists outside the 'central industrial region', more than half, in 1924 and 1947 alike, were supplied by the cities of Dundee and Aberdeen. Even so, neither the Highlands nor Southern Scotland could today be described, without exaggeration, as being 'practically devoid of Trade Unionism'. Had we, moreover, been able for 1947 to include in the regional survey the general workers' unions, with their representation of the agricultural workers, the textile workers of the Borders, the fishermen, quarrymen and other isolated groups, it is likely that the position in the outlying areas would have become even more favourable.

The final column of Table 136 attempts to assess the changes in regional distribution of the last twenty-five to thirty years. The fall in membership in the Lothians and eastern Border counties, and the small increase in the Fife area are probably the result of those deficiencies in the 1947 survey to which attention has already been drawn. Perhaps, too, the increase in Ayr, Lanark and Renfrew has in fact been greater than is here shown. Some useful conclusions can, however, be drawn. The four cities, with the exception of Dundee, show high rates of increase, until today very nearly half of the total membership in Scotland is to be found within their boundaries. The other areas which come out best are the more remote regions—the Highlands, the South-western counties (especially, it would seem, Dumfries), and the North-East—and the northern fringe of the 'central industrial region' in the counties of Dunbarton and Stirling, with a possible extension into Perth and Angus (outside Dundee). It is this 'northern fringe', indeed, which shows the greatest increase of all, though the figures may be inflated by the favourable representation of shipbuilding (Clydebank) and the metal-working industries (the Falkirk area) within the 1947 sample.

The development since 1924 can be summarized as showing a continued and accelerated spread of trade unionism to the previously remote and unorganized areas, and within the industrialized parts of the country a movement towards the cities. One might also have expected to find some reflection in the trade union statistics of that shift in the bias of location of Scottish industry from west to east—or, more exactly, perhaps, from the centre of the industrial region to its periphery—which is undoubtedly taking place. The performance of Stirling does suggest it, and the tendency might have been more plainly revealed had it not been for the omission in 1947 of the miners of Fife, Ayr and the Lothians, and for the association of Stirling with Dunbarton and of Ayr with Lanark and Renfrew in the regional groupings of 1924.

Comparisons for regions within Scotland between the numbers of trade union members and those of insured employees can only be tentative, because of the qualifications which affect both sets of figures. The indications, however, are that the density of organization ranges from around 60 % in the industrial belt to 30 % or less in the Highlands and some Border districts. A more detailed comparison was provided in *The Strength of Trade Unionism in Scotland* between the estimates of trade union membership for the various cities and counties and their populations. When the necessary allowances for inadequate statistics have been made, a trade union percentage of 20 or over seems probable in the counties of Lanark, Renfrew, Dunbarton, Stirling, Clackmannan, and Angus, with Aberdeen, Ayr, Fife, West Lothian and Midlothian in the 15–20 % range.[1] At the other extreme, the percentage is less than 5 in Sutherland and Kinross, and probably also in Ross and Cromarty, Kincardine, Berwick and Kirkcudbright. Of these, only two are Highland counties; the uniting factor with the others would seem to be their proportionately low burghal populations. Outside the mining villages, trade unionism is still something of an urban phenomenon.

The above analyses of the industrial and of the geographical distribution of trade unionism show similar results—a marked but diminishing concentration in particular sectors, and a significant tendency for organization to spread to new industries and new localities. These parallel developments in the industrial and regional composition of trade union membership are very largely parts of a single process. The industries whose relative importance in the trade union world has declined are usually highly localized. It has been pointed out above how preponderant in the Scottish trade union movement of 1892 were the metal workers of all kinds. In the 1947 survey it was

[1] The cities are included in their respective counties in these calculations.

estimated that three-quarters of the trade unionists in the 'Metals, machines and conveyances' group were to be found in the counties of Lanark, Renfrew, Dunbarton, Stirling and Ayr. On the other hand, the industries in which trade unionism has expanded rapidly, or has newly entered, in the last sixty years are often industries in which employment is spread evenly over the country, more or less in proportion to population. This will be true, for example, of the railwaymen, teachers, local government employees and post office workers, and of many of the groups of employees within the ranks of the general workers' unions. Even so, the existence in urban and industrial areas of a climate of opinion favourable to trade unionism means that these groups also attain their highest degree of organization there.

SIZES OF UNIONS

The development of trade unionism in remote areas and previously un-organized industries has been facilitated by the emergence of large national organizations with secure funds and efficient administrations. The progress of amalgamation has, in fact, been one of the outstanding and best-known features of the evolution of trade unionism in the last sixty years, and, more especially, since the end of the first world war. In 1892 there were 1,233 separate trade unions in the United Kingdom with a total membership of 1,576,000. By 1920, a slightly greater number of unions, 1,384, contained 8,348,000 members. At the end of 1951, 9,480,000 members were distributed amongst only 704 separate unions, and, of these, the seventeen largest con-tributed almost exactly two-thirds of the total.

Table 137 shows the similar position which has been reached within Scotland. The 1947 survey certainly included all the larger organizations within its scope (none with over 5,000 members in Scotland could have escaped, and probably very few with more than 1,000) but equally certainly

Table 137. *Sizes of trade unions in Scotland*, 1947

Membership range	Number of unions	Number of members	Percentage of number of unions in Scotland	Percentage of all trade union members in Scotland
Under 1,000	53	20,932	42·4	2·4
1,000–5,000	36	89,404	28·8	10·2
5,000–10,000	14	96,335	11·2	10·9
10,000–25,000	14	202,963	11·2	23·0
Over 25,000	8	471,568	6·4	53·5
Total	125	881,202	100·0	100·0

SOURCE: Material collected by the author.

excluded some of those with only a few Scottish members. The actual numbers of unions in the lower ranges of membership, therefore, will be somewhat greater than the table gives. On the other hand, against the additional membership which the excluded unions would bring to this end of the table must be offset probable understatements of the membership of some of the larger unions. The percentages in the final column should represent pretty accurately the actual state of affairs.

In 1947, slightly more than two-fifths of the trade unions operating in Scotland accounted for less than one-fortieth of the membership. At the other extreme, the eight largest unions, or about one-sixteenth of the total number, contained more than half the total membership. The seventeen largest unions in Scotland, in fact, contained just over 70 % of the total membership, so that the degree of concentration is, if anything, even higher than in the United Kingdom, with its two-thirds proportion.

Of the eight largest unions in Scotland, the first seven were also, in 1947, the seven largest in the United Kingdom—the Transport and General Workers' Union, the National Union of General and Municipal Workers, the Amalgamated Engineering Union, the National Union of Mineworkers, the National Union of Railwaymen, the Union of Shop Distributive and Allied Workers and the Amalgamated Society of Woodworkers—although individual rankings by size were different. In eighth place came the largest of the 'independent' Scottish organizations, the Educational Institute of Scotland.

PURELY SCOTTISH TRADE UNIONS

The amalgamation movement has, clearly, been no great respecter of the Anglo-Scottish border. Nevertheless, there still exists a significant group of organizations whose membership is confined to Scotland. Table 138 gives some idea of their extent and influence. Together, it will be seen, they contain about one-seventh of all trade union members in Scotland. In other words, they are, in the aggregate and by the test of membership alone, about as important in the trade union life of Scotland as the single largest union, the Transport and General Workers', is in that of the United Kingdom. 'Independent' Scottish trade unionism is, even so, much weaker than it was in 1924 when, out of a total of 227 unions with 536,432 members, 90 purely Scottish unions had a membership of 213,469. Much of the change, however, can be ascribed to the formation of the National Union of Mineworkers and to the absorption of the Scottish Farm Servants' Union by the Transport and General Workers' Union.

Many of the surviving 'independent' unions are purely local rather than Scottish in character, and, with the exception of textiles, it is only in those groups of industries where unions covering the whole of Scotland are found that they contain significant percentages of the group memberships. This is true of the teachers—among whom the two Scottish associations are virtually without competition—the printers, the painters and some other building tradesmen, the road transport workers, the bakers and the clerks. On the other hand there would seem nowadays to be no separate Scottish unions at all in pottery and glass, tailoring and clothing, agriculture, water transport, railway service, commerce and distribution or banking and insurance.[1]

Table 138. *'Independent' Scottish trade unions*, 1947

Industrial group	Affiliated to the T.U.C.		Not affiliated to the T.U.C. but affiliated to the S.T.U.C.		Not affiliated to either Trades Union Congress		Total		Membership as percentage of total group membership in Scotland
	No.	Mem-bership	No.	Mem-bership	No.	Mem-bership	No.	Member-ship	
Coal-mining	1*	6,170	—	—	—	—	1	6,170	9·4
Metals, machines and conveyances	2	3,460	1	85	1	29	4	3,574	2·0
Textiles	3†	6,500	4	6,207	7	2,495	14	15,202	48·7
Boot and shoe	—	—	—	—	2	52	2	52	1·5
Printing and paper	1	6,291	—	—	—	—	1	6,291	23·0
Building, contracting and woodworking	3‡	13,474	3	4,482	1	150	7	18,106	23·6
Other transport, agriculture and general labour	1	20,000	1	5,200	—	—	2	25,200	11·9
National government	—	—	—	—	3	443	3	443	1·0
Local government	—	—	1	340	2	923	3	1,263	4·4
Teaching	—	—	—	—	2	28,639	2	28,639	99·9
Entertainment and sports	—	—	—	—	1	617	1	617	8·3
All other groups	2	16,946	—	—	3	10,456	5	27,402	68·7
Total	13	72,841	10	16,314	22	43,804	45	132,959	15·1§

* The Scottish Colliery Enginemen, Boilermen and Tradesmen's Association which is, in fact, a section of the National Union of Mineworkers (although enjoying considerable autonomy) and, as such, affiliated to the T.U.C. The Association affiliates separately to the S.T.U.C.

† Includes the Scottish Lace and Textile Workers' Union which is affiliated to the T.U.C. as part of the British Lace Operatives' Federation.

‡ Includes the Edinburgh and District Coopers' Society (which is, in fact, a branch of the National Trade Union of Coopers) and the Amalgamated Society of Coopers, both of which are affiliated to the T.U.C. as part of the Coopers' Federation of Great Britain and Ireland. The Amalgamated Society is the only purely Scottish union which has a link with the T.U.C., but not with the S.T.U.C.

§ Percentage of 881,202.

SOURCE: J. D. M. Bell, op. cit.

[1] One could also include coal-mining—see Table 138.

THE SCOTTISH TRADES UNION CONGRESS

Their separate classification in Table 138 is not intended to convey the quite misleading impression that the purely Scottish unions regard themselves as, in any important sense, a group apart. The larger of them—apart from the teachers and the clerks—affiliate to the British, as well as to the Scottish, Trades Union Congress. The Scottish trade union movement is not, nor, with a few possible exceptions, does it wish to be, completely separate and divided from its counterpart in the rest of the United Kingdom. It does, however, enjoy a considerable measure of 'devolution' through the existence of the Scottish Trades Union Congress.

This organization dates from 1897. In part, its origin lay in the exclusion of trades councils from direct affiliation to the British Trades Union Congress in 1895, a decision which the Scottish trades councils, led by Aberdeen, resolved to combat, but it was perhaps inevitable that a separate Scottish body should sooner or later emerge, especially as the accepted conception of the proper function of a Trades Union Congress moved from that of an annual debating forum to that of a co-ordinating central authority for the whole trade union movement. The Scottish Trades Union Congress has, accordingly, grown in influence and prestige, not in competition with the T.U.C., but step by step with it. In 1918 G. D. H. Cole was able to discuss the S.T.U.C. as a 'much less responsible' body even than the unreformed T.U.C. of those days.[1] Two years later, a new constitution conferred upon the T.U.C. the undisputed leadership of the British Trade Union Movement. It was in pursuit of that example that the S.T.U.C. was, in its turn, strengthened by a new constitution in 1923, and, under the long and brilliant secretaryship of William Elger, 1922–46, slowly attained its present status within the Scottish movement.

Today the S.T.U.C. has affiliated to it not only purely Scottish unions— some of which make this their only Congress affiliation—but also the Scottish membership of the great majority of unions which are affiliated to the T.U.C. and have members on this side of the Border. There is, indeed, little difference between the percentage of Scottish trade unionists whose organizations belong to the S.T.U.C. and that of trade unionists in the United Kingdom who are directly connected with the work of the T.U.C.—about 85–90 % in each case. As in England and Wales, the teachers' organizations, the powerful National and Local Government Officers' Association and a number of civil service unions do not affiliate to trades union congresses, but, the Scottish Clerks' Association apart, these are the only large 'outsiders'.

The organization and methods of the S.T.U.C. in many ways resemble those developed by the T.U.C., although it retains such distinctive features

[1] G. D. H. Cole, *An Introduction to Trade Unionism* (1918), p. 21.

as the direct affiliation of trades councils,[1] the absence of the 'card vote' procedure at its congresses, and the election of the General Council by the whole congress, not in industrial sections. It works closely with the T.U.C. on all matters where Scottish interests are directly affected, although it remains a completely distinct organization. The S.T.U.C. is today, then, a widely representative body, performing for its affiliated organizations and members in Scotland many services which, by its remoteness, the T.U.C. would be unable to undertake as effectively, and for which no conceivable alternative organization (for example, a federation of Scottish trades councils) would be likely to have the necessary equipment and prestige.

[1] There are forty-eight affiliated trades councils (*S.T.U.C. Report, 1953*). Some cover, not individual towns, but the whole, or parts, of counties. Of these, those for Mid-lothian, Peebles-Selkirk and West Lothian have 'burgh committees' in the principal centres.

CHAPTER 20

THE CHURCHES

By JOHN HIGHET

Like other nations, Scotland has had applied to her a number of clichés of description and conventional attributes. Of these, one of the most firmly entrenched is that Scotland is a 'church-minded' nation. Even those Scots who would today hesitate to echo this sentiment will be found reflecting, 'Still, if there is anything to what our fathers and grandfathers assert, it would appear that we once were "church-minded"'.

What in fact is the position in Scotland today, and how does it compare with the situation, say, fifty and eighty years ago? And how does Scotland compare in this respect with its neighbours, England and Wales? In this chapter we shall discuss these questions mainly in the frame of reference appropriate to the statistical emphasis of this book: that of the numerical strengths of the various Christian denominations. Let it be said at once that we are far from imagining that strength in numbers is the most important thing that can be said about a religious association: this is indeed in some ways the least important, as the record of, for example, the Society of Friends sufficiently testifies. The quantitative measure is, nevertheless, by no means irrelevant or valueless, even if it says nothing about the intensity of the religious feeling or the quality of the Christian witness of those enumerated.

The data used in this inquiry are in most cases the official 'exact' figures published by denominations, in some the official estimates supplied by church officials, and in a few others 'unofficial' estimates which are nevertheless based on such relevant information as is available.[1]

CHURCH MEMBERSHIP IN 1950/51

In Scotland there are just over two million 'full', 'official', or communicant members of the thirty-odd Christian denominations represented within its borders. This represents 58 % of the adult population of 3,486,000 in 1950.[2]

---

[1] See 'Note on Sources', pp. 314–15.

[2] The fact that there are some 'under-20's' on the rolls of most Protestant denominations means that we are not being quite exact in expressing membership throughout this chapter as a percentage of the adult population. But to express it as a percentage of the total population is unsatisfactory, while to take as the base the population aged, say, 16 and over would understate the percentages.

During a visit to Glasgow in the spring of 1947, the Rev. Professor Reinhold Niebuhr told the *Glasgow Herald* that in his opinion the American people were probably more

In addition, most denominations have a number of adherents: persons who attend religious services fairly regularly and have the welfare of the congregation at heart, but who for one reason or another stand aside from full or official membership. No one knows the aggregate numerical strength of this category; its magnitude in relation to full membership varies so much from denomination to denomination that it is impossible to do more than guess at a total for the country. Probably 500,000 would be fairly near the mark. If so, members and adherents would together form about 70 % of the adult population.

It is with full membership that this study is primarily concerned. But the remaining 30 % is not necessarily made up of convinced atheists or agnostics, hostile in greater or lesser degree to the Christian churches. A third order of identification with religious bodies must be recognized. There are an unknown number of people who, while neither members nor adherents, would declare that in any fundamental ideological conflict they would be found 'on the side of the angels'. This category recruits some at least of its number from the 'four-wheel Christians'—those whose only attendances at church are when they are wheeled there for baptism in a perambulator, arrive in a taxi for the solemnization of their marriage, wheel their children to church for their baptism and, finally, are driven to church or chapel in a hearse. If a religious census of Scotland were taken on the model of some European countries, the proportion professing religious affiliations of some degree of intensity would probably be somewhere between 90 % and 95 % of the adult population.[1]

Just over one-and-a-half million—43 % of the adult population—belong to Protestant denominations, while half a million adults, or 14·5 %, are Roman Catholics. Thus three-quarters of the church membership is Protestant. Scotland's religious community is also predominantly Presbyterian, for almost two-thirds is of that order (Table 139). Although, however, there are, for various historical reasons, six Presbyterian bodies in Scotland (see Table 141), the five other than the Established Church account for only 3 % of the Presbyterian total. Much has been made of Scotland's history of

'church-minded' than any other nation, with the possible exception of the Scots. The latest edition of the *Year Book* of the American Churches puts the total church membership in the United States in 1951 at 88·7 m. This total, which includes members of Jewish congregations and all baptized persons in the Roman Catholic, Eastern Orthodox and Protestant Episcopal Churches, is 58 % of the estimated population of the United States. The comparable total for Scotland is about 2¼ m. (including all Catholics)—approximately 45 % of the total population. In this respect, then, Scotland must take second place to the United States at least.

[1] Sir John Sinclair's *Analysis of the Statistical Account of Scotland* (1826) contains a table of religious 'professions' relating to 1821, but there are no recent or contemporary figures against which to set them. Sinclair's table allocates the entire population to one denomination or another, making no allowance for profession of atheism or agnosticism.

ecclesiastical schisms, disruptions and secessions, but this is an interesting measure of the extent to which Presbyterians have returned to the main fold of the Established Church,[1] which with 1,271,247 members is now numerically by far the strongest Protestant body in the country.

Table 139. *Estimated Christian Church membership in Scotland and in England and Wales, 1950/51*

Scotland				England and Wales			
Denominational groupings	Membership	Percentage of adult population (1950)	Percentage of church membership	Denominational groupings	Membership	Percentage of adult population (1950)	Percentage of church membership
Presbyterian	1,309,100	37·6	64·9	Anglican	3,161,600	10·0	43·9
Non-Presbyterian	202,100	5·8	10·0	Others	2,007,500	6·4	27·9
Protestant	1,511,200	43·4	74·9	Protestant	5,169,100	16·4	71·8
Roman Catholic (adults)	505,200	14·5	25·1	Roman Catholic (adults)	2,034,600	6·4	28·2
Total	2,016,400	57·8	100·0	Total	7,203,700	22·9	100·0

When we turn to consider the position in England and Wales, two striking points of contrast with the Scottish situation immediately emerge. The first is the contrast between the proportions of estimated church membership to adult population (1950). In England and Wales this proportion is 22·9 %, compared with 57·8 % in Scotland. Whereas the adult population of England and Wales is nine times that of Scotland, church membership is only a little more than 3½ times the Scottish total. The second point of contrast is that whereas the Church of Scotland claims 36·5 % of the adult population, with all other Protestant denominations forming 6·9 %, only 10 % of the adult population of England and Wales appear to be closely associated with the Anglican Communion made up, within these geographical boundaries, of the Church of England and the Church in Wales, while the other Protestant denominations claim a proportion—6·4 %—which is slightly smaller than the equivalent percentage for Scotland.

The figure given in Table 139 of the Anglican Communion in England and Wales—3,161,600—is made up of an estimated 196,400 for the Church in

---

[1] The latest and most substantial reunion took place in 1929, when the United Free Church (itself a reunion of the Free Church and the United Presbyterians) merged with the Church of Scotland. The five small contemporary Presbyterian bodies are composed of the minorities standing aside from reunions over many years. For an account of the principles distinguishing the Presbyterian denominations, the reader may be referred to the writer's *The Churches in Scotland To-day* (Glasgow: Jackson, 1950).

Wales and the total on the 1950 Electoral Roll of the Church of England, 2,965,200. In respect of the Church of England the alternative is to cite the total of Easter Week communicants. In 1950, this number was 1,984,215. The Electoral Roll total has been chosen here partly because it is the larger by almost one million, but also because, in the judgment of Mr Robert Stokes,[1] Editorial Secretary of the Church Information Board, it is slightly less misleading than the other. We can, however, take the Easter Week communicants figure as the number of Church of England members who communicated at least once in the year. This number is 6·7 % of the adult population. In 1950, all but twenty-two Church of Scotland congregations sent in a return of those who had communicated at least once during the year. They amounted to 863,174, or 24·8 % of the Scottish adult population.[2] Even on this basis of comparison, then, the Church of Scotland would appear to be in a stronger position.[3]

Table 140 shows that in England and Wales denominational strengths are more evenly distributed over church membership than is the case in Scotland. While the 'national' ecclesiastical order—Presbyterianism—accounts for 64·9 % of Scottish membership, the equivalent 'national' order south of the Border—Anglican Episcopalianism—accounts for only 43·9 %. Methodism claims 10·4 % in England and Wales as against 0·6 % in Scotland; Congregationalism 3·2 % as against 1·7%; the Baptist Churches 4·3 % as against 1·0%; and 'Other Independent and Free Churches' 2·4 % as compared with 0·2 %. These and other facts provide striking confirmation of the observation by a Commission of the Church Assembly, in their report, *Church and State*:[4]

In Scotland the National Church is far more nearly co-extensive with the Christian element in the nation. With the possible exception of the Roman Catholics—and as a nation Scotland is unquestionably Protestant—the members of other religious bodies are relatively few in number. In England there is something like an even balance.

[1] In correspondence with the writer. See also 'Note on Sources', pp. 314–15.
[2] While it is true that the English 'count' relates to a restricted period, these two terms may be taken as roughly comparable, for two reasons. First, Easter Week as an occasion for taking communion has a greater significance for Anglican members than any single day or week has for members of the Church of Scotland. Second, although the Church of Scotland has on its rolls a few communicants under the age of 20, there are extremely few in the 16 and 17 age-groups and none at all in the lower groups, whereas it would appear that in the Church of England children of 14 or 15 as well as young people aged 16–19 can be confirmed and so may be included in the number of Easter communicants.
[3] A further point of interest is that the 1950 Easter Week communicants figure is 67 % of the Church of England membership (regarded as the number on the Electoral Roll), while the Church of Scotland figure of 'once-a-year-communicants' is 68 % of the total membership. In this respect at least there would appear to be little to distinguish the two national Churches.
[4] *Church and State* (Church Information Board of the Church Assembly, 1952), p. 27.

Table 140. *Distribution of main denominational groupings in Scotland and in England and Wales, 1950/51*

Denominational grouping	Scotland			England and Wales		
	Membership	Percentage of adult population, 1950	Percentage of church membership	Membership	Percentage of adult population, 1950	Percentage of church membership
Presbyterian:						
Church of Scotland	1,271,200	36·5	63·0	} 229,303	0·7	3·2
Other Presbyterian	37,900§	1·1	1·9			
Episcopalian	56,382	1·6	2·8	3,161,600	10·0	43·9
Methodist*	13,024	0·4	0·6	745,849	2·4	10·4
Baptist	19,686	0·6	1·0	313,023	1·0	4·3
Congregationalist	35,140	1·0	1·7	229,825	0·7	3·2
Other 'Independent' and 'Free' Churches†	3,209	0·1	0·2	176,442	0·6	2·4
'New' Churches and other miscellaneous denominations‡	74,630§	2·1	3·7	313,050§	1·0	4·3
Protestant	1,511,200§	43·4	74·9	5,169,100§	16·4	71·8
Roman Catholic‖	505,200§	14·5	25·1	2,034,600§	6·4	28·2
Total	2,016,400§	57·8	100·0	7,203,700§	22·9	100·0

* The figure for England and Wales includes Methodist Church, Independent Methodist Church, and Wesleyan Reform Union.

† The Scottish figure includes Churches of Christ, Society of Friends, and Unitarians; and the figure for England and Wales includes the fore-going and the Moravian Church and the Union of Welsh Independents.

‡ Includes those listed under *Others* in Table 141 except the Society of Friends.

§ Estimated.

‖ Adults only.

The Roman Catholic Church is, however, a more definite 'exception' in this regard than the Commission appear to realize. The Roman Catholic population of Scotland in 1951 is officially stated to have been 748,463.[1] This figure cannot be used as it stands for our present purpose of comparison, since it includes infants, children, and young people in their early 'teens. If, however, we apply to the Catholic total the ratio of under-20-years to over-20-years in the population as a whole, we get 505,200 as an estimate of the number of adult Catholics. Applying the English-plus-Welsh age-group ratio to the figure of 2,837,700 reported[2] as the Roman Catholic population in England and Wales in 1951, we get 2,034,000 as the estimated adult Catholic population south of the Border.

If these estimates are accepted—and it should be noted that they may well overestimate the number of adult Catholics—the proportion of the adult population in Scotland who are Roman Catholics is 14·5 %, as against 43·4 % who are Protestants. Again, adult Roman Catholics make up one-quarter of the total church membership. There can be no doubt that these proportions, while confirming the general impression that Scotland is a Protestant nation, present a situation which the Protestant bodies cannot but regard as challenging. In England and Wales, however, the Protestant Churches must surely regard the position as even more challenging, for there, although adult Catholics form only 6·4 % of the population, the Protestant proportion is only 2½ times, whereas in Scotland it is 3 times, the Catholic proportion; and the adult Catholic community represents 28·2 % of church membership.

The Roman Catholic population in Scotland is densest in the Clyde Valley area. The chief factor in this has been the influx of Irish Catholics into that area and the concentration there of their descendants. The Province of Glasgow, including the Archdiocese of Glasgow and the Dioceses of Paisley and Motherwell, accounts for nearly 70 % of Catholics in Scotland of all ages. The area of the Province is made up largely of the three counties of Dunbarton, Lanark and Renfrew. In Lanark, a quarter of the population is Catholic, in Dunbarton 22 % and in Renfrew 21·5 %; and of the population in these three counties as a group, 24·8 % is Catholic. In terms of density of Catholic population, Coatbridge leads the large burghs with 43·9 % of its population Catholic. Airdrie is next with 35·6 %, Greenock third with 31 % and Motherwell and Wishaw fourth with 28·4 %. Then follow Glasgow (26·2 %), Clydebank (24·7 %) and Paisley (22·8 %). Dundee, with 20·5 %, and Stirling, with 17·1 %, are the only large burghs outside the Clyde Valley area with anything like a comparable proportion of Catholics.[3]

A detailed list of denominations in Scotland and in England and Wales,

---

[1] *The Catholic Directory for Scotland*, 1952, pp. 265–6.
[2] *The Catholic Directory*, 1952, p. 589.
[3] Cf. *The Catholic Directory for Scotland*, 1952, pp. 266–9.

Table 141. *Christian church membership in Scotland and in England and Wales, 1950/51*

Scotland		England and Wales	
Denomination	Membership	Denomination	Membership
PROTESTANT		PROTESTANT	
Presbyterian		*Presbyterian*	
Church of Scotland	1,271,247*	Presbyterian Church of England	69,676
United Free Church	24,566*	Presbyterian Church of Wales	159,627§
Free Church	10,000‡		
Free Presbyterian Church	680†		
United Original Secession	1,926*		
Reformed Presbyterian	704	*Anglican communion*	
Anglican communion		Church of England	2,965,200‖
Scottish Episcopal Church	56,382*	Church in Wales	196,389§
Methodist and Independent Churches		*Methodist and other members of Free Church Federal Council*	
Congregational Union	35,140	Congregational Union	229,825
Baptist Union	19,686	Baptist Union	313,023
Methodist Church	13,024	Methodist Church	730,592
		Union of Welsh Independents	125,336
		Independent Methodist	8,963
		Wesleyan Reform Union	6,294
Churches of Christ	1,818	Churches of Christ	7,717¶
Unitarian Churches	1,000†	Unitarian Churches	20,000†
		Moravian Church	2,957
Others		*Others*	
Greater World Christian Spiritualist League	2,700†	Greater World Christian Spiritualist League	24,300†
Churches of the Spiritualists' National Union	2,138*	Churches of the Spiritualists' National Union	16,834
Jehovah's Witnesses	2,000†	Jehovah's Witnesses	27,000†
Church of the Nazarene	788	Church of the Nazarene	460
Elim Foursquare	700†	Elim Foursquare	14,000†
Assemblies of God	500†	Assemblies of God	20,000†
New Church	435	New Church	4,260¶
Society of Friends	391	Society of Friends	20,432
Seventh-Day Adventists	364	Seventh-Day Adventists	6,214¶
Miscellaneous	65,000‡	Miscellaneous	200,000‡
Protestant total (est.)	1,511,200	Protestant total (est.)	5,169,100
Roman Catholic (adults)	505,200‡	Roman Catholic (adults)	2,034,600‡
Grand total (est.)	2,016,400	Grand total (est.)	7,203,700

* 1950.   † 'Official' estimate.
‡ 'Unofficial' estimate. The Miscellaneous figures include two large bodies, the Christian Brethren (about 35,000 in Scotland and 80,000 in England and Wales) and the Salvation Army (about 23,000 and 100,000 respectively).
§ 1938: latest available figure.   ‖ Electoral Roll figure.
¶ 1951.

303

with their membership totals—either 'exact' or estimated—is furnished in Table 141. Of the denominations listed under the heading 'Others', only the Church of the Nazarene and the Churches of the Spiritualists' National Union are relatively stronger in Scotland than in England and Wales; the former, indeed, whose British headquarters is in Glasgow, finds its birthplace in Scotland, being the 'legal successor' of the Pentecostal Church in Scotland. It has 23 members per 100,000 of the adult population in Scotland, as compared with 1 per 100,000 in England, while the Churches of the S.N.U. have 61 members per 100,000 in Scotland as against 52 per 100,000 in England. The Greater World Christian Spiritualist League, with 77 per 100,000 of each population, would appear to be in equal favour on each side of the Border. While we have only unofficial estimates to go on, it would seem that the Christian Brethren (commonly called Plymouth Brethren) are relatively stronger in Scotland, where their membership is about 1 % of the adult population, compared with 0·3 % in England and Wales. Within Scotland this sect finds most of its support in Ayr and Central Scotland, and there is some evidence that it is at its most active in small towns and mining centres in these areas, and that it has some following among fisherfolk in the North-East. On the whole, however, neither it nor the other 'new' or 'unorthodox' denominations have much influence on Scottish social life. The Salvation Army, although small numerically, has left its mark in the poorer districts of the cities through its extensive social welfare work, which is missionary in character.

Before we pass to a historical comparison, it is worth noting that in the four years between 1947 and 1951 the proportion of total church membership to adult population in Scotland has increased by about 2 %. Most of the Protestant bodies have recorded slight increases, the most substantial being the 15,000 increment of the Church of Scotland. During the same period the Roman Catholic adult population increased by about 46,000—a numerical advance of nearly twice that of the Protestant bodies put together.

THE POSITION IN 1901 AND 1871

We turn now to consider the Churches' position in 1901 and 1871 and to compare it with the situation today. The year 1871 has been chosen for the very practical reason that it is the census year closest to the mid-nineteenth century for which information and guidance as to numbers are available.[1]

The majority of the 1901 figures have been taken from official records, but in some cases—those of the smaller Presbyterian bodies in particular—resort has had to be made to estimates supplied by officers of the bodies concerned.

---

[1] A few 'exact' totals and some estimates have been obtained for 1851, but they are insufficient for the present purpose.

In the case of 1871, the figures for the Presbyterian Churches, the Congregational Union, and the category 'Others' are based on figures supplied by the Rev. James Johnston in his pamphlet, *The Ecclesiastical and Religious Statistics of Scotland.*[1] The others—half the entries—are official figures, official estimates, or estimates on the basis of official 'guides'.

It will be seen from Table 142 that eighty years ago 58·7 % of the adult population of Scotland were Christian Church members, compared with 62·5 % fifty years ago and 57·8 % now.

Table 142. *Estimated Christian church membership in Scotland,*
1871, 1901 *and* 1951

Denominations and denominational groupings	Membership			Percentage of adult population			Percentage of church membership		
	1871	1901	1951	1871	1901	1951	1871	1901	1951
Church of Scotland	390,000	668,300	1,271,200	21·8	26·5	36·5	37·1	42·4	63·0
Other Presbyterian churches	405,200	509,300	37,900	22·6	20·2	1·1	38·5	32·3	1·9
Total Presbyterian	795,200	1,177,600	1,309,100	44·4	46·7	37·6	75·5	74·7	64·9
Non-Presbyterian Protestant churches	85,300	153,800	202,100	4·7	6·1	5·8	8·1	9·8	10·0
Total Protestant	880,500	1,331,400	1,511,200	49·1	52·8	43·4	83·6	84·5	74·9
Roman Catholic (adults)	172,200	244,100	505,200	9·6	9·7	14·5	16·4	15·5	25·1
Grand total	1,052,700	1,575,500	2,016,400	58·7	62·5	57·8	100·0	100·0	100·0

At first glance, there would seem little warrant in the data presented in Table 142 for what is almost certainly the accepted belief that fifty and eighty years ago the Scots were a much more 'church-minded' people than they are today. A difference in proportion of aggregate membership to adult population of 1 % over eighty years, and of 4·7 % in the last fifty years, hardly betokens the kind of catastrophic set-back to—though it does evidence a deterioration in—the churches' strength which the older generation of Scots, and a good many clergymen, frequently assert has taken place.[2]

[1] Glasgow: Bryce, 1874.
[2] The figures of membership, however, do not tell the whole story. They have to be viewed in conjunction with information as to any fall in frequency of attendance or deterioration in the quality of members' Christian witness. It would be a mistake, however, to suppose that in earlier years all seemed well to ministerial observers of the contemporary scene. Johnston's main motive in writing the pamphlet already referred to was to bring to the Churches' attention the fact that a considerable section of the nation were 'patently godless'. Scattered throughout the earlier sources are frequent references to the low spiritual state of the country, and to other contemporary grounds—as they seemed—of disquiet.

But a closer examination reveals some justification for Protestant and in particular for Presbyterian concern. For the chief factor in keeping the current proportion within nodding distance of those for 1871 and 1901 has been the growth of the Roman Catholic Church. Whereas fifty and eighty years ago about one in every ten adults in Scotland was a Catholic, the proportion is now one in seven. Consequently, while the Protestant percentages for 1871 and 1901 show virtually the same increase (3·7 %) as do those for total membership (3·8 %) in these years, there is a greater fall in the Protestant proportions—from 52·8 % to 43·4 %—than in the total membership proportions—from 62·5% to 57·8%—between 1901 and 1951. The Protestant churches can now claim as members only a little more than two-fifths of the adult population, whereas fifty years ago they claimed slightly more than half and eighty years ago very nearly half.

This absolute and relative Catholic expansion finds expression also in the comparative percentages the main divisions bear to total church membership. In 1871 the Protestant-Catholic ratio was in the region of 5 to 1. By 1901 it was virtually the same, the slight change being in the Protestants' favour. Now, however, it is 3 to 1.

An interesting point which emerges from Table 142 is that although the non-Presbyterian Protestant Churches' share of total church membership rose from 8·1 % in 1871 to 9·8 % in 1901, today at 10 % it is only slightly higher. In the last fifty years, then, they have been the constant focal point round which distribution has varied between the Presbyterian churches and the Catholics. Further, they have been making inroads into the Presbyterian share of the Protestant aggregate membership. Whereas in 1871 the Presbyterians could claim 90·3 % of Protestant membership, this had dropped to 88·4 % in 1901 and is now 86·6 % (Table 143).

Moreover, when the necessary adjustments called for by Presbyterian re-unions have been carried out, it would appear that, within the Presbyterian family, the setback has been borne exclusively by the Established Church. For 1871 and 1901 the proportions of adjusted Church of Scotland membership to adult population are, respectively, 43·8 % and 46·1 %. The proportion is 36·5 % now. The point can be more graphically expressed by saying that for the Church of Scotland to show the same proportion to population now as it claimed in 1901, 335,000 members would have to be added to its rolls—an increase of 26 %.

The fall away, then, has been from what in the last 400 years has come to be regarded as the traditional form of Scottish religious attachment, while the overall position has been partially righted only by attachment on the part of an increasing section of the populace to the pre-Reformation order. This movement, however, has had little to do with conversions, which have not in any case been exclusively in the one direction; and it is highly unlikely that in relation to a population not fed by Irish Catholic immigration and the higher Catholic birth-rate a comparable strengthening of the Roman Catholic position in Scotland would have manifested itself.

Table 143. *Trends in relative position of non-Presbyterian Protestant churches in Scotland, 1871 to 1950/51*

Frame of reference	1871	1901	1950/51
Percentage of adult population	4·7	6·1	5·8
Percentage of total church membership	8·1	9·8	10·0
Percentage of Protestant membership	9·7	11·6	13·4

ATTENDANCES IN 1851 AND 1951

For the first and only time, the Census of Population in 1851 had associated with it a voluntary inquiry on attendance at church on Sunday 30 March of that year.[1] The numbers who attended a place of worship on Census Sunday in Scotland were: morning, 943,951 or 32·7 % of the total population; afternoon, 619,863 or 21·5 %; evening, 188,874 or 6·5 %. In England and Wales the proportions of attenders to population were: morning, 25·9 %; afternoon, 17·7 %; evening, 17·1 %. Since, of course, an unascertainable number would attend on at least two occasions during the day, it is impossible to obtain a ground for overall comparison between the two communities. We can say, however, that as times for public worship, the morning was more and the evening less popular among Scottish churchgoers than they were in the south.

How does attendance 100 years ago compare with attendance today? If we assume that church membership between 1851 and 1871 grew in relation to the adult population at much the same pace as it did between 1871 and 1901 we can hazard the guess that the total in 1851 was about 870,000. This is much less than the total of nearly 950,000 persons who attended church on the morning of 30 March 1851. Since every church member cannot have been in church on that morning, well over 100,000 of those who were in church cannot have been full members but must have been adherents and adolescents (including children). Even so, it is likely that at the very least something like three-quarters of the total membership were at public worship. There are no official figures on contemporary churchgoing habits, but recent social survey estimates point to a maximum number of regular attenders in Scotland of about 20 % of the population, or about one million persons.[2] Attendance

---

[1] The results have been published in a report, *Religious Worship and Education in Scotland* (H.M.S.O., 1854), which also reproduces the results of a similar inquiry carried out in England and Wales.

[2] Surveys agree in estimating the percentage for England and Wales at between 15 and 20. For some areas, notably London, the figure is put at about 10 % or less.

20-2

nowadays is thus at most equal to half the total church membership, and would be a good deal less than half if adherents and children were deducted from the survey estimates.

The 1851 Census also revealed that at the time there was seating accommodation in the 3,395 places of worship in Scotland for 1,834,805 persons, or 63·5 % of the population.[1] On that particular Sunday morning, then, the Scottish churches were only about half full, and in the afternoon about one-third full, while in the evening only 10 % of seating capacity was in use. While these figures tell us that any conception of packed churches 100 years ago has little substantiation, the reason for this would seem to be, not that attendance was poor by any reasonable standards, but that accommodation was more than adequate for normal needs. Indeed, it was estimated in 1851 that accommodation for 58 % of the population was sufficient 'for all practical purposes'.

In short, there can be little doubt that while there is no very marked difference in the proportions of the adult populations who are church members now and were members 100 years ago, there has been a considerable falling-off in regularity of attendance of both members and non-communicant supporters. Against this, it is true, has to be set the trend towards the new pattern of fireside worship—listening to religious broadcasts. The Rev. Francis House, head of Religious Broadcasting at the B.B.C., stated recently that on a typical Sunday something like one-third of the adult population of Britain heard at least one religious broadcast, and that the total estimated audience for all religious services on a Sunday was over 18,000,000. The proportion of the population who listened was, he said, lowest in the London and Birmingham areas and highest in Scotland and Wales.[2] But while most churchmen would be found to welcome this as better than no communication whatsoever with absentees from church, and as indicating that the religious state of the nation may not be what the empty pews might suggest, few will regard it as a finally acceptable substitute for public worship as our fathers and grandfathers knew it.

CHARGES, MANPOWER AND MONEY

For all its limitations, the criterion of membership strengths is the best quantitatively-expressible guide to the changing religious state of the nation. There are, however, a number of other pointers, such as the number of parishes or charges, ministerial manpower, the monetary rewards of the profession, and the financial support given by congregations. We shall do no more than touch on these, and even then as pertaining almost exclusively to the Church of Scotland.

One result of Scotland's ecclesiastical history is that there are—or have

---

[1] In England there was accommodation for 57 %.
[2] *Manchester Guardian*, 11 Sept. 1952.

been until recently—a great many small areas with what seems at least a proliferation of churches, in the sense of buildings. Some of these at one time served devotees of distinct denominations; but now that the great bulk of the Presbyterian following is reunited, they have become the meeting-places of somewhat attenuated congregations of the one Church. It is no uncommon thing to find in the cities four or five Church of Scotland churches grouped within an area bounded by not many more streets of moderate length. Many of these churches, even when well-attended, have still unused seating accommodation which would go a long way to meet the needs of the regular attenders of the neighbouring congregation, while in the new housing areas many small hall-churches are packed to capacity. Faced with the necessity to economize in both costs and manpower, and with the material difficulties of building new churches to meet the needs of population movements, the Church has in the last twenty-odd years tackled this problem of uneconomic duplication with resource and yet with an understanding of the ties of loyalty that have made many church people reluctant to break their association even with 'the stone and lime of the old building'. Since the Union of 1929 between the then United Free Church and the Established Church, over 600 unions of charges have taken place, and there has been a net decrease of 521 in the number of parishes or charges from 2,869 in 1929 to 2,348 at the end of 1950, about two-thirds of the reduction occurring in the first ten years. Some of the buildings of 'closed' charges have been moved stone by stone for re-erection on sites in the new housing estates.

One reason for this policy of amalgamation has been the shortage of ministers. The relevant data concerning the manpower situation in the Church of Scotland in recent years are set out in Table 144.

Although the number of students at the four Church of Scotland Divinity Halls rose between the end of the war and 1951, and the number of licentiates has been steadily increasing, little headway has been made with the task of filling vacant charges. It was not until 1950 that any material increase was recorded in the number of probationers elected to home charges, and while this played a part in reducing the number of vacancies by twenty-two, there were still, at the end of that year, 142 charges without a minister. The main reason for the failure to reap the full benefit of these improvements has been the magnitude of the 'wastage' in recent years: deaths and resignations since the war have been more numerous than in the pre-war period. Since the average age of ministers in parochial charges is now higher than it has been for some time, and many will reach the normal retiring age within the next five years,[1] there is no immediate prospect of a diminution of losses, and it is to an adequate supply of new entrants to the profession that the Church must continue to look for a solution of its manpower problem.

[1] *Reports to the General Assembly of the Church of Scotland*, 1950, p. 610.

Table 144. *Manpower in the Church of Scotland: supply, wastage and vacant charges, 1947–51*

	1947	1948	1949	1950	1951
Number of students taking theology course in the four Divinity Halls	153	210	260	262	222
Number of probationers on Roll at 31 March of previous year	104	85	71	62	70
Number of students licensed (including ministers admitted from other churches) during year to 31 March	32	43	56	90	113
	136	128	127	152	183
Number elected to home charges	45	45	46	77	73
Number elected to overseas charges or otherwise removed from Roll	6	12	19	5	19
Total removed from Roll during year to 31 March	— 51	— 57	— 65	— 82	— 92
Number on roll at 31 March	85	71	62	70	91
At end of previous year					
Number of charges	2,410	2,387	2,377	2,357	2,348
Number of ministers	2,246	2,243	2,218	2,193	2,206
Vacancies	— 164	— 144	— 159	— 164	— 142
By March:					
Number elected to home charges	45	45	46	77	
	119	99	113	87	
'Wastage' during year	25	60	51	55	
Vacancies at end of year	144	159	164	142	

It is true that, while the number of probationers and ordained assistants on the Roll in March of recent years has been either less than, or just about, half the number of vacancies at the end of the preceding year, there was an improvement in 1951, when ninety-one probationers formed a potential supply to be set against the 142 vacancies brought forward from the previous year. But for some years up to 1951 a substantial proportion of students preparing for the ministry were students taking the special war-service course, and since this type of student is no longer available, a marked reduction in the number of licentiates after 1952 is to be anticipated. Further, the average number of students per year taking the theology course since the war—205—is considerably below the average of 301 for the years 1930 to 1939: even the highest post-war figure of 263 in 1949/50 is below that of any year in the 1930's with the exception of 1930/31 and 1932/33.

In recent years the Committee on the Use of Ministerial Resources in the Church has given much thought to this decline in the numbers preparing for the ministry. It is not, in their view, to be traced to a single cause. One important cause has been 'the growing demands made on the comparatively small section of the population receiving University education and the disparity in the emoluments between the ministry and a number of professions open to students'. Much more significant, however, in the Committee's view, have been 'the general temper of our age and the drift from religion which has become increasingly apparent'. To this the Committee added: 'The Church's supply of students depends primarily on its own vitality. No quick remedy can be prescribed when a revival of religion is the only certain cure'.[1]

As everyone knows, at one time in Scotland the ministry was one of a very limited number of professions open to the university graduate, and the clergy-man shared with the schoolmaster and the medical practitioner the distinction of being the only university men with any direct and widespread connexion with the people. Indeed, of the three the minister was probably, even in the smallest parish, the man of highest attainments and widest scholarship. Certainly he was the linch-pin of the community. The contrast between this and the present situation, in which the minister, however estimable and respected, does not and cannot occupy anything like so central a position, affords one of the sharpest insights into the changed characteristics of a much more populous and complex society. This slow social change has almost certainly had its effect on the attractiveness of the ministry as a vocation. And the effect, like the process, has itself been slow. While it is only in recent years that the manpower shortage has become pressing, it is a mistake to suppose that the contemporary problem has had no rudimentary precursor. There was a temporary manpower decline at the turn of the century, when for a few years the annual supply of probationers fell below the demand made by vacancies. Reflecting on this—as they later termed it—'ominous fact', the Committee on Probationers in 1900 found one of the causes to be that 'there seems to exist in many minds a much lower estimate than formerly of the ministry as a vocation'. Of this, in turn, one of the causes, in their view, was the 'straitened incomes' of the clergy, 'the existence of so many livings under £200 a year'; and 'ecclesiastical disputes and controversies' might be another. But, the Committee stated, 'deeper than any other cause may be a certain, observable ebb in spiritual life'.[2]

Here, then, are two factors—monetary rewards and a lowering of the spiritual temperature of the time—which different committees at different times found to be common in the manpower situation they were examining. Of these, we shall discuss further the first only.

[1] *Reports*, 1948, p. 530.
[2] *Report on the Schemes of the Church of Scotland*, 1900, p. 973.

In 1951, 814 charges—more than a third of the total—were at the minimum stipend of £475 plus a manse in 'ordinary' charges and £525 plus a manse in the four large Scottish cities and in Shetland, and in Church of Scotland charges in London, Liverpool and Newcastle.[1]

At the time of the Union the minimum stipend was £300 and a manse in 'ordinary' charges, and it was recognized by the Church that, in the light of conditions then prevailing, it should be increased by £100 in order that ministers 'should have a reasonable maintenance'. This goal, however, eluded the Church for many years. The first increase was in 1937—of £5; the next, again of £5, was in 1940; and a year later brought the figure to £315. It reached £330 in 1942, £350 in 1943, and £370 in 1944. In 1947 it was £400, but it is only in a superficial sense that that year can be said to have achieved the aim the Church set itself in 1929. If account is taken of the rise in the cost of living, that aim has not been fulfilled even yet.

Fifty years ago the minimum aimed at by the Church was £200. In the year 1900/01, out of 1,376 charges there were 261 'livings' below that limit— 165 between £180 and £200; 81 between £160 and £180; 11 between £140 and £160; and 4 under £140. Fifty years before that—in 1851—the incomes of Church of Scotland ministers were on average about £200.[2] The general range of stipends in the United Presbyterian Church was from £90 to £200, but some of the larger charges in the cities had stipends varying from £300 to £500[2]— the level not reached even yet by the minimum stipend of the Established Church.[1] The minimum stipend of the Episcopal Church in Scotland was increased by £20 to £400 in 1953. The Free Church 'equal dividend' is now £360. The country stipend of the Baptist Union of Scotland is £290 and the city stipend £300, manse and rates being additional. In 1952 the Congregational Union of Scotland increased their minimum stipend by £40, to bring it up to £400.

It is interesting to compare these emoluments with those available in what is commonly said to be the poorest paid of the other graduate professions, namely, school-teaching, and with industrial earnings. On the new Scottish teachers' salary scale which came into operation on 1 August 1952, the starting-point for men graduates with ordinary degrees is £475, rising to £765 in the eighteenth year, while men graduates with first or second class honours degrees start at £575 and rise to £915 in the eighteenth year. Many ministers in the denominations mentioned above may still be on the minimum stipend after

---

[1] For 1952 the minimum stipend was raised to £500 in 'ordinary' charges and £550 in the other cases.

[2] J. H. Dawson, *The Abridged Statistical History of the Scottish Counties*, 1862, pp. xlix and lii. According to an extract from the *Edinburgh Almanac*, 1850, reproduced by Thomas Downie in his stimulating booklet, *Economics, Ethics and Stipends* (Blackwood, 1945), the average Church of Scotland stipend in 1791 was £103 and in 1841, £233. Sinclair's *Analysis* (1826) puts the average at £220.

a good deal longer service than eighteen years, and consequently receiving much less than the ordinary graduate's £765 after that period. In Scotland in 1906 the average earnings of adult male workers in industrial occupations were less than £2 a week; by 1951 the average had risen to over £8 a week. These compare, respectively, with about £4 and £9. 10s. a week (plus a manse) paid to Church of Scotland ministers on the minimum stipend. While it is not to be supposed that monetary rewards are or are ever likely to be the deciding factor in choosing the career of the ministry, it is equally unrealistic to expect intending recruits to be completely oblivious to that aspect of their profession.

If the general membership of the Established Church as well as their annual forum—the General Assembly—see in this one of the reasons for the present shortage of ministers, a large part of the remedy is in their own hands. At present less than half of the money put to stipend needs comes from endowments; the rest comes direct from congregational givings. All congregations—alike those who pay the whole of their ministers' above-the-minimum stipend and those who cannot pay the whole minimum—are under obligation to contribute to the support of the ministry. There exists a fund known as the Annual Fund or the Maintenance of the Ministry Fund, but not all congregational givings for stipend purposes pass through its accounts; many congregations pay all the stipend of the minister direct, while others give all their contributions to the Fund and some pay partly to the Fund and partly direct to the minister. As an official publication of the Church puts it, 'the mainstay of the Minimum Stipend is the Annual Fund, and the mainstay of the Annual Fund, congregational contributions'.[1] Any increase in the minimum stipend must come largely from this latter source. The rate of contribution per member has been about 3s. for several years (see Table 145). It was 3s. in 1950, when congregational aid to the Fund amounted to £192,342.[2]

It must be kept in mind, however, that rates of contribution per member to the Maintenance of the Ministry Fund are not, for reasons already given, the rates of total stipend contribution per member. Still less do the above rates represent the average annual financial contribution of the membership to the Church's life and work as a whole. The approach to that average is through the figure known as the total of Christian Liberality. This, while excluding donations from individuals received direct by the General Treasurer, comprises all contributions received by congregations from members and congregational organizations; proceeds of sales of work (which, however, usually involve circuitous givings or givings in kind by members); and whatever income may be received from invested funds belonging to the congregation. Table 145 gives Christian Liberality figures for some years between 1929 and 1950.

[1] *Year Book of the Church of Scotland, 1952*, p. 59.
[2] As we have seen, the minimum stipend for 1952 was raised to £500. This means that givings to the Fund in 1952 were about 4s. per member.

Table 145. *Church of Scotland: Christian Liberality and contributions to the Maintenance of the Ministry Fund in selected years*

Year	Total Christian Liberality	Average Liberality per member	Contributions per member to Maintenance of the Ministry Fund* (part of Liberality per member)
	£	£ s. d.	s. d.
1900	(490,343)†	(14 10)†	—
1930	1,856,295	1 9 2	3 6
1939	1,779,313	1 7 7	2 10
1947	2,546,000	2 0 6	3 0
1948	2,755,000	2 3 7	3 0
1949	2,779,206	2 3 10	3 1
1950	2,826,087	2 4 5	3 0

* See p. 313.   † Estimated.

There has, then, been a steady increase in the rate of giving per member since 1947; and the rate in that year was higher than in the last years of the 1930's and well above the average at the turn of the century. Nevertheless, an annual payment to the Church which is not much more than (if not indeed under) what many members subscribe to sports and recreational clubs, and is much less than the annual outlay of the average football pools investor, can hardly be regarded by church members as evidencing a very generous financial support of a cause that supposedly lies close to their hearts.

NOTE ON SOURCES

The sources of the majority of Protestant membership statistics are the official annual reports or year-books of the denominations concerned. In some cases, where no 'exact' figures are otherwise accessible, estimates supplied by officers of churches have been used (these are referred to as 'official' estimates); and in the case of the few bodies who do not divulge membership statistics or whom the writer failed to contact, estimates have been taken from or based on D. P. Thomson's *The Scottish Churches Handbook* (1933), *The World Christian Handbook* (1949), and *A Christian Year-Book* (1950). These 'unofficial' estimates, and to a lesser degree the 'official' estimates, should be treated with caution. Every attempt has been made, in the case of marked differences in the basis of membership, to obtain equivalent figures.

On Church of England figures, Mr Robert Stokes, Editorial Secretary of the Church Information Board, states that while the Electoral Roll figure is less misleading than the number of Easter Week communicants, it is not a true guide to membership, primarily because there is at present 'no generally effective force reminding and persuading people who have moved to put their names on the

Electoral Roll of their new parish'. But there are few religious bodies who could not with justification adduce the same argument; and in any case no better index of Anglican membership exists.

Roman Catholic publications provide figures of the Catholic population, including infants and children, but no breakdown into age-groups. The writer has been assured by the Rev. John Gogarty, Secretary of the Archdiocese of Glasgow, that no basis exists for a more reliable estimate of the adult Catholic population than that adopted here. Since it is all but finally established that the Catholic birth-rate is higher than that for the community as a whole, the estimates here used may well overstate Catholic adult strength.

Acknowledgment is due to the many churchmen and lay officers who, on occasion at much cost to themselves in time and labour, furnished the writer with indispensable or helpful information.

INDEX OF NAMES AND PLACES

INDEX OF SUBJECTS

Housing (*cont.*)
 density of occupation, 197–8
 finance, 204–11
 subsidies, 6, 207–9
Household budgets, 171–4, 175–7, 203–4

Immigration, 15–17, 20
Imports (Scottish), Ch. 10 passim
Income, Ch. 5 passim
 distribution of, 5–6, 54–5, 62, 153, 155–6, 168
 from property, 53–5, 56, 62, 154
 from work, 53–5, 55–6, 62, 154
 real, 50–1, 55–8, 61, 63
Industrial growth, rate of, 69, 71–5, 83
Infant mortality, 23–5, 215–16

Juvenile Advisory Committees, 278
Juvenile delinquency, 237–9
Juvenile labour, Ch. 18 passim
Jute trade, 125, 127, 128, 129

Landowners, 103–5
Leather trades, Ch. 6 passim, 127
Linen trade, 125, 127, 128
Linoleum industry, 82, 129
Livestock, 86, 88
Local Government
 capital expenditure, 188–90
 debt, 190–2
 expenditure, total and by services, 181–8 passim
 revenue, total and by source 181–8 passim
 services, Ch. 13 passim

Manpower, Ch. 4 passim
 age-distribution, 36–9
 changes in occupational distribution, 40–2
 distribution by industries, Ch. 6 passim
 male and female, 35, 36–9, 42–3
 See also Population, working
Manufacturing, general and miscellaneous trades, Chs. 6 and 9 passim
Marriage habits, 27–9
Marriage-rates, 27–9
Metal trades, 3, 4, 5, Ch. 6 passim, 118–24
Migration, 13–19, 20
Mining and quarrying, Ch. 6 passim
Morbidity, 8, Ch. 15 passim
 causes of, 218–19
 occupational, 221
 regional differences, 221–3
 cost of, 224–6
Mortality, causes of, 212–16
 See also Death-rates

National Coal Board, 112, 114, 115, 117
National Health Insurance, 218, 219–20
National Health Service, 224, 225, 226
New industries, 3, 4, 5, 45, Chs. 6 and 9 passim

Overcrowding, 6, 196–7, 202

Paper and printing, 74, 78, 131
Population
 birthplaces, 17
 distribution of, 1–2, 9–13, 14–15, 19, 20
 growth, 2, 9–11, 20, 21
 working, 56, 57, 62, 63
 See also Manpower
Presbyterians, Ch. 20 passim
Probation, 241–2
Productivity, 71, 73–4, 83
 in coalmining, 113, 115–17
Profits, Ch. 5 passim
Protestants, 31, Ch. 20 passim

Rates, 181–8 passim, 204–10, 259
Rent, 171, 186, 203–11 passim
Reproduction rates
 gross, 26–7, 32
 net, 32
Retail sales, 174–5
Roman Catholics, 31, Ch. 20 passim
Rubber industry, 82, 131–2

Salaries, Ch. 5 and 11 passim
Scholarships, 260–1
School leaving practice, 249–50
Schools
 types of, 246–9, 251–2
 size of classes, 253
Scottish development area, 76
Service trades, Ch. 6 passim
Shipbuilding, 4, 71, 118, 120, 121
 wages, 163–4
Steel consumption, 122–3
Steel industry, 3, 120, 121–3

Taxes, direct, 57–8, 62
Teachers
 shortage of, 252–5
 graduate, 255–6
 women, 255–6
Tenements, 6, 194–6
Textile trades, Ch. 6 passim, 124–8
 wages, 150, 153, 166–7
Trade (Scottish), Ch. 10 passim
 composition, 135–7
 direction of, 137–8